Workplace Spirituality

Management, Spirituality and Religion

Series Editor
Yochanan Altman

Volume 1

Workplace Spirituality

Making a Difference

Edited by
Yochanan Altman, Judi Neal and Wolfgang Mayrhofer

DE GRUYTER

ISBN 978-3-11-071129-5
e-ISBN (PDF) 978-3-11-071134-9
e-ISBN (EPUB) 978-3-11-071140-0
ISSN 2700-7790
DOI https://doi.org/10.1515/9783110711349

Library of Congress Control Number: 2021951625

Bibliographic information published by the Deutsche Nationalbibliothek
The Deutsche Nationalbibliothek lists this publication in the Deutsche Nationalbibliografie; detailed bibliographic data are available on the internet at http://dnb.dnb.de.

Cover Image: Ion Jonas, based on an idea by Yochanan Altman
Typesetting: Integra Software Services Pvt. Ltd.
Printing and binding: CPI books GmbH, Leck

MIX
Papier aus verantwortungsvollen Quellen
FSC www.fsc.org FSC® C083411

www.degruyter.com

Acknowledgements

In expressing our gratitude to the Fetzer Institute for championing the publication of this volume, we would like to highlight the support they have extended to us throughout its materialization. In particular we to wish to note their moral, emotional and material support during the Covid-19 pandemic, which required necessary changes to the project. We hope that this collection will serve both as an endorsement as well as reinforcement of Fetzer's mission to help build the spiritual foundation for a loving world. Please visit www.fetzer.org to learn more.

We wish to acknowledge the International Association of Management, Spirituality & Religion (IAMSR) and its membership's foundational role in developing academic scholarship pertinent to the domain of workplace spirituality/religion. Their know-how and insights have greatly benefited this project.

We also wish to record our thanks and appreciation to the Vienna University of Economics and Business (WU Vienna), Austria. As a dependable partner, not only for the conference linked to this edited volume, they have also been at the forefront of facilitating scholarship in the domain of management, spirituality and religion, hosting the inaugural conference of the IAMSR and pioneering the first German speaking gathering on the subject. We express special appreciation to Gisela Ullrich-Rosner and Michaela Schreder for their detailed attention to the preparation of the manuscript for this book. Michaela and Gisela are wonderful examples of workplace spirituality in action.

https://doi.org/10.1515/9783110711349-202

Foreword

This book is extremely relevant and timely. Faith and spirituality have been a foundational aspect of the human experience throughout the ages. Yet how they are experienced and expressed continues to change with the times. For example, in the United States (U.S.) context, a recent Gallup survey shows that Americans' membership in houses of worship (e.g., synagogue, church, or mosque) has fallen to 47% – the lowest in the survey's 80-year history and down from 70% in 1999 (Jones, 2021). This represents a steady decline since the start of the 21st century. This trend is being driven by two factors: more adults expressing no religious affiliation and declining church membership among those who are religiously affiliated. Beneath these trends are population or generational differences, with younger age cohorts expressing less religious affiliation (7% of traditionalists – U.S. adults born before 1946; 13% of baby boomers (1946-64); 20% of those in Generation X (1965-80) and 31% of millennials (1981-1996)).

Simultaneously, the Fetzer Institute supported a Study of American Spirituality that sought to better understand what spirituality means to Americans and how it informs their social lives and civic action (Fetzer Institute, 2020). The study included participants of diverse, including no, religious affiliation or spiritual identification. It found that "Spirituality is a complex, diverse, and nuanced phenomenon that people of all spiritual and religious self-identifications experience." (Fetzer Institute, 2020) More specifically, 86% of people consider themselves to be spiritual and 68% of people believe that their spirituality guides how they act in the world. These numbers include people who identify as part of a faith tradition and those who do not.

What are we to make of these two seemingly contradictory reports? I offer these data as a foundation for the importance and relevance of spirituality in the workplace. To many, spirituality in the workplace is inappropriate. And yet, as these studies demonstrate, many people acknowledge the importance of spirituality in their lives even as their connection to structures and places through which to express their spirituality is shifting. At the same time, many organizations and workplaces are inviting people to bring their 'whole selves', including their spirituality, to work for increased wellbeing, engagement, creativity, and effectiveness (Kegan &Lahey, 2016; Neal, 2013). Indeed, for those who are spiritually unaffiliated *and* for those whose faith and spirituality are central to their lives, the workplace – where many adults spend the majority of their time outside of the home – may be an important location for the expression and fulfillment of their values. Further, organizations are often the structural mechanisms through which societies organize and accomplish their most important and complex social, economic, and technical goals. They are both drivers and representations of societal life and values. Given this, they

https://doi.org/10.1515/9783110711349-203

remain a critical focus site for and potential driver of personal growth and development and human flourishing.

Recognizing all of this, at the Fetzer Institute (the Institute), we strive to live our mission and values by creating a spiritually-grounded workplace community – which we call a Community of Freedom (COF). Our COF is the spiritual ground of our work to transform ourselves and society in an authentic and effective way. The individual and communal ways of being and practices expressed through the COF – and rooted in our core organizational values of love, trust, authenticity, and inclusion – support the Institute in cultivating the necessary culture to enact our mission of helping build the spiritual foundation for a loving world. One of the structures we use to remain grounded in our mission and vision are our community of freedom gatherings (COFG). The COFGs consist of weekly, three-hour gatherings of all staff – from our groundskeepers and program staff to our finance and information technology staff and leaders. During COFGs we bring in outside facilitators and spiritual teachers to help us engage in individual and communal spiritual exploration and community building. We also offer sessions by staff and provide space and resources for staff to pursue their personal paths. Examples of sessions include suites of contemplative practices, the science of wellbeing, conversational capacity, and being with collective grief and mourning. Sessions usually include didactic and experiential components, along with opportunities for small and large group discussions which allow staff to share deeply with one another. In 2016, the Institute commissioned an independent case study to learn more about the early lights, shadows, and impacts of the COFG. Some of the key learnings were that staff felt an increased sense of trust, morale, connection, and ability to navigate relational difficulties from the work. The case study also surfaced staff questions and concerns around the purpose of the COFGs as it relates to our external work, use of inclusive language and framing around the COFG and its offerings, and how the gatherings translate into larger organizational policies and practices. Some of these questions have been answered as we have deepened our work as a community and others we continue to inquire around and grow into.

Not only is the Institute committed to cultivating our own spiritually grounded workplace, but we also seek to learn with likeminded others in cultivating workplace cultures that support human development and flourishing; and that enable organizations to operate from and according to their deepest vision and values towards a more loving world. It is this commitment that animates our support of the work being done by the International Association of Management, Spirituality and Religion (IAMSR), including this volume. Those of us seeking to create workplaces that are robust containers for human flourishing and the world we want to inhabit require support and fellow travelers. Many of us are grappling with similar inquiries around the lights and shadows of bringing spirituality into the workplace.

There is so much we have learned over the past twenty years of experimenting in this area and so much more to learn. This volume offers some of the best thinking and practice from thought leaders in the field. May it serve as inspiration and fuel our collective imaginations and efforts around what is possible.

Shakiyla Smith, VP, Organizational Culture
Fetzer Institute
November 10, 2021

References

Fetzer Institute. (September 2020). *Study of Spirituality in the United States*. Report retrieved from https://spiritualitystudy.fetzer.org/sites/default/files/2020-09/What-Does-Spirituality-Mean-To-Us_%20A-Study-of-Spirituality-in-the-United-States.pdf

Jones, J.M. (2021). *U.S. Church Membership Falls Below Majority for First Time*. Gallup. Retrieved from https://news.gallup.com/poll/341963/church-membership-falls-below-majority-first-time.aspx

Kegan. R., Lahey, L.L. (2016). *An everyone culture: Becoming a deliberately developmental organization*. Harvard Business Review Press.

Neal. J. (2013). *Creating enlightened organizations: Four gateways to spirit at work*. Palgrave Macmillan.

Contents

Introduction

Judi Neal, Yochanan Altman, Wolfgang Mayrhofer

1 The Past, Present and Future of Workplace Spirituality

Introduction

In this introductory chapter we offer a brief history of IAMSR, a brief history of the field of workplace spirituality, and a broad overview of the trends in the field. We, the three editors of this book, will each conclude this chapter with offering our own views of workplace spirituality and what we see emerging in the future.

A Brief History of IAMSR

The International Association of Management, Spirituality and Religion (IAMSR) was established in 2010 by Yochanan Altman in response to an emerging need from informed practitioners who did not 'feel at home' with the *Journal of Management, Spirituality and Religion* (JMSR) community, as an exclusive academic forum. Since then, IAMSR has primarily acted as a bridge between academia and practice through its biennial conferences, which cater to both communities, running two parallel tracks – one academic, one practitioner, on a common theme, with frequent exchange and mutual fertilization. In 2020 IAMSR established a book series titled *Management, Spirituality and Religion* in partnership with De Gruyter, of which this book is its first title.

To date, IAMSR has held five international conferences. Following the inaugural conference in Vienna in 2010 on the theme 'Spirituality and Management: Strangers no More?', we held conferences in Bangalore, India on 'The Indian Challenge to Western Management' in 2012, in Lourdes, France on 'Miracles & Management' in 2013, on 'Creativity and Spirituality' in Barcelona, Spain in 2015 and on 'Leadership, Spirituality & Education' in Fayetteville, Arkansas, US in 2017.

The conferences have been guided by the motto "to be informed and inspired by the context." The context refers to the situ of the conference. Hence, we wish to refer to the location as well as season in which the event takes place. In Vienna it was around its famed Christmas markets (and Hanukkah occasioned at the same time too); in Bangalore, renown for its spiritual heritage, we were visited by no less than three gods (gurus); in Lourdes, a Marian site, we held the conference during the religious holiday of Pentecost; in Barcelona the conference was planned around its national Sant Jordi day and in Fayetteville we benefited from engagement with the Christian culture of the Deep South. Over the years the conferences evolved in length and structure. The last two conferences were three days events that ran two

https://doi.org/10.1515/9783110711349-001

parallel streams: an academic track and practitioner-oriented workshops with joint keynotes.

IAMSR participants come from academia (mostly, but not only, from business schools), training and consultancy firms, practicing managers as well as faith ministries. The conferences are strictly professional events, open to all faiths and none and to participants from all countries. The conferences have been held under the auspices of the Management, Spirituality and Religion Special Interest Group of the Academy of Management (AoM).

We had planned to hold the sixth conference in Vienna in September 2020, seeing this as an opportunity to celebrate the tenth-year anniversary of IAMSR conferences. Our vision was to invite eminent scholars to present their perspectives on the trends in the field of workplace spirituality over the past ten years and to strategically think about the future of the field for the next ten years. We had intended to have participants submit chapters to a book following the conference. The Covid-19 pandemic changed our plans, and as of this writing, we hope to now hold that conference in September 2022.

Challenges also present opportunities, so we decided that since the date of the conference was delayed, we would instead invite selected scholars with unique perspectives on the field to submit chapters before the conference. Thus, this book. Over thirty authors from around the world share their expertise and scholarship on the past and current trends in workplace spirituality and they offer many suggestions for future research and the future of the field itself.

The twenty chapters in this book are divided into five parts. Part I, "Introduction," includes this introductory chapter and an overview chapter of the field of workplace spirituality. Part II includes seven important themes that are essential lenses on the field: (1) leadership, (2) ethics, (3) strategic management, (4) organizational change, (5) organizational behavior, (6) human resource management, and (7) gender and diversity. Part III focuses in on three sectors where workplace spirituality has been implemented, describing both research and practice in these settings. Part IV is titled "Key Issues" and the three chapters in this section delve more deeply into ways of thinking about and enacting workplace spirituality that are not yet in the mainstream but that expand this field in valuable directions. Part V consists of four chapters on essential epistemologies and methodologies of interest to theory development and empirical research: (1) indigenous studies, (2) relational ontologies, (3) ethnography, and (4) psychodynamics.

This book is not a textbook for an introductory course on workplace spirituality. Nor does it purport to completely cover all aspects of the field. Instead, this is meant to be an update and a snapshot on what is presently unfolding is the workplace spirituality domain since the inaugurating IAMSR conference. It is also designed to provoke collaborative dialogue among scholars who will attend the next IAMSR conference. It is our hope that those who read this book will find their thinking, their research, and their community expanded and enriched.

Brief History of Workplace Spirituality

In 1970, Robert Greenleaf, who is often acknowledged as the instigator of the Servant Leadership movement, published an essay titled *The Servant as Leader.* This pamphlet was published a few years after Greenleaf retired as the Director of Management Research after 38 years at AT&T. A few years later he founded the Greenleaf Center for Servant Leadership. His concept of servant leadership was inspired by Herman Hesse's book *Journey to the East* (1956) that reminded Greenleaf of the role of prophecy in Christianity. The adoption of servant leadership grew over time and is still in practice in many organizations today. However, even though the servant leadership movement was founded as a result of a spiritual book, and even though Greenleaf was a deeply religious man, the servant leadership movement cannot be portrayed as the beginning of the workplace spirituality movement, since it was not explicit about spirituality or faith in any way.

The same is true of the seminal contribution of Abraham Maslow. Known as the founding father of **humanistic psychology** he could conceivably be considered a founding father of workplace spirituality, with books such as *Towards a Psychology of Being* (1962) and *Religions, Values and Peak-Experiences* (1970). Of Jewish upbringing, his concepts of *peak experience* and *self-actualization* have profoundly influenced **positive psychology** and the **positive organizational scholarship** movement, an important constituent of our field; and his *hierarchy of needs* has been pivotal to human resource management and organizational behavior. Greenleaf and Maslow were both of the Abrahamic faiths (the latter considered himself an atheist), embodying an implicit bias of the field of workplace spirituality to this day – its monotheistic and Western outlooks, though Maslow was deeply influenced by indigenous spiritualities (Stine, 2019).

Thus, both Greenleaf and Maslow laid the groundwork for what was to come later.

An extensive review of the workplace spirituality literature did not report any references before 1970, and few between 1970 and the early 1990s. However, in the early nineties, the field of workplace spirituality began to blossom (Neal, 2018).

Mitroff et al. (1994) published a seminal article in the *Academy of Management Executive,* recommending that corporations create a "World Service/Spiritual Center" to help them face global challenges in a turbulent world. An online search does not turn up any organizations that created this kind of center, but this article was an early step in legitimizing the emerging field of workplace spirituality. There are two reasons for this legitimization: (1) Ian Mitroff is a highly respected management scholar and practitioner, particularly for his work in systems theory and crisis management, and (2) the *Academy of Management Executive* is a highly ranked journal for scholar/practitioners. A few years later, Mitroff and Denton (1999) published seminal research on the state of the field from a corporate perspective, and this work is still among the most widely referenced.

Three other seminal works were published in 1994 including Dehler and Welsh (1994), McCormick (1994) and Neck and Milliman (1994). Dehler and Welsh contrasted the fields of organizational development and organizational transformation, declaring that attention to emotion and spirituality distinguish the field of organizational transformation. McCormick wrote about managerial challenges in workplace spirituality and examined five themes: compassion, right livelihood, selfless service, work as a form of meditation, and the problems of pluralism. Neck and Milliman focused on the inner work of workplace spirituality, describing "Thought self-leadership." Scholars continued to build on their work throughout the nineties, resulting in a significant increase in publications in the field.

In 1995, the business media began to pay attention to workplace spirituality from a practitioner perspective. Neal (2018, p. 13) documents:

> In June of that year, *Business Week* published an article titled "Companies hit the road less travelled: Can spirituality enlighten the bottom line?" (Galen & West, 1995). Over the next year or so, there were articles on workplace spirituality in most of the major business publications (cf. Laabs, 1995; Murray, 1995; Osborne, 1995; Segal, 1995; Brandt, 1996) and in many international newspapers. In my observation, that was when workplace spirituality became a movement. A glance at any comprehensive bibliography in the field (cf. Neal, 2016) will show a smattering of scholarly and popular press publications before 1995, and a dramatic increase from 1995 on.

Most of the publications during the nineties were in one of the following categories: (1) descriptions of organizational practices, (2) attempts to define workplace spirituality, and (3) theory development. A major criticism of scholarly work during this early period was the lack of empirical research, particularly quantitative research (Gibbons, 2000; Giacalone & Jurkiewicz, 2003; Dent et al., 2005). This is typical for a new field of study.

By the mid-nineties, it became common for professional scholarly organizations such as the Organizational Behavior Teaching Society, the US regional Academies of Management and the Management Education Division (MED) at the Academy of Management to list workplace spirituality presentations in their conference programs. The majority of these were experiential, and they drew scholars who had a deep personal interest in spirituality. They tended not to be research based at that early stage. However, a handful of doctoral students began doing dissertations in the field. The first of these was David Trott's dissertation (1996), titled *Spiritual well-being of workers: An exploratory study of spirituality in the workplace*. At that time, faculty support for this kind of research was nearly non-existent. Tackney et al. (2017) interviewed a number of pioneers in the field and quoted Trott describing the challenges of doing research on workplace spirituality as a doctoral student:

> When the professor asked me what my topic was, I didn't even get the whole title out before he grinned from ear to ear, slammed a 10-dollar bill on the table and said, "I'll bet you nobody is going to care about that topic in 5 years." Literally, the very next second the dismissal bell rang. I stood up and my head was down as I walked out of the room. My inner voice was

> whirling around thinking "what am I going to do"? I hadn't walked 100 strides before I said "I don't care what he says – even if I have to leave this university, I'm going to pursue this.
> (Tackney et al., 2017, p. 141)

When Trott conducted his research, there were no measures of spirituality in the workplace, so he used Ellison's (1983) psychological assessment of spiritual well-being. However, the following year Hamilton Beazley (1997) completed his dissertation titled *Meaning and measurement of spirituality in organizational settings: Development of a spirituality assessment scale*. Both dissertations helped to lay the groundwork for empirical research from that point on. Several years later Kinjerski and Skrypnek (2004) developed the Spirituality at Work Survey (SAWS) which is still widely used in quantitative studies.

A turning point for the professionalization of the field was a symposium on workplace spirituality organized by Lee Robbins in 1997, sponsored by the MED division of the Academy of Management. Panelists included Judi Neal, Lee Bolman and David Cooperrider. The session was standing room only and Lee Robbins, Jerry Biberman and Judi Neal created a mailing list of interested attendees with the idea of potentially creating a new interest group at the Academy of Management. The high level of energy and interest at that symposium led to the creation of other events at AOM in the next two years where petitions for forming an interest group were circulated. The application for interest group status was approved by the Academy in 2000, and the first sessions of the MSR group were conducted in 2001.

In the early 2000s, one of the hindrances to increased recognition of the field was the difficulty of getting published in mainstream journals that were either skeptical about the field or found the topics it engages with too threatening (King, 2008). As more and more scholars began conducting research in the field, Jerry Biberman and Judi Neal created a proposal for a new journal and then learned that Yochanan Altman was considering doing the same thing. Altman became the founding editor of the *Journal of Management, Spirituality and Religion* (JMSR) and Biberman was its first senior editor. For the first six years (2004–2009), Altman published the journal as an independent publication and over the following ten years (2010–2020) as a partnership between IAMSR (constituted in 2010) and Routledge, of the Taylor & Francis Group. Starting 2021 the *Journal of Management, Spirituality and Religion* is once again independent; its publishing platform is IngentaConnect (https://www.ingentaconnect.com/content/jmsr/rmsr20). With 70+ published issues JMSR is the largest repository of academic knowledge in the field and widely considered its leading journal. JMSR currently publishes 5 issues a year and offers its services as an ad-hoc publisher to like-minded professional groups. In 2021 the journal publishes an Open Access special issue in partnership with AITIA Institute (https://www.aitiainstitute.org) in addition to its regular issues.

As well as the organizational sponsor of JMSR and organizer of the biennial conferences, IAMSR established in 2020 a book series in partnership with De Gruyter.

This book is the first in the series and at the time of going to press two additional books are in the pipeline (https://www.degruyter.com/serial/MSR-B/html).

Since the early 2000s the field has matured substantially. While early research was primarily descriptive, definitional, and non-empirical, current research is more rigorous, more international, and more widespread. One sign of maturing is the recent partnership between the Management, Spirituality and Religion (MSR) interest group and Fetzer Institute. Fetzer Institute is one of the premier foundations in the U.S. supporting research on faith, spirituality, and consciousness. Their mission is to help build the spiritual foundation for a loving world. In 2018 they worked with MSR leadership to create the MSR Fetzer Scholarship for Emerging Scholars and New Faculty. Each year since 2019, Fetzer Institute, a sponsor of this book, has supported 20 doctoral students and new faculty in attending the annual Academy of Management conference, with a focus on involvement in MSR events. The fact that is has been easy to find at least 20 highly qualified scholars each year for this scholarship is strong evidence that work in this field is now widespread. Recipients of this scholarship come from all over Europe, from African countries, from Asia and the Asia Pacific, the Middle East, Australia, Latin America and North America. They are a diverse group representing a variety of religious and spiritual perspectives as well as fields of study. Twenty years ago, it would have been impossible to find anywhere near this number of scholarship recipients each year.

Some Observations of Trends in the Field Since the First IAMSR Conference

This section discusses some of the trends we have seen since the first IAMSR conference. As you read the chapters in this book, there will be additional descriptions of trends in the recent past as well as authors' views of what could or what should emerge as we move ahead in the development of this field.

1. The Maturing of the Field of Workplace Spirituality

We have already discussed the growth of MSR and the wider acceptance of workplace spirituality research in the Academy of Management, and the growth of the *Journal of Management, Spirituality and Religion.*

This book also represents the maturing of the field from an early focus on generic workplace spirituality or generic research on faith at work to finer distinctions. For example, in the "Themes" section of this book, authors explore specific connections between spirituality and different aspects of the field of management such as leadership, ethics, strategy, family business, and so on. The authors here also explore specific applications of workplace spirituality in various sectors such as policing and health and wellbeing. Other edited volumes have chapters that describe various religious and faith tradition perspectives (cf. Dhiman, 2018; Neal, 2013).

2. Levels of Analysis

In the early stages of this field, most of the research and publications focused on the individual level of analysis. As the field developed, the level of analysis also began to include group dynamics, organizational systems, and patterns across organizations. As will be discussed below, there is now an increasing interest on the role of workplace spirituality in the development of global consciousness.

3. Religious Discrimination Lawsuits

One challenge that has emerged in recent years is the growth in the U.S. of religious discrimination lawsuits (Sullivan, 2013). From 2002 until 2010, the International Center for Spirit at Work gave the annual International Spirit at Work Award to organizations that had specific policies, practices or programs that nurtured the human spirit at work (Neal, 2013). But after 2010, the awards committee was not able to find any organizations willing to apply for the award. They were concerned that receiving the award might give them too much visibility for their emphasis on spirituality or religion, opening them up to potential lawsuits from employees (Point et al., 2019)

4. Evolution of Language

As Marie Holm describes in this book, mindfulness has become a major trend in the workplace spirituality field. There are a few reasons for this including that early mindfulness programs at Aetna demonstrated a strong correlation between decrease in healthcare costs and increases in employee productivity. Aetna estimated that they saved about $2000 per employee per year in healthcare costs and gained about $3000 per employee per year in productivity (Pinkser, 2015). Chade-Meng Tan, a software engineer at Google, built upon the success of the mindfulness programs at Aetna (Giang, 2015; Tan, 2012), bringing a sense of Silicon Valley coolness to mindfulness in the workplace. After that, a large number of corporations jumped on the bandwagon and this is now the most common approach to workplace spirituality. The use of the term "mindfulness" creates a lot less resistance than terms such as "workplace spiritualty." Indeed, Altman found in the first seminar for Human Resource Managers on workplace spirituality he convened in London in 2008 that participants could not bring themselves to utter 'spirituality' and instead referred to the 'S word'.

We should point out, however, that there is a much greater acceptance of spiritually-based language in scholarly settings than there is in corporate settings. This also varies widely by geographic region and culture. For instance, in China and France, there is low tolerance for explicitly spiritual language, in both cases due to its alignment with religion: in the former religion is outlawed, in the latter it conflicts with the country's constitution as laic; and so scholars and practitioners find other terms to describe the phenomena ranging from philosophical to scientific terminology.

Language around "leadership" also seems to be changing. Jody Fry is probably the most recognized scholar on spiritual leadership (Fry & Nisiewicz, 2012), and his work has been the inspiration for many workplace spirituality dissertations. But just as the term "workplace spirituality" can create resistance, particularly in corporations, there seems to be increasing resistance to using the term "spiritual leadership." So people use more secular language to describe the same phenomena, including terms like authentic leadership, self-leadership, inner leadership, quantum leadership and conscious leadership.

5. Scholar/Practitioners

Another trend we will discuss here is the rise of the Scholar/Practitioner in the field of workplace spirituality. Twenty to thirty years ago, scholars had little connection to practitioners and were not very aware of what was going on in organizational practice. At the same time, practitioners were unaware of the research in the field and were unlikely to read the journal articles or attend academic conferences and were not guided by research discoveries. Now, not only are the interconnections between scholars and practitioners much stronger, it is not uncommon for the scholar to be doing consulting and coaching in the field, many practitioners hold Ph.D.s and conduct applied research in their organizational settings.

6. Impact: Making a Difference

A major trend we have evidenced in management academe is a new focus on research that has a positive impact on the world in some way, also known as Management Research Mode 2 (Bartunek, 2011). The same is true within MSR and within the field of workplace spirituality. In the past, the focus has frequently been on whether or not explicit spiritual approaches even exist within organizations. If they exist, then scholars tend to describe them, but only more recently have begun to explore the outcomes of programs and approaches. Typically, the outcomes focus on benefits for the individual or benefits for the organization. More recently, scholars and practitioners are starting to ask themselves questions about the impact of workplace spirituality on all stakeholders, including communities, families, the environment, indigenous people. Broader issues such as racism, oppression, colonialism, social justice, gender equality, environmental degradation, and humanity's relationship with non-human stakeholders have become a part of the conversation. The bottom line is that increasing numbers of people who work in this workplace spirituality domain are more interested in making a difference than in getting published, getting promoted, or having more power.

This section has discussed six macro-trends in the field of workplace spirituality. This is not all- inclusive and you are encouraged to explore the trends that are described in the chapters that follow. All of these trends and more show up in one or more chapters, and will hopefully expand your thinking about your own work in new ways.

Individual Perspectives on What is Emerging in Workplace Spirituality

This final section of our introductory chapter takes a brief look at emerging trends that each of us sees from our own particular lens. These three emerging trends are based on our personal experiences, our professional interests, and our commitment to doing work that makes a difference.

Workplace Spirituality and Global Consciousness – Judi Neal

Vaclav Havel, in an address to the U.S. Congress made a statement that is even more relevant today, over thirty years later:

> Without a global revolution in the sphere of human consciousness, nothing will change for the better in the sphere of our being as humans, and the catastrophe toward which this world is headed – be it ecological, social, demographic, or a general breakdown of civilization will be unavoidable. (Havel, 1990)

I believe that we are entering a "global revolution in the sphere of human consciousness," and it is essential that we do. This global revolution is both impacted by workplace spirituality and has an impact on workplace spirituality.

As scholars and practitioners, we live in a global, interconnected world. The world needs leaders who are capable of thinking and acting with global awareness and a commitment to the greater good. Yet there are few resources available to support the development of globally conscious leaders in academia or in corporate leadership development. There are no university courses or programs on global consciousness and it is not considered a field of study in academia, or as a field of practice in organization. But it is essential for the world we find ourselves in.

The wicked problems we face require humanity to collectively respond in ways that will transform complex, messy situations such as the Covid-19 pandemic, political polarization, and climate change into a world that provides well-being and flourishing for all (Tsao & Laszlo, 2019). Mitroff (2021) states that these wicked, messy, complex problems require a new mode of inquiry, which he calls "Heroic Inquiry." Heroic Inquiry requires a sense of wholeness, interconnectedness and oneness in order to understand and solve wicked problems rather than the prevailing materialistic scientific approach of taking something apart to analyze its elements.

The field of workplace spirituality has studied phenomena at the individual, team and organizational level. It is now beginning to explore interconnections at the global level from a systems dynamic perspective (Meadows, 1991). One of the first initiatives to take this approach was the Fowler Center for Business as an Agent of World Benefit at Case Western University led by David Cooperrider. Using an Appreciative Inquiry (Cooperrider & Whitney, 2005) approach, students develop case studies showcasing businesses that are having a positive impact on the world with a focus on human flourishing. Their work demonstrates the importance of a shift in consciousness in organizational leadership. The research on quantum leadership by Tsao and Laszlo makes this connection with global consciousness even clearer (Tsao & Laszlo, 2019).

As a new field of inquiry in the domain of workplace spirituality, definitions are important at this early stage. I offer three definitions as a way of providing an initial map of the territory and inviting different but complimentary forms of scholarship and programmatic actions.

1. Global Consciousness as an Individual Stage of Development

Global consciousness can reside in an individual as a stage of human development beyond ego-centric and tribal-centric. The individual feels a sense of deep connection, interdependence, and oneness to humanity and the planet. There are countless stage theories of stages of human development, and of the development of levels of consciousness. Some examples include Trust Theory (Gibb, 1978), Spiral Dynamics (Beck & Cowan, 2014), and Integral Theory (Wilber, 2001). The highest level of consciousness in these models goes by terms such as global consciousness, oneness consciousness, or non-dual consciousness. In these theories there are usually bifurcation points where a quantum shift in self-identity occurs. Tsao and Laszlo describe this as a shift from consciousness of separation to consciousness of connectedness (2019).

2. Global Consciousness as an Aspect of Leadership Development

Global consciousness is an aspect of leadership development where people are trained in wisdom practices, connectedness practices, and linear and non-linear ways of knowing. The goal is to create a critical mass of leaders with a deep awareness of connectedness and interdependence.

In business in the past, terms like "global consciousness" or "global mindset" have been framed as cross-cultural sensitivity, which is cognitive and behavioral based, or as international management, which is strategic. Egel and Fry (2019) take an expanded view of global leadership in a complex environment, which they call "Being-centered leadership." They argue that a commitment to the spiritual journey is essential for developing the kind of global mindset that recognizes the dignity and commonality of the human experience and includes the ability to reconcile and transcend apparent opposites.

Leadership development programs, such as Tsao and Laszlo's (2019) Quantum Leadership program, have been developed to provide experiences, wisdom, practices, models and guidance to help leaders move to higher levels of consciousness in a way that positively impacts their personal and professional lives, their organizations, humanity, and the planet. It would be valuable to document these programs and to learn more about best practices and their impacts.

3. Global Consciousness as a Collective Phenomenon

Global consciousness is a collective phenomenon whereby the human race perceives itself collectively within and inseparable from nature and commits to the greater good. There is an emergence of international and cross-functional projects and organizations working in this domain. They are working together to solve the climate crisis, and to support world peace, well-being of all living things, and economic, social, and environmental justice.

There have been occasional examples of the experience of global consciousness as a collective phenomenon. New Year's Eve 2000 millennial angst is one example. This was a time when the industrialized world was concerned about the negative potential of Y2K on the computer-centric world. But for a 24-hour period, television viewers could see the new year roll in, country by country around the world. It was as if, for just a moment, all of humanity was celebrating the start of a new year, a new century, and a new millennium. And they were also celebrating the fact that computers and the internet kept working and that it wasn't the "end of the world."

Currently we are in the midst of several global "wicked problems." Everyone is impacted and it will take small and large actions from each and every person, as well as interconnected and coordinated effort from major institutions to transform these shared crises into a more loving world where all can flourish.

Workplace Spirituality and New Technologies – Wolfgang Mayrhofer

It is a no-brainer that new technologies are here to stay and continue to have a strong impact on the world of work. How we organize work at the collective and individual level, e.g. within various societies, in organizations, and in our personal lives, heavily depends on available technologies that support production and service as well as the relationship between individual and/or collective actors. Take, for example, the technology induced changes that have occurred over the past decades with regard to automated production processes, tracking information about shipped goods, and the possibilities to communicate with each other across large geographical distances. Computer-controlled machinery that requires fewer individuals with different kinds of qualifications, the role of electronic data bases providing real-time information about traffic jams, alternative routes and delays in train, plane, and tram connections as well as various ways of communicating via mobile phones, computers and sophisticated conference software with team members across the globe, are just the tip of the iceberg. As a result, at least three crucial issues arise, all of which have consequences for the future of workplace spirituality.

Decoupling of space and performance. Due to the broad array of recent technology and its impact on the world of work, an increasing number of jobs no longer depend on a specific spatial setting that the individual has to be in. True, this is not the case for a number of professions such as, e.g., physiotherapists, police officer patrolling streets, and room cleaners. Nevertheless, the global COVID-19 pandemic from the early 2020s clearly demonstrates the enormous potential to work, for the better or the worse, outside a workplace that the employing organization has provided.

Real-time self- and other-monitoring. The broad diffusion of various kinds of technology allows continuous surveillance of different aspects of individual, group, and organizational behavior. There is plethora of examples for this, including the use of embodied computing that uses tangible technology on, in, and around the body such as intelligent wristbands, epidermal electronics, and implantables/ingestibles; the availability of various key performance indicators at the team/organizational unit related to, for example, sales and customer contact; and the broad array of indicators, often in 'dashboard style', that show various organizational performance indicators such as turnover, market share, waste, and energy consumption on a day-to-day basis.

Optimizing oneself and others. Linked to the above, figures that seem to exactly capture vital aspects of individuals, groups, and organizations are not simply 'available'. Rather, the embeddedness of our lives in a capitalist society where efficiency, effectiveness, and merit are part of the individual and collective canon that governs many parts of our lives seems to require the use of such information to further optimize what is at hand. The 'magic of numbers' does its work and seduces us to use the available figures and their development over time to guide our action and measurably develop ourselves.

Against this backdrop, a number of developments should – and partially already do – emerge in the area of workplace spirituality. The following are of specific importance.

1. Increasing emphasis on the body

While approaches to spirituality vary in their view of what is constitutive for a holistic view of the individual, many would regard the body as an essential element of the configurational web that forms human beings. Workplace spirituality is affected, for example, by the decoupling between the space that one occupies during working hours and the unit that one's performance is attributed to since this gap raises concerns about issues such as accountability, feeling wholeness, and meaning. While for thousands of years the immediate link between action and outcome at least in spatial terms has been relatively strong, the developments of the past two decades are very recent and require massive individual and collective reorientation. Workplace spirituality can further guide such a reorientation.

2. Supporting the here-and-now beyond functionalization

The current popularity of approaches such as mindfulness are but one indicator for a growing and widespread uneasiness with the strict regime that – often with good intentions – we as well as our peers, supervisors, and organization apply to optimize 'outcome'. The well-known adage of 'unintentional intentionality' comes to mind – workplace spirituality, in many, but not all practical appearances not tied to the dictum of performance and outcome, has a worthy area to cover new ground. Opening up avenues where individuals, groups, and organizations can consciously spend time exploring and experiencing the spiritual realm becomes ever more important under conditions that relentlessly seem to require efficient, effective, and goal-oriented use of one's resources.

3. Establish, defend and enlarge sacred spaces

The concept of the sacred is a traditional part of most spiritual traditions and practices. While, of course, the concrete form of, justification for, and significance of the sacred varies greatly, arguably a common characteristic is its isolation from the ordinary that pervades our daily life. New technologies have a tendency to usurp many, if not all areas of the individual and collective life. This is especially true for working environments and lives where the demands are high and there is the implicit assumption that at least during – often way beyond – working hours the person fully is a part of the economic system. Silent rooms, prayer breaks, meditation zones, inner and outer pilgrimages etc. are a few examples how workplace spirituality can create and use sacred spaces both in their material and immaterial sense.

These are well-trodden as well as partially new paths. New technologies' emergence and, some would argue, intrusion into our working lives require workplace spirituality to cover many bases in order to contribute to a fuller and more holistic individual and collective existence.

Confronting Dark Spiritualities: Antisemitism As a Case in Point – Yochanan Altman

The workplace spirituality movement is commonly portrayed in bright colors, since its aim (writ large) is to create a better world, the workplace included. With the passage of time though, its temporal attributes come to light. Workplace spirituality, as a scholarly field and its practice equivalents, emerged in the 1990s and the first decade of the 2000s. The same period also sees the beginnings of the academic fields of positive psychology and positive organizational scholarship; a time of increasing wealth and prosperity in the West, when liberal democracy and the human rights and civil liberties it advocates triumphed, pro LGBT legislation became canonical and diversity management at the workplace has come to be normative practice. Introducing *positive psychology*, Martin Seligman, in his 1998 APA presidential address foresaw this new domain as "building of the most positive qualities of an individual: optimism, courage, work ethic, future mindedness, interpersonal skill, the capacity for pleasure and insight, and social responsibility" (Seligman, 1999, p. 561). And so it did, possibly culminating in the establishment of *happiness studies* as a scholarly domain and practice.

At the onset of the 2020s we find ourselves with a different worldview, or perhaps in a different world mood. In Europe, from where I am writing, multiculturalism has been replaced by nationalism as the leading rhetoric and 'illiberal democracy' is no longer a clandestine term, but the official policy of Viktor Orbán in Hungary, whose long stint in power and success in eroding civil liberties, resembles that of Recep Erdoğan in Turkey and Vladimir Putin in Russia (not a conclusive list). Under the heading *Democracy Under Siege* Freedom House's survey of world politics sums up the present situation: "As a lethal pandemic, economic and physical insecurity, and violent conflict ravaged the world, democracy's defenders sustained heavy new losses in their struggle against authoritarian foes, shifting the international balance in favor of tyranny". And the report elaborates: . . . "the long-term democratic decline has become increasingly global in nature . . . in 2020, the number of Free countries in the world reached its lowest level since the beginning of a 15-year period of global democratic decline, while the number of Not Free countries reached its highest level." (Repucci & Slipowitz, 2021) And Gandesha (2018, p. 49) notes "We appear to be living in an age of populism", of both the right and the left.

With hindsight, signs of things to come were already evident at the time workplace spirituality took its first steps on the academic and practitioner scenes. Zakaria (1997) warned of the 'rise of illiberal democracies'; and populist right-wing policies were advocated, among others, by Le Pen in France, Haider in Austria and Lega Nord in Italy since the 1980s, drawing growing public support. By then, Laclau and Mouffe's theories on left-wing populism (Laclau & Mouffe, 1985) were well articulated and closely studied in political left circles.

A key development of the past decade – the rapid spread of social media and its wide use (and misuse) – is a major contemporary current in public discourse with evident political overtones. The impact of social media in creating and enacting grassroot movements such as *#me too, black lives matter* and modern anti-slavery campaigns, with obvious workplace implications, are hard to ignore. The point is this. Whatever our views and beliefs, it has become difficult to disentangle workplace spirituality from the politics of the times. Thus, for example, organizing the fifth IAMSR international conference in Fayetteville, Arkansas in May 2017, the organizers were faced with the calamity that delegates from Muslim countries were prevented from attending due to President Trump issuing executive order 13780 shortly before the conference took place, banning entry to the USA from these countries. This was anathema to the philosophy of an institution and a movement predicated on engaging with religion and its relevance to work, management and organizations. Taking a stand on issues that are in the public domain and that may be controversial thus becomes difficult to avoid. I am not talking about having a principled position on sustainability or climate change or corporate social responsibility – these have become by now accepted truisms, much like – as the saying goes, motherhood and apple pie. I am talking about taking a stand against dark spiritualities.

By dark spiritualities I refer to deep seated prejudices, widely accepted negative stereotypes implicitly shared by many, woven into societies' cultural fabric from time immemorial and acted upon in our day to day, often subconsciously and sometimes without malicious intent. I wish to differentiate these dark spiritualities which are often taken for granted, 'because this is the way things are', from the discourse on the dark side of organizations (Vaughan, 1999) – such as, bullying and harassment, blatant discrimination, corruption and nepotism, sabotage; as well as the dark side of workplace spiritualty, often attributed by critical management scholars (Lips-Wiersma & Mills, 2014), since these tend to be specific and episodic; whereas the dark spiritualities I refer to tend to be diffused and universal.

An example of a dark spirituality is Nazism, the darkest of all 20th century dominant spiritualities. As a radical humanist movement, Nazism put center stage the creation of a 'new' breed of human being that required the extermination of 'unwanted' elements in society, like the physically and mentally handicapped, homosexuals, and most and foremost – Jews; culminating in the Final Solution of the Jewish Question, i.e. the Shoah (Holocaust). At the core of Nazi ideology was Antisemitism, that is the hatred and fear of Jews. Nazism was routed but not uprooted and its foundation – Antisemitism, remains intact. Whether Nazism was a direct continuation of German (and European) Antisemitism of the 19th century, or a new departure for this age-old hatred has been a matter for debate.

Antisemitism as a generalized anti-Jewish attitude (whether against Jews as individuals, Jews as a collective, or 'Jews' as an abstract concept) has been around since at least the birth of Christianity – of relevance to a scholarly movement for which religion is a point of departure. Its intensity fluctuates, but it has never completely disappeared and is present also in geographies bereft of Jews ('Antisemitsm without Jews') resurfacing under favorable circumstances. Justin Welby, Archbishop of Canterbury, said as much in evidence before the Home Affairs Select Committee at the House of Commons (2016, p. 19):

> we have to recognize that antisemitism has been the root and origin of most racist behavior for the past 1,000 years . . . It seems to be something that is latent and under the surface, and it bubbles to the surface very, very easily indeed. I think it is one of those things that, when we see it, tells us that there are strains and stresses in society. It is the canary in the mine.

The world has experienced considerable strains and stresses over the past decade or so, and lo and behold, Antisemitism has mushroomed in all corners of the world and intensified, aided by social media and the darknet. A 2016 survey found that an antisemitic post is uploaded to social media every 83 seconds (WJC, 2017). Antisemitic incidents include physical harm and loss of life, attacks on places of worship, vandalism to cemeteries, harassment and intimidation of persons in public spaces. More recently Jews were accused as both creators of the Covid-19 pandemic and financially benefiting from its cure (EJC, 2021).

Whilst extensively studied by historians and political scientists, and of interest to social psychologists, Antisemitism seems to have escaped the attention of business & management scholars (Altman et al., in press). Consequently, bar the occasional scandal, we know next to nothing how Antisemitism as an attitude and behavior pattern may affect individuals at work or infuse an organizational culture. The former may be of personal concern for anyone perceived to be Jewish – whether they are Jews or not; the latter, as was the case with the British Labour party, found to be institutionally antisemitic in an official enquiry (EHRC, 2020), caused grave injury to individuals and profoundly damaged a century old institution.

The challenge presented to the workplace spirituality movement is the opportunity to engage in the here and now combating centuries old hatreds, such as Antisemitism, thereby widening our reach as a scholarly and applied movement aiming to do good. And whilst a logo colored rainbow for a Gay Pride parade doesn't necessarily make a workplace safe for LGBT+ employees, nor does a corporate Juneteenth celebration imply Black workers are treated equitably, there are signs of willingness by both the corporate and significant others to confront our deepest prejudices at the workplace. Contribution through research, theorizing and developing applications for practice, would be a worthwhile undertaking for workplace spirituality scholars and practitioners.

References

Altman, Y., Koll, J., Mayrhofer, W., Mueller-Camen, M., & Schneebaum, A. (in press). Contours of workplace Antisemitsm. In A. Lange, K. Mayerhofer, D. Porat, & L. H. Schiffman (Eds.), *An End to Antisemitism!* (Vol. 4). De Gruyter.

Bartunek, J. M. (2011). What has happened to mode 2? *British Journal of Management, 22*(3), 555–558. https://doi.org/10.1111/j.1467-8551.2011.00773.x

Beazley, H. (1997). *Meaning and measurement of spirituality in organizational settings: Development of a spirituality assessment scale* [Doctoral dissertation, The George Washington University]. UMI Microform 9820619.

Beck, P. D. E., & Cowan, C. C. (2014). *Spiral Dynamics: Mastering Values, Leadership and Change.* John Wiley & Sons. https://books.google.at/books?id=w7PwBwAAQBAJ

Brandt, E. (1996). Corporate pioneers explore spirituality: Peace; Developing spirituality within the company. *HR Magazine, 41*(4), 82–87.

Cooperrider, D. L., & Whitney, D. K. (2005). *Appreciative Inquiry: A Positive Revolution in Change.* Berrett-Koehler.

Dehler, G. E., & Welsh, M. A. (1994). Spirituality and organizational transformation: Implications for the new management paradigm. *Journal of Managerial Psychology, 9*(6), 17–26. https://doi.org/10.1108/02683949410070179

Dent, E. B., Higgins, M. E., & Wharff, D. M. (2005). Spirituality and leadership: An empirical review of definitions, distinctions, and embedded assumptions. *The Leadership Quarterly, 16*(5), 625–653. https://doi.org/10.1016/j.leaqua.2005.07.002

Dhiman, S. (Ed.). (2018). *The Palgrave Handbook of Workplace Spirituality and Fulfillment.* Palgrave. https://doi.org/10.1007/978-3-319-62163-0

Egel, E., & Fry, L. W. (2019). Cultivating a global mindset through "being-centered" leadership. In J. Neal (Ed.), *Handbook of Personal and Organizational Transformation* (pp. 981–1000). Springer.

EHRC. (2020). *Investigation into Antisemitism in the Labour Party.* Equality and Human Rights Commission. https://www.equalityhumanrights.com/en/publication-download/investigation-antisemitism-labour-party
EJC. (2021). *Antisemitism worldwide 2020.* European Jewish Congress, Kantor Center Tel-Aviv University.
Ellison, C. W. (1983). Spiritual well-being: Conceptualization and measurement. *Journal of Psychology and Theology, 11*(4), 330–338. https://doi.org/10.1177/009164718301100406
Fry, L. W., & Nisiewicz, M. S. (2012). *Maximizing the Triple Bottom Line Through Spiritual Leadership.* Stanford University Press.
Galen, M., & West, K. (1995, June 5). Companies hit the road less travelled: Can spirituality enlighten the bottom line? *Business Week*, 82–85.
Gandesha, S. (2018). Understanding right and left populism. In J. Morelock, *Critical Theory and Authoritarian Populism* (pp. 49–70). University of Westminster Press. https://doi.org/10.16997/book30.d
Giacalone, R. A., & Jurkiewicz, C. L. (2003). *Handbook of Workplace Spirituality and Organizational Performance.* M.E. Sharpe. https://books.google.at/books?id=qmbBeAac-acC
Giang, V. (2015). *Inside Google's insanely popular emotional intelligence course.* Accessed on Sept 23 2016 at http://www.fastcompany.com/3044157/the-future-of-work/inside-googles-in sanely-popular-emotional-intelligence-course?utm_source
Gibb, J. R. (1978). *Trust: A New View of Personal and Organizational Development.* Guild of Tutors Press.
Gibbons, P. (2000). Spirituality at work: Definitions, measures, assumptions, and validity claims. In J. Biberman & M. D. Whitty (Eds.), *Work and Spirit: A Reader of New Spiritual Paradigms for Organizations* (pp. 111–131). Univesity of Scranton Press.
Havel, V. (1990, February 22). *Address to the U.S. Congress.* Accessed on May 28, 2021 at https://www.vhlf.org/havel-quotes/speech-to-the-u-s-congress/
Hesse, H. (1956). *The Journey to the East.* Picador.
House of Commons. (2016). *Antisemitism in the UK:* Tenth *report of session 2016-17.* Accessed July 11, 2021. https://publications.parliament.uk/pa/cm201617/cmselect/cmhaff/136/136.pdf
King, J. E. (2008). (Dis)Missing the obvious: Will mainstream management research ever take religion seriously? *Journal of Management Inquiry, 17*(3), 214–224. https://doi.org/10.1177/1056492608314205
Kinjerski, V. M., & Skrypnek, B. J. (2004). Defining spirit at work: Finding common ground. *Journal of Organizational Change Management. Special Issue "Research That Matters: Helping Organizations Integrate Spiritual Values and Practices.," 17*(1), 26–42. https://doi.org/10.1108/09534810410511288
Laabs, J. (1995). Balancing spirituality and work. *Personnel Journal. September 18, 74*(9), 60.
Laclau, E., & Mouffe, C. (1985). *Hegemony and Socialist Strategy.* Verso.
Lips-Wiersma, M., & Mills, A. J. (2014). Understanding the basic assumptions about human nature in workplace spirituality: Beyond the critical versus positive divide. *Journal of Management Inquiry, 23*(2), 148–161. https://doi.org/10.1177/1056492613501227
Maslow, A. (1962). *Towards a Psychology of Being.* Van Nostrand Reinhold Company.
Maslow, A. (1970). *Religions, Values and Peak-Experiences.* Penguin Books.
McCormick, D. W. (1994). Spirituality and management. *Journal of Managerial Psychology, 9*(6), 5–8. https://doi.org/10.1108/02683949410070142
Meadows, D. H. (1991). *The Global Citizen.* Island Press.
Mitroff, I. I. (2021). My lifelong love affair with philosophy: Coping with wicked messes. *Psychology Today.* Accessed March 2, 2021 at https://www.psychologytoday.com/us/blog/crisis-manage ment/202102/my-lifelong-love-affair-philosophy

Mitroff, I. I., & Denton, E. A. (1999). *A Spiritual Audit of Corporate America: Multiple Designs for Fostering Spirituality in the Workplace*. Jossey-Bass.

Mitroff, I. I., Mason, R. O., & Pearson, C. M. (1994). Radical surgery: What will tomorrow's organizations look like? *Academy of Management Perspectives*, *8*(2), 11–21. https://doi.org/10.5465/ame.1994.9503101062

Murray, M. (1995, October 19). Tackling workplace problems with prayer. *Wall Street Journal, Eastern Edition*, B1, B12.

Neal, J. (2013). *Creating Enlightened Organizations*. Palgrave Macmillan.

Neal, J. (2016). *Annotated workplace spirituality bibliography*. Unpublished document supported by a grant from Fetzer Institute.

Neal, J. (2018). Overview of workplace spirituality research: A literature review. In S. Dhiman (Ed.), *The Palgrave Handbook of Workplace Spirituality and Fulfillment* (pp. 3–57). Palgrave. https://doi.org/10.1007/978-3-319-62163-0_45

Neck, C. P., & Milliman, J. F. (1994). Thought self-leadership: Finding spiritual fulfilment in organizational life. *Journal of Managerial Psychology*, *9*(6), 9–16. https://doi.org/10.1108/02683949410070151

Osborne, R. (1995). Company with a soul. *Industry Week*, *244*(9). https://search.ebscohost.com/login.aspx?direct=true&db=buh&AN=9505192290&site=ehost-live

Pinkser, J. (2015). Corporations' newest hack: Meditation. *The Atlantic (Online)*. http://www.theatlantic.com/business/archive/2015/03/corporations-newest-productivity-hack-meditation/387286/. Accessed 11 Nov 2016

Point, S., Altman, Y. H., & Neal, J. A. (2019, August 1). *In search of spiritual organizations*. Presented at the Academy of Management, Boston, MA.

Repucci, S., & Slipowitz, A. (2021). *Democracy under siege*. https://freedomhouse.org/report/freedom-world/2021/democracy-under-siege. Accessed July 11, 2021

Segal, D. (1995). Trying to profit from parables. *The Washington Post*, D12+.

Seligman, M. E. P. (1999). The president's address. *The American Psychologist*, *54*, 559–562.

Stine, B. S. (2019). *It's so old it is new: Native self actualization placement assessment*. https://www.cdu.edu.au/sites/default/files/the-northern-institute/first_nations_symposium_-_27_sep_2019.pdf accessed 10 June, 2021

Sullivan, P. M. (2013). EEOC best practices support best practices for spirit and religion at work. In J. Neal (Ed.), *Handbook of Faith and Spirituality in the Workplace* (pp. 19–31). Springer. https://doi.org/10.1007/978-1-4614-5233-1_2

Tackney, C. T., Chappell, S. F., & Sato, T. (2017). MSR founders narrative and content analysis of scholarly papers: 2000–2015. *Journal of Management, Spirituality & Religion*, *14*(2), 135–159. https://doi.org/10.1080/14766086.2017.1295879

Tan, C.-M. (2012). *Search Inside Yourself: The Unexpected Path to Achieving Success, Happiness (and World Peace)*. HarperCollins.

Trott, D. (1996). *Spiritual well-being of workers: An exploratory study of spirituality in the workplace* [Doctoral Dissertation]. University of Texas at Austin.

Tsao, F. C., & Laszlo, C. (2019). *Quantum Leadership: New Consciousness in Business*. Stanford Business Books, an imprint of Stanford University Press.

Vaughan, D. (1999). The dark side of organizations: Mistake, misconduct, and disaster. *Annual Review of Sociology*, *25*(1), 271–305. https://doi.org/10.1146/annurev.soc.25.1.271

Wilber, K. (2001). *A Theory of Everything: An Integral Vision for Business, Politics, Science and Spirituality*. Shambhala Press. https://books.google.at/books?id=juxkSiDpHD0C

WJC. (2017). https://www.worldjewishcongress.org/en/news/watch–the-rise-of-anti-semitism-on-social-media-summary-of-2016-6-1-2017 Accessed July 13, 2021

Zakaria, F. (1997). The rise of illiberal democracy. *Foreign Affairs*, *76*(6), 22–43.

Roger Gill

2 Introduction to Spirituality

Introduction

In this chapter we introduce spirituality and its place in the workplace and in organizations more generally. We look at the relationships between spirituality and science and between spirituality and religion. We strike a note of caution: there is a dark side to workplace spirituality. The chapter concludes with the future of spirituality and suggestions for further study and research.

What is Spirituality?

First, let us dispose of a common but eccentric notion of spirituality: its frequent confusion with *spiritualism*. Spiritualism is a theory that the "spirit" exists separately from matter, for instance the body, and that the only reality is spirit. It is associated, for example, with astrology, mediums, séances, tarot cards and the practice of supposedly communicating with the dead. Spirituality, whether based on religion or secular humanism, can be an antidote to many of today's societal problems; spiritualism may well reflect or even contribute to them. Kristy Hesketh (2020) has suggested that a spiritualist movement based on spiritualism has grown rapidly as a result of the formation and development of the mass media and the associated rise of "fake news" and misinformation. Understanding what animates people to believe the unbelievable, just as understanding what animates people to do anything, is clearly an ongoing challenge, not least for "spiritually intelligent" leaders.

Misunderstanding of what spirituality is can create negative prejudice that hinders productive learning and application of knowledge about the essence of being human and motivation and well-being. Judi Neal (2018) speaks of her experience in the 1970s when she broached the subject of spirituality in one of her organizational behaviour classes at Yale University: "[I] was immediately shut down by the professor who proclaimed that anyone who thought they had any kind of transcendent experiences was delusional, probably schizophrenic and needed to be in therapy." And Lieutenant-Commander Justin Top of the US Marine Corps says that many leaders simply shy away from the talk of spirituality altogether because of the controversial nature of religious topics, yet "such a reaction can be an unfortunate neglect of a powerful and important tool for leadership" (Top, 2019, p. 66), which we discuss in the next chapter.

The Latin root of "spirituality" is *spiritus*, meaning "breath". Early use of the term, in the 5th century CE, for Christians, referred to the influence of God in human lives – the Holy Spirit. By the 12th century CE, it had come to refer, in modern

https://doi.org/10.1515/9783110711349-002

parlance, to the psychological aspects of human experience. And in its modern sense, it is associated with *la nouvelle spiritualité* of Madam Jeanne-Marie Bouvier de la Motte Guyon, a controversial mystic anathema to the Catholic Church, in 17th-century France (Wakefield, 1988, pp. 184, 361–363). By the 20th century the word came into widespread usage in many languages and in relation both to all religious traditions and to secular and humanist traditions too. However, spirituality has remained without a satisfactory common defnition (Wakefield, 1988, pp. 184, 362–363; Cross & Livingstone, 1997, p. 1532; Wulff, 1997, p. 5). A universally accepted definition is required for proper scientific study. In the absence of this, it is important and helpful to state and justify what one means by a term before proceeding to any exploration or discussion of the concept it denotes.

Spirituality for me and for the purposes of this chapter concerns the human spirit in the sense of a person's animating principle and what this means for management and leadership in organizations. It therefore concerns what relates to, or affects, the emotions and personality of a person in relation to mood, courage, determination and energy. Spirit is what drives people. It is a synergy of meaning, purpose, beliefs and values (in particular, moral values or virtues), a sense of community and belonging, and a sense of value or worth in one's life that, together, animate us in what we seek and do and thereby leads to our fulfilment and happiness. It is consistent with the human need or desire both to understand human experience and for self-actualization (in terms of Maslow's hierarchy of needs) (Milliman et al., 2017). Individual spirituality, for Rocha and Pinheiro (2020), is a personal identity:

> . . . a way of life that represents habits, the pursuit of meaning and purpose, search for transcendence, connection with the others, and the divine in all aspects and areas (personal and work). It is also a component of workplace spirituality because of interactions of spirituality within the organization occur in the workplace as the members search for meaning in their work.

By the early 2000s more and more people in the United States and the United Kingdom and elsewhere, especially managers, were seeking meaning, value or worth in what they do and are willing to forsake material wealth for this higher level of being (Overell, 2002, p. 2; Chalofsky, 2003; Hoar, 2004; Nash & Stevenson, 2004). Value comes from a profound feeling of well-being from work or other activity that results from a belief that one is making a contribution, making a difference, and connecting to others and to something beyond, and greater than, oneself through pursuing a common purpose (Kaizen Solutions, n.d.). And purpose in life, management philosopher Charles Handy (1997, p. 108) says, gives people "energy for the journey". As the German philosopher Nietzsche said: "He who has a why to live can bear with almost any how" (Allport, 1983, p. 12).

Spirituality may take a humanistic (secular) form or – relating to a transcendent higher power – a religious form. Chris Cook (2004), psychiatrist, ordained Anglican priest and Professor of Spirituality, Theology & Health at Durham University, comments:

> Spirituality is a distinctive, potentially creative and universal dimension of human experience arising both within the inner subjective awareness of individuals and within communities, social groups and traditions. It may be experienced as relationship with that which is intimately 'inner', immanent and personal, within the self and others, and/or as relationship with that which is wholly 'other', transcendent and beyond the self. It is experienced as being of fundamental or ultimate importance and is thus concerned with matters of meaning and purpose in life, truth and values.

Cook (2020) also says, in respect of spirituality in the field of psychiatry: "Spirituality (whether religious or not) has become a fourth dimension of clinical concern, alongside the psychological, social and biological."

A study of 414 postgraduate students in three different schools – science, management, and social sciences and humanities – at Pondicherry University in India showed a positive significant correlation between spirituality and subjective happiness, meaning in life and satisfaction with life (Deb et al., 2020). The pursuit of happiness is a widespread human phenomenon. Agnieszka Bojanowska and Anna Zalewska (2016) explain how well-being is associated with happiness. They found that people associate happiness mainly with health and relationships but also with knowledge, work, material goods and freedom. Those who associated happiness with work displayed greater positive feelings. Happiness associated with relationships predicted greater life satisfaction. And happiness associated with material goods predicted lower life satisfaction. Yet happiness has been shown to be associated with being a "taker", meaningfulness with being a "giver", concerned with the needs of others (Baumeister et al., 2013). Laszlo Zsolnai and Bernadette Flanagan (2019, p. 3) note that "numerous studies document that the more people prioritize materialistic goals, the lower their well-being and the more likely they are to engage in manipulative, competitive, and ecologically degrading behaviours".

Based on our definition of spirituality we can define spiritual well-being as a state of well-being characterized by positive thoughts, feelings and behaviour in one's relationships with one's work in respect of meaning, purpose, belonging and value or worth in what we do (Robertson & Cooper, 2015; Anglim & Grant, 2016), and Gomez and Fisher (2003) say that spirituality is "a state of being that reflects positive feelings, behaviours and cognitions of relationships with oneself, others, nature and the transcendent, which provides the individual with a sense of identity, wholeness, satisfaction, joy, contentment, beauty, love, respect, positive attitudes, inner peace and harmony, and purpose and direction in life."

Houghton et al. (2016) define spirituality in the context of work organizations as the nurturing of employees' inner selves, connectedness and community, and meaning and purpose. Alewell and Moll (2018, pp. 33–46) define individual spirituality as connecting with other people and to the sacred and transcendent and the personal attitudes and abilities that enable or facilitate it, for example love. Group cohesion and identity are often enhanced by spirituality and religion in leadership (Price & Hicks, 2006), thus providing a feeling of belonging. Rabell and Bastons

(2020) point out that spirituality orientates the human being to the needs of others and to an intellectual and affective openness to them that reinforces cooperation, acting as a "social glue". A survey of 2,230 people by Caroline Liu and Peter Robinson (2011) found three inter-correlated but distinct constituent factors of connectedness: interconnection with human beings, interconnection with nature and all living things, and interconnection with a higher power. Their conceptualization of spirituality "incorporates and transcends religiousness".

In his reflections on his incarceration and survival of the Holocaust during the Second World War, the Austrian neurologist and psychiatrist Viktor Frankl (1984) concluded that our striving to find a meaning in one's life is the primary motivational force in human beings. While one may argue that a more fundamental driving force in life is the need to stay alive, the need for meaning in life is indisputable. The meaningfulness of events, goals, tasks, actions and situations in the workplace is determined significantly by personal values, beliefs and needs. Meaning in life, King and Hicks (2021) say, poses a challenge to study, and, to make sense of it in a way that is useful, it needs to be distinguished from the "the meaning of life", which is best left to philosophers and theologians. They suggest that the current scholarly consensus on the nature of meaningfulness in life is that it entails comprehension or coherence of one's experience; purpose driven by one's values, identity and associated goals; and existential significance in terms of one's belief that one's life is valued and makes a difference to the world in some way. Religion for many people provides meaning in life and indeed the meaning *of* life because it provides guidance in how to live one's life in accordance with God's plan. Ecklund and colleagues (2020) are exploring how religion intersects with aspects of people's social location, such as social class, income, race and gender, in shaping the experiencing of workplace conflict. More broadly, this could include spirituality and humanism.

By the start of the third decade of the twentieth century, according to Marianna Fotaki and colleagues (2020), the fragmentation of meaning in our world has reached new heights." They point out that the world faces multiple crises in relation to economic differences, finance, food, water, energy, climate, migration and security, as well as a blurring of the boundaries between truth and lies, honest and dishonesty, fact and fiction. Further issues concern the struggle between democracy and autocracy, populism, the resurgence of hegemonic imperialism, xenophobia, the rise of anti-Semitism, the spread of Islamophobia, racism, corruption and a host of dysfunctional cultural differences. Fotaki and colleagues (2020) suggest that the reason is that "there is an absence of shared understanding of their causes and of ways to address them . . . partly due to the fragmentation of meaning and the failure of imagination." They argue that new ways of thinking about these issues, communicating about them and imagining solutions to them and the role of organizations and management in our societies are needed. In addition to envisioning possible attractive futures, storytelling and contributions from philosophy, theology and anthropology, spiritual narratives offer strategies for doing so too.

Meaninglessness in life is troubling. Its causes include boredom, but also a lack of purpose and a lack of power to control or change a situation. Finding more meaning in life when there are spiritual struggles – with self-doubt, moral conflict and a lack of meaning – is associated with low neuroticism; and finding meaning predicts greater well-being in terms of satisfaction with life, self-esteem, and less depression and anxiety (Wilt et al., 2016). Neal Chalofsky (2003) suggests that meaningful work – work that expresses one's inner being – depends on several factors, among them:

- Knowing one's purpose in life and how work fits with that purpose
- Having a positive belief about one's ability to achieve that purpose and pursuing
- the opportunity to do so through work
- Empowerment – autonomy and control over one's environment
- Recognizing and developing one's potential through learning
- The nature of work itself

Having a purpose and meaning in life increases overall well-being and life satisfaction, improves mental and physical health, enhances resilience, enhances self-esteem, and decreases the chances of depression (Arnold et al., 2007; Smith, 2013). And having a sense of purpose in one's life even predicts greater income and net worth (Hill et al., 2016). When employees feel a lack of congruence with their organization's purpose, they become disengaged, resulting in a lack of motivation and commitment and consequential poor performance at both individual and organizational level (Benefiel & Abbott, 2019, p. 274). Having a sense of purpose in life is associated with several personality characteristics; in order of magnitude these are conscientiousness, low neuroticism, extraversion, agreeableness and openness (Anglim & Grant, 2016).

Spiritual well-being is an aspect of spirituality. The extent to which a person perceives or derives a sense of well-being from spirituality is important. It is therefore useful to assess this. Spiritual well-being is not the same as mental health or physical health but it is closely related. A useful inclusive definition of spiritual well-being is that it is a state of wholeness in that all aspects of life are in balance and one feels confident, creative and fulfilled, both within oneself and with other people, giving one a sense of purpose, meaning, belonging and value or worth in everyday life. The leadership challenge in this respect is to empower and engage people – followers, subordinates or others – in pursuing and achieving this state of wholeness.

It is widely held, then, that spirituality is associated with good mental health and well-being (Koenig et al., 2012). However, a causal link is less clear, for several reasons:

- Variations in the definition of spirituality and in its measurement
- Evidence that an agreeable temperament and sociability (which correlate with spirituality) may be the key personality characteristics that predispose people to

be spiritually orientated and that these characteristics, rather than spirituality in itself, contribute to well-being
- Evidence that the benefits associated with spirituality may be largely due to being a member of a close-knit community

In other words, spirituality just may be a consequence of spiritual well-being rather than a cause of it. Michael King (2014) cautions that spiritual *experience* should not be conflated with its *outcomes*. A study exploring inconsistencies in research findings on the connection between spirituality and well-being concluded that personality (a preference for intuitive cognition rather than analytical cognition) exerts an important influence in any positive well-being (salutogenic) effects from spirituality or religiosity (Czekóová et al., 2018).

Spirituality, Science and Religion

Religion and science have long been a battleground for argument. But spirituality and science have an overlapping and complementary relationship, according to Oliver Robinson (2018, 2020). Both developed, he says, as "expressions of the modern values of progress, questioning, innovation and individual empowerment". However, their characteristics are opposites, or contrasts. As management and leadership both draw on science and the arts, this relationship is of interest for the study of spirituality and leadership. Robinson presents a model of multiple overlapping dialectics (MODI) comprising seven polarities (Table 2.1).

Table 2.1: Robinson's seven dialectical polarities of science and spirituality (adapted from Robinson, 2018, 2020).

Science	Spirituality
Outer knowing	Inner knowing
Impersonal encounter	Personal encounter
Cultivating thinking	Cultivating feeling
Empirical focus	Transcendental focus
Verbal knowledge	Ineffable human experience
Understanding mechanism	Grasping ultimate purpose
Explanation	Contemplation

The MODI model has parallels with philosophical theories of spirituality (Chinese yin-yang philosophy and Western alchemy, for example Jung's *Sol* and *Luna* (Jung, 1963)), psychological theories (theories of cognition) and neurological theory (McGilchrist, 2011, 2012). It has potential for understanding the differences and relationship between management and leadership, the nature of effective leadership, and the similarities and differences in the contemporary wide range of leadership theories.

Spirituality for many people, however, is grounded in religion. Emile Durkheim (1915/1995, p. 62) defines religion as "a unified system of beliefs and practices relative to sacred things, that is to say, things set apart and forbidden – beliefs and practices which unite into one single moral community called a Church, all those who adhere to them". The concept of spirituality at work for others has come to transcend religiousness or even to replace it with a secular or humanist view that also involves looking inward at oneself (Liu & Robertson, 2011). There is the view that spirituality is necessary for religion but religion is not necessary for spirituality, and that altruistic love – regard or devotion to the interests of others – is the common bridge between them (Fry, 2003), and is an influence for good in leadership (Gill & Negrov, 2021). The Dalai Lama (1999, p. 22) says:

> Religion I take to be concerned with faith in the claims of one faith tradition or another, an aspect of which is the acceptance of some form of heaven or nirvana. Connected with this are religious teachings or dogma, ritual prayer, and so on. Spirituality I take to be concerned with those qualities of the human spirit – such as love and compassion, patience, tolerance, forgiveness, contentment, a sense of responsibility, a sense of harmony – which brings happiness to both self and others . . . This is why I sometimes say that religion is something we can perhaps do without. What we cannot do without are these basic spiritual qualities.

In distinguishing between religion and spirituality, the Dalai Lama describes religions characteristically as including rituals in their practice (although spiritual practices, such as meditation, may also involve them). Emma Thompson (2021, p. 66), a solicitor (lawyer) and writer, says: "Physical gatherings and ceremonies are essential in every civilisation and religion. Rituals can formally reflect our values, aspirations and beliefs, investing them with solemnity and a sense of spiritual presence. Adding sensory beauty to a special occasion with clothes, flowers, music and language is something like taking a photograph for the soul, entrenching memories."

This view also makes a connection between religion and spirituality in that religion can be a precursor to spirituality. However, as a leading exponent of spiritual leadership, Louis (Jody) Fry (2005, pp. 47–83), has suggested, individuals can develop their personal qualities and values without being dependent on any religious or metaphysical belief systems and that workplace spirituality can be either inclusive or exclusive of religious beliefs or practices or theories.

Morally binding values such as those grounded in a religion, and even spiritual values, may alter organizational decision-making and ethical behaviour, for example in family-owned firms (Astrachan et al., 2020). However, whether people who hold religious beliefs are more or less likely to behave ethically than non-believers is not clear: the evidence appears to be ambivalent (Rashid & Ibrahim, 2008). Paul Tracey (2012) pointed out in his substantial review of trends and future directions in the relationship between religion and organization that, while religion has played a profound role in shaping contemporary societies, its relationship with organizations and their management has not been explored much. For example, he says: "The idea that objects become sacred in a given organization because of the collective meaning ascribed to them by a particular community has important implications for the study of organizations, both religious and secular." In discussing Karl Marx's well-known view of religion as "the opium of the people", in which religion and economics are intertwined and religion is masked as control and "exploitation that infuses capitalism", Tracey suggests that Marx ignored the positive aspects of religion, such as its role as the basis of almost all workers' uprisings as well as its actually greater influence on the ruling classes than on workers.

Being able to express and explore our religion or spirituality is a basic human need and a universal human right applied to everyone and enshrined in European and UK law, based on the Universal Declaration of Human Rights (Mental Health Foundation, 2014). Religion is an important part of life for many Americans in particular (Ecklund et al., 2020). In 2008, Bertelsmann Stiftung's Religion Monitor, examining the responses from 21,000 people around the world from all the major religions, found that there was very much greater religiosity in the United States than in most of Europe, including Germany (Joas, 2010, pp. 317–334). More recently, the Pew Research Center (2015) found that over 75 percent of Americans are affiliated with a religious tradition, mostly Christian (59 percent). And a large-scale study in the United States found that 20 per cent of employees at all levels overall see their work as a spiritual calling (a perception that one's work has meaning or purpose such that it is directed toward a greater good), whereas 58% do not do so, with variations among ethnic groups, gender (24 percent of women and 17 percent of men), position in the organization (26 percent at the top and 16 percent at the bottom).

There was an interesting reverse difference among Americans according to income and religious identity: Protestant Christians and Muslims highest (26 to 33 percent), followed by Roman Catholics (18 percent) and Jews (16 percent); figures were 19 percent for other religions and 8 percent for no religion (Ecklund et al., 2020). Tracey's review of the literature on religion and organization found that religion is important for identity, self-evidently so in religious organizations, with well-known examples of the relationships between the Palestinian and Jewish people in Israel and between Roman Catholics and Protestants in Northern Ireland, though more research is needed into this role in secular organizations (Tracey, 2012).

While being able to express and explore our religion is a universal human right, people at work may experience conflict between their faith and the demands of their job. In the American study above, some 20 percent overall were found to do so occasionally (Ecklund et al., 2020). More black respondents than white respondents did so; more lower-paid than high-paid employees did so; and more Muslims than other Christians also did so. There were no significant differences by gender or organizational position. Muslims (62 percent) and Jews (54 percent) experienced most religious discrimination, feeling that they had been treated unfairly most often because of their faith, compared to other faiths and none.

Buddhism is not only a religion but also a philosophy for a spiritual way of life, according to Kriger and Dhiman (2018). As a religion, they say that, through the role model of the Buddha and The Way (*Dharma*), it connects human beings, and society as a whole, to the nature of reality. And as a way of life, it values ethical norms for living with wisdom and in harmony with others. In a sense Buddhism is a pragmatic religion or philosophy in that, if personal experience does not concur with any aspect of Buddhist theory or philosophy, then that aspect should be discarded. Mai Vu (2018) carried out a study of the Buddhist approach to spiritual leadership in Vietnam in which she discovered that this entailed a process of self-transformation and operated as a skilful means to respond to contextual challenges in flexible and mindful ways. Kriger and Dhiman (2018) describe aims of Buddhism as the creation of enduring happiness, the cessation of suffering and an enduring balance in all aspects of self and society as well as the creation of "a harmonious society based on equanimity, loving-kindness, compassion, and reciprocal joy for oneself and others". As they say, these aims have important implications for engaged spirituality in the workplace.

The "New Spirituality" is a term coined by Gordon Lynch (2007) for a spirituality based on "progressive values and practices informed by conceptual, material and social resources associated with established belief systems but detached from their institutional roots", such as religion (Bell et al., 2020). This movement, Lynch (2007, pp. 3–4) says, has been particularly apparent in Britain, Canada, Scandinavia, and Australia and New Zealand but not so much in the United States and many Roman Catholic societies in Western Europe. Bell and colleagues (2020) present the new spirituality as an interdisciplinary approach to understanding different forms of contemporary spirituality and neoliberalism. They chart the lives and experiences of social actors in engaging with new and alternative forms of spirituality in a neoliberal capitalist context. Examples are individualism expressed in mindfulness and outdoor management development, commodification of spirituality, the enchantment of gardens and gardening, and the "contemporary faith of innovationism".

"Many roads Thou hast fashioned: all of them lead to the Light", wrote Rudyard Kipling (1906) in his "A Song to Mithras", the Roman god of the rising sun, war, justice and contracts who some scholars suggest had first appeared in ancient polytheistic Persian religion. Ananda Coomaraswamy (1944), the great art historian, used the phrase "paths that lead to the same summit" to refer to the world's range of religious faiths and conceptions of spirituality that have given us the timeless and universal wisdom found everywhere that is known as the perennial philosophy (Sotillos, 2020, p. xii), which was popularized by Aldous Huxley (1945) in an anthology. The study of comparative religions underpins this view (Bouquet, 1962). Samuel Sotillos (2020,

p. 5) says: "The perennialist critique of the modern and postmodern world is concerned with the loss of the sense of the sacred and the spiritual crisis that has developed in its wake . . . with its destructive consequences." Sotillos is referring to religions here rather than secular or humanist conceptions of spirituality, but a spiritual crisis that concerns rises in geopolitical conflict, materialism, consumerism and human suffering has led to renewed and increasing attention to spirituality, both religious and secular.

In discussing the conservation of resources and the legacy of Prince Philip, the Duke of Edinburgh, Rabbi Jonathan Wittenberg (2021, p. 28) says: "To the mystics of all religions, and for many with no formal faith, God is not some distant deity, up with the fairies in heaven. The sacred dwells in all life, in every human being, in the animals, birds, trees, and the elements themselves, the flowing water and fertile soil." And he quotes Prince Philip: "If God is in nature, nature itself becomes divine." Wittenberg adds: "We therefore have a responsibility not to harm it, not just for our own selfish interests, but as a duty." It hardly needs to be said, but the implications for management and leadership in government and business in respect of human consumption, conservation of resources and protection of the environment are clear: in Wittenberg's words, we are not proprietors of the planet but its trustees.

There are many paths to the same summit, but what do these paths have in common and how do they differ? Perhaps understanding this – the multitude of religions and spiritual practices – would help us to better understand workplace spirituality, especially in doing international business and in multinational teams, and in forging a spiritual synergy for the common good. Since the religiously inspired 9/11 attacks in the United States in 2001, there has been a growing movement arguing that religion is harmful to humanity, though the proponents have been criticised for cherry-picking their evidence (Whitehouse, 2019). Resolving this issue, Oxford social anthropologist Harvey Whitehouse (2019) argues, depends on clarity about what is meant by "good" and "bad" and investigating the role, if any, that religion has played "in establishing the cooperative behaviours that have allowed human societies to grow from small hunter-gatherer groups to vast empires and nation states". We might add vast business corporations and other organizations of all kinds that employ people. Early spiritual leaders and prophets include Buddha, Confucius and Zrathustra, who arguably did this through preaching their moralistic ideologies. Sacred rituals have served as a kind of social glue in encouraging cohesion and cooperation among people.

Mubbasher Khanzada (2005) explored the views of leaders from the three monotheistic religions – Judaism, Christianity and Islam – on what characterised their faiths, with a view to developing a holistic view. He found that there is much in common among these religions in terms of values and ethics, morality, and principles and rules for interacting with people. A fundamental principle that emerged, and is endorsed in studies of comparative religion, is "Do to others what you would have them do to you" – commonly called the Golden Principle or the Golden Rule, which dates at least from Confucian and Ancient Greek times and is enshrined in virtually all religions of the world as well as humanism. It has a perhaps more useful corollary: "Do not do to others what you would not wish them to do to you." Either way it should be noted that principle depends for its utility on knowing how others wish to be treated. Further key principles that emerged are faith (in the oneness of God or the oneness of humanity), belief, truth, love, hope, justice, forgiveness, humility and tolerance.

The differences that emerged among the three Abrahamic religions concern the views of the nature and personality of God and who conveyed the message – the prophets. Khanzada (2005, p. 70) says: "What divides us has to do more with ignorance, intolerance, misguided and misinformed perceptions than with actual reality. Open-minded communications and dialogues without prejudice and hatred would let rationality take its route and we *can* converge to the same focal point that is the will of God." Again, the lessons for management and leadership in government and business are self-evident. A start could be made in the UK by improving religious education in schools, which, according to the government's education watchdog, Ofsted, are "implanting unhelpful misconceptions about religion and failing to prepare pupils for a multi-religious and multi-secular society" (M. Davies, 2021). There is a wider issue with teaching and learning in respect of religion. According to Donald Wiebe, the philosophy of religion scholar, the academic study of religion in colleges and universities in Europe and North America is almost always beset by religious bias (Wiebe, 2021). His analysis suggests that the boundary between the objective (scientific) study of religion and religious education for the purpose of societal improvement has become blurred. He maintains that the objective and scientific study of religion should not be encumbered by religious or moralizing influences: rigour and honesty are crucial to knowledge and the integrity of its teaching, learning and application.

While spirituality has often been equated to religion, it has increasingly come to include a non-religious, secular form in recent times. Humanism, for example, is a philosophy whereby people shape their own lives because they believe it is the only life we have: there is no after-life (T. Davies, 2008). We make sense of the world, it posits, through logical reasoning and evidence and believe in treating those around us with warmth, understanding and respect: in other words, with love. Humanism draws on science rather than revelation from a supernatural source in understanding the world and it focuses on human agency. Humanism typically is non-religious and is usually aligned with secularism. However, the term "secular spirituality" is controversial. Secularism has been said by some to have increased during the twentieth century at the expense of religion.

There is some evidence that people who are spiritual but not religious are more prone to mental health problems than those who are spiritual and religious and those who are neither spiritual nor religious (M. King, 2014). This research, Cook and Powell (2013) point out, did not and could not prove any causal association, and cultural context may be moderating factor (e.g. religious USA v. secular UK), so it cannot be said that spirituality is bad for one's health. Its author, Michael King (2013), however, maintains that "a religious or spiritual life confers no advantage in terms of mental health". Meanwhile, a clinical case has been made for individualised personal healthcare in which it is the recipient who determines the importance of religion and spirituality rather than any imposed formal policy or practice (Timmins et al., 2016). This is endorsed in leadership research, in particular Bass and Avolio's model of transformational leadership and one of its four key constructs, individualised consideration: treating individuals according to their needs and recognising their uniqueness (Bass, 1985, 1990; Bass & Avolio, 1994).

Organizational and Workplace Spirituality

We have so far defined spirituality that is personal, but can an organization be "spiritual"? The notion of spirit was introduced into discussions about organizational health in 2001 by sociologist John Bruhn, defining it, consistent with our definition in relation to individuals, as "the core or heart of an organization . . . what makes it vibrant, and gives it vigor" (Bruhn, 2001, p. 17). The nature of the work that people carry out, how they perceive it and how they do it are integral to their self-concept (Geh, 2014). Pawar (2017) sees work itself, individual spirituality and workplace spirituality as together constituting organizational spirituality.

Russ Moxley (2000, p. 39) contrasts what he calls a "spirited organization" with a "dispirited" one (Table 2.2).

Table 2.2: Spirited and dispirited organizations (reprinted by permission of the publisher, Jossey-Bass/John Wiley & Sons).

Dispirited Organizations	Spirited Organizations
Use physical and mental energy	Use four forms of energy: physical, mental, emotional and spiritual
Work is a job	Work is a vocation
Sense of separation and disconnected-ness	Sense of connectedness to others
More competition than cooperation and Community or family used as a community	Community or family used as a metaphor
Lack of congruence between personal and organizational mission and values	Congruence between personal and organizational mission and values
Lack of meaning and purpose; workers drained of energy	Work has meaning and purpose: energized, animated workers
Leadership exercised in a top-down way	Workers involved in the activity of leadership

EILEEN FISHER, Inc., an American women's fashion company established in 2000, is an exemplary organization in terms of workplace spirituality, according to a case study by Bonita Betters-Reed et al. (2020). The founder's personal values, including spiritual values, Judi Neal (2013) says, are seen as central to having established the company as a values-based organization in which these values are translated into organizational practices and embedded in the culture, and a sense of meaning and purpose is nurtured. The dignity and value of each and every person in the company "drives everything from hiring practices to leadership style to customer service".

The meaningfulness of work is an important aspect of workplace spirituality. Richard Hackman and Greg Oldham (1976, 1980) define meaningfulness in this context as a function of skill variety, task identity and task significance:

- Skill variety – the extent to which the job requires use of a range of skills and offers a variety of tasks to perform
- Task identity – the extent to which a job-holder is able to complete a whole and identifiable piece of work
- Task significance – the extent to which the job is perceived to have an impact on others and their lives in the organization or in general

John Milliman and colleagues (2017) provide a useful analysis of the relationship between workplace spirituality and the fit between the person and the environment (Table 2.3):

Table 2.3: Workplace spirituality and person-environment fit (based on Table 1, Milliman et al., 2017).

Level of P-E Fit	Aspect of Workplace Spirituality
Person-Job Fit	Meaningful work
Person-Group Fit	Sense of belongingness and community
Person-Organization Fit	Alignment with organizational vision, purpose and values

Human well-being is a key goal of ethical leadership: in a group or team at work or play, in an organization, in a nation, in our world. Daniel Siegel (2012, p. 459) defines general well-being as "a state of optimal regulation and adaptive functioning of body, mind, and relationships". Examples of unsatisfactory physical well-being, he gives, include difficulty in working or other physical activities because of physical ill-health. Unsatisfactory psychological well-being includes inability to work because of emotional problems. And unsatisfactory relational well-being includes lack of communication and intimacy with others. In a study of work-family conflict, Selvarajan, Singh and colleagues (2020) found that spirituality mitigated its negative effects on well-being.

Studies of the relationship between spirituality and organizational performance and effectiveness are sparse (Houghton et al., 2016). One reason may be because both concepts are defined in a variety of different ways. Most measures of organizational performance and effectiveness are financial in nature. Nidhi Sharma and Reetesh Singh (2020) used Petchsawanga and Duchon's Workplace Spirituality Measure (Petchsawang & Duchon, 2009) and Taylor and Bower's scale (Taylor & Bowers, 1972) to measure organizational effectiveness in terms of group functioning, job satisfaction and goal integration in a sample of academics in the higher-education sector in India. They established an association between the two measures, spirituality and organizational effectiveness, and the universality of the association across several demographic factors.

The Dark Side of Spirituality

Spirituality, organizational spirituality in particular, has a dark side. There are examples of its distortion and exploitation for instrumental purposes, such as cynical impression management, control and domination, and the hope and expectation of making more money (Case & Gosling, 2010; Tourish, 2013, pp. 59–76). Dennis Tourish and Naheed Tourish (2010) argue that the workplace spirituality movement "promotes constricting cultural and behavioural norms and thus seeks to reinforce the power of leaders at the expense of autonomy for their followers". Employees and followers may come to realise that they are being manipulated deceitfully for the benefit of the organization, not themselves. In turn this can lead to distrust, cynicism, disgust with management, and disengagement – the very opposite of spirituality's more honourable and ethical characteristics – and, potentially, even industrial action and sabotage.

The history of management and leadership is littered with the debris of intrinsically useful and ethical innovations such as job enrichment, quality circles, empowerment, spirituality, mindfulness, unconscious bias and the rest because of their cynical and mostly unsuccessful exploitation. Inspired by Buddhist teachings, mindfulness, for example, is an individual practice people use to cultivate wisdom in order to help them resolve problems causing suffering and to enhance personal development. However, in the secular context, corporate or organizational mindfulness is largely recognised as a company's effort to bring a heightened awareness of its employees to each moment and to help them to discern and respond to threats quickly, and it has been commodified and commercialized accordingly (Vu & Gill, 2018).

Moreover, what may be desirable and progressive has an obverse face: what is undesirable and harmful. How best to impart spiritual meaning without imposing one's religious beliefs or atheism on others remains ideologically controversial and a challenge in resolving it (Holland et al., 2016) – in both the corporate world and government. Religion, spirituality and spiritual leadership are no exception. According to UK all-party parliamentary group's report on religion in the media, many religious people believe that journalists are "indifferent towards religion and belief and actively biased against people of faith at worst" (All-party Parliamentary Group's on Religion in the Media, 2021). Journalists focus too much on liturgy, doctrines and rituals, the report says, and not enough on people's lived experience, namely religious literacy, while Humanists UK caution that there must be freedom to criticise religious beliefs and ideas (Zeffman, 2021, p. 4).

Whither Spirituality?

A better understanding of how work contributes to meaning in our lives (L. A. King & Hicks, 2021), workplace spirituality, and organizational spirituality in general (Rocha & Pinheiro, 2020) is needed. As King and Hicks (2021) say, there are many opportunities at work for this. For example, confidence that our actions and behaviour are valued and matter to other people can be instilled by meeting challenges, overcoming obstacles and recognition for doing so. And seeing how our goals at work may contribute to a higher purpose, such as the common good, also provides meaning in life. However, while we know that meaning in one's work has both personal and organizational benefits, we need to know more about how organizations can foster this.

A major review of research into workplace spirituality by Judi Neal covered its historical trends, research methodologies employed, organizational exemplars of workplace spirituality, spiritual practices in the corporate sector, the consequences of spirituality, and recommendations for further research (Neal, 2018). Neal recommends further study of the evolution and relationships of the fields of spirituality and psychology, spirituality and healthcare, both of which are relatively mature, and workplace spirituality and theology, an emerging phenomenon (Tackney, 2018). This book hopefully is a step in that direction. Neal (2018) identifies three movements in workplace spirituality: the spirit at work, faith at work, and conscious capitalism. She says that the spirit at work movement is mainly secular and influenced particularly by Eastern traditions and practices such as mindfulness, meditation and yoga (Neal, 2013). The faith at work movement is championed mainly by Protestant Christian business leaders and scholars (Miller, 2007). And the conscious-capitalism movement is driven mainly by CEOs and exemplary business practices (Mackey & Sisodia, 2013).

More research is needed into the characteristics and inter-relationships of individual, workplace and organizational spirituality: Rocha and Pinheiro (2020) point out that most of the extant literature is theoretical rather than empirical (including their own model of organizational spirituality). Research is also hampered by lack of clear and commonly accepted definitions, a problem in the field of leadership research too.

It is, of course, helpful for researchers to state what they mean by "spirituality", but the wide variety of definitions they use makes creating a general theory of spirituality almost impossible. Mixed-method approaches in research are the most likely ones to throw more light on the nature and inter-relationships of spirituality, management and religion. Avenues to explore further include the effects of spirituality not just on immediate stakeholders but also on the wider communities, the influences of the environment – economic conditions, crises and disasters, climate change, war, terrorism, conflict and peace, diversity, and corruption on spirituality. Similar concerns apply to the role and importance of the institution of religion in organization theory, with its narrow focus on corporations (Tracey et al., 2014).

Considerable progress has been made in studying the outcomes of spirituality at work, such as, for example, meaningfulness of work, sense of purpose, sense of connectedness ad belonging, recognition, fulfilment, satisfaction, well-being, happiness, commitment, and organizational performance and productivity, and indeed the greater good of society. Further progress could be made in respect of cross-cultural similarities and differences, both sectoral and national, and the reasons for them. Differences in values and beliefs and associated behaviour, are the cause of many conflicts, often based on misunderstanding. But despite this progress, the spiritual needs of people at work still pose a growing challenge to those in leadership positions in business, government and society at large (Gill, 2014). The issues are their awareness and understanding of these needs and their willingness, desire and ability to respond to them. This is a major challenge for leadership and management today, and it needs to be addressed. Spiritual leadership may hold the key.

References

Alewell, D., & Moll, T. (2018). Spiritualität am Arbeitsplatz: Ein Thema auch für die Personalarbeit in Deutschland. In H. H. Surrey & V. A. Tiberius (Eds.), *Die Zukunft des Personalmanagements: Herausforderungen, Lösungsansätze und Gestaltungsoptionen* (pp. 33–46). vdf.

All-party Parliamentary Group's on Religion in the Media. (2021). *Learning to listen – Inquiry into religious literacy in print and broadcast media*. London: UK Government, April.

Allport, G. W. (1983). Preface. In V. E. Frankl (Ed.), *Man's Search for Meaning* (p. 12). Washington Square Press.

Anglim, J., & Grant, S. (2016). Predicting psychological and subjective well-being from personality: Incremental prediction from 30 facets over the big 5. *Journal of Happiness Studies, 17*(1), 59–80. https://doi.org/10.1007/s10902-014-9583-7

Arnold, K. A., Turner, N., Barling, J., Kelloway, E. K., & McKee, M. C. (2007). Transformational leadership and psychological well-being: The mediating role of meaningful work. *Journal of Occupational Health Psychology, 12*(3), 193–203. https://doi.org/10.1037/1076-8998.12.3.193

Astrachan, J. H., Binz Astrachan, C., Campopiano, G., & Baù, M. (2020). Values, spirituality and religion: Family business and the roots of sustainable ethical behavior. *Journal of Business Ethics, 163*(4), 637–645. https://doi.org/10.1007/s10551-019-04392-5

Bass, B. M. (1985). *Leadership and Performance Beyond Expectations*. Free Press.
Bass, B. M. (1990). From transactional to transformational leadership: Learning to share the vision. *Organizational Dynamics, 18*(3), 19–31. https://doi.org/10.1016/0090-2616(90)90061-S
Bass, B. M., & Avolio, B. J. (1994). Introduction. In B. M. Bass & B. J. Avolio (Eds.), *Improving Organizational Effectiveness through Transformational Leadership*. SAGE Publications.
Baumeister, R. F., Vohs, K. D., Aaker, J. L., & Garbinsky, E. N. (2013). Some key differences between a happy life and a meaningful life. *The Journal of Positive Psychology, 8*(6), 505–516. https://doi.org/10.1080/17439760.2013.830764
Bell, E., Gog, S., Simionca, A., & Taylor, S. (Eds.). (2020). *Spirituality, Organization and Neoliberalism: Understanding Lived Experiences*. Edward Elgar.
Benefiel, M., & Abbott, M. (2019). Spirituality and leadership. In L. Zsolnai & B. Flanagan (Eds.), *The Routledge International Handbook of Spirituality in Society and the Professions* (p. 274). Routledge. https://books.google.at/books?id=AC2NDwAAQBAJ
Betters-Reed, B., Harvey, S., & Neal, J. (2020). Nurturing the soul of the company at Eileen Fisher, Inc. *Journal of Management, Spirituality & Religion, 17*(3), 211–222. https://doi.org/10.1080/14766086.2020.1752994
Bojanowska, A., & Zalewska, A. M. (2016). Lay understanding of happiness and the experience of well-being: Are some conceptions of happiness more beneficial than others? *Journal of Happiness Studies, 17*(2), 793–815. https://doi.org/10.1007/s10902-015-9620-1
Bouquet, A. C. (1962). *Comparative Religion: A Short Outline* (6th ed.). Penguin Books. https://books.google.at/books?id=zQ49AAAAIAAJ
Bruhn, J. G. (2001). *Trust and the Health of Organizations*. Kluwer Academic/Plenum Publishers.
Case, P., & Gosling, J. (2010). The spiritual organization: Critical reflections on the instrumentality of workplace spirituality. *Journal of Management, Spirituality & Religion, 7*(4), 257–282. https://doi.org/10.1080/14766086.2010.524727
Chalofsky, N. (2003). Meaningful work. *Training & Development*, 52–58.
Cook, C. C. H. (2004). Addiction and spirituality. *Addiction, 99*(5), 539–551. https://doi.org/10.1111/j.1360-0443.2004.00715.x
Cook, C. C. H. (2020). Mental health in the kingdom of God. *Theology, 123*(3), 163–171. https://doi.org/10.1177/0040571X20910700
Cook, C. C. H., & Powell, A. (2013). Spirituality is not bad for our mental health. *British Journal of Psychiatry, 202*(5), 385–386. https://doi.org/10.1192/bjp.202.5.385
Coomaraswamy, A. K. (1944). Paths that lead to the same summit: Some observations on comparative religion. *Motive, 4*(8 May), 29–32, 35.
Cross, F. L., & Livingstone, E. A. (1997). *The Oxford Dictionary of the Christian Church* (3rd ed., p. 1532). Oxford University Press.
Czekóová, K., Shaw, D. J., & Urbánek, T. (2018). Personality systems, spirituality, and existential well-being: A person-centered perspective. *Psychology of Religion and Spirituality, 10*(4), 307–317. https://doi.org/10.1037/rel0000109
Dalai Lama (the 14th), & Gyatso, T. (1999). *Ethics for the New Millennium*. Putnam.
Davies, M. (2021, May 12). RE teaching falls short of Ofsted standards . . . again. *Church Times*.
Davies, T. (2008). *Humanism* (2nd ed.). Routledge.
Deb, S., Thomas, S., Bose, A., & Aswathi, T. (2020). Happiness, meaning, and satisfaction in life as perceived by Indian University students and their association with spirituality. *Journal of Religion and Health, 59*(5), 2469–2485. https://doi.org/10.1007/s10943-019-00806-w
Durkheim, E. (1915). *The Elementary Forms of the Religious Life. Trans. K. E. Field, 1995*. Free Press.
Ecklund, E. H., Daniels, D., Bolger, D., & Johnson, L. (2020). A nationally representative survey of faith and work: Demographic subgroup differences around calling and conflict. *Religions, 11* (6),287. Available online: https://doi.org/10.3390/rel11060287. Accessed on 19 April, 2021.

Fotaki, M., Altman, Y., & Koning, J. (2020). Spirituality, symbolism and storytelling in twentyfirst-century organizations: Understanding and addressing the crisis of imagination. *Organization Studies*, *41*(1), 7–30. https://doi.org/10.1177/0170840619875782

Frankl, V. E. (1984). *Man's Search For Meaning: An Introduction to Logotherapy* (3rd ed.). Simon & Schuster. https://books.google.at/books?id=W3q8R4dRZTwC

Fry, L. W. (2003). Toward a theory of spiritual leadership. *The Leadership Quarterly*, *14*(6), 693–727. https://doi.org/10.1016/j.leaqua.2003.09.001

Fry, L. W. (2005). Toward a theory of ethical and spiritual well-being, and corporate social responsibility through spiritual leadership. In R. A. Giacalone & C. L. Jurkiewicz (Eds.), *Positive Psychology in Business Ethics and Corporate Responsibility* (pp. 47–83). Information Age Publishing.

Geh, E. Z. (2014). Organizational spiritual leadership of worlds "made" and "found": An experiential learning model for "feel." *Leadership & Organization Development Journal*, *35*(2), 137–151. https://doi.org/10.1108/LODJ-04-2012-0052

Gill, R. (2014). Spirituality at work and the leadership challenge. *Journal for the Study of Spirituality*, *4*(2), 136–148. https://doi.org/10.1179/2044024314Z.00000000028

Gill, R., & Negrov, A. (2021). Love as an influence for good in leadership. *Theology of Leadership* 4(1), 28–53.

Gomez, R., & Fisher, J. W. (2003). Domains of spiritual well-being and development and validation of the spiritual well-being questionnaire. *Personality and Individual Differences*, *35*(8), 1975–1991. https://doi.org/10.1016/S0191-8869(03)00045-X

Hackman, J. R., & Oldham, G. R. (1976). Motivation through the design of work: Test of a theory. *Organizational Behavior and Human Performance*, *16*(2), 250–279. https://doi.org/10.1016/0030-5073(76)90016-7

Hackman, J. R., & Oldham, G. R. (1980). *Work Redesign*. Addison-Wesley.

Handy, C. (1997). *Hungry Spirit: Beyond Capitalism – A Quest for Purpose in the Modern World*. Hutchinson.

Hesketh, K. A. (2020). Spiritualism and the resurgence of fake news. In K. Dalkir & R. Katz (Eds.), *Navigating Fake News, Alternative Facts, and Misinformation in a Post-Truth World* (pp. 222–237). IGI Global. https://doi.org/10.4018/978-1-7998-2543-2

Hill, P. L., Turiano, N. A., Mroczek, D. K., & Burrow, A. L. (2016). The value of a purposeful life: Sense of purpose predicts greater income and net worth. *Journal of Research in Personality*, *65*, 38–42. https://doi.org/10.1016/j.jrp.2016.07.003

Hoar, R. (2004, May). Work with meaning. *Management Today*, 44–53.

Holland, K. J., Lee, J. W., Marshak, H. H., & Martin, L. R. (2016). Spiritual intimacy, marital intimacy, and physical/psychological well-being: Spiritual meaning as a mediator. *Psychology of Religion and Spirituality*, *8*(3), 218–227. https://doi.org/10.1037/rel0000062

Houghton, J. D., Neck, C. P., & Krishnakumar, S. (2016). The what, why, and how of spirituality in the workplace revisited: A 14-year update and extension. *Journal of Management, Spirituality & Religion*, *13*(3), 177–205. https://doi.org/10.1080/14766086.2016.1185292

Huxley, A. (1945). *The Perennial Philosophy*. Harper & Brothers.

Joas, H. (2010). The religious situation in the United States. In Bertelsmann Stiftung (Ed.), *What the World Believes: Analyses and Commentary on the Religion Monitor 2008*. (pp. 317–334). Bertelsmann Stiftung.

Jung, C. G. (1963). *Mysterium Coniunctionis: An Inquiry into the Separation and Synthesis of Psychic Opposites in Alchemy*. Routledge.

Kaizen Solutions. (n.d.). *Spirit at Work*. Kaizen Solutions. www.kaizensolutions.org/saw.html (accessed 6 May 2014).

Khanzada, M. S. (2005). *Leadership principles from the divine* [Thesis submitted in partial fulfilment of the requirements for the degree of MBA]. University of Strathclyde Graduate School of Business.

King, L. A., & Hicks, J. A. (2021). The science of meaning in life. *Annual Review of Psychology, 72*(1), 561–584. https://doi.org/10.1146/annurev-psych-072420-122921

King, M. (2013). Reply to Cook and Powell. Spirituality is not bad for one's health. *British Journal of Psychiatry, 202*(5), 386. https://doi.org/10.1192/bjp.202.5.386

King, M. (2014). The challenge of research into religion and spirituality (Keynote 1). *Journal for the Study of Spirituality, 4*(2), 106–120. https://doi.org/10.1179/2044024314Z.00000000026

Kipling, R. (1906). A song to Mithras. In *Puck of Pook's Hill*. Macmillan.

Koenig, H. G., King, D. E., & Carson, V. B. (Eds.). (2012). *Handbook of Religion and Health* (2nd ed.). Oxford University Press. https://books.google.at/books?id=NiRZcCVbkZ4C

Kriger, M., & Dhiman, S. (2018). A Buddhist theory of organizational leadership. In G. E. Roberts & J. E. Crossman (Eds.), *The Palgrave Handbook of Workplace Spirituality and Fulfillment* (pp. 127–152). Palgrave Macmillan. https://doi.org/10.1007/978-3-319-62163-0_53

Liu, C. H., & Robertson, P. J. (2011). Spirituality in the workplace: Theory and measurement. *Journal of Management Inquiry, 20*(1), 35–50. https://doi.org/10.1177/1056492610374648

Lynch, G. (2007). *The New Spirituality: An Introduction to Progressive Belief in the Twenty-first Century*. I. B. Tauris.

Mackey, J., & Sisodia, R. (2013). *Conscious Capitalism: Liberating the Heroic Spirit of Business*. Harvard Business Review Press.

McGilchrist, I. (2011). *Can the Divided Brain Tell Us Anything About the Ultimate Nature of Reality?* Royal College of Psychiatrists. https://www.rcpsych.ac.uk/docs/default-source/members/sigs/spirituality-spsig/iain-mcgilchrist-can-the-divided-brain-tell-us-anything-about-the-ultimate-nature-of-reality.pdf?sfvrsn=a1e381e1_2

McGilchrist, I. (2012). *The Master and His Emissary: The Divided Brain and the Making of the Western World*. Yale University Press.

Mental Health Foundation. (2014, June 25). *Spirituality*. London: Mental Health Foundation. Downloaded from http://www.mentalhealth.org.uk/dhelp-information/mental-health-a-z/S/spirituality/ on 25 June 2014

Miller, D. W. (2007). *God at Work: The History and Promise of the Faith at Work Movement*. Oxford University Press.

Milliman, J., Gatling, A., & Bradley-Geist, J. C. (2017). The implications of workplace spirituality for person–environment fit theory. *Psychology of Religion and Spirituality, 9*(1), 1–12. https://doi.org/10.1037/rel0000068

Moxley, R. S. (2000). *Leadership and Spirit: Breathing New Vitality and Energy into Individuals and Organizations* (1st ed). Jossey-Bassand Center for Creative Leadership.

Nash, L., & Stevenson, H. (2004). Success that lasts. *Harvard Business Review, 82*(2), 102–109.

Neal, J. (2013). *Creating Enlightened Organizations: Four Gateways to Spirit at Work*. Palgrave Macmillan.

Neal, J. (2018). Overview of workplace spirituality research. In S. Dhiman, G. E. Roberts, & J. E. Crossman (Eds.), *The Palgrave Handbook of Workplace Spirituality and Fulfillment* (pp. 1–56). Palgrave Macmillan. https://doi.org/10.1007/978-3-319-61929-3_45-1

Overell, S. (2002, September 13). The search for corporate meaning. *Financial Times*, 12.

Pawar, B. S. (2017). The relationship of individual spirituality and organizational spirituality with meaning and community at work: An empirical examination of the direct effects and moderating effect models. *Leadership & Organization Development Journal, 38*(7), 986–1003. https://doi.org/10.1108/LODJ-01-2016-0014

Petchsawang, P., & Duchon, D. (2009). Measuring workplace spirituality in an Asian context. *Human Resource Development International*, *12*(4), 459–468. https://doi.org/10.1080/13678860903135912
Pew Research Center, J. (2015). *America's changing religious landscape*. Available at https://org/2015/05/12/americas-changing-religious-landscape (accessed on 19 April 2021).
Price, T. L., & Hicks, D. A. (2006). A framework for a general theory of leadership ethics. In G. R. Goethals & G. L. J. Sorenson (Eds.), *The Quest for a General Theory of Leadership* (pp. 123–151). Edward Elgar Publishing, Incorporated. https://books.google.at/books?id=NEpkPgAACAAJ
Rabell, B. M., & Bastons, M. (2020). Spirituality as reinforcement of people-focused work: A philosophical foundation. *Journal of Management, Spirituality & Religion*, *17*(5), 403–418. https://doi.org/10.1080/14766086.2020.1764380
Rashid, Md. Z., & Ibrahim, S. (2008). The effect of culture and religiosity on business ethics: A cross-cultural comparison. *Journal of Business Ethics*, *82*(4), 907–917. https://doi.org/10.1007/s10551-007-9601-3
Robertson, I., & Cooper, C. (2015). *The bank on your people partnership. Bank on your people: Wellbeing and productivity in the financial sector*. Robertson and Cooper Ltd.
Robinson, O. C. (2018). *Paths Between Head and Heart: Exploring the Harmonies of Science and Spirituality*. O Books.
Robinson, O. C. (2020). A dialectical approach to understanding the relationship between science and spirituality: The MODI model. *Journal for the Study of Spirituality*, *10*(1), 15–28. https://doi.org/10.1080/20440243.2020.1726045
Rocha, R. G., & Pinheiro, P. G. (2020). Organizational spirituality: Concept and perspectives. *Journal of Business Ethics*, published online on 21 February 2020 and accessed on May 10, 2021 at. https://doi.org/10.1007/s10551-020-04463-y
Selvarajan, T. T. R., Singh, B., Stringer, D., & Chapa, O. (2020). Work-family conflict and well-being: Moderating role of spirituality. *Journal of Management, Spirituality & Religion*, *17*(5), 419–438. https://doi.org/10.1080/14766086.2020.1796768
Sharma, N., & Singh, R. K. (2020). Workplace spirituality and organizational effectiveness: Exploration of relationship and moderators. *Journal of Management, Spirituality & Religion*, 1–20. https://doi.org/10.1080/14766086.2020.1829011
Siegel, D. J. (2012). *Pocket Guide to Interpersonal Neurobiology: An Integrative Handbook of the Mind*. Norton. https://www.overdrive.com/search?q=EA13A89A-5DF7-421E-B5DF-6422CC69BB25
Smith, E. E. (2013, January 9). There's more to life than being happy. *The Atlantic*. Downloaded from https://www.theatlantic.com/health/archive/2013/01/theres-more-to-life-than-being-happy/266805/ on 27 January 2016.
Sotillos, S. B. (2020). *Paths That Lead to the Same Summit: An Annotated Guide to World Spirituality*. The Matheson Trust.
Tackney, C. T. (2018). Authenticity in employment relations: A theology of the workplace analysis. *Journal of Management, Spirituality & Religion, Special issue on research methods*, *15*(1), 82–104. https://doi.org/10.1080/14766086.2017.1417153
Taylor, J. C., & Bowers, D. G. (1972). *Survey of Organizations: A Machine-Scored Standardized Questionnaire Instrument*. Center for Research on Utilization of Scientific Knowledge, University of Michigan.
Thompson, E. (2021, April 10). We need our old rituals to help us recover meaning. *The Times*, 66.
Timmins, F., Caldeira, S., Naughton, M., Plakas, S., & Koenig, H. (2016). A commentary on Michael King. "The challenge of research into religion and spirituality". *Religions*, *7*(4), 39. https://doi.org/10.3390/rel7040039

Top, J. (2019, August). *Marine Corps Gazette (USA), August.*

Tourish, D. (2013). *The Dark Side of Transformational Leadership: A Critical Perspective.* Routledge.

Tourish, D., & Tourish, N. (2010). Spirituality at work, and its implications for leadership and followership: A post-structuralist perspective. *Leadership*, *6*(2), 207–224. https://doi.org/10.1177/1742715010363210

Tracey, P. (2012). Religion and organization: A critical review of current trends and future directions. *Academy of Management Annals*, *6*(1), 87–134. https://doi.org/10.5465/19416520.2012.660761

Tracey, P., Phillips, N., & Lounsbury, M. (Eds.). (2014). *Religion and Organization Theory. Research in the Sociology of Organizations, Vol. 41.* Emerald Group Publishing. http://www.emeraldinsight.com/books.htm?issn=0733-558x&volume=41

Vu, M. C. (2018). *Spiritual leadership: A Buddhist approach* [Thesis submitted for the degree of PhD, Durham University]. Durham theses, Durham University. Available at Durham E-Theses Online: http://etheses.dur.ac.uk/12773/

Vu, M. C., & Gill, R. (2018). Is there corporate mindfulness? An exploratory study of Buddhist-enacted spiritual leaders' perspectives and practices. *Journal of Management, Spirituality & Religion*, *15*(2), 155–177. https://doi.org/10.1080/14766086.2017.1410491

Wakefield, G. S. (Ed.). (1988). *A Dictionary of Christian Spirituality* (pp. 184, 362–363). SCM Press.

Whitehouse, H. (2019). Has religion been good or bad for humanity? *New Scientist*, *242*(3224), 36–39. https://doi.org/10.1016/S0262-4079(19)30604-9

Wiebe, D. (2021). *The Learned Practice of Religion in the Modern University.* Bloomsbury.

Wilt, J. A., Grubbs, J. B., Exline, J. J., & Pargament, K. I. (2016). Personality, religious and spiritual struggles, and well-being. *Psychology of Religion and Spirituality*, *8*(4), 341–351. https://doi.org/10.1037/rel0000054

Wittenberg, J. (2021, April 17). Duke of Edingburgh's conservation plea was a mission from God. *The Times*, 28.

Wulff, D. M. (1997). *Psychology of Religion: Classic and Contemporary* (2nd ed.). John Wiley & Sons.

Zeffman, H. (2021, May 7). Call to protect free speech as MPs accuse media of anti-religious bias. *The Times*, 4.

Zsolnai, L., & Flanagan, B. (2019). Introduction. In L. Zsolnai & B. Flanagan (Eds.), *The Routledge International Handbook of Spirituality in Society and the Professions* (p. 3). Routledge. https://books.google.at/books?id=AC2NDwAAQBAJ

Themes

Roger Gill

3 Leadership and Spirituality

Introduction

The major challenges facing humanity in the third decade of the twenty-first century are spiritual in nature. In meeting them successfully, leadership – spiritual leadership in particular – holds the key. How, then, do spirituality and leadership relate to each other? And how do they together contribute to the performance and well-being of people at work? Let is first consider what they have in common? One answer is that neither term has a single, universally accepted definition. The consequence is that discussion and research concerning spirituality or leadership, or the relationship between them, are at best at high risk of being fragmented and confusing and at the worst fruitless. One antidote to this problem is that any discussion or research concerning spirituality and leadership starts with a proposal for a clear and precise definition of each term and a justification for it.

The purpose of this chapter is to review the state of the art in this field, the challenges ahead, and some suggestions for further research. In doing this I aim to show how spirituality is fundamental to ethical and effective leadership and how spiritual leadership is a development of "conventional" concepts of leadership and spirituality and, as a result, our hope for the future of humanity.

What is Leadership?

It is commonly said that there are as many definitions of leadership as there are those defining it, and they come from a diverse range of backgrounds – politics, business, public service, the armed forces, sport, the media, the arts and, not least, academia. The quest for a general theory of leadership has been a challenging one and unsuccessful so far but a fascinating and useful one (Goethals & Sorenson, 2006). The least we can do is to say what we mean by the term and then write about it, as I do with "spirituality". Leadership, like spirituality, and indeed many words, such as beauty and love, is what I call a "Humpty Dumpty" word:

> When I use a word, Humpty Dumpty said, in a rather scornful tone, it means just what I choose it to mean – neither more nor less. The question is, said Alice, whether you can make words mean so many different things. The question is, said Humpty Dumpty, which is to be master – that's all. (Carroll, 1871, p. 87)

My definition, then, is that *leadership is showing the way and helping or inducing others to pursue it* (Gill, 2011, p. 9). The rationale for this I present elsewhere in detail

https://doi.org/10.1515/9783110711349-003

(Gill, 2011, pp. 2–11). In brief, this is, first, that it draws on its etymology, which in this particular case eschews the well-known "etymological fallacy" simply because it is very helpful to do so: etymology can aid clarification where there is confusion and the development of helpful conventions. Second, it represents a distillation of the wide range of extant definitions that have led to misunderstanding and confusion. Leadership is very much more than the basic and most common definition: "a process whereby an individual influences a group of individuals to achieve a common goal" (Northouse, 2013, p. 5). In my model (Gill, 2011, pp. 99–106), showing the way and helping or inducing others to pursue it entails envisioning a desirable future (a vision); promoting a clear purpose or mission, supportive values and intelligent strategies; and empowering and engaging all those concerned – six core themes and practices (Figure 3.1).

An initial version of this model (Gill, 2006) has been independently validated (Rupprecht et al., 2013), and the development and validation of the revised version is underway.

Research into how long-term well-being develops has revealed that job resources predict a high level of job-related well-being. Baran Metin and colleagues (Metin et al., 2016) investigated aspects of empowerment focusing on the relationship between work resources such as autonomy, management and colleague support, and knowledge and skills together with job demands and employee engagement and the role of authenticity – employees' ability to experience their "true selves". They found that authenticity was positively associated with engagement, job satisfaction and job performance and it was also a mediator between job resources (empowerment) and those outcomes.

Research on job resources has explored job control (autonomy and participation in decision making) and supportiveness of the organizational climate in terms of perceptions of the quality of communications and social support (Mäkikangas et al., 2016). Other research also shows that empowerment clearly affects employee engagement and that empowerment is itself a strategy for enhancing employee engagement by providing more meaningful work (Rudolph & Baltes, 2017; Tanskanen et al., 2016).

Engagement – influencing, motivating or inspiring people to want to do what needs to be done – is the focus of most theories of leadership. However, it is only one piece in the jigsaw puzzle that is leadership. Viewing leadership as *only* about engaging people at work is a mistake, though it is clearly a necessary and probably the most important element as the consequence of the other five core practices of leadership. Engagement is the extent to which people are motivated or inspired to willingly, even eagerly, give of their discretionary effort over and above doing what they *have* to do (Gill, 2011, p. 257). Jim Dethmer and colleagues allude to *spirit* in saying: "[Employee engagement] is all about allowing the flow of life force or energy in individuals and in an organization' [which] 'is directly related to their vitality, passion, focus, creativity, innovation, intuition, clarity, and vision" (Dethmer et al., 2014).

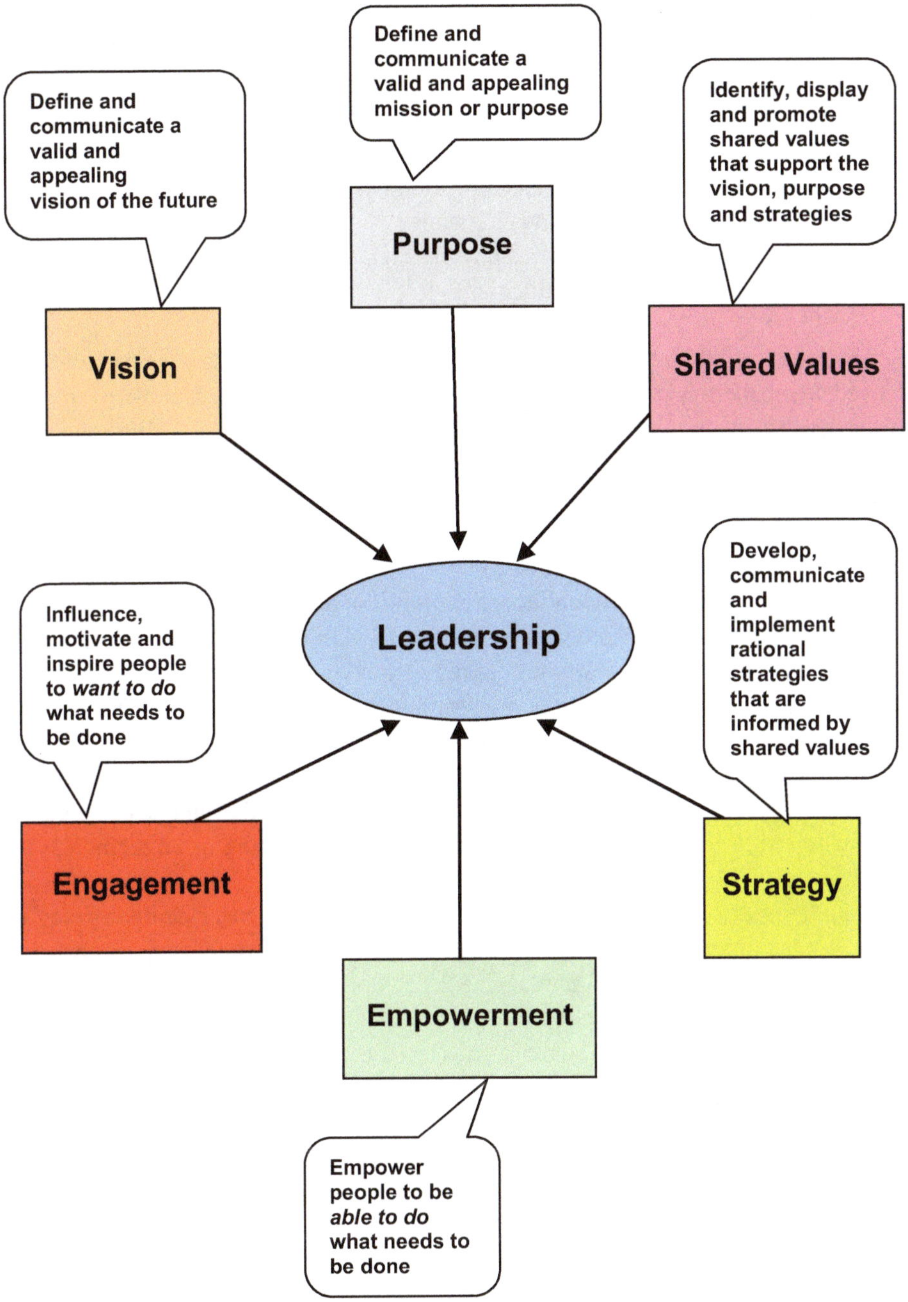

Figure 3.1: A model of six core themes and practices of leadership (Gill, 2011, p. 101).

Schaufeli and colleagues (2002) found that employee engagement is a positive, fulfilling and affective-motivational state of work-related well-being that is displayed during task performance by:

- Absorption (a cognitive dimension) – maintaining high levels of concentration and involvement
- Dedication (an emotional dimension) – showing high levels of involvement, enthusiasm, inspiration, pride and challenge
- Vigour (a physical dimension) – showing high levels of energy, persistence and effort, despite setbacks and difficulties

Engagement is akin to 'flow': a high degree of engagement is experienced and displayed when there is undistracted, concentrated absorption in an activity which is rewarding in itself as greatly pleasurable, joyous, even rapturous (Nakamura & Csikszentmihalyi, 2014, pp. 239–263). There is empirical evidence for the mediating effect of meaning in work in the relationship between leadership and engagement (Ghadi et al., 2013). And meaningfulness of work is associated positively with psychological well-being (Arnold et al., 2007). One particular feature of engagement – affective commitment (emotional attachment to the organization) – is a direct predictor of employees' psychological well-being (Rivkin et al., 2018). And a positive relationship was found in a study in a large HR services organization in Germany between leaders' own engagement and employee engagement (and performance), with quality of leader-member exchange (LMX) as a mediator (Gutermann et al., 2017). Much evidence exists for the association between employee engagement and employee well-being (Guest, 2014). It is a salutary thought that making money for the owners of a business (its purpose) never was motivating or engaging for its employees.

Much research has focused on why employees are unengaged or disengaged at work. Tomas Chamorro-Premuzic (2016, p. 13) says that research suggests two reasons: those in leadership and management positions do not understand what people really want from work and too many managers are simply incompetent leaders. He says that "employees will be more engaged if their accomplishments are valued by the organisation, if they can form meaningful relationships with their colleagues, and if the rules of conduct are transparent and enforced fairly. Conversely, if they feel unappreciated, isolated or treated unfairly, they will become disengaged, alienated and burnt out."

There are individual differences in what employees emphasize with respect to their values that influence or determine their behaviour. There is wide variation in the extent to which these differences are understood and responded to by competent leaders and managers. Despite the plethora of expensive and time-consuming leadership development programmes, there are still far too many managers failing as leaders. There are a variety of reasons for this: faulty selection and promotion practices, self-interest, sycophancy, narcissism, vanity, and sheer lack of aptitude for leadership. It may well be the case that those who need leadership development most are those who desire and undertake it least. And leadership development programmes appear to be largely designed for those who need it least.

Just like spirituality itself, engagement in practice has its downside. High levels may lead to excessive stress – physical, physiological or psychological – and "presenteeism", whereby an employee attends work despite sickness and not fully functioning because of a high degree of commitment to the job, company or supervisor. There is an association, Kelly McGonigal (2015) says, between stress and meaningfulness: those people who experience stressful life or work events tend to be those who also consider their lives or work to be most meaningful. She notes: "Stress seems to be an inevitable consequence of pursuing goals that feed our sense of purpose". Moreover, leadership that inspires excessive employee engagement is likely to rebound, with increased absence due to sickness (K. Nielsen & Daniels, 2016).

In her introduction of a special issue on quantum management in the *Journal of Management, Spirituality and Religion,* Kathryn Pavlovich (2020) brings together current thinking about management and leadership that draws on quantum physics. Quantum management, she say, posits a universe that is an "inexplicable wholeness and connectedness that is governed through entanglement, potentiality, and indeterminism . . . [and] enables us to radically reframe our understanding of reality through eliminating dichotomies." Quantum management is dependent on our "direct-intuitive experience [so] our personal experiences and practices are central to this shift in awareness." Increased awareness in turn enables us to critique how our actions and behaviour impact on other people and on the world in general. Quantum managers and leaders, it is argued, are then more likely to be able to "focus on enhancing human flourishing and societal well-being".

Quantum theory applied to leadership emerged in the 1990s. Drawing on both Western and Easter thought quantum leadership entails expanding and transforming human consciousness – awareness of the mind of itself and of the world around us – through enhanced connectedness (Tsao & Laszlo, 2019). Connectedness, which is more or less a form of mindfulness, entails empathy and compassion. This deepens intuition by combining personal experience with analytical cognitive development. The benefits are many in terms of greater personal effectiveness and well-being at work. Our bodies, minds and spirit are in synchrony – working together simultaneously – and we are in tune with others around us and our natural environment in oneness and wholeness. Examples of its outcomes are greater creativity, collaboration, ability to inspire people, and sustainable transformation. Quantum leadership is also claimed to enhance productivity and profit in business organizations. However, its obviously spiritual aspects are worthy of continuing exploration.

Spiritual Leadership

Spirituality concerns the human spirit in the sense of a person's animating principle: spirituality is what drives people. Gilbert Fairholm (1996) suggested a spiritual dimension to leadership as associated with integrity, independence and justice, one that is concerned with meeting people's needs for meaning and value in what they do. Spirituality concerns what relates to, or affects, the emotions and personality of a person in relation to mood, courage, determination and energy. I define spirituality as a synergy of meaning, purpose, beliefs and values (in particular, moral values, or virtues), a sense of community or belonging, and a sense of value or worth in one's life. This synergy animates us in what we seek and do, leading to fulfilment and happiness.

What we now call spiritual leadership may serve both an organization's vision, purpose, values and strategies and its employees' psychological needs (Steger, 2012, p. 232). Indeed, it may be a strategy in its own right. Spiritual leadership encompasses sense making or "meaning making" (Weick, 1995), for example interpreting the environmental complexities – the threats and opportunities of the organization's external environment and the strengths and weaknesses of its internal environment.

No form of effective moral or ethical leadership coerces people to change or compromise deeply held personal values and beliefs. Instead, true spiritual leadership enables employees to find meaning, purpose, belongingness, and a sense of value or worth in their work without imposing this on them. This contributes to employees' spiritual well-being and their happiness in their lives, their performance at work and the performance and well-being of their organization and is the spiritual challenge to leadership today (Gill, 2014). Weber suggested that the old paradigm of the bureaucratic organization is a recipe for "parcelling out the souls of workers" (Weber, 1964) – alienated, powerless, non-fulfilled, estranged from their own selves and emotionally homeless (Blauner, 1964) – characterised by laissez-faire and transactional leadership (management-by-exception and contingent reward) and a lack of transformational leadership (Gill et al., 1998).

Research in a Canadian healthcare setting by Margaret McKee and colleagues found a significant relationship between transformational leadership and employees' mental and spiritual well-being (McKee et al., 2011). This relationship was mediated by workplace spirituality, in particular employees' sense of community. McKee and colleagues (2011) say: "Leaders influence individual well-being through their ability to enhance employees' sense of community in the workplace". Feeling disconnected from colleagues – from the social aspects of work – may adversely affect well-being at work, e.g. remote working in the virtual organization and 'hot desking'. This has been highlighted in organizations, for example, by the 2020–21 Covid-19 pandemic. Kelly-Ann Allen (2020) explored how social isolation and loneliness are on the rise and describes how meaningful connections are instrumental in developing a sense of belonging and our consequential sense of identity and well-being.

How can spiritual leadership induce altruistic love and intrinsic motivation among diverse members within an organization without being regarded as really yet another covert, sophisticated form of corporate exploitation of human vulnerability? Vu and Gill (2019b) explored an approach to spiritual leadership from a Buddhist perspective that focuses on the power of skilful means to tackle such concerns. In organizations pursuits such as reputation, power, winning, dominance, profit, recognition and even leader–follower relationships are the basis for objectives and expectations. This is known in Buddhism as "attachment". Attachment also characterises preoccupation with physical appearance, fame and celebrity.

In Buddhism any kind of attachment is believed to be a potential source of suffering and other negative consequences. Vu and Gill (2019b) explain how the Buddhist metaphor of "the raft", the emphasis on non-attachment and other Buddhist stories of skilful means contribute to our understanding of spiritual leadership cross-culturally. And they suggest that an issue that could usefully be explored is the cultural difference concerning attitudes to human relationships between the Buddhist emphasis on non-attachment and the Western emphasis on belonging. They also suggest that "fusion leadership" is an approach to integrating Eastern and Western values and mind-sets that may effectively respond to the challenges and dilemmas in spiritual leadership, and leadership more generally, in the context of globalization (Vu & Gill, 2019a).

Research with hospital nurses in Indonesia showed that for them (a) spiritual leadership has a significant effect on workplace spirituality but not on their job satisfaction or on *ihsan* behaviour (doing well or doing one's best); (b) workplace spirituality has a significant effect on job satisfaction but not on *ihsan* behaviour; and (c) job satisfaction has a significant effect on *ihsan* behaviour (Supriyanto et al., 2016).

We turn now to the first of two major theories of spiritual leadership – servant leadership.

Servant Leadership

"Servant leadership" is a theory put forward by Robert Greenleaf that postulates that leaders emerge who have the personal characteristics and skills to serve the needs of others – their group, organization or society – at a given time (Greenleaf, 1977). In the Bible it is clear that Moses knew that leadership is about servitude and that his only authority was that granted freely to him by those whom he led (Greenleaf et al., 2003). His inspirational leadership style was, in contemporary terms, illustrative of contingency leadership theory, integrating servant leadership with the leadership of the visionary, the teacher and the shepherd (Ben-Hur & Jonsen, 2012).

Socrates and his pupil Xenophon had also seen leadership as serving others and meeting their needs (Adair, 1989, p. 39). And in the Bible St Paul said, " . . . I have made myself every man's servant, to win over as many as possible" (1 Corinthians 9:9). As Major-General (Rtd) Tim Cross has said,"'[Jesus] served those who served the cause . . . but He certainly wasn't a doormat, rather a man of tremendous physical and moral courage" (Cross, 1998). It is no coincidence that the motto of the UK's Royal Military Academy at Sandhurst is *Serve to Lead* and that the Service prayer says, " . . . help us to be masters of ourselves that we may be servants of others, and teach us to serve to lead". An example in the world of business comes from the founder of SouthWest Airlines, Herb Kelleher, who said: "Leadership is being a faithful, devoted, hard-working servant of the people you lead and participating with them in the agonies as well as the ecstasies of life" (Quoted in *Annual Report 1998*, Center for Effective Organizations, Marshall School of Business, University of Southern California, Los Angeles, 13.). How many leaders today would see themselves as servants?

Robert Greenleaf by all accounts, Donald Valeri says, was a deeply moral person who was influenced by the Quaker religion (Valeri, 2007). Joe Anderson says Greenleaf also dabbled in Methodism, Unitarianism and Buddhism but was never committed to any particular variety in the Christian tradition and, indeed, once said that he was never "a pious Christian" (Anderson, 2008). Anderson also says that he believed strongly in the capability of the human spirit but never understood the Holy Spirit "that dwells in the heart of those that are born again – those that experience the second birth" (Anderson, 2008). However, he suggests that Greenleaf's ideas about servant leadership are clearly rooted in the Bible and Judeo-Christian heritage. And Valeri (2007) points out that Greenleaf spent his life in a contemplative, spiritual search for truth and meaning, which contributed to his own code of moral behaviour which he never imposed on others, preferring to follow a path of "gentle but firm persuasion". Yet, as Don Frick says, as a natural introvert he never promoted himself (Frick, 2004).

Effective leaders show the way and help or induce others to pursue it (Gill, 2011, p. 9). In helping or inducing employees or followers along the way, servant leaders focus on serving their needs because they care for them. They are concerned for their needs, their aspirations and growth as human beings, and their well-being – physical, mental, emotional and spiritual. In its highest manifestation this concern is driven by love for their employees or followers. Altruistic love, disinterested and selfless concern for the well-being of others, is central to servant leadership (Gill & Negrov, 2021). The virtue of generosity as distinctive in servant leadership reflects the virtue of altruistic love, the basis of all other virtues: "the source from which virtuous leadership comes" (Bocarnea et al., 2018).

The effects of servant leadership on employees' life satisfaction and the mediating role of work engagement and self-esteem in this relationship were investigated in a study of Pakistani employees in a large tractor manufacturing company (Chughtai,

2018). Servant leadership was found to be positively related to both work engagement and self-esteem, which, in turn, were both positively related to life satisfaction. Work engagement and self-esteem mediated the effects of servant leadership on life satisfaction. Perceptions of servant leadership in Chinese employees have been shown to predict their levels of work engagement (R. Yang et al., 2017). And a meta-analysis of 130 independent studies found that servant leadership had incremental predictive validity over transformational, authentic and ethical leadership and that behavioural outcomes were significantly explained by the level of trust in the leader and the leader-follower relationship (Lee et al., 2020).

A combination of personal traits, motivation to lead and a need to serve others characterizes servant leaders, according to Van Dierendonck (2011). He sees servant leadership as empowering and developing people by expressing humility, authenticity, interpersonal acceptance and stewardship and by providing direction. The mediating processes of trust and fairness are important to encouraging self-actualization, positive job attitudes, performance and a strong organizational focus on sustainability and corporate social responsibility.

The servant leader, Danah Zohar and Ian Marshall (2001, p. 33) say, "serves the ultimate source of meaning and value". Examples are Mahatma Gandhi, Mother Theresa, Nelson Mandela, Martin Luther King, Jr, and the Dalai Lama. They can equally be called spiritual leaders. Less well known is Katsuhiko Yazaki, the Japanese owner of a global mail-order company, Felissimo. Zohar and Marshall describe how, after becoming wealthy through an inherited business, Yazaki emerged from a monastery with a new self-awareness and a vision of the "proper" role of business as enhancing human happiness (Zohar & Marshal, 2001, pp. 262–263). He pursued this vision by helping his customers to imagine and achieve more fulfilling lifestyles and investing his money in educational projects and saving the environment.

Servant leadership, despite its appeal to many scholars and practising managers, has not met with universal acclaim. Mitch McCrimmon (2010), a psychologist and executive development consultant, has argued vehemently that servant leadership is paternalistic and, paradoxically, an impediment to employee engagement. He argued that workers need to be empowered to think for themselves and take more ownership, not be "served" by their managers. It may be appropriate, he says, in those situations where leaders are elected – such as politics or clubs where such leaders are expected to serve the wishes, needs or interests of the people they represent or be voted out of office – but not in business, where managers are usually expected to serve their companies' owners first and foremost (or be fired):

> The harsh reality in business is that employees are a means to an end. Effective managers will, of course, do all they can to engage, motivate, consider and include employees but that does not amount to being their servant. The truth is that while managers fire employees who aren't performing, no servant can fire his master. Therefore, this sense of servant leadership is interesting but clearly false.

McCrimmon also says that servant leadership adds no value to a multitude of post-heroic leadership models that abandon traditional notions of autocratic and hierarchical leadership in favour of emphasis on teamwork, community, involvement in decision making, caring and selflessness. He says that servant leadership, in transactional analysis terms the nurturing parent (Berne, 1964), also risks the same adverse consequences – demotivation and disengagement – as autocratic leadership (the critical parent). McCrimmon argues as well that servant leadership is less empowering for employees – and therefore less engaging – than employees serving their managers. And a rationale for servant leadership from religion, such as Jesus Christ as a role model, he says, is based merely on personal values rather than on business value. What McCrimmon overlooks or downplays, however, is the possibility that leadership may entail serving an abstract but compelling cause (a mission or purpose) such as one's nation – "Serve to Lead".

Understanding of servant leadership has increased in recent years, according to a systematic review (Nathan et al., 2019), cautioning that there are still "lingering questions" about the conceptual and empirical research that suggests, not surprisingly, an overlap between servant leadership and transformational, ethical and authentic leadership as well as limitations and shortcomings in research design. Perhaps servant leadership makes more of a practical moral and spiritual contribution than a theoretical one at present.

Our second review concerns the most well-known and widely accepted model of spiritual leadership.

Fry's Model of Spiritual Leadership

Since the turn of the twenty-first century, spiritual leadership has become established as a new approach to leadership, or perhaps a development of it. A central contribution came from Louis (Jody) Fry and his colleagues, arguing for spiritual leadership in embracing commitment to ethical business practices, employee well-being, sustainability and social responsibility (Fry, 2003; Fry & Nisiewicz, 2013; Fry et al., 2017). Fry (2003) believed that the spiritual dimension of human existence had been ignored by leadership scholars in their attention to its behavioural, cognitive, social and emotional aspects.

The importance of the spiritual dimension in human life came into stark relief for him personally during his journey through difficult times, beginning in 1999 and involving a helicopter crash, a car wreck, and a divorce, revealed in an interview in 2013 (Fry, 2013). This experience, together with his discovery and reading of Horton's inspirational book entitled *God* (Horton, 1950), led him to become a born-again Christian. Horton's view of God was that of "an ideal source of help and object of devotion: a being so much greater, more enduring, and more worthy than ourselves that we may confidently lean on it for support and unreservedly give ourselves to its service"

(Horton, 1950, pp. 4–5). This view of God as "a higher power on a continuum from atheism (there is no God; one has no sense of calling or membership; all is evil, hopeless and rooted in sorrow, distress, despair, and calamity) to complete pantheism (everything is God; all is good and rooted in joy, peace, serenity" (Fry, 2003, pp. 706–707) formed the basis for his spiritual leadership theory. Despite this allegiance, Fry remains objectively eclectic in his portrayal of religion and spirituality in his writings. Fry (2003) summarises his original model thus:

> A causal theory of spiritual leadership . . . within an intrinsic motivation model that incorporates vision, hope/faith, and altruistic love, theories of workplace spirituality, and spiritual survival. The purpose of spiritual leadership is to create vision and value congruence across the strategic, empowered team, and individual levels and, ultimately, to foster higher levels of organizational commitment and productivity.

Fry's model is based on the interaction of intrinsic motivators of leaders and followers that comprise hope, faith, vision and altruistic love (Figure 3.2).

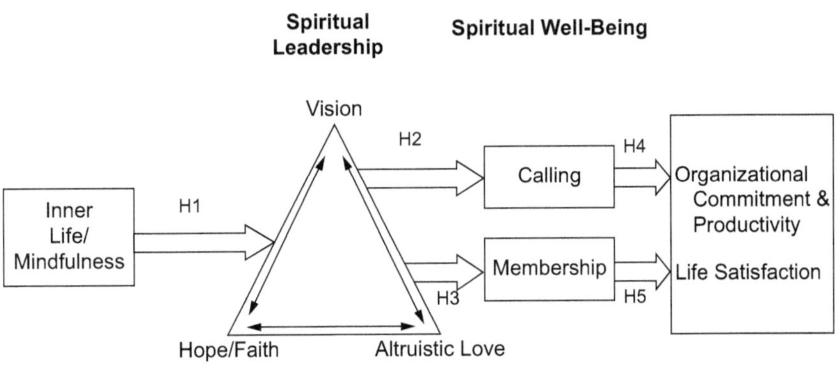

Figure 3.2: Fry's original model of spiritual leadership (Fry et al., 2017, reprinted by permission of the publisher).

Faith, hope and love are the so-called Christian Triad posited by St Paul in 1 Corinthians 13 (Gill & Negrov, 2021). Altruistic love is characterized by the values of forgiveness, kindness, integrity, empathy and compassion, honesty, patience, courage, trust, loyalty and humility. Hope and faith elicit effort or motivation in terms of endurance, perseverance, pursuit of stretch goals, the desire to "do what it takes", and the expectation of a reward or victory. These motivators determine calling and membership, which in turn (in other versions of the model) lead to organizational and personal outcomes of organizational commitment, employee life satisfaction, corporate social responsibility and financial performance. The latter three outcomes are known as the Triple Bottom Line: people, planet and profit (Fry & Nisiewicz, 2013, p. 5).

A study of medical laboratory workers by Yang and Fry (2018) using Fry's model found general support for the spiritual leadership model's positive influence on organizational commitment and unit productivity and life satisfaction and that organizational membership mediated the relationship between spiritual leadership and employee burnout. A number of other studies have validated Fry's model, not only in the USA and Western cultures but also in a range of other cultures, such as Taiwan (Chen & Yang, 2012; Chen et al., 2012), China (Chen et al., 2012), South Korea (Hunsaker, 2016), Iran (Javanmard, 2012) and Pakistan (Bodla & Ali, 2012). In some cases religious beliefs and practices are central to employees in their work. For example, Egel and Fry (2017) have adapted the spiritual leadership model for Islamic leadership based on Islamic tenets (Figure 3.3).

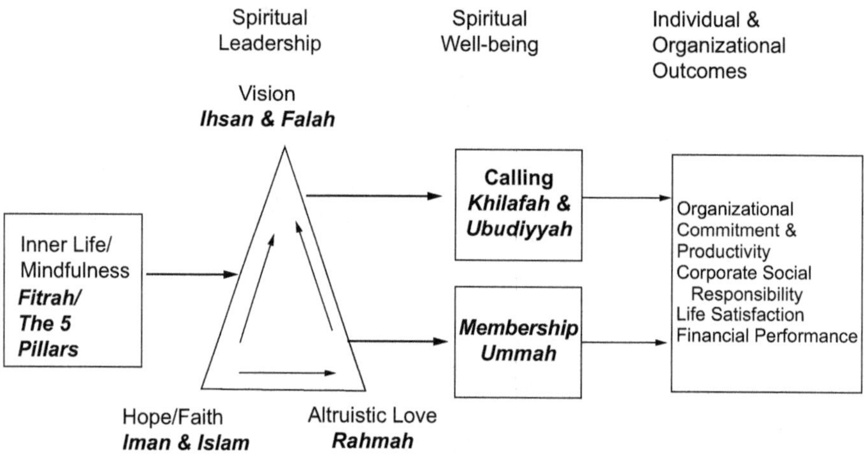

Figure 3.3: Theoretical transposition of the components of Fry's spiritual leadership model into a model for Islamic leadership (Egel & Fry, 2017, reprinted by permission of the publisher).

In a study of Islamic perspectives on leadership, many aspects of transcendental leadership were found in the *Qur'an*, particularly prophetic leadership, suggesting the importance of inter-connectedness of the leader, followers and altruism for leadership effectiveness (AlSarhi et al., 2014).

Fry's spiritual leadership theory (SLT) is not without its critics. For example, there are inconsistencies in the definition and use of the term "spirituality" as well as in the different versions of his model that are portrayed. Bruce Avolio and colleagues suggest that Fry does not provide an acceptable working definition of spirituality and that he does not help to explain what constitutes spirituality and leadership and how they relate to each other (Avolio et al., 2009). The underpinning research is criticized for its single-method usage rather than a multi-method approach. Peter Case and colleagues criticize Fry not only for superficial theorizing but also for a too rational and positivistic treatment of spirituality (Case et al., 2012). They argue that Fry's SLT promotes spiritual leadership without a proper philosophical and theological conception of spirituality.

In 2010 Fry and colleagues introduced a Balanced Scorecard for spiritual leadership, drawing on management and business theory and practice (Fry et al., 2010). Fry's approach to spirituality focuses on organizational commitment, productivity and financial performance, which, in Marjolein Lips-Wiersma's view, is counterintuitive (Lips-Wiersma, 2003). The issue here is whether spirituality has anything to do with material gain – making money. Studies have shown a relationship between spirituality and economic benefits. But just because there may be such a relationship does not justify the hijacking of spirituality specifically for that purpose. Case, French and Simpson (2012) see the SLT as subsumed in consumerism, with the "go-getting" attitude that promotes "egocentric notions of leader/follower relations" and may place "the employee under the performative auspices of managing spirituality". All of this raises ethical questions with its implications of top-down management, the exploitation and control of employees (Rozuel & McGhee, 2012) that we discussed earlier.

A systematic and critical analysis of 59 empirical studies by Johye Oh and Jia Wang (2020) at Texas A&M University produced a holistic, comprehensive model of spiritual leadership incorporating Fry's model (Figure 3.4, overleaf).

Inner life as an antecedent of spiritual leadership in this model concerns one's spiritual values and self-reflective practices such as prayer, meditation and religious traditions, in other words one's individual and social identity (Duchon & Plowman, 2005). "Confucian mindset" refers to social order and harmony. In addition to the factors in Fry's model of spiritual leadership, this factor, in particular social order, appeared significant in the South Korean context (Hunsaker, 2014a). Social order is characterized by the expectation of reciprocal moral obligations and associated behaviour within the social hierarchy of relationships in a group or organization. A cautionary note comes from Denis Diderot, the French philosopher: "Watch out for the fellow who talks about putting things in order. Putting things in order always means getting other people under your control." (Diderot, D. (1796). Harmony is focused on interpersonal attitudes and behavior among individuals within a unit whereby members are expected to pursue conformity and group consensus – a practice increasingly manifest in China but likely to be controversial in other cultures. In the West one is more likely to meet "productive conflict" instead, with its creative outcomes. It is likely that a Confucian mindset is significant to spiritual leadership elsewhere in other parts of East Asia.

However, Mai Vu (2018), in a study of spiritual leadership in Vietnam, a developing country in transition with a Communist government, suggested that a Buddhist perspective prevalent there today is different not only from that in the West but also from that elsewhere in East Asia despite a hitherto long tradition of Confucianism there as a remnant of Chinese rule. She found that Buddhist-enacted leadership is essentially a process of self-transformation using skillful means – a way of teaching knowledge and applying learning according to the context and the particular people

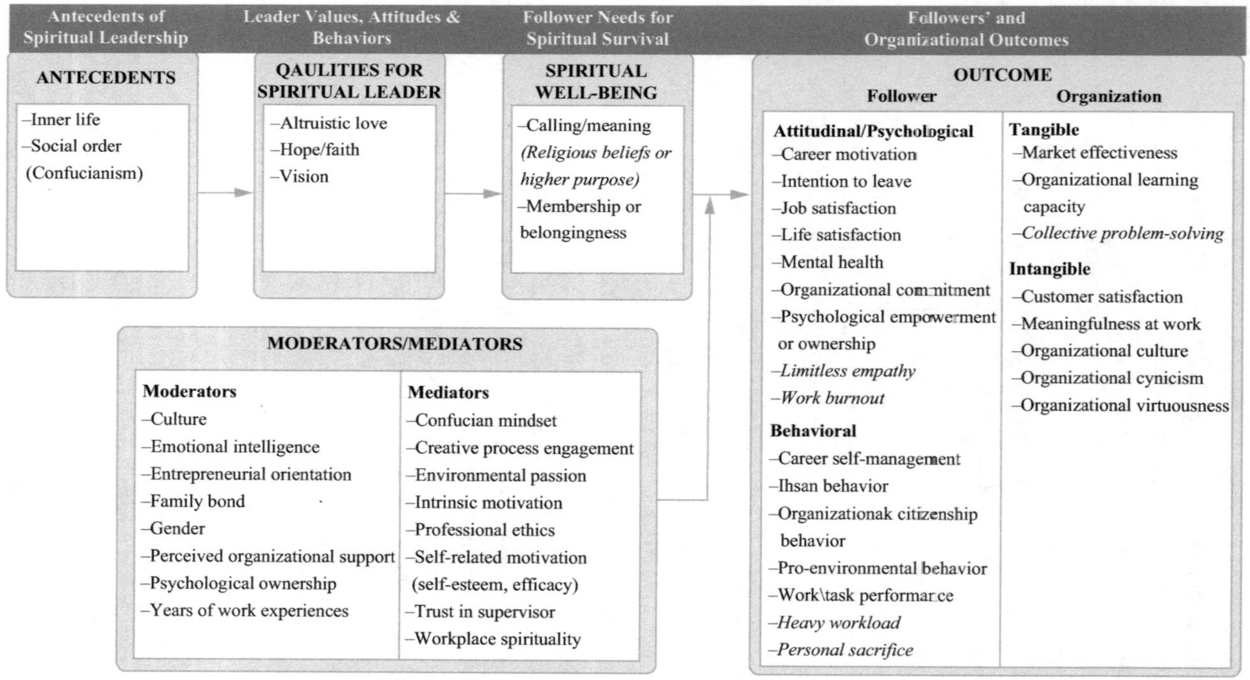

Figure 3.4: Oh and Wang's holistic model of spiritual leadership (2020) (reprinted by permission of the publisher).
Notes:1. Factors in italics were identified from qualitative studies.2. *Ihsan* behaviour in Islam is a virtue-based discretionary behaviour that enhances the well-being of the organization and its members. In simple language it refers to doing well or doing one's best (Supriyanto et al., 2016).3. Mediators provide information about how or why variables are strongly associated, while moderators explain the circumstances that cause a weak or ambiguous association between variables that were expected to have a strong relationship.

concerned – involving multiple leadership identities and responding to contextual challenges with mindfulness and flexibility.

Spiritual Leadership and Spiritual Intelligence

Drawing on the concept of spirituality in this chapter, we can define spiritual intelligence (known as SQ) as understanding that human beings have an animating need for purpose (a sense of calling), meaning, and a sense of belonging, virtue and worth in what they seek and do. Spiritual leadership is characterized by responding appropriately to that need. While Howard Gardner (1999, pp. 59–66) expressed concerns that it is difficult to separate spiritual intelligence from its religious connotations and that there was insufficient empirical evidence to separate it from other forms of intelligence, it has gained empirical support and credibility from research in psychology, neurology, anthropology and cognitive science, according to its key proponents, Danah Zohar and Ian Marshall (2001, pp. 11–13). How does SQ relate to emotional intelligence? They contrast SQ with EQ: "My emotional intelligence allows me to judge what situation I am in and then to behave appropriately within it . . . But my spiritual intelligence allows me to ask if I want to be in this particular situation in the first place. Would I rather change the situation, creating a better one?" (Zohar & Marshal, 2001, p. 5).

Emotional intelligence (known as 'EQ', as distinct from SQ and IQ) is the extent of our self-awareness, our ability to manage our own feelings, our awareness of the needs and feelings of other people, and our ability to respond appropriately (Gill, 2011, pp. 298–299). It is closely related to, if not an aspect of, spiritual intelligence. Zohar and Marshall (2001, p. 285) point out that: "Self-awareness is one of the highest criteria of high spiritual intelligence but one of the lowest priorities of our . . . culture." And Robert Furey (1986, p. 126) suggests that: "A person does not seek to encounter the spiritual dimension of his being until he has developed a healthy sense of humility" (through self-awareness).

Humility, then, is a spiritual value. A growing body of research has shown how humility in leadership is associated with a range of positive outcomes for followers, employees, teams, organizations, and leaders themselves (Swain & Murray, 2020). Examples of such outcomes are the following:

- Increased follower self-efficacy or confidence, motivation and performance (Mao et al., 2019)
- Reduced emotional exhaustion in high-stress occupations and environments (L. Wang et al., 2018)
- Improved information sharing (Y. Wang et al., 2018)
- Enhanced follower creativity (Gonçalves et al., 2015)
- Greater feedback-seeking behaviour by subordinates (Qian et al., 2018)

- Improved group and organizational performance and effectiveness (Ou et al., 2018; Rego et al., 2018; Owens & Hekman, 2016)
- Lower employee turnover (Owens et al., 2013)
- Prosocial and altruistic behaviour in the members of groups, such as helpfulness (LaBouff et al., 2012)
- Encouragement of shared leadership (Chiu et al., 2016; Lindsay et al., 2018)
- Increased self-control in the leader (Tong et al., 2016)Greater liking of leaders by subordinates (Swain, 2018)
- Strengthening of social relationships (R. Nielsen & Marrone, 2018)
- Greater individual resilience (Brazil & Dunham, 2018)
- Better overall self-rated physical health (Krause, 2010)

Methods for assessing humility have comprised self-report, implicit association tests, reports by others, and a combination of these (Swain & Murray, 2020). Though useful, these methods suffer from well-known weaknesses of these methods in general, not least the lack of consensus on the definition of humility. However, there are promising developments ongoing.

Zohar and Marshall (2004) argue that spiritually intelligent leaders can move people from a state of acting from "lower" motivations – fear, greed, anger and self-assertion – to acting from higher forms – exploration, cooperation, personal power, mastery and higher service. This is reminiscent of transformational leadership. Research at Regent University in the USA found that managers in local government who displayed greater servant leadership and spiritual intelligence also reported lower levels of stress and higher levels of workforce engagement with their jobs and organization (Roberts, 2013). Aydın Söylemez and Mustafa Koç (2019) in a study in Turkey found that spiritual intelligence has a positive influence on meaningfulness and life satisfaction. And Muneeba Ali (2019) in Pakistan argues that spiritual leadership based on spiritual intelligence may play an important part in effective change management and organization transformation by contributing to a sense of meaning, well-being, vision and a culture of love in which people feel loved, appreciated and cared for, but that empirical research is needed.

Assessment of Spirituality and Spiritual Leadership

How do we assess spirituality and develop spiritual leadership in the workplace? Clearly this is useful to do as a basis for understanding and fostering employee empowerment and engagement with the ultimate aim of enhancing or sustaining employee well-being and happiness as well as organizational performance and effectiveness. There are many instruments available for assessing spirituality and spiritual well-being, though they are mostly for clinical or religious situations.

Much research in spirituality has employed questionnaires custom-designed for the specific topic under investigation, and few instruments serve a universal purpose, which is no doubt related to the issue of a universal definition of spirituality. The same problem besets leadership assessment. Some examples follow.

The Spiritual Well-Being Scale (SWBS) emerged as a development from the quality-of-life movement in the early 1980s, combining two dimensions of life: the existential and the religious (Paloutzian & Ellison, 1982; Bufford et al., 1991; Genia, 2001; Paloutzian et al., 2012, pp. 353–358). It recognised that the religious dimension had been ignored as an element in well-being and that both dimensions "occupy an important place in human life as motivating and harmonizing forces" (addressed specifically in the Turkish context in a different assessment instrument with the same name) (Ekşi & Kardaş, 2017). The SWBS has been translated into several languages and consists of two 10-item sub-scales – religious well-being (RWB) and existential well-being (EWB) – covering well-being in a variety of areas, including physical and mental health, psychological adjustment, and assertiveness.

The Spiritual Formation Inventory (SFI), developed by Bruce Baker and Donghun Lee, is non-religious, focused on observable prosocial behaviour, and suitable for workplaces in general (Baker & Lee, 2020). Spiritual formation is defined as fostering a workplace culture of high engagement. The SFI consists of 19 items assessing three factors – honouring individuals, nurturing relationships, and serving with integrity, which are significantly correlated with workplace engagement, which was measured by the Utrecht Work Engagement Scale (UWES) (Schaufeli et al., 2011). The 17-item UWES itself assesses work engagement characterized by vigour, dedication and absorption in work and is available in several languages.

The Intrinsic Spirituality Scale is a six-item intrinsic spirituality scale that assesses the degree to which spirituality serves as an individual's primary driving force (Hodge, 2003). It is suitable for both theistic and non-theistic populations.

The Spiritual Leadership Scale developed by Louis Fry and colleagues based on his Spiritual Leadership Theory consists of 34 items covering seven factors: vision, hope/faith, altruistic love, meaning/calling, membership, organizational commitment, and productivity (Fry et al., 2005).

Petchsawanga and Duchon's Workplace Spirituality Measure comprising 22 items, developed in Thailand to measure compassion, meaningful work, mindfulness and transcendence (Petchsawang & Duchon, 2009).

The Integrated Spiritual Intelligence Scale (ISIS). A scale consisting of 83 items and a 45-item, 22-subfactor short form (Amram & Dryer, 2008).

Servant Leadership Behavior Scale (SLBS-6) (Sen et al., 2019) includes a spiritual dimension, a distinguishing feature that shows servant leadership as a holistic and distinctive leadership approach (Nathan et al., 2019). The inclusion of spirituality faithfully reflects both Greenleaf's initial theorizing (Greenleaf, 1977) and Graham's subsequent analysis (Graham, 1991) that servant leadership relies on spiritual insights and humility as its source of influence.

The Lee Kum Sheung Center for Health and Happiness at Harvard University (CenterHealthHappiness@hsph.harvard.edu) has compiled a repository of psychological well-being scales that primarily relate to the health sector, though some scales overlap the area of spirituality and may be helpful in relation to spiritual assessment and leadership. The Center defines spiritual well-being together with psychological and social aspects of well-being as constituting subjective wellbeing as a whole.

How spiritual leaders and spiritual leadership develop has been studied in a limited way in three religion-based organizations in Australia. Low and Ayoko (2020) documented the process for 26 spiritual leaders in three such organizations, revealing four phases: (1) awareness of a spiritual calling, associated with interest and opportunity through formal appointment; (2) the learning process associated with personal characteristics, social family and organizational environment, self-development, a deep relationship with a higher being (God), and formal training; (3) the characteristics of spiritual leaders and spiritual leadership in terms of inspiration, humility, authority, spiritual lifestyle, and follower-based leadership; and (4) outcomes in terms of spiritual leaders' personal development, followers' development, and organizational development. This work needs extending to using larger and wider-ranging samples and covering broader demographics and contexts.

The Challenges Ahead and the Needs for Further Research

A fundamental contribution of future research to the field of spirituality and leadership would be made by finding satisfactory definitions for both terms that meet consensual approval. I have suggested definitions for both leadership and spirituality for consideration. At least then we would all be researching and writing about the same thing! And that would make the difference between disappointment and delight in the impact of leadership development programmes.

While many studies have shown a positive significant correlation between spirituality (however defined) and spiritual well-being in the population as a whole, a causal link needs to be investigated: is spirituality a cause of spiritual well-being or a consequence of it?

In addition to the well-established quantitative methods that have characterized most research into spirituality and leadership, Oh and Wang say that we now need to supplement these with a diverse range of qualitative methods. They say that, to advance spiritual leadership research, we need more studies using different methodologies and methods. For example, researchers may consider using the case study approach to collect stories of exemplary spiritual leaders, the phenomenological approach to understand spiritual leaders' lived experiences, [and] the grounded theory approach to develop new theories and explanations of spiritual leadership (Oh & Wang, 2020).

Research into how spirituality informs ethical and effective leadership in general can be usefully further explored, focusing on extant theories and models of leadership such as the GILL (General Inventory for Lasting Leadership) (Gill, 2006, 2011; Rupprecht et al., 2013). The GILL, for example, includes the core leadership themes and practices of empowerment and engagement, also identified by Hunsaker (Hunsaker, 2014a), and shared values (in addition to vision, purpose/mission and strategy). Other mediators and moderators can be researched as well as outcomes and measures such as corporate social responsibility, the psychological contract, and organizational performance including profitability and shareholder value (Hunsaker, 2014a), product and service quality, stakeholder satisfaction, and, not least, employee well-being. Faith and hope and altruistic love feature in Fry's and Oh and Wang's models of spiritual leadership, and love has been shown to be an influence for good in leadership (Gill & Negrov, 2021), so it would be interesting and potentially useful to explore what other values that characterize cultures in which different religions and life philosophies such as Buddhism and humanism prevail inform their concepts and practices of spirituality and spiritual leadership.

Most of the research on spiritual leadership carried out in recent years has concerned Fry's SLT. Most of the empirical studies in the field of spirituality in organizations and spiritual leadership have been quantitative rather than qualitative or mixed-method in nature. And most of these studies have explored the impact on organizational performance and effectiveness and, frequently, financial measures. Benefiel and colleagues say that there is growing concern over the appropriateness of aggregating empirical individual-level data to group and organizational levels in exploring how valid constructs are (Benefiel et al., 2014). To move research on workplace spirituality and spiritual leadership beyond the nascent stage, compared to the more developed management and leadership fields, requires new and more creative multi-method approaches, including qualitative methods. As John Antonakis (2017) says, qualitative research can contribute contextual insights into leadership phenomena, for example in countries in political or economic transition.

Fry and his colleagues (Fry et al., 2017) have recommended further studies of the validity of his spiritual leadership model, among them:

- Longitudinal studies across different populations to test for changes over time in key variables and performance measures
- Studies to explore the efficacy of the model in different national cultures, both religious and secular, political ideologies and stages of economic development
- Studies of outcomes of spiritual leadership at individual, team and organizational levels and the depth of its general validity
- Studies of other stakeholder outcomes, concerning psychological well-being, product and service quality, customer satisfaction, corporate social responsibility, and measures of financial performance and other appropriate performance indicators

- Use of measures from other leadership theories as control measures, such as such as transformational leadership, authentic leadership, ethical leadership, and servant leadership

Areas of exploration of spirituality at work and spiritual leadership to be addressed include generalisability of theories and models and the influence of context – national, organizational, industry-sectoral, professional and team culture; ideology, politics and religion; and social culture, particularly diversity in respect of gender, black and minority ethnic groups. Consequential issues to be addressed concern bias, unfair discrimination and accommodation (Krishnakumar et al., 2015). And empirical research is needed into the potential contribution of spiritual leadership and spiritual intelligence to organizational change and transformation.

Cheryl Hunt at the University of Exeter in the UK says that, in academia, "discussing and studying spirituality is certainly not widely encouraged" (Hunt, 2020). Reasons for this may be how research publications are viewed within an assessment scheme; the place and status of inter-disciplinary and multi-disciplinary research; the lack of clarity and the confusion in the understanding of spirituality, for example its confusion with spiritualism; and its domination by religion that is perceived in a largely secular audience (in the UK at least). As David Rousseau (2019, p. 19) says, there is "a tendency in science to diminish or devalue what it cannot explain" and that highlighting the significance of people's experiences provides an antidote to this. A renewed encouragement of inter-disciplinary or multi-disciplinary research in the field of spirituality across the arts, humanities, sciences and business is needed. A potential contribution to this in relation to spirituality and science comes from Robinson (2020). Empirical research is needed to validate Robinson's MODI model and its utility in leadership theory and practice and a subsequent assessment system.

Oh and Wang (2020) say that spiritual leadership researchers have focused, almost exclusively, on followers' well-being and other outcomes, overlooking the benefits and consequences for leaders themselves, and they call for research to uncover the mutual benefits of spiritual leadership, especially leaders in work organizations. Very few studies have examined the antecedents of spiritual leadership (Fry, 2003; Dede & Ayranci, 2014; Fry et al., 2017; Hunsaker, 2014a, 2014b). Oh and Wang (2020) suggest that, given the theoretical background of spiritual leadership in motivation, ethics, religions and values, these elements could be explored in depth as antecedents that predict spiritual leadership behaviour.

Research into spirituality and leadership, including spiritual leadership, in a diverse range of contexts has been sparse so far. This needs to be extended across cultures, nations and industries. This would contribute to a universal understanding of the relationship between spirituality and leadership and cross-cultural differences that exist. For example, the relationship between leadership, spirituality and harmony and altruistic love and how to measure it; other aspects of Confucianism in relation to leadership; and that between other Asian philosophies and religions such as Taoism, Hinduism and Buddhism and leadership (Vu & Gill, 2019a; Hunsaker, 2014a).

Empirical research to validate and develop Oh and Wang's model of spiritual leadership, itself a development of Fry's model, would be worthwhile. Oh and Wang (2020) say: "Only a handful of studies [have] looked at the links between spiritual leadership and other constructs, such as organizational citizenship behavior, psychological empowerment and organizational learning capacity. These constructs clearly relate not only to spiritual leadership but also leadership more generally. More studies are needed.

Earlier I discussed humility in leadership and I mentioned that ways of assessing it are ongoing. Promising areas include assessment of non-verbal cues such as posture and voice and other body language, assessment of observable choices of academic courses, word choice in writing (such as inclusivity of language) and psychometric personality assessment (Swain & Murray, 2020). More research and development are needed here too.

Investigation is recommended of the relationship between spirituality and Bass and Avolio's Full-Range Leadership model (which is probably the most widely accepted theory of leadership, and in particular the relationship with spirituality of the four "Is": individualised consideration, intellectual stimulation, inspirational motivation and idealised influence (Bass, 1985; Avolio & Bass, 2001).

A survey by the Chartered Institute of Personnel and Development reported in 2017 showed how employee empowerment and engagement were identified by more than half of human resource professionals as somewhat or very ineffective in the public and private sectors taken together and 40 percent thought that this was a major need for attention over the following three years (Table 3.1):

Table 3.1: Percentage of human resource professionals identifying current effectiveness in empowering and engaging people in the public and private sectors in the United Kingdom.

	Empowerment	Engagement
Very effective	5	4
Somewhat effective	42	42
Somewhat ineffective	29	35
Very ineffective	24	18

Note: Based on Figure 4, p.15, *HR Outlook Survey,* Chartered Institute of Personnel and Development, (2017).

Further research is needed on how leaders can develop and introduce an organizational culture that is based on those values, attitudes and competencies that reflect a spiritual philosophy and associated practices. We need to do this through a

creative mixed-methods research approach, in ways that are both different and better than currently and in exercising leadership ourselves in doing this:
- showing the way – developing and communicating a clear, meaningful, shared vision, shared purpose, shared values, and clear strategies
- helping or inducing people to pursue it through empowering and engaging them in what needs to be done

Fry and Altman (2013) have shown that integration of spiritual leadership into training has led to positive outcomes, such as team empowerment, overcoming resentment, conflict and fear, and consensus-based decision making. Spirituality and leadership therefore can form part of leadership development activity, and further research can help us to do this both effectively and ethically (Oh & Wang, 2020).

Conclusion

In her conclusion to the quest for a general theory of leadership, Joanne Ciulla (2006, pp. 232–233) says: "Leadership is ultimately a moral endeavor. When it is done right, leaders help to create the conditions for people to flourish physically, mentally, and as human beings, and they do so without harming others or the world around them." I concur, and I would only add – "and flourish spiritually, whether religious or secular."

Spirituality in leadership and management, and in particular in management education and leadership development programmes and activities, is sorely lacking in both the public sector and business enterprises around the world. The consequence is employee disengagement, spiritual desolation, and psychological and physical ill-health. It is gratifying to see, however, that awareness of this need – and attention to it – is gradually increasing. The potential outcome of such efforts is what I view as the supreme goal for humanity: our spiritual well-being. The area of the workplace, work itself and its management are the theatre in which this drama plays out.

Spiritual well-being of people at work is both instrumental for organizational effectiveness, however defined and measured, and a socially and morally responsible and desirable end in itself. Workplace spirituality is causally related in various ways to employees' spiritual well-being. Spiritual leadership creates workplace spirituality and ultimately spiritual well-being, partly, but significantly, through employee empowerment and engagement. We need to help or induce employers and other group and organizational leaders to enhance their understanding and practice of leadership, in particular spiritual leadership, in their organizations. Research, education and training are crucial in this effort to improve the wellbeing of human beings, the organizations that employ them, and ultimately the societies in which we all live.

References

Adair, J. (1989). *Great Leaders*. The Talbot Adair Press.

Allen, K.-A. (2020). *The Psychology of Belonging*. Routledge.

AlSarhi, N., Salleh, L. M., Mohamed, Z., & Amini, A. (2014). The West and Islam perspective of leadership. *International Affairs and Global Strategy*, *18*, 42–56.

Amram, Y., & Dryer, C. (2008). *The Integrated Spiritual Intelligence Scale (ISIS): Development and Preliminary Validation*. Institute of Transpersonal Psychology.

Anderson, J. (2008, May). *The writings of Robert K. Greenleaf: An interpretive analysis and the future of servant leadership*. Paper presented at the Servant Leadership Research Roundtable, School of Global Leadership & Entrepreneurship, Regent University, School of Global Leadership & Entrepreneurship, Regent University, Virginia Beach, USA.

Antonakis, J. (2017). On doing better science: From thrill of discovery to policy implications. *The Leadership Quarterly*, *28*(1), 5–21.

Arnold, K. A., Turner, N., Barling, J., Kelloway, E. K., & McKee, M. C. (2007). Transformational leadership and psychological well-being: The mediating role of meaningful work. *Journal of Occupational Health Psychology*, *12*(3), 193–203. https://doi.org/10.1037/1076-8998.12.3.193

Avolio, B. J., & Bass, B. M. (Eds.). (2001). *Developing Potential Across a Full Range of Leadership: Cases on Transactional and Transformational Leadership*. Lawrence Erlbaum.

Avolio, B. J., Walumbwa, F. O., & Weber, T. J. (2009). Leadership: Current theories, research, and future directions. *Annual Review of Psychology*, *60*, 421–449.

Baker, B. D., & Lee, D. D. (2020). Spiritual formation and workplace engagement: Prosocial workplace behaviors. *Journal of Management, Spirituality & Religion*, *17*(2), 107–138.

Bass, B. M. (1985). *Leadership and Performance Beyond Expectations*. Free Press.

Benefiel, M., Fry, L. W., & Geigle, D. (2014). Spirituality and religion in the workplace: History, theory, and research. *Psychology of Religion and Spirituality*, *6*(3), 175–187. https://doi.org/10.1037/a0036597

Ben-Hur, S., & Jonsen, K. (2012). Ethical leadership: Lessons from Moses. *Journal of Management Development*, *31*(9), 962–973.

Berne, E. (1964). *Games People Play New York*. Grove Press.

Blauner, R. (1964). *Alienation and Freedom*. Chicago University Press.

Bocarnea, M., Henson, J., Huizing, R., Mahan, M., & Winston, B. E. (2018). Fruitful leadership: Leading with love. In M. Bocarnea, J. Henson, R. Huizing, M. Mahan, & B. E. Winston (Eds.), *Evaluating Employee Performance through Christian Virtues* (pp. 7–22). Palgrave Macmillan.

Bodla, M. A., & Ali, H. (2012). Workplace spirituality: A spiritual audit of banking executives in Pakistan. *African Journal of Business Management*, *6*(11), 3888–3897. https://doi.org/10.5897/AJBM10.1242

Brazil, D., & Dunham, Y. G. (2018). Resilience and overcoming failure. In S. Smith, C. Brazil, B. Britt, & E. Elinger (Eds.), *West Point Leadership*. Rowan Technology Solutions.

Bufford, R. K., Paloutzian, R. F., & Ellison, C. W. (1991). Norms for the spiritual well-being scale. *Journal of Psychology and Theology*, *19*(1), 56–70. https://doi.org/10.1177/009164719101900106

Carroll, L. (1871). *Through the Looking-Glass and What Alice Found There* (New Edition 2003). Puffin Classics.

Case, P., French, R., & Simpson, P. (2012). From theoria to theory: Leadership without contemplation. *Organization*, *19*(3), 345–361. https://doi.org/10.1177/1350508412437072

Chamorro-Premuzic, T. (2016, March 10). Leaders must learn to behave better to boost engagement. Talent management. *Raconteur*, 13.

Chartered institute of personnel and development. (2017). *HR Outlook Survey* (HR Outlook Survey). Chartered Institute of Personnel and Development.

Chen, C.-Y., & Yang, C.-F. (2012). The impact of spiritual leadership on organizational citizenship behavior: A multi-sample analysis. *Journal of Business Ethics*, *105*(1), 107–114. https://doi.org/10.1007/s10551-011-0953-3

Chen, C.-Y., Yang, C.-Y., & Li, C.-I. (2012). Spiritual leadership, follower mediators, and organizational outcomes: Evidence from three industries across two major Chinese societies. *Journal of Applied Social Psychology*, *42*(4), 890–938. https://doi.org/10.1111/j.1559-1816.2011.00834.x

Chiu, C.-Y. C., Owens, B. P., & Tesluk, P. E. (2016). Initiating and utilizing shared leadership in teams: The role of leader humility, team proactive personality, and team performance capability. *Journal of Applied Psychology*, *101*(12), 1705–1720. https://doi.org/10.1037/apl0000159

Chughtai, A. A. (2018). Examining the effects of servant leadership on life satisfaction. *Applied Research in Quality of Life*, *13*(4), 873–889. https://doi.org/10.1007/s11482-017-9564-1

Ciulla, J. B. (2006). What we learned along the way: A commentary. In G. R. Goethals & G. L. J. Sorenson (Eds.), *The Quest for a General Theory of Leadership* (p. 3968). Edward Elgar Publishing. https://doi.org/10.4337/9781847202932.00017

Cross, T. (1998, July 5). *Christian leadership* [Speech at Wellbeck College].

Dede, N. P., & Ayranci, E. (2014). Exploring the connections among spiritual leadership, altruism, and trust in family businesses. *Quality & Quantity*, *48*(6), 3373–3400. https://doi.org/10.1007/s11135-013-9962-x

Dethmer, J., Chapman, D., & Klemp, K. W. (2014). *The 15 Commitments of Conscious Leadership: A New Paradigm for Sustainable Success*. Conscious Leadership Group (www.conscious.is) and KWK Kayley Warner Klemp (www.kaleyklemp.com).

Diderot, D. (1796). *Supplement to Bougainville's "Voyage."*

Duchon, D., & Plowman, D. A. (2005). Nurturing the spirit at work: Impact on work unit performance. *The Leadership Quarterly*, *16*(5), 807–833. https://doi.org/10.1016/j.leaqua.2005.07.008

Egel, E., & Fry, L. W. (2017). Spiritual leadership as a model for Islamic leadership. *Public Integrity*, *19*(1), 77–95. https://doi.org/10.1080/10999922.2016.1200411

Ekşi, H., & Kardaş, S. (2017). Spiritual well-being: Scale development and validation. *Spiritual Psychology and Counselling*, *2*(1), 73–88.

Fairholm, G. W. (1996). Spiritual leadership: Fulfilling whole-self needs at work. *Leadership & Organization Development Journal*, *17*(5), 11–17. https://doi.org/10.1108/01437739610127469

Frick, D. M. (2004). *Robert K. Greenleaf: A Life of Servant Leadership*. Berrett-Koehler Publishers.

Fry, L. W. (2003). Toward a theory of spiritual leadership. *The Leadership Quarterly*, *14*(6), 693–727. https://doi.org/10.1016/j.leaqua.2003.09.001

Fry, L. W. (2013, January 7). *Interview with National Public Radio, USA, Quidity/Benedictine University*. [Interview]. Accessed at www.youtube.com/watch?v=89T8dK9ZpPQ on March 4, 2021

Fry, L. W., & Altman, Y. (2013). *Spiritual Leadership in Action: The CEL Story Achieving Extraordinary Results Through Ordinary People*. Information Age Publishing.

Fry, L. W., Latham, J. R., Clinebell, S. K., & Krahnke, K. (2017). Spiritual leadership as a model for performance excellence: A study of Baldrige Award recipients. *Journal of Management, Spirituality & Religion*, *14*(1), 22–47. https://doi.org/10.1080/14766086.2016.1202130

Fry, L. W., Matherly, L. L., & Ouimet, J. -Robert. (2010). The spiritual leadership balanced scorecard business model: The case of the Cordon Bleu-Tomasso Corporation. *Journal of Management, Spirituality & Religion*, *7*(4), 283–314. https://doi.org/10.1080/14766086.2010.524983

Fry, L. W., & Nisiewicz, M. S. (2013). *Maximizing the Triple Bottom Line Through Spiritual Leadership*. Stanford University Press. https://doi.org/10.1515/9780804784290

Fry, L. W., Vitucci, S., & Cedillo, M. (2005). Spiritual leadership and army transformation: Theory, measurement, and establishing a baseline. *The Leadership Quarterly*, *16*(5), 835–862. https://doi.org/10.1016/j.leaqua.2005.07.012

Furey, R. J. (1986). *So I'm Not Perfect: A Psychology of Humility*. Alba House.

Gardner, H. E. (1999). *Intelligence Reframed: Multiple Intelligences for the 21st Century*. Basic Books.

Genia, V. (2001). Evaluation of the spiritual well-being scale in a sample of college students. *International Journal for the Psychology of Religion*, *11*(1), 25–33. https://doi.org/10.1207/S15327582IJPR1101_03

Ghadi, M. Y., Fernando, M., & Caputi, P. (2013). Transformational leadership and work engagement: The mediating effect of meaning in work. *Leadership & Organization Development Journal*, *34*(6), 532–550.

Gill, R. (2006). *Theory and Practice of Leadership*. SAGE Publications.

Gill, R. (2011). *Theory and Practice of Leadership* (2nd ed.). SAGE Publications.

Gill, R. (2014). Spirituality at work and the leadership challenge. *Journal for the Study of Spirituality*, *4*(2), 136–148. https://doi.org/10.1179/2044024314Z.00000000028

Gill, R., Levine, N., & Pitt, D. C. (1998). Leadership and organizations for the new millennium. *Journal of Leadership Studies*, *5*(4), 46–59. https://doi.org/10.1177/107179199900500405

Gill, R., & Negrov, A. (2021). Love as an influence for good in leadership. *Theology of Leadership*, *4*(1), 28–53.

Goethals, G. R., & Sorenson, G. L. J. (Eds.). (2006). *The Quest for a General Theory of Leadership*. Edward Elgar. https://books.google.at/books?id=NEpkPgAACAAJ

Gonçalves, L., Ribeiro, P., & Rego, A. (2015, June). *How leaders' humility predicts team creativity: An empirical study*. Paper presented at the IMC 2015 International Management Conference, Bucharest, Romania.

Graham, J. W. (1991). Servant-leadership in organizations: Inspirational and moral. *The Leadership Quarterly*, *2*(2), 105–119. https://doi.org/10.1016/1048-9843(91)90025-W

Greenleaf, R. K. (1977). *Servant Leadership. A Journey into the Nature of Legitimate Power & Greatness*. Paulist Press.

Greenleaf, R. K., Beazley, H., Beggs, J., & Spears, L. C. (Eds.). (2003). *The Servant-Leader Within: A Transformative Path*. Paulist Press.

Guest, D. (2014). Employee engagement: A sceptical analysis. *Journal of Organizational Effectiveness: People and Performance*, *1*(2), 141–156.

Gutermann, D., Lehmann-Willenbrock, N., Boer, D., Born, M., & Voelpel, S. C. (2017). How leaders affect followers' work engagement and performance: Integrating leader–member exchange and crossover theory. *British Journal of Management*, *28*(2), 299–314. https://doi.org/10.1111/1467-8551.12214

Hodge, D. R. (2003). The intrinsic spirituality scale: A new six-item instrument for assessing the salience of spirituality as a motivational construct. *Journal of Social Service Research*, *30*(1), 41–61. https://doi.org/10.1300/J079v30n01_03

Horton, W. R. (1950). *God (9th printing)*. Association Press.

Hunsaker, W. D. (2014a). Relationship of confucian values to spiritual leadership in a South Korean context. *Asian Social Science*, *10*(12), 130–141. https://doi.org/10.5539/ass.v10n12p130

Hunsaker, W. D. (2014b). Spiritual leadership in South Korea: A multi-sample analysis of the brokerage sector. *Life Science Journal*, *11*(7), 84–88. http://www.lifesciencesite.com/lsj/life1107s/014_24409life1107s14_84_88.pdf.

Hunsaker, W. D. (2016). Spiritual leadership and organizational citizenship behavior: Relationship with Confucian values. *Journal of Management, Spirituality & Religion*, *13*(3), 206–225. https://doi.org/10.1080/14766086.2016.1159974

Hunt, C. (2020). Celebrating ten years of the *Journal for the Study of Spirituality*. *Journal for the Study of Spirituality*, *10*(1), 1–5. https://doi.org/10.1080/20440243.2020.1731789
Javanmard, H. (2012). The impact of spirituality on work performance. *Indian Journal of Science and Technology*, *5*(1), 1961–1966.
Krause, N. (2010). Religious involvement, humility, and self-rated health. *Social Indicators Research*, *98*(1), 23–39. https://doi.org/10.1007/s11205-009-9514-x
Krishnakumar, S., Houghton, J. D., Neck, C. P., & Ellison, C. N. (2015). The "good" and the "bad" of spiritual leadership. *Journal of Management, Spirituality & Religion*, *12*(1), 17–37. https://doi.org/10.1080/14766086.2014.886518
LaBouff, J. P., Rowatt, W. C., Johnson, M. K., Tsang, J.-A., & Willerton, G. M. (2012). Humble persons are more helpful than less humble persons: Evidence from three studies. *The Journal of Positive Psychology*, *7*(1), 16–29. https://doi.org/10.1080/17439760.2011.626787
Lee, A., Lyubovnikova, J., Tian, A. W., & Knight, C. (2020). Servant leadership: A meta-analytic examination of incremental contribution, moderation, and mediation. *Journal of Occupational and Organizational Psychology*, *93*(1), 1–44. https://doi.org/10.1111/joop.12265
Lindsay, D. R., Bond, D., & Smith, D. (2018). Shared leadership: Understand the power of leader-ful organizations. In D. R. Smith & J. E. Swain (Eds.), *West Point Leadership*. Rowan Technology Solutions.
Lips-Wiersma, M. (2003). Making conscious choices in doing research on workplace spirituality: Utilizing the "holistic development model" to articulate values, assumptions and dogmas of the knower. *Journal of Organizational Change Management*, *16*(4), 406–425. https://doi.org/10.1108/09534810310484163
Low, J. J. Q., & Ayoko, O. B. (2020). The emergence of spiritual leader and leadership in religion-based organizations. *Journal of Business Ethics*, *161*(3), 513–530. https://doi.org/10.1007/s10551-018-3954-7
Mäkikangas, A., Schaufeli, W., Leskinen, E., Kinnunen, U., Hyvönen, K., & Feldt, T. (2016). Long-term development of employee well-being: A latent transition approach. *Journal of Happiness Studies*, *17*(6), 2325–2345. https://doi.org/10.1007/s10902-015-9696-7
Mao, J., Chiu, C. (Chad), Owens, B. P., Brown, J. A., & Liao, J. (2019). Growing followers: Exploring the effects of leader humility on follower self-expansion, self-efficacy, and performance. *Journal of Management Studies*, *56*(2), 343–371. https://doi.org/10.1111/joms.12395
McCrimmon, M. (2010). Why servant leadership is a bad idea. *Management.Issues, 16 August*. https://www.management-issues.com/opinion/6015/why-servant-leadership-is-a-bad-idea/
McGonigal, K. (2015). *The Upside of Stress*. Vermilion (Random House Group).
McKee, M. C., Driscoll, C., Kelloway, E. K., & Kelley, E. (2011). Exploring linkages among transformational leadership, workplace spirituality and well-being in health care workers. *Journal of Management, Spirituality & Religion*, *8*(3), 233–255. https://doi.org/10.1080/14766086.2011.599147
Metin, U. B., Taris, T. W., Peeters, M. C. W., van Beek, I., & Van den Bosch, R. (2016). Authenticity at work – a job-demands resources perspective. *Journal of Managerial Psychology*, *31*(2), 483–499. https://doi.org/10.1108/JMP-03-2014-0087
Muneeba, A. (2019). Effect of spiritual intelligence on effective change management: A review of selected researches. *Electronic Research Journal of Social Sciences and Humanities*, *1*, 30–47.
Nakamura, J., & Csikszentmihalyi, M. (2014). The concept of flow. In M. Csikszentmihalyi (Ed.), *Flow and the Foundations of Positive Psychology* (pp. 239–263). Springer Netherlands. https://doi.org/10.1007/978-94-017-9088-8_16
Nathan, E., Mulyadi, R., Sen, S., van Dierendonck, D., & Liden, R. C. (2019). Servant leadership: A systematic review and call for future research. *The Leadership Quarterly*, *30*(1), 111–132. https://doi.org/10.1016/j.leaqua.2018.07.004

Nielsen, K., & Daniels, K. (2016). The relationship between transformational leadership and follower sickness absence: The role of presenteeism. *Work & Stress. An International Journal of Work, Health & Organisations*, *30*(2), 193–208. https://doi.org/10.1080/02678373.2016.1170736

Nielsen, R., & Marrone, J. A. (2018). Humility: Our current understanding of the construct and its role in organizations. *International Journal of Management Reviews*, *20*(4), 805–824. https://doi.org/10.1111/ijmr.12160

Northouse, P. G. (2013). *Leadership: Theory and Practice* (6th ed.). SAGE Publications.

Oh, J., & Wang, J. (2020). Spiritual leadership: Current status and agenda for future research and practice. *Journal of Management, Spirituality & Religion*, *17*(3), 223–248. https://doi.org/10.1080/14766086.2020.1728568

Ou, A. Y., Waldman, D. A., & Peterson, S. J. (2018). Do humble CEOs matter? An examination of CEO humility and firm outcomes. *Journal of Management*, *44*(3), 1147–1173. https://doi.org/10.1177/0149206315604187

Owens, B. P., & Hekman, D. R. (2016). How does leader humility influence team performance? Exploring the mechanisms of contagion and collective promotion focus. *Academy of Management Journal*, *59*(3), 1088–1111. https://doi.org/10.5465/amj.2013.0660

Owens, B. P., Johnson, M. D., & Mitchell, T. R. (2013). Expressed humility in organizations: Implications for performance, teams, and leadership. *Organization Science*, *24*(5), 1517–1538. https://doi.org/10.1287/orsc.1120.0795

Paloutzian, R. F., Bufford, R. K., & Wildman, A. J. (2012). Spiritual well-being scale: Mental and physical health relationships. In M. Cobb, C. Puchalski, & B. Rumbold (Eds.), *Oxford Textbook of Spirituality in Healthcare* (pp. 353–358). Oxford University Press.

Paloutzian, R. F., & Ellison, C. W. (1982). Loneliness, spiritual well-being and the quality of life. In L. A. Peplau & D. Perlman (Eds.), *Loneliness: A Sourcebook of Current Theory, Research and Therapy. Journal of Psychology and Theology* (Vol. 11, pp. 330–340).

Pavlovich, K. (2020). Introduction to the special issue on quantum management. *Journal of Management, Spirituality & Religion*, *17*(4), 299–300. https://doi.org/10.1080/14766086.2020.1789309

Petchsawang, P., & Duchon, D. (2009). Measuring workplace spirituality in an Asian context. *Human Resource Development International*, *12*(4), 459–468. https://doi.org/10.1080/13678860903135912

Qian, J., Li, X., Song, B., Wang, B., Wang, M., Chang, S., & Xiong, Y. (2018). Leaders' expressed humility and followers' feedback seeking: The mediating effects of perceived image cost and moderating effects of power distance orientation. *Frontiers in Psychology*, *9*, 563. https://doi.org/10.3389/fpsyg.2018.00563

Rego, A., Cunha, M. P. e., & Simpson, A. V. (2018). The perceived impact of leaders' humility on team effectiveness: An empirical study. *Journal of Business Ethics*, *148*(1), 205–218. https://doi.org/10.1007/s10551-015-3008-3

Rivkin, W., Diestel, S., & Schmidt, K.-H. (2018). Which daily experiences can foster well-being at work? A diary study on the interplay between flow experiences, affective commitment, and self-control demands. *Journal of Occupational Health Psychology*, *23*(1), 99–111. https://doi.org/10.1037/ocp0000039

Roberts, G. E. (2013). Leadership coping skills: Servant leader workplace spiritual intelligence. *Journal of Strategic Leadership*, *4*(2), 52–69.

Robinson, O. C. (2020). A dialectical approach to understanding the relationship between science and spirituality: The MODI model. *Journal for the Study of Spirituality*, *10*(1), 15–28. https://doi.org/10.1080/20440243.2020.1726045

Rousseau, D. (2019). Spirituality and philosophy. Chapter 2. In L. Zsolnai & B. Flanagan (Eds.), *Routledge International Handbook of Spirituality in Society and the Professions*. Routledge.

Rozuel, C., & McGhee, P. (2012). Investigating the convergence of corporate social responsibility and spirituality at work. *Australian Journal of Professional and Applied Ethics*, *14*(1), 47–62.

Rudolph, C. W., & Baltes, B. B. (2017). Age and health jointly moderate the influence of flexible work arrangements on work engagement: Evidence from two empirical studies. *Journal of Occupational Health Psychology*, *22*(1), 40–58. https://doi.org/10.1037/a0040147

Rupprecht, E. A., Waldrop, J. S., & Grawitch, M. J. (2013). Initial validation of a new measure of leadership. *Consulting Psychology Journal: Practice and Research*, *65*(2), 128–148.

Schaufeli, W. B., Salanova, M., González-romá, V., & Bakker, A. B. (2002). The measure of engagement and burnout: A two-sample confirmatory factor analytic approach. *Journal of Happiness Studies*, *3*(1), 71–92. https://doi.org/10.1023/A:1015630930326

Schaufeli, W. B., Salanova, M., González-Romá, V., & Bakker, A. B. (2011). *Utrecht Work Engagement Scale –17. PsycTESTS* [Data set]. American Psychological Association. https://doi.org/10.1037/t07164-000

Sen, S., Nathan, E., Butar Butar, I., Mulyadi, R., & Castles, S. (2019). SLBS-6: Validation of a short form of the servant leadership behavior scale. *Journal of Business Ethics*, *156*(4), 941–956. https://doi.org/10.1007/s10551-017-3594-3

Söylemez, A., & Mustafa, K. (2019). Studying spiritual intelligence as a predictor on meaningfulness and life satisfaction. *Spiritual Psychology and Counseling*, *4*(2), 109–122.

Steger, M. F. (2012). Spiritual leadership. In P. C. Hill & B. J. Dik (Eds.), *Psychology of Religion and Workplace Spirituality* (pp. 223–238). Information Age Publishing.

Supriyanto, A. S., Soetjipto, B. E., & Maharani, V. (2016). The effect of spiritual leadership on workplace spirituality, job satisfaction and ihsan behaviour: A study on nurses of Aisyiah Islamic hospital in Malang, Indonesia. *International Journal of Applied Business and Economic Research*, *14*(11), 7675–7688.

Swain, J. E. (2018). Effects of leader humility on the performance of virtual groups. *Journal of Leadership Studies*, *12*(1), 21–37. https://doi.org/10.1002/jls.21552

Swain, J. E., & Murray, E. D. (2020). Assessing leader humility. *Journal of College and Character*, *21*(3), 204–211. https://doi.org/10.1080/2194587X.2020.1781657

Tanskanen, J., Taipale, S., & Anttila, T. (2016). Revealing hidden curvilinear relations between work engagement and its predictors: Demonstrating the added value of generalized additive model (GAM). *Journal of Happiness Studies*, *17*(1), 367–387.

Tong, E. M. W., Tan, K. W. T., Chor, A. A. B., Koh, E. P. S., Lee, J. S. Y., & Tan, R. W. Y. (2016). Humility facilitates higher self-control. *Journal of Experimental Social Psychology*, *62*, 30–39. https://doi.org/10.1016/j.jesp.2015.09.008

Tsao, F. C., & Laszlo, C. (2019). *Quantum Leadership: New Consciousness in Business*. Stanford University Press.

Valeri, D. P. (2007). *The Origins of Servant Leadership* [Dissertation submitted for the degree of Doctor of Philosophy]. Greenleaf University.

van Dierendonck, D. (2011). Servant leadership: A review and synthesis. *Journal of Management*, *37*(4), 1228–1261. https://doi.org/10.1177/0149206310380462

Vu, M. C. (2018). *Spiritual leadership: A Buddhist approach* [Thesis submitted for the degree of PhD, Durham University]. Durham theses, Durham University. Available at Durham E-Theses Online: http://etheses.dur.ac.uk/12773/

Vu, M. C., & Gill, R. (2019a). Fusion leadership: A transcultural interpretation and application. *International Journal of Cross Cultural Management*, *19*(2), 140–159. https://doi.org/10.1177/1470595819847229

Vu, M. C., & Gill, R. (2019b). "Letting go of the raft" – The art of spiritual leadership in contemporary organizations from a Buddhist perspective using skilful means. *Leadership, 15*(3), 360–380. https://doi.org/10.1177/1742715018761931

Wang, L., Owens, B. P., Li, J. J., & Shi, L. (2018). Exploring the affective impact, boundary conditions, and antecedents of leader humility. *Journal of Applied Psychology, 103*(9), 1019–1038. https://doi.org/10.1037/apl0000314

Wang, Y., Liu, J., & Zhu, Y. (2018). Humble leadership, psychological safety, knowledge sharing, and follower creativity: A cross-level investigation. *Frontiers in Psychology, 9*, 1727. https://doi.org/10.3389/fpsyg.2018.01727

Weber, M. (1964). *The Theory of Social and Economic Organization*. The Free Press.

Weick, K. E. (1995). *Sensemaking in Organizations* (Vol. 3). SAGE Publications.

Yang, M., & Fry, L. W. (2018). The role of spiritual leadership in reducing healthcare worker burnout. *Journal of Management, Spirituality & Religion, 15*(4), 305–324. https://doi.org/10.1080/14766086.2018.1482562

Yang, R., Ming, Y., Ma, J., & Huo, R. (2017). How do servant leaders promote engagement? A bottom-up perspective of job crafting. *Social Behavior and Personality: An International Journal, 45*(11), 1815–1827. https://doi.org/10.2224/sbp.6704

Zohar, D., & Marshal, I. N. (2001). *Spiritual Intelligence: The Ultimate Intelligence*. Bloomsbury Publishing.

Zohar, D., & Marshall, I. N. (2004). *Spiritual Capital: Wealth We Can Live by*. Berrett-Koehler.

Laszlo Zsolnai

4 Ethics and Spirituality

The paper discusses the relationship between ethics and spirituality in business and management context. It shows that business ethics lacks a deeper existential-spiritual foundation which causes inadequate and ineffective functioning of ethics in business and management. The paper argues for spiritual-based business ethics and presents some research tracks, namely Integral Ecology, Indian Ethos in Management, and Buddhist Economics which create meaningful connections between ethics and spirituality. Finally, the paper discusses the challenges of the Anthropocene era for ethics and spirituality in business and management and the corresponding tasks for research and action.

Ethics Is Devoid of Spirituality

Mainstream paradigms of ethics including business ethics are devoid of any reference to spirituality or religion. They employ a materialistic and individualistic conception of human nature in which humans are materialistic beings having only materialistic desires and motivations. Contemporary "laic" ethics suggests that ethical action is a cognitive enterprise. Today's dominant ethical theories provide abstract models to be applied or followed by moral agents. But the main problem of ethical behavior is not ethical knowledge but ethical motivation as recent findings of moral psychology show.

Stanford psychologist Albert Bandura (2016) discovered a number of psychosocial mechanisms by which considerate moral agents can enter in harmful and socially injurious conduct. These moral disengagement mechanisms include moral justification, euphemistic labeling, advantageous comparison, displacement of responsibility, diffusion of responsibility, disregarding or distorting the consequences, dehumanization, and attribution of blame.

Spiritually-based or spiritually-inspired ethics makes people less likely to employ moral disengagement mechanisms (Baron et al., 2015) and provides them with greater opportunities for effective moral functioning. Empirical evidence suggests that spiritual experiences help the persons to transcend their narrow self-conceptions and enable them to exercise genuine empathy with others and to take an all-encompassing perspective.

Spiritual experiences involve authentic experimental identification with people, animals, plants and various other aspects of nature and the cosmos. (Grof, 1998) Despite the diversity of spiritual experience, the main ethical message is always the same: love and compassion, deep reverence for life, and empathy with all sentient

https://doi.org/10.1515/9783110711349-004

beings. Spiritual experiences allow people to "develop a new system of values that is not based on conventional norms, precepts, commandments, and fear of punishment" but "understanding of the universal order". People realize that they are an integral part of creation and that by hurting others they would be hurting themselves. (Grof, 1998, S. 129)

The Ethics Management Paradox

Reducing ethics to a functional and instrumental management tool may crowd out genuine moral feelings and moral commitment that can result in less ethical functioning. We must be aware of the paradox of ethics management when substituting ethics for technocratic management devices.

The core idea of the Ethics Management Paradox can be stated as follows. (Bouckaert, 2006; Bouckaert & Zsolnai, 2021) By creating new regulations to temper opportunistic behavior in and among organizations, we often reinforce the underlying roots of opportunism. We introduce economic incentives like benefits, such as premiums or tax relief for those who respect the new regulations, but by doing this, we substitute moral feelings for economic calculations. Hence, the paradox appears: the more ethics management, the less ethics in management. Preaching moral concepts such as trust, responsibility or democracy on the basis of calculative self-interest or as conditions of systemic functionality is ambiguous. It opens the door for suspicion and distrust because calculations and systemic conditions can easily be manipulated. When the fox preaches, guard your geese.

It is fascinating to see how trust, value-driven leadership and democratic stakeholding have become part of Western management theory. But we must be aware of its paradoxical characteristics. The more economic democracy can be sustained by a rational and economic discourse, the more it risks crowding out the moral commitment, which is a necessary condition for sustaining genuine entrepreneurship and stakeholding. Thus we must put forward not only the question of how to make business ethics operational, but also the question of how to make it genuinely ethical.

The ethics management paradox discloses the gap between expectations that ethics management improves the ethicality of business and the reality that this is not always the case. Remember the cases of Enron, Webcom, Parmalat, Ahold, Lernout and Hauspie. In 2008 a second bubble busted out and brought us the banking crisis followed by an economic recession. The surprising point is that before the crisis a lot of the involved companies and banks had invested in programs of corporate social responsibility and business ethics. But these efforts failed because ethics management was reduced to a business management tool.

The Ethics Management Paradox implies a search for spirituality as a way to transcend instrumental rationality that creates the paradox. Spirituality – as an inner experience of deep interconnectedness with all living beings – opens a space of distance from the pressures of the market and the routines of business as usual. This distance seems to be a necessary condition for developing innovative ethical ideas and practices. It may restore intrinsic motivation and provides a long time horizon. Unfortunately, spirituality is not yet a mainstream concept in the business world. In business the instrumental and utilitarian rationality is still the dominant perspective, whereas spirituality is anchored in a deeper, non-instrumental and non-utilitarian experience of life. Business can be renewed and transformed into a progressive social institution if it enriches itself by taking spirituality seriously at the core of its activities. (Bouckaert & Zsolnai, 2011)

Ethical codes and professional ethics formulate rights and duties for all relevant stakeholders to avoid a clash of interests. But there is a zone of wicked problems or what Schumacher calls divergent problems that remain unsolvable and difficult to overcome (Schumacher, 2004). By divergent problems Schumacher refers to problems which are linked with antagonistic and unconciliatory value premises. Ethical codes which mostly protect the interests and power of the regulating authorities, do not solve this kind of problems. At best, they help us to keep value conflicts under control. We need other ways to overcome deeply rooted conflicts of values.

Spirituality as a discipline has the potential to disclose meaning and purpose in life that overcomes the drive for self-interest, polarization and conflicts of values. We can consider spirituality as intuitive and non-rational thinking that opens our mind to the co-creation of meaning in life. Its methods include empathy, dialogical thinking, story-telling, symbolic visualizations, meditation, self-reflection, prayer etc. Spirituality helps to go beyond the blocked problems and discloses new perspectives that enable us to transcend them and to find new ways of being and acting.

The interlinked ecological, social and economic crisis clearly show the inadequacy of the materialistic management paradigm. Materialistic management is based on the belief that the primary motivation of doing business is money-making and success should be measured by the generated profit only. (Zsolnai, 2015) A post-materialistic management paradigm is emerging and characterized by frugality, deep ecology, trust, reciprocity, responsibility for future generations, and authenticity. Within this framework profit and growth are no longer ultimate aims but elements of a wider set of values. In a similar way cost-benefit calculations are no longer the essence of management but are part of a broader concept of wisdom in leadership.

Research Tracks Reconnecting Ethics and Spirituality

In the last decades we could see the emergence of initiatives which represent promising attempts to reconnect ethics with spirituality. The most important of them are

Integral Ecology, Indian Ethos in Management, and Buddhist Economics which have a number of implications for business and management.

Integral Ecology, proposed by the Pope's encyclical "Laudato si'", integrates the concerns for people and the planet. (Pope Francis, 2015). An integral and transdisciplinary understanding of the world links up science to human values and sees the world as a systemically connected ecology, economy, equity and justice. Integral ecology shows a path to sustainable development through frugal consumption and the acknowledgement of the intrinsic value of nature.

In the encyclical the Pope underlines the human origins of the ecological crisis and proposes fundamental changes in the organization of our economic and social life. Among the important suggestions by the Pope are frugality in consumption and recognition of the intrinsic value of nature. Both these propositions pose serious challenges to economics and business.

In the encyclical we see a condemnation of the current "use and throw away" culture which "generates so much waste, because of the disordered desire to consume more than what is really necessary". (Pope Francis, 2015 para 123) It calls for "modifying consumption, developing an economy of waste disposal and recycling, protecting certain species and planning a diversified agriculture and the rotation of crops". (Pope Francis, 2015 para 180)

Pope Francis (2015 para 203) fears that "we have too many means and only a few insubstantial ends". He encourages to develop "more sober lifestyles, while reducing their energy consumption and improving its efficiency". (Pope Francis, 2015 para 193) He believes that "a decrease in the pace of production and consumption can at times give rise to another form of progress and development". (Pope Francis, 2015 para 191)

Christian spirituality underlined in the encyclical proposes "an alternative understanding of the quality of life, and encourages a prophetic and contemplative lifestyle, one capable of deep enjoyment free of the obsession with consumption. . . . We need to take up an ancient lesson, found in different religious traditions and also in the Bible. It is the conviction that 'less is more'." It is a return to simplicity "which allows us to stop and appreciate the small things, to be grateful for the opportunities which life affords us, to be spiritually detached from what we possess, and not to succumb to sadness for what we lack". (Pope Francis, 2015 para 222) "Happiness means knowing how to limit some needs" (Pope Francis, 2015 para 223)

Pope Francis (2015 para 140) urges us to accept the *intrinsic value* of *nature* and to express appreciation for it. Natural beings and ecosystems "have an intrinsic value independent of their usefulness. Each organism, as a creature of God, is good and admirable in itself; the same is true of the harmonious ensemble of organisms existing in a defined space and functioning as a system".

The encyclical emphasizes that "environmental protection cannot be assured solely on the basis of financial calculations of costs and benefits. The environment is one of those goods that cannot be adequately safeguarded or promoted by market forces". (Pope Francis, 2015 para 190)

The Integral Ecology vision of Pope Francis has already inspired a lot of discussion, research initiatives and practical actions. (Jakobsen & Zsolnai, 2017; *LSRI*, 2020; *Economy of Francesco*, 2020)

Indian Ethos in Management is a movement initiated by S. K. Chakraborty, the Founder of Management Centre for Human Values at the Indian Institute of Management, Calcutta.

The crash between the globalized, market directed business forces and Indian spiritual values and ethics based on the Vedanta was the "Leitmotif" of Chakraborty for his decades long endeavor with inspired zeal to establish and promote an Indian Model of Management built on the indigenous knowledge of India. His seminal contribution has been in anchoring a solid spiritual foundation to human values and leadership using insights from Indian ethos and its modern proponents like Rabindranath Tagore, Swami Vivekananda, Mahatma Gandhi, and Sri Aurobindo. (Chakraborty, 1997, 2014; Chakraborty & Chakraborty, 2008; Mukherjee & Zsolnai, 2021)

Indian Ethos in Management aims to bring India's indigenous concepts into the professional Indian management. While doing so, Chakraborty published dozens of books on values, ethics and leadership; He founded three journals and two institutions, and inspired many business students in India and abroad, and thousands of corporate executives and professionals who have gone through his management development programs. Of special mention is the Journal of Human Values, of which Chakraborty was the Founder Editor-in-Chief, published biannually by Sage Publications.

Chakraborty's effort to root business ethics in the traditions of Indian spirituality, particularly in the Vedantic heritage, is challenging for Western ethicists who usually think in terms of theories of rights, social contract, and utility maximization. Introducing spirituality in the field of business and managerial ethics creates a shift from external rule-directed behavior toward an inner-directed, existential search for meaning. What is missing in conventional business and managerial ethics is a deep, intersubjective intuition of the Presence of Life that guides thoughts and actions. Chakraborty calls such an ethic based on re-connection with the inner source of Life, consciousness ethics, which he rightly distinguishes from compliance ethics and cognitive ethics.

This new focus has not only led to broader concepts of purpose and success than traditionally associated with management. It has also given rise to deeper existential questions as to the identity and responsibility of corporations and their leaders, questions very similar in nature to those faced by persons with a spiritual quest. (Pruzan, 2009; Mukherjee, 2020)

Chakraborty emphasized that the mainstream materialistic value-orientation of today's business can hardly be reconciled with any genuine spirituality. The dominant understanding of economic rationality, namely individualistic, self-interest maximization should be replaced with a broader notion of reason. Nobel Prize winning economist Amartya Sen (2004) suggested that rationality requires subjecting one's choice of action, including objectives, values, and priorities to reasoned scrutiny. In this way spiritually inspired choices may not be incompatible with the demands of human reason. Business actors can rationally pursue their objectives based on spiritual values and priorities.

Indian Ethos in Management can serve as inspiration for academics, business leaders and management professionals to rethink their roles and responsibilities in transforming business into a more human and ecological enterprise. This has contemporary relevance in a world ridden with an alarming crisis caused by global spread and attack of Covid-19 virus. The importance of upholding and pursuit of Indian Ethos in the global combat against this killer virus suggest alternative ways of thinking and living for a safe, sane and sustainable future for the self, the organization, the community, society, nations and the planet at large.

Buddhist Economics has been developed to create an alternative worldview that challenges the main underlying assumptions of Western economics. (Zsolnai, 2011; Tideman, 2016; Magnuson, 2016; Brown, 2017)

In his best-selling book, "Small is beautiful" E. F. Schumacher (1973) emphasized that the task and aims of economizing are to provide peace and permanence. Buddhist economics is dedicated to this dual task. The main goal of a Buddhist life is liberation from all suffering. Nirvana, which can be approached by want negation and the purification of the human character, is the final state.

Values central to Buddhist economics are simplicity and non-violence. From a Buddhist point of view the optimal pattern of consumption is to reach the highest level of human satisfaction by means of the lowest rate of material consumption. This allows people to live with less pressure and strain. People living simple lifestyles are less prone to aggressive behavior than those heavily dependent on scarce natural resources.

While modern Western economics promotes doing business based on individual, self-interested, profit-maximizing ways, Buddhist economics suggests an alternative strategy. The underlying principle of Buddhist economics is to minimize suffering of all sentient beings, including non-human beings. From a Buddhist viewpoint a project is worthy of being undertaken if it can reduce the suffering of all those who are affected. Any change in economic-activity systems that reduces suffering is to be welcomed.

Modern Western economics cultivates desires. People are encouraged to develop new desires for things to acquire and for activities to do. The profit motive of companies requires creating more demand. Buddhist economics suggests that we do not multiply but simplify our desires. Once the minimum standards of material comfort, which include enough food, clothing, shelter, and medicine, have been achieved it is wise to try to reduce one's desires. Wanting less could bring substantial benefits for the person, for the community, and for nature. Buddhist economics recommends moderate consumption and is directly aimed at changing one's preferences through meditation, reflection, analysis, autosuggestion and the like.

Modern Western economics aims to introduce market solutions wherever social problems need to be solved. This leads to the process of marketization by which spheres of society became subordinated to the market mechanism. Non-violence ("ahimsa") is the main guiding principle of Buddhism for solving social problems and it is a basic requirement that an act does not cause harm to the doer or the receivers. Non-violence prevents doing actions that directly cause suffering to oneself or others and urges that participative solutions are found.

In modern Western economics the value of an entity (be it a human being, other sentient being, object or anything else) is determined by its marginal contribution to the production output. A project is considered worthy of undertaking if and only if its discounted cash flow is positive. To get the best from the partners requires taking genuine care of their existence. Caring organizations are rewarded for the higher costs of their socially responsible behavior by their ability to form commitments among owners, managers and employees and to establish relationships of trust with customers and subcontractors. (Frank, 2004)

Western economic man is allowed to consider the interest of others only if it serves his or her own interest. The self-interested, opportunistic behavior often fails. Generosity, suggested by Buddhism, would work in business and social life because people are, in fact, "homo reciprocans" – we tend to reciprocate what we get and often give back more in value than we receive. (Bowles & Gintis, 2011)

Buddhist economics does not aim to build an economic system of its own. Rather, it represents a strategy which can be applied to any economic setting at any time. It helps to create livelihood solutions that reduce the suffering of all sentient beings through want negation, non-violence, caring and generosity. (Zsolnai, 2008)

Challenges for the Future

The new reality of the Anthropocene (Steffen et al., 2011, 2018) generates big challenges for ethics, business and management. Literally, the continuation of the existence of humanity and other life forms is at stake (McKibben, 2020).

(i) How can a life-affirmative ethics be developed and translated into business and management practices?

(ii) How can spiritually-rooted business and economic models be created, implemented and scaled up to preserve nature and to serve human well-being?

(iii) How can ethics and spirituality contribute to the resilience and well-being of human communities in the age of ecological degradation and breakdown?

To solve these and other related problems genuine commitment and extraordinary creativity is needed from scholars and practitioners alike. We need unique combination of good heart and skillful mind to cope with the enormous ecological and social calamities to come.

References

Bandura, A. (2016). *Moral Disengagement: How People do Harm and Live with Themselves*. Worth Publishers, Macmillan Learning.

Baron, R. A., Zhao, H., & Miao, Q. (2015). Personal motives, moral disengagement, and unethical decisions by entrepreneurs: Cognitive mechanisms on the "slippery slope". *Journal of Business Ethics*, *128*(1), 107–118. https://doi.org/10.1007/s10551-014-2078-y

Bouckaert, L. (2006). The ethics management paradox. In L. Zsolnai (Ed.), *Interdisciplinary Yearbook of Business Ethics* (Bd. 1, S. 191–194). Peter Lang Academic Publishers. https://books.google.at/books?id=-siHU8HeRCYC

Bouckaert, L., & Zsolnai, L. (Eds.). (2011). *The Palgrave Handbook of Spirituality and Business* (Bd. 17). Palgrave Macmillan. http://www.tandfonline.com/doi/abs/10.1080/08963568.2012.711964

Bouckaert, L., & Zsolnai, L. (2021). The ethics management paradox and spiritual-driven businesses. *Journal of Management, Spirituality and Religion (forthcoming)*.

Bowles, S., & Gintis, H. (2011). *A Cooperative Species: Human Reciprocity and Its Evolution*. Princeton University Press. https://doi.org/10.1515/9781400838837

Brown, C. (2017). *Buddhist Economics: An Enlightened Approach to the Dismal Science*. Bloomsbury Press. https://books.google.at/books?id=WHC7DAAAQBAJ

Chakraborty, S. K. (1997). *Ethics in Management: Vedantic Perspectives*. Oxford University Press.

Chakraborty, S. K. (2014). *Human Values and Ethics*. Himalaya Publishing House.

Chakraborty, S. K., & Chakraborty, D. (2008). *Spirituality in Management: Means or End?* Oxford University Press.

Economy of Francesco. (2020). https://francescoeconomy.org/

Frank, R. H. (2004). *What Price the Moral High Ground?: Ethical Dilemmas in Competitive Environments*. Princeton University Press.

Grof, S. (1998). *The Cosmic Game: Explorations of the Frontiers of Human Consciousness*. State University of New York Press. https://books.google.at/books?id=PANEMQvjEMAC

Jakobsen, O., & Zsolnai, L. (Eds.). (2017). *Integral Ecology and Sustainable Business*. Emerald. https://books.google.at/books?id=84A0DwAAQBAJ

LSRI. (2020). http://www.campion.ox.ac.uk/?q=lsri

Magnuson, J. (2016). *From Greed to Wellbeing: A Buddhist Approach to Resolving Our Economic and Financial Crises*. Policy Press. https://books.google.at/books?id=KwVpDwAAQBAJ

McKibben, B. (2020). 130 Degrees" New York Review of Books. August 20, 2020. *New York Review of Books*.

Mukherjee, S. (2020). *Looking East. Indian Wisdom for Modern Management*. Peter Lang Publishers.

Mukherjee, S., & Zsolnai, L. (Eds.). (2021). *Indian Spirituality and Management. The Legacy of S. K. Chakraborty*. Springer.

Pope Francis. (2015). *Praised Be: On the Care of Our Common Home*.

Pruzan, P. (2009). *Rational, Ethical and Spiritual Perspectives on Leadership: Selected Writings.* Peter Lang Publishers. https://books.google.at/books?id=kDXLWR1QsgUC

Schumacher, E. F. (1973). *Small Is Beautiful: Economics as if People Mattered.* Abacus.

Schumacher, E. F. (2004). *A Guide for the Perplexed.* Harper Perennial.

Sen, A. (2004). *Rationality and Freedom.* Harvard University Press. https://books.google.at/books?id=DaOY4DQ-MKAC

Steffen, W., Persson, Å., Deutsch, L., Zalasiewicz, J., Williams, M., Richardson, K., Crumley, C., Crutzen, P., Folke, C., Gordon, L., Molina, M., Ramanathan, V., Rockström, J., Scheffer, M., Schellnhuber, H. J., & Svedin, U. (2011). The anthropocene: From global change to planetary stewardship. *AMBIO*, *40*(7), 739–761. https://doi.org/10.1007/s13280-011-0185-x

Steffen, W., Rockström, J., Richardson, K., Lenton, T. M., Folke, C., Liverman, D., Summerhayes, C. P., Barnosky, A. D., Cornell, S. E., Crucifix, M., Donges, J. F., Fetzer, I., Lade, S. J., Scheffer, M., Winkelmann, R., & Schellnhuber, H. J. (2018). Trajectories of the earth system in the anthropocene. *Proceedings of the National Academy of Sciences*, *115*(33), 8252–8259. https://doi.org/10.1073/pnas.1810141115

Tideman, S. (2016). *Business as an Instrument for Societal Change: In Conversation with the Dalai Lama*. Greenleaf Publishing.

Zsolnai, L. (2008). Buddhist economic strategy. In L. Bouckaert, H. Opdebeeck, & L. Zsolnai (Eds.), *Frugality: Rebalancing Material and Spiritual Values in Economic Life* (S. 279–303). Peter Lang. https://books.google.at/books?id=leERnTUc8VcC

Zsolnai, L. (2011). *Ethical Principles and Economic Transformation – A Buddhist Approach.* Springer. https://books.google.at/books?id=78rtvM2i1UoC

Zsolnai, L. (2015). Post-materialistic business: Spiritual value-orientation in renewing management. Palgrave Macmillan.

Kathryn Pavlovich

5 Spirituality and Religion: Influencing the Strategic Management Field of Research

Introduction

> On August 19, 2019, the Business Roundtable (BRT) – a group of prominent CEOs of companies, including JPMorgan Chase, Amazon, Apple, and Walmart, among others – released a statement declaring that the purpose of the corporation no longer gives shareholders special consideration, but rather that corporations should serve the interests of all of their stakeholders.
>
> (Harrison et al., 2020, p. 1223)

This declaration signals an important shift occurring in the strategic management field. This announcement by the BRT acknowledges a change in awareness from understanding the purpose of an organisation as solely concerned with increasing shareholder wealth to a purpose where organisations are at the forefront of creating a more economically, socially, environmentally and spiritually responsible planet. As Frederick stated back in 1998, it is unfortunate that we continue to see the corporation as the "central star in the solar system" (p.42), around which society revolves. Rather, we should see organisations as an integral part of society.

The focus of this chapter is to review the influence of spirituality and religion on the strategic management field. Before turning to this review, and acknowledging that while the terms spirituality and religion are often used interchangeably, each has its own distinctive characteristics. Spirituality encompasses an individual transcendent search for meaning and purpose that stems from inner-based contemplative practices (Ashmos & Duchon, 2000; Driver, 2005); whereas religion is seen as an organized institutional belief system with some degree of faith in a transcendent hereafter (Ashmos & Duchon, 2000; Gümüsay, 2019). The chapter examines this domain intersection in three sections. The first examines the impact of spirituality and religion on the traditional strategic management process; the second section examines the person as an agent of emergent strategic change; and the third section examines a more contemporary and dynamic perspective of strategic management that now extends the firm's role and purpose as being an integral part of society.

Strategic Management As a Process

Strategic management is the process of guiding an organisation into a desired and created future, realised through two central elements: the creation of a strategy that best aligns the organisation's activities with the external environment, and the

https://doi.org/10.1515/9783110711349-005

implementation of this strategy through resource allocations (Barney, 1991; Newbert, 2007). Both of these elements are moderated by ongoing planning, monitoring, analysis and assessment of all activities to evaluate whether the organisation is on target to meet its strategic vision and alignment with the dynamic and changing external environment. Strategic management includes sub-fields of diversification, mergers and acquisitions, strategic alliances, competitive dynamics and interfirm rivalry.

This review regarding the impact of spirituality and religion on strategic management was undertaken through a google search using the terms Strategic Management, Strategy, Spirituality, Religion, and also a manual search using the same keywords through leading journals that included the *Strategic Management Journal, Academy of Management Review, Academy of Management Journal, Academy of Management Perspectives, Journal of Management Studies,* and relevant journals that include: *Journal of Business Ethics, Business and Society, Business Strategy and the Environment, and Journal of Management Spirituality and Religion.*

Surprisingly, there were very few studies that directly link spirituality and religion with the strategic management process. Most of the references to the above key words referred to functional level management such as 'coping as a strategy'; 'spirituality as a strategy' or "strategies for religious entities'. The most prominent research article that emerged from this search was Barron and Chou's (2017) work whereby they explore corporate level strategy through a spiritual lens. They focus on the four stages of the strategic management process: the development of an organisation's vision and mission that should focus, they argue, on perpetuity from a perspective of transcendence – enabling the organisation to look into the future beyond physical limitations and barriers. The second stage, that of assessing environmental conditions, can be attained through relying on an inexhaustible source of will; the third stage involves finding alternative strategic scenarios and they argue, these can be sourced through the supreme power. Finally, implementation of the strategy can be achieved through focus on a sense of oneness within humanity. Barron and Chou (2017) clearly make a connection between the four stages of strategic decision making and being guided by a supreme force. However, the practical application of this conceptual framework is not clear and it remains a descriptive framework, rather than a theoretical contribution that extends the field.

In terms of the leading journals, the *Strategic Management Journal* has acknowledged the importance of religion in two articles. The first was an investigation by Miller back in 2002 who argued that religious organisations should engage with competitive strategies, particularly from a perspective of resource complexity and institutional theory. This prompted a wider debate on the appropriability of applying economic theory that underlies strategic management concepts – such as value creation and competitive markets – to religious organisations. Indeed, Gomez and Moore (2006) argued that the use of strategic management concepts is a paradox for religious organisations. For example, attendees of certain churches are unlikely to 'switch' religions as they would cell phone or toothpaste brands. They argue that attendees of churches are therefore not customers in the economic sense and hence the issue of interfirm rivalry is undermined. Gomez and Moore also question how value can be explained in terms of product/market services when it is one's religious beliefs that is at stake. These critiques aside, Miller's (2002, 2006) work is the first to conceptually link religious organisations within a strategic management framework and prompted discussion around these dichotomies.

More recently, Damaraju and Makhija (2018) examined CEO selection based upon social proximity, using a database of India's various castes/religions. This research recognises that the values and beliefs of the CEO impacts on corporate strategy and organisational direction, and may well spark a future conversation. In 2019, the *Academy of Management Perspectives* published a symposium on "With or Without Spirit" but these research articles focus on leadership and entrepreneurship. They do not specifically address corporate level strategy.

There have been references to spirituality as a source of sustained competitive advantage in the Resource-Based View (RBV) framework, but again, despite describing the possibility, there has not been any in-depth analysis of how religion and spirituality as a source of inimitability and nonsubstitutablity could be developed and sustained (Arbaugh, 2001, 2006; Barron & Chou, 2017; Miller, 2002). Arbaugh (2001) maintains that since resources are "bundled" from an individual level up to the organisation level, the inimtiablity and tacitness of religious values can play a key part in the formation of an organisation's dynamic capabilities. Belief systems that stem from spirituality could very well differentiate the strategic positioning of one organisation from another, with the assumption that the integration and interconnectedness that stems from ethical and socially responsible behaviour becomes embedded into the cultural values of the organisation (Driscoll et al., 2019).

Some discussion exists on the role of religion on firm governance and performance data. Using a large sample of firms domiciled across 12 European countries, Alsaadi (2021) found that religious-based index membership was often used as an impression management tool to attract further investment. In another study using panel data of 806 U.S. firms, Xu and Ma (Xu & Ma, 2021) found that in their ratings of corporate social responsibility (CSR) performance, firms with top managers who had attended religiously associated schools outperformed firms with no such managers. The positive relationship between religious school attendance (RSA) and CSR performance was stronger among firms with lower levels of community religiosity. These studies confirm that trust relationships are developed as a consequence of shared religious experiences, acting as a form of social capital development (Marks & Mudely, 2021). However, these studies above have not extrapolated these findings to how these religious-based relationships affect corporate level strategy.

Thus, there has been very little influence of spirituality and religion on the mainstream strategic management field. Pavlovich and Markman (2021) contend that the absence of spirituality and religion in mainstream journals may possibly be a reluctance by researchers to openly acknowledge a belief in something beyond the self, as it challenges our fundamental beliefs regarding the rationality of science. Acknowledging our spirituality would ask us to revisit our ontological assumptions regarding the nature of our research and our role in the world. This may indeed be why few have attempted to integrate corporate level strategy with the faith-based mystical elements of spirituality and religion.

Strategic Management As Agency – Emergent Process

If we move from a functional view of strategic management and examine the more emergent aspects of strategic management as agency, there have been a small number of contributions that explore the creation of strategic direction from a) a leadership perspective and b) from the impact of personal spirituality. Both of these approaches view strategy as an emergent process rather than the above more planned approach.

From a leadership viewpoint, the link with corporate level strategy has been noted, but this research does not clearly pull together the strategy process and spirituality. In a review on the literature on spiritual leadership, Oh and Wang (2020) found that motivating people to pursue the organisation's vision and mission was one of the three central contributions to the leadership field. Interestingly, they found that most of the research examined the impact on followers and their organisational commitment, not the impact of the leader's spirituality itself. In a second study, Phipps (2012) proposed a framework describing how the personal spiritual beliefs of a top level leader can influence strategic decision making. She provided a multi-level schema examining how these leaders filter and frame information for strategic decision making through these meta-beliefs. However, this framework is quite generic and difficult to see how it has a direct impact on strategic decisions. In the research on CEO selection noted earlier, Damaraju and Makhija (2018) found that caste/religion played an important role in CEO selection, i.e., as a form of information or "positive discrimination." While this is not directly related to strategic management, the impact of leader choice clearly has a direct impact on corporate level strategy. Thus, the question of how spirituality and religious beliefs influence this process has been rarely examined, yet has the potential to play a significant role in the future aspirations of the organisation.

Strategic Management As Purpose – Linking Organisations and Society

Despite the absence of studies integrating strategic management with spirituality and religion, the field is in the process of redefining itself away from the primacy of shareholder wealth to one that recognises the significant role that business can play in redefining and recreating society. Thus, the field is realigning from the corporate strategy question of "how might organisations position themselves in the future to increase shareholder wealth?" towards "how might organisations lead the creation of an ethical and sustainable societal future?" Of course, the planning processes of strategic management remain important, as does looking after shareholder investments, but there is a shift in emphasis in terms of the weaving together of the organisation-society interface – acknowledging that organisations are not the central star in the solar system (Frederick, 1998). In the following sections, I explain this evolution in terms of connectedness (a stakeholder view) and interconnectedness (a spiritual view).

A Stakeholder View

This exciting shift now places a higher order purpose at the core of the organisation's activities. From a spiritual perspective, this higher order purpose is a *directional envisioned future that is moral and transcendent.* It is a higher order construct that is future-oriented, distinguishing it from the low-level short term goals of daily life (Costin & Vignoles, 2020). It is also directional in that it acts like a compass steering decision making and actions, somewhat like being guided by the north star when the path ahead is hazy (Kaipa, 2012). As a higher order process, purpose acts as a moral guide for developing transcendent actions with the rightness or wrongness of conduct ultimately judged on the outcomes and consequences of those actions.

This evolution in awareness regarding the overarching purpose of organisations is readily witnessed in strategic management research that now intersects business and society through collective action groups that include – to name a few –the sharing economy, benefit corporations (B Corps), responsible management, grand challenges, etc. These new forms of institutions place the betterment of society at the core of the organisation's purpose with strong engagement with stakeholders that create networks of connectedness. For instance, Scherer and Voegtlin (2020) contend that many businesses are now active partners in multi-party collaborations with public and civil sectors, endeavouring to attend to growing concerns over the unsafe extension of planetary boundaries. Williams, Whiteman and Parker (2019) make a case for such collaborations as necessary to tackle the complexity and scale of these challenges. Placing networks of stakeholders at the core of strategic management's 'setting future direction' conversation then becomes important in enabling society to include economic, social, environmental and spiritual imperatives.

Despite this change in direction, it is important to note that not all are engaged in this shift. There are many who are still convinced by the primacy of shareholder wealth. Harrison et al. (2020) give examples of courts that have legally insisted that maximising shareholder wealth is the core function of organisation. They also note a second example of Delaware jurists who called for shareholder wealth maximisation to be enforced. Nevertheless, despite these objections, there is mounting evidence that including stakeholders into the strategic management process results in higher firm performance. For example, in a study of 26 goldmines over the period of 1993–2008, Henisz, Dorobantu & Nartey (2014) found that increasing stakeholder support enhanced the financial valuation of a firm. Chen and Kelly (2015) too found that benefit corporations (B-Corps) had a statistically significant revenue growth rate that outpaced the average revenue growth of the public companies that operate in the same 4-digit Standard Industrial Classification (SIC) code.

As these new institutional forms embrace collective interest at the core of their purpose, connectedness is now a leading influence in the strategic management field. For instance, in a study on corporate endorsement of the sustainable development goals, Williams et al. (2019) found that successful multi-partnership outcomes were most dependent on social bonds and dense sets of relations for bridging, bonding and connecting. I use these examples not to demonstrate the influence of spirituality and religion, but as markers that demonstrate a major shift in attitudes and understandings within strategic management.

Interconnectedness: Beyond Stakeholders

While the above research does not explicitly reference spirituality and religion, it illustrates an evolution from the centrality of the organisation, to the connectivity of stakeholders and ultimately, I argue, towards the interconnectedness of all things – a central element of spirituality. The above stakeholder approach to corporate level strategy opens the conversation on firm boundaries and the nature of value-creation. An important question related to connectedness and collective issues – which is where the current stakeholder conversation resides –relates to who is a stakeholder and who is not. Downing, Kang and Markman's (2019) research has demonstrated that organisations need to be aware of actions that not only include direct rivals, but also second- and third-degree indirect competitors. Beyond that, their research indicated, stakeholders have no direct influence. However, my point is that spirituality is about interconnectedness that extends beyond networks and boundaries. Thus, stakeholder engagement focuses on networks of connectedness – which is an instrumental part of strategic management's evolution – but I argue that the influence of spirituality and religion and its associated moral code will increasingly be about interconnectedness.

Liu and Robertson (2011) characterise interconnectedness as the highest end of the spirituality continuum in that it transcends boundaries and demonstrates a sense of interconnection with human beings, nature, all living things, and with a higher power. In the interconnected world, everyone and everything is a stakeholder as boundaries are entangled, permeable and become indeterminate webs of relationships (Pavlovich, 2020). This absence of boundaries highlights how religion and spirituality – as a sense of oneness – act as a macro-level organizing mechanism at a cosmological level– which highlights the imperative of system interdependence (Frederick, 1998). In acknowledging our interdependence, spirituality recognises the sacredness of life, ourselves, our relationships, the world around us, and our potential for societal transcendence.

There are moments when interconnectedness is starting to appear in strategic management research. Scherer and Voegtlin (2020) argue for responsible governance, arguing that the assumption that business is disconnected from society is untenable. They extend the debate on the purpose of the organisations questioning whose interests should be most taken into account – shareholders or stakeholders? Importantly, they extend the shareholder – stakeholder debate to include political governance that includes reflexive and participative actions that extend beyond the corporation boundaries. These purpose-driven participatory governance structures, while not influenced directly by spirituality, begin the conversation on the role and purpose of the organisation through interconnectedness. They illuminate how organisational values and social good is visible in the organisation's image, mission and vision underlying a higher order purpose.

Such a perspective is also promoted by Cunliffe (2011) who argues for an organisation studies that is embedded by a radical reflexive sense of Otherness. While she does not explicitly mention spirituality and religion, the notion of engaging within an intersubjective and interconnected space calls us to consider our self-Other relationships – where we see ourselves as embedded in an inherently relational world, where knowing, action and change are created between people by working together to create new ways of seeing, doing and knowing. These reflexive and participative modes of engagement also identified by Scherer and Voegtlin (2020) ask us to rethink our interconnectedness that goes beyond simply connecting. They acknowledge that we are entangled in a self-Other world where boundaries are fluid, mutually enforcing and dynamic.

Finally, in a study that acknowledges the power of religion, Martinez, Peattie and Vazquez-Brust (2019) suggest that a 'syncretic' theory may be helpful in attending to the complexity of sustainability and economic outcomes. They claim that syncretic approaches integrate multiple disciplines with their source ideas drawn from cultural and religious foundations. Thus, it has the ability to integrate humanity and nature, and morality and truth. Such an approach places finding constructive connections through values and belief systems at the basis of corporate level conversations and strategy development. This research draws on the importance of a moral code as the guiding source of future actions for the organisation.

While not comprehensive, these examples illustrate the evolution of the field where the nature of organisational relationships within an interconnected world become important in the creation and enactment of flourishing futures.

Conclusion

Despite spirituality and religion being generally overlooked by our scientific community, religion is overwhelmingly about interconnectedness – even more so than science that focuses primarily on understanding and explaining how parts work. Rather spirituality and religion focus on system effects of the whole through a metaphysical impulse that entangles all living things, with humans being just a part of this interdependent ecosystem.

In this chapter, I have argued that the strategic management field has evolved from a sole focus on the organisation's interests to one of connectedness, acknowledging that stakeholders play a key role in the organisation's activities. I suggested that future research trends are likely to examine the influence of spirituality and religion through the sphere of interconnectedness, acknowledging a deep awareness that all actions are entangled and impact on the whole system. While spirituality and religion have not explicitly influenced the field, there is increasing awareness that organisations are an integral and embedded part of the solar system – not the central star. Such relationships are spiritual, interdependent and entangled (Pavlovich, 2020). As the strategic management literature acknowledges these multi-level interdependent partnerships as imperative to addressing collective issues such as grand challenges, there is an awareness that organisations have a responsibility to act as catalysts for change. This means a return to a moral code that drives organisational purpose as stewards who uphold the flourishing of an interconnected planetary system.

References

Alsaadi, A. (2021). Can inclusion in religious index membership mitigate earnings management? *Journal of Business Ethics*, *169*(2), 333–354. https://doi.org/10.1007/s10551-019-04280-y

Arbaugh, J. B. (2001, August 7). *Reversing the spirituality lenses: Challenges and opportunities for developing a spiritual perspective on strategy*. Academy of Management Meeting, Washington, DC. http://www.leaderu.com/offices/ben_arbaugh/ben_arbaugh-reversing.html

Arbaugh, J. B. (2006). Dialogue on Miller's (2002) "Competitive strategy of religious organizations": An introduction. *Journal of Management, Spirituality & Religion*, *3*(3), 194–198. https://doi.org/10.1080/14766080609518624

Ashmos, D. P., & Duchon, D. (2000). Spirituality at work: A conceptualization and measure. *Journal of Management Inquiry*, *9*(2), 134–145. https://doi.org/10.1177/105649260092008

Barney, J. (1991). Firm resources and sustained competitive advantage. *Journal of Management*, *17*(1), 99–120. https://doi.org/10.1177/014920639101700108

Barron, K., & Chou, S. Y. (2017). Toward a spirituality mode of firm sustainability strategic planning processes. *Society and Business Review*, *12*(1), 46–62. https://doi.org/10.1108/SBR-01-2016-0008

Chen, X., & Kelly, T. F. (2015). B-corps – A growing form of social enterprise: Tracing their progress and assessing their performance. *Journal of Leadership & Organizational Studies*, *22*(1), 102–114. https://doi.org/10.1177/1548051814532529

Costin, V., & Vignoles, V. L. (2020). Meaning is about mattering: Evaluating coherence, purpose, and existential mattering as precursors of meaning in life judgments. *Journal of Personality and Social Psychology*, *118*(4), 864–884. https://doi.org/10.1037/pspp0000225

Cunliffe, A. L. (2011). Crafting qualitative research: Morgan and Smircich 30 years on. *Organizational Research Methods*, *14*(4), 647–673. https://doi.org/10.1177/1094428110373658

Damaraju, N. L., & Makhija, A. K. (2018). The role of social proximity in professional CEO appointments: Evidence from caste/religion-based hiring of CEOs in India. *Strategic Management Journal*, *39*(7), 2051–2074. https://doi.org/10.1002/smj.2787

Downing, S. T., Kang, J.-S., & Markman, G. D. (2019). What you don't see can hurt you: Awareness cues to profile indirect competitors. *Academy of Management Journal*, *62*(6), 1872–1900. https://doi.org/10.5465/amj.2018.0048

Driscoll, C., McIsaac, E. M., & Wiebe, E. (2019). The material nature of spirituality in the small business workplace: From transcendent ethical values to immanent ethical actions. *Journal of Management, Spirituality & Religion*, *16*(2), 155–177. https://doi.org/10.1080/14766086.2019.1570474

Driver, M. (2005). From empty speech to full speech? Reconceptualizing spirituality in organizations based on a psychoanalytically-grounded understanding of the self. *Human Relations*, *58*(9), 1091–1110. https://doi.org/10.1177/0018726705059038

Frederick, W. C. (1998). Moving to CSR: What to pack for the trip. *Business & Society*, *37*(1), 40–59. https://doi.org/10.1177/000765039803700103

Gomez, P.-Y., & Moore, R. (2006). From strategy of religions to religion of strategy: Comments on Miller's "Competitives strategies of religious organizations." *Journal of Management, Spirituality & Religion*, *3*(3), 199–213. https://doi.org/10.1080/14766080609518625

Gümüsay, A. A. (2019). Embracing religions in moral theories of leadership. *Academy of Management Perspectives*, *33*(3), 292–306.

Harrison, J. S., Phillips, R. A., & Freeman, R. E. (2020). On the 2019 business roundtable "Statement on the purpose of a corporation." *Journal of Management*, *46*(7), 1223–1237. https://doi.org/10.1177/0149206319892669

Henisz, W. J., Dorobantu, S., & Nartey, L. J. (2014). Spinning gold: The financial returns to stakeholder engagement. *Strategic Management Journal*, *35*(12), 1727–1748. https://doi.org/10.1002/smj.2180

Kaipa, P. (2012). What wise leaders always follow. *Harvard Business Review*, 1–23.

Liu, C. H., & Robertson, P. J. (2011). Spirituality in the workplace: Theory and measurement. *Journal of Management Inquiry*, *20*(1), 35–50. https://doi.org/10.1177/1056492610374648

Marks, J., & Mudely, S. (2021). The role of religion in the formation of trust-based relationships amongst South African entrepreneurs. In K. Pavlovich & G. Markman (Eds.), *Spirituality, Entrepreneurship and Social Change*. World Scientific Publishing Company.

Martinez, F., Peattie, K., & Vazquez-Brust, D. (2019). Beyond win–win: A syncretic theory on corporate stakeholder engagement in sustainable development. *Business Strategy and the Environment*, *28*(5), 896–908. https://doi.org/10.1002/bse.2292

Miller, K. D. (2002). Competitive strategies of religious organizations. *Strategic Management Journal*, *23*(5), 435–456. https://doi.org/10.1002/smj.234

Miller, K. D. (2006). A case for including religious organizations in management research. *Journal of Management, Spirituality & Religion*, *3*(3), 214–230. https://doi.org/10.1080/14766080609518626

Newbert, S. L. (2007). Empirical research on the resource-based view of the firm: An assessment and suggestions for future research. *Strategic Management Journal*, *28*(2), 121–146. https://doi.org/10.1002/smj.573

Oh, J., & Wang, J. (2020). Spiritual leadership: Current status and agenda for future research and practice. *Journal of Management, Spirituality & Religion*, *17*(3), 223–248. https://doi.org/10.1080/14766086.2020.1728568

Pavlovich, K. (2020). Quantum empathy: An alternative narrative for global transcendence. *Journal of Management, Spirituality & Religion*, *17*(4), 333–347. https://doi.org/10.1080/14766086.2019.1706626

Pavlovich, K., & Markman, G. (2021). *Spirituality, Entrepreneurship and Social Change*. World Scientific Publishing Company.

Phipps, K. A. (2012). Spirituality and strategic leadership: The influence of spiritual beliefs on strategic decision making. *Journal of Business Ethics*, *106*(2), 177–189. https://doi.org/10.1007/s10551-011-0988-5

Scherer, A. G., & Voegtlin, C. (2020). Corporate governance for responsible innovation: Approaches to corporate governance and their implications for sustainable development. *Academy of Management Perspectives*, *34*(2), 182–208. https://doi.org/10.5465/amp.2017.0175

Williams, A., Whiteman, G., & Parker, J. N. (2019). Backstage interorganizational collaboration: Corporate endorsement of the sustainable development goals. *Academy of Management Discoveries*, *5*(4), 367–395. https://doi.org/10.5465/amd.2018.0154

Xu, B., & Ma, L. (2021). Religious values motivating CSR: An empirical study from corporate leaders' perspective. *Journal of Business Ethics*. https://doi.org/10.1007/s10551-020-04688-x

Giuseppe Delmestri, Doris Schneeberger

6 Organizational Change and Work Spirituality: Expanding the Moral Circle

Work spirituality is a broad academic tent under which two rather different 'camps' gather. On one side there are scholars and practitioners wishing to measure and augment the "spiritual capital" of organizations in order to foster innovation, efficiency and profits (Zohar & Marshall, 2004); on the other those who advocate for the betterment of the human condition in organizations and a re-enchantment of nature beyond any instrumental reasons (Bøje et al., 2012); Case & Gosling, 2010). The ones, the 'instrumentalists,' advance the *business case for spirituality*; the others, the 'critical spiritualists,' advance instead a *spiritual case for business*, which would lose legitimacy if it prevented the spiritual flourishing of individuals and communities. Organizational change is framed in the two camps according to an analogous epistemological-axiological difference, the ones aiming at identifying objective best practice examples of "spiritual organizations" leading to higher efficiency and profits (Mitroff & Denton, 1999), the others studying the role of spiritual leadership and practices to emancipate individuals within communities in organizations (Dent et al., 2005; Mabey & Mayrhofer, 2015). What is common to the two camps is their teleological and activist flavor evident in the belief that, by aligning the spiritual values of the employees to those of the organization or by elevating their spiritual awareness, positive change will almost spontaneously come true (Dehler & Welsh, 1994).

We share Case and Gosling's (2010, p. 276) preoccupation that the spiritual organization, as an instrumentalist ideal type, risks "representing a sinister attempt on the part of capitalist organizations to harness, manipulate and control the soul of employees." Our aim in this chapter is thus to contribute to the critical spiritualist discussion in its attempt to "seek more transformative connections . . . with nature and with the planet" (Neal, 2013a, p. 735) and in its pursuit of a "non-anthropocentric ethics" (Gosling & Case, 2013). Within this research program, however, we recognize a blind spot. In the purportedly non-anthropocentric flight forward towards a "post-humanist approach" for the re-enchantment of an undefined nature (Bøje, 2012, p. 266) we risk disregarding the trees for the forest.

The 'trees' are billions of individual sentient beings exposed to terrible suffering and painful death amassed in factory farms (Lever & Evans, 2017). We agree with Taylor and Bell (2012, p. 569) that "spirituality must be made to work within but against modernity, challenging and transcending the foundations of efficiency and calculability that are inherent to disenchanted organizational norms" and consider nonhuman animals (NHAs) to be victims of a modernist system of objectification that transforms them into raw materials to be efficiently processed

https://doi.org/10.1515/9783110711349-006

(Fischer, 2020). In these firms, NHAs are considered like machines producing under a pure economic logic goods for human consumption despite the fig leave offered by marginal welfare improvements within organic and 'humane' protocols (Lever & Evans, 2017). The new generations, the millions of children and young adults who woke up politically to fight against climate change have mostly embraced a plant-based diet following scientific evidence on the negative climate effects of animal products (Willett et al., 2019) and a moral repulsion towards the mainstream practices in animal husbandry (Elder, 2020). This generation, soon equipped with higher negotiation power due to current demographic trends (Goodhart & Pradhan, 2017), is entering organizations and increasingly pushing for change, e.g., not only plant-based food in canteens but a whole different approach to our relationship with NHAs. The field of workplace spirituality cannot remain deaf, as it mainly has so far, to this spiritual awakening that is expanding the moral circle to include NHAs seen in their individuality – not just part of an undefined 'nature' or members of species whose biodiversity we must protect for anthropocentric reasons. This new expanded sensitivity to suffering and compassion goes hand in hand with spiritual practices such as meditation and community exchange interestingly combined more with rationality and science than with religion.

The purpose of this chapter is hence not only to offer a bird's eye view on the understanding of organizational change within workplace spirituality literature and on the reception of work spirituality within the organizational change literature, but also to point to the need for future research in addressing the role of NHAs in contemporary organizations. In the following, we first discuss the sparce reception of workplace spirituality in organizational change by analyzing two important handbooks and two specialized journals. We then analyze two work spirituality handbooks and the *Journal of Management, Spirituality and Religion (JMSR)* to ascertain how organizational change is treated in this field. Further, we focus on how the relationship between human and nonhuman animals has been framed and theorized within the workplace spirituality literature. Finally, we sustain that "care, compassion and support of others" (MSR Division, 2018, p. 2) would require the recognition of suffering as a common experience across the species including sentient NHAs among the "others" for whom we should feel compassion. We advance that such extended care and compassion, as well as a longtermist ethical approach, should be adopted in the quest for the universalizing stage of spiritual development (Fowler, 1981). We complement these considerations with personal observations derived from our own involvement as participants or researchers in climate movements.

Workplace Spirituality in the Organizational Change Literature

The *Journal of Organizational Change Management* is a primary outlet also for the work spirituality field. This overlapping in readership would suggest a strong integration of the topics of change and spirituality, but the journal is a place where scholars of both fields publish maintaining mostly the disciplinary distinction. We found indeed 208 articles with the search term "spiritual*". However, as the topics refer to mindfulness practices, spiritual capital measures, authentic leadership or leadership for sustainability, they do not directly address organizational change as usually understood, i.e., "organizational change as a difference in form, quality, or state over time in an organizational entity" (Poole & Van de Ven, 2004, p. xi). Searching within these articles for the word 'change' in the title and abstract we could only find Long and Mills (2010) theoretical paper, that address organizational change in some more substantial way. The authors offer a critique of an instrumental interpretation and use of workplace spirituality as a means to achieve material gains by forging a more performing common culture. When framed instrumentality, Long and Mills (2010) argue, workplace spirituality becomes a subtle tool for imposing managers' values on employees, trying to control their minds and devaluing opportunities of spiritual self-realization outside of the organizational context. For them, a project of critical spirituality should develop "the capacity to operate within the context of diverse values, rather than try to operate from the misguided belief that spiritual values will unify the organization" (p. 337). Long and Mills (2010, p. 338), hence, consider the project of introducing spirituality at work ethically justified only if it aims at promoting "an elevated social consciousness necessary to reconstruct the workplace in a manner that challenges the structural inequalities, exploitive tendencies, unsustainability and marginalization produced by modern managerial practices in the pursuit of material gain."

In the *Journal of Change Management*, sixteen articles include the word "spiritual*" but few of them treat the topic in a more substantial way. Apart from articles that address the spiritual component of transformative leadership (Gill, 2002), or that mention spirituality in passing while framing the need for organizational change to reach system level in order to address climate sustainability (Benn & Baker, 2009), notable is Boje's (2012) call for a new ontology that considers our interconnection with nature. However, the main attention to spirituality in this journal comes from practitioners, consultants, or management gurus like Scharmer (2020). The debate on Scharmer's "Theory U" as a practical change management approach or as an "esoteric" management fashion also addresses this (Kühl, 2020). Scharmer's Theory U focuses on community, self-transcendence and awareness, i.e., a terminology close to the spiritual vocabulary. It states the explicit need for society to transform itself to overcome "spiritual disruption" referring to mindfulness practices as "new methods and tools that help leaders and change-makers create containers for evolving the self, i.e. for shifting the awareness in a system from ego to eco" (Scharmer, 2020, p. 329).

The analysis of *The Routledge Companion to Organizational Change* edited by David M. Boje, Bernard Burnes and John Hassard (2012) let the following topics emerge. The chapter by Bushe (2012) on Cooperrider's Appreciative Inquiry (AI) refers to what seems to be the first consideration of spirituality in the organizational change discipline. AI is centered on discovering what "gives life" to any organizational system and in this "might be considered a spiritual practice" (Bushe, 2012, p. 94). And indeed, in a recent interview with Sandra Waddock (2015, p. 164, passim), Cooperrider himself emphasizes that the spiritual underpinnings of AI are aimed at appreciating "the miracle of life" inspired by Albert Schweitzer's book *Reverence for Life*. For Schweitzer (1947; cit. by Kawall, 2003, p. 340), who was inspired by the Janisim's concept of *ahimsa* (non-violence towards every being), reverence for life affords the "fundamental principle of morality, namely that good consists in maintaining, assisting and enhancing life, and that to destroy, to harm, or to hinder life, is evil." Cooperrider's spiritual position grounds a meta-ethic that combines ontological, epistemological and ethical stances: the social world is a miracle of cooperation, science should be generative, and "we need a reconnection with the miracle of life on this planet, where we see things again in living systems, alive and miraculous and filled with emergent potential" (interview with Waddock, 2015, p. 249). In a similar vein, Boje (2012, p. 520), reconnects to some of these ideas about the ontology of our world and prefigures "a future that is about ecological sustainability and ontic ties to nature" and of "rediscovering enchantment [of] . . . the natured world", in what he calls a "posthumanist approach."

One entire chapter of this *Companion* is devoted to the relationship between spirituality at work and organizational change (Taylor & Bell, 2012). The authors define spirituality at work as a movement aimed at re-enchanting our organizations made meaningless by the dominance of a purely instrumental rationality. Given the level of disenchantment and the instrumentality of managerial approaches to organizational culture, only a transformational approach can have an effect against the total absence of metaphysical and transcendent issues speaking to the magic, mystery, or enchantment of our social and personal worlds. However, they also point to the risk that this movement could merely produce a '*disenchanted* re-enchantment'. Its modernist approaches might be hijacked by management and transformed into a "a means of colonizing the self in a way which extends ever deeper into individual subjectivities" (p. 571). They conclude with a more positive, although paradoxical, take on the role of spirituality in our organizations: "spiritualities enable the development of subjects who are able to reconcile reason and emotion, remaining relational and attached while simultaneously rooted in enlightenment norms of critical thinking" (Taylor & Bell, 2012, p. 576).

In the 2004 edition of the *Oxford Handbook of Organizational Change and Innovation* edited by Marshall Scott Poole and Andrew Van de Ven, there is no mention of work spirituality, and religion was mentioned only as an institutional logic. In the 2nd edition, schedule to be published in mid-2021, workplace spirituality, judging from the authors and table of contents, again doesn't seem to receive consideration. We now turn to an analysis of how organizational change ideas, theories and methods were received within the work spirituality literature.

Organizational Change in Work Spirituality Literature

Although change is ubiquitous in the *Handbook of Faith and Spirituality in the Workplace* edited by Judi Neal (2013c), it is here mainly meant in the sense of transformative spiritual change that is supposed to have positive effects on organizations. Similarly, change is conceived in the sense of a movement towards a "a spiritually rich and spiritually friendly workplace" by Stoner (2013, p. 495). A chapter by Russell (2013) on spiritual leadership touches upon the role of leaders as spiritual change agents. Stead and Stead (2013, p. 271) focus on the transformative role of spirituality to empower change towards sustainability and "the creation of spiritual capital in organizations, a kind of wealth earned by serving humankind and the planet." Major (2013) describes the downsizing and change of a division at Hewlett-Packard and uses work spirituality vocabulary such as "belonging" (community), "purpose" (meaning) and "transcendence." Waddock and Steckler (2013, p. 287) investigate the role of wisdom and spirituality to ground valuable social entrepreneurship towards the challenges of our times such as "climate change and lack of sustainability, population growth and inequity, and food, security, and energy crises." They envision disruptive social change agents working towards systemic social change by challenging existing business models.

In the *Palgrave Handbook of Workplace Spirituality and Fulfillment* edited by Satinder Dhiman, Gary Roberts and Joanna Crossman (2018), organizational change or change management are mentioned in ten chapters, but mostly tangentially, e.g., servant leadership, individual spirituality and mindfulness practices are considered in different chapters as conducive to greater engagement and as preconditions for effective organizational change. Only in three chapters there is a broader and more original treatment. Bucci (2018) suggests an interesting scriptural approach to change management based on the transposition of reflections by Christian authors on the process of individual conversion. His central idea is that sustainable change can only occur if individuals go through a process of conversion led by deeply held spiritual values and translates this insight into a stage model for change. Neal (2018) refers in her overview of workplace spirituality research to Dehler and Welsh's (1994) integration of Porras and Silvers' (1991) model of organizational transformation with the notions of emotion and spirituality going beyond the purely cognitive focus of organizational development. Finally, Burton, Jeong and Saini (2018, p. 3) address the problem of "dark spirituality", a situation where "a state of darkness that 'masquerades' as good . . . ultimately works against the growth and development of an organization and the common good."

In the *Journal of Management, Spirituality and Religion* (JMSR) we could find six articles that explicitly address organizational change or change management. Goltz (2018) frames in an instrumental way the mindfulness practices of Buddhism as "allowing safe space for experiencing the discomfort associated with resistance to change and transcending the discomfort." In a similar instrumental perspective, Geh and Tan (2009, p. 296) see organizational change management as aiming "to help employees meet new and existing performance targets rapidly and effectively" and suggest "that individuals who experience the spiritual foundation of life can grow and develop in ways consistent with organizational goals." In a less instrumental fashion, Whitney (2010, p. 78) explicitly frames Appreciative Inquiry as an organizational change approach that, by creating spiritual resonance in the workplace, "fosters high collaboration, that is collaboration for the greater good, rather than simply collaboration to get the job done." Case and Gosling (2010, p. 259) criticize such instrumental views that "treat spirituality in ahistorical and apolitical terms as yet another neutral resource to be harnessed and husbanded by the erstwhile custodians of organizational performance." Pavlovich (2020, p. 333) offers instead a theorization of "quantum empathy" as "a macrolevel organizing mechanism" based on inner work (mindfulness practices), connectedness (reflexivity), and transcendence (empathy) explicitly not conceived as "a tool-kit for organizational change" but as a spiritual way to reimagine a future beyond exploitative capitalist forms. Groen (2007, p. 310) mentions organizational change management in comparing a religious workplace with a secular one and finds a "remarkable similarity as one considers the various ideals of a spiritually infused workplace, such as vocation, ethics, interconnectedness, and being responsible to our local and global community."

Work Spirituality, Nonhuman Animals and Food

In the introduction, we anticipated that our focus in this chapter will be the spiritual awakening of millions of children and young adults in science-based social movements. In our own participation in these climate movements we could observe the prevalence of plant-based food as well as the importance of communitarian forms of meditation and getting together linked with a strong longtermist rational orientation. Although we consider the recognition of this expanding moral circle to include future generations and nonhuman animals in non-instrumental ways as a blind spot in the workplace spirituality literature, notwithstanding the above presented review of this literature, where concepts such as "ecological sustainability" (Bøje, 2012, p. 520), "transformative connections" with nature (Neal, 2013a, p. 735) and "non-anthropocentric ethics" (Gosling & Case, 2013) are central, reveals that an integration of a new ethical and spiritual consideration of nonhuman animals should not be a distant call for spirituality scholars.

Indeed, already Neal (2013b, p. 4) refers to the book *Blessed Unrest* by Paul Hawken (2007, p. 12) who interprets these movements dedicated to creating a sustainable and just world as expressing "the needs of the majority of people on earth to sustain the environment, wage peace, democratize decision making and policy, rejuvenate public governance . . . and improve their lives" (cit. by Stead & Stead, 2013, p. 273). Neal (2013a, p. 735), in this respect, emphasizes in the concluding chapter of her *Handbook* the need for the work spirituality field to "seek more transformative connections." In the same place she reports feeling a spiritual connection with nature: "I felt the Earth as a living being, and saw the wind as the breath of Gaia. I felt an overwhelming love for the planet, and suddenly understood why some people were so passionate about sustainability." She ends the chapter with an optimistic referral to Steven Pinker's TED Talk *"The Myth of Violence"*, where the Harvard professor provides "overwhelming documentation for the decline of violence in humankind" (p. 736). What Neal does not mention is that at the end of the talk Pinker introduces Peter Singer's notion of expanding moral circles to include not only future generations but also NHAs: indeed, while violence within humankind has drastically declined especially after WWII, it is exactly in the second half of the past century that intensive animal agriculture in factory farms has emerged, to a point that, according to FAO data, 136 billion farmed NHAs are killed every year after a short and painful life (Elder, 2020, p. 548; Lever & Evans, 2017).

Before coming back to the theme of the expanding moral circle in the next section, we report here our analysis of how NHAs and, relatedly, food, are considered in the workplace spirituality literature. In Neal's (2013c) *Handbook of Faith and Spirituality in the Workplace*, we found the word "animal(s)" mentioned only on eight pages in six chapters: as the Jewish *mitzvah* 'commandment' to be kind to them (Lurie, Ch. 6), as avoiding products that use animal testing and food made with rennet in devotional yoga practice (Greene, Ch. 10), as interconnection in the creation through breath with animals and plants in Maori religiosity (Spiller and Stockdale, Ch. 11), as totemic ancestors and possible entities in which a person's spirit could be reborn in indigenous Australian spirituality (Miley and Read, Ch. 12), as named by Adam (Russel, Ch. 15), and as part of the ecosystem to be included together with plants, waterways and air in the circle of stakeholders of conscious capitalism (Wigglesworth, Ch. 43). Food instead is mentioned on 30 pages: as gratitude for the Chairman of Tyson Foods, one of the world's largest producers of NHA products, as a case study of a Canadian food company selling NHAs product, as ritual practices involving food, as food security and food scarcity, as offer to the needy, and as symbol of gratitude and caring. The term “vegetarian” is mentioned only once in the context of devotional yoga practice (Greene, Ch. 10) while “vegan” is never mentioned.

In the *Palgrave Handbook of Workplace Spirituality and Fulfillment* edited by Dhiman and colleagues (2018), the term “animal*” is mentioned on 21 pages in 14 chapters. Apart from casual mentions such as that of the Oxford English dictionary of the soul as “the principle of life in man or animals” (p. 62), of animal rights in relationship to the pharmaceutical industry (p. 402), or of animals in a zoo, more substantial mentions refer again to the faith-friendly company Tyson Foods and to the religious understandings of the relationship between human and nonhuman animals in Christianity, Buddhism or Hinduism. Dhiman and Kriger (2018, p. 91), for instance, summarize this relationship as follows:

> *Vedānta* promotes harmonious living via a vision of the oneness of all existence. Outwardly, various forms of life such as plants, animals, birds, and human beings seem to be different from one another, but their underlying life principle of pure awareness, the consciousness principle, is one and the same. From the spiritual standpoint, while interacting with the world and the myriad beings, we are to remember that they are all none but our own true Self. If we perceive someone as different from us, we may have aversion or fear, but if we have the vision of oneness, we will see the other as related and just another aspect of our own Self.

Similarly, Pandey and Navare (2018, p. 107) highlight that in yoga humans have an obligation “toward all nonhuman forms of life . . . by protecting them or feeding them . . . where our planet is addressed as mother earth.” Maheshwari and Gupta (2018, p. 495) state that the “Vedic scriptures offer a way of harmonious living with other humans, animals, and the cosmos leading to a scenario of all being happy.” Interesting is also Burchard’s (2018) discussion of the Biblical concept of the gardener-priest in the chapter *Cultivating a Garden of Beauty and Meaning* that also includes the reign over animals understood as responsibility. While the terms “vegetarian” and “vegan” are never mentioned in this handbook, the term “food” is mentioned in twenty chapters on 41 pages as offering, ritual gift, shortage, nutrition, fast food, and product of companies.

In the *Journal of Management, Spirituality and Religion* the search in titles and abstracts for the terms “animal*” and “food” was unsuccessful. Searching everywhere in the text for the term “animal*”, we could find 198 rather casual mentions mainly referring to ritual slaughter, Halal, our purported superiority in dignity to NHAs, but also respect for them. The term “vegetarian” hits four times including Boje’s (2005a, 2005b) reporting his conversion to Janisim and to a vegan diet as part of his spiritual journey and Peter Pruzan, interviewed by Laszlo Zsolnai (2019, p. 228), addressing the problem of the incapacity of Western consumers to act on scientific evidence: “the huge consumption of meat is a major contributor to the ongoing disruption of the global climate . . . and the destruction of biotypes [. . . however] the percentage of the populations in such well-informed societies that are vegetarian or vegan is small.”

We also searched eight bibliographies on the MSR Division Resources Bibliographies and Annotated Bibliographies webpage (https://msr.aom.org/ourlibrary/new-item) and found only one reference from a search of the words "animal" OR "food" in Rao (no date: 32) *Creativity and Personal Mastery. Annotated Bibliography* where he mentions Robbins' (2001) book as "a searing indictment of factory farming as well as the treatment of animals generally" and as "mak[ing] the case that our food industry, especially the meat-poultry part of it, is destructive of your health and well-being . . . lay[ing] out economic and environmental reasons for a change in our diet away from animals as food."

Hence, our analysis shows that NHAs have received only scant attention in the workplace spirituality literature and mainly from authors associated with Far Eastern religious traditions. The importance given to the case study of Tyson Foods as a spiritual organization, despite being "the world's largest processor and marketer of chicken, beef, and pork" (2018, p. 29), is significant and evident also in the objectified used of words to denote chickens, cows and pigs. This gap, however, as we have argued at the beginning of this section, could easily be filled as we discuss in the next section.

Expanding the Moral Circle: NHAs As Moral Subjects and Longterminism

New generations are increasingly involved in movements that question existing economic and social practices because they threaten human and nonhuman survival on this planet. Movements like the youth movement Fridays 4 Future, its adult equivalent Extinction Rebellion, the supportive scientists' movement Scientists 4 Future, to name but a few, are mounting more and more pressure worldwide on political and economic institutions (Etchanchu et al., 2021). In advocating for their own survival and that of future generations as well as for the preservation of biodiversity and the respect for other sentient beings, they expand their moral circle (the circle of beings that demand moral consideration for, both in the dimensions of time, future generations, and of species, nonhuman animals).

"[F]uture generations will outnumber us by thousands or millions to one; of all the people who we might affect with our actions, the overwhelming majority are yet to come. Those people have the same moral value as us in the present. So in the aggregate, their interest matter enormously" (John & MacAskill, forthcoming, p. 1). The rationale of the idea of longtermism is clear. Future generations of humans will be impacted significantly by our actions (due to climate change, environmental degradation, and depletion of natural resources, for example). John and MacAskill (forthcoming, p. 2) see the root cause of this shortcoming in political short-termism and suggest institutional reforms in order to "increase the time horizons" of governments.

They propose to install “government research institutions and archivists”, “posterity impact assessments”, “future assemblies”, and “legislative houses for future generations” (see also Zsolnai, 2006).

Currently, whether political and economic systems cause future harm or not tends not to be taken into account – at least not enough. Our conduct tends to be morally flawed in the sense that we tend not to extend our moral circle in the temporal dimension. Moreover, we tend to exclude those who do not belong to our own species, and thus cause considerable harm and suffering. Peter Singer (2011, p. 120) is a famous voice in the philosophic ethics discourse calling for an inclusion of NHAs into our moral circle. He points out that “the pleasures and pains of non-human animals are no less significant because the animals are not members of the species Homo sapiens.”

The practices we observed in our individual experiences in the social movements trying to expand our moral circles in the temporal and species dimensions seem consistent with the ethical idea of expanding our moral circle. We observed meditation and mindfulness derived from the Buddhist meditation tradition, but also forms of religious syncretism and shamanism (as in the Signal group “Spirit of XR” where spirituality is discussed also in ‘secular’ terms). The sharing of vegetarian or vegan food (even freegan meals recovered from food items others would have or have thrown out) is also a central component in communitarian gatherings as well as rituals of so-called “check-ins” and “check-outs” in which activists not only share a meal but also their current personal emotional states in order round off their activities with a further communitarian aspect. This combination of mindfulness and communitarian values confirms the different meanings that such practices have in these movements in comparison to the more individualist reception of yoga and New Age meditation in older generations (Munir et al., 2021). Indeed, du Plessis and Just (2021) see in the recent reception of mindfulness in these movements a transformative and progressive potential. Moreover, these practices and the strong values of respect for nature and compassion for all sentient beings are not combined with irrational beliefs, but, paradoxically, with beliefs in rational scientific principles – an observation that confirms Taylor and Bell’s (2012, p. 576) reflection that contemporary spiritualities enable individuals “to reconcile reason and emotion,” relationality and critical thinking (to be sure, not a totally new phenomenon, as also Christian philosophers like Thomas Aquinas based faith on reason). In other words, in these, “[t]he experience of a transformative connection” (Lurie, 2013, p. 91) assumes a different spiritual form.

Conclusions

In this chapter we have argued that (critical) work spirituality studies should extend their understanding of spirituality to encompass more philosophical value-based approaches that argue for the expansion of our moral circle. It is worth taking note of the diffusion of science-based practices of meditation and community in social movements where millions of young and less-young people are socialized to political life and action. Because a new relationship with NHAs considered as sentient beings is central in this new rational spiritual orientation, our academic understanding of NHAs and organizational practices towards them will have to be rethought completely. Organizations will be flooded by this new generation and will have to react in many ways if they want to maintain their legitimacy. The decision if we should completely abolish NHA farming and all go vegan or if we should 'only' drastically reduce meat and dairy consumption and resort for the rest to high-welfare small-scale NHA agriculture (Bruckner, 2020) and to cultured meat[1] and dairy (Elder, 2020) is still debated also with reference to geographical and socio-economic conditions (Smith, 2016; Jairath et al., 2021). However, factory farms are the source of 99 percent of NHA products in industrial societies (Lever & Evans, 2017). Those places, in which profitability rather than animal welfare is prioritized, undoubtedly represent the dark side of human mastery of nature. The appalling suffering in slaughterhouses and factory farms should provide us with ample reason to expand our moral circle to include nonhuman sentient beings. As is emphasized in the ethical stance of longtermism, next to nonhumans, also the fate of future generations of humans depends on our ethical conduct. We'd like to conclude this chapter with Judi Neal's (2013c) opening longtermist dedication in her *Handbook*: "May the work that we are doing today help create a better world for you and for at least seven generations."

1 Interestingly, Tyson Foods has recently diversified its lines of business and has invested in the development of zero-suffering alternative proteins like plant-based and cultured meat. Tom Hayes, President and Chief Executive Officer at Tyson Foods, framed this move not as an "either or" but as a "yes and" scenario (2018) focusing on the growing need of sustainable proteins for a growing world population. No mention is made of farm animal welfare as a motivation. The company slaughters approximately 155,000 cows, 461,000 pigs and 45,000,000 chickens every week (*Tyson Sustainability Report 2019*, 2019, https://www.tysonsustainability.com/downloads/Tyson_2019_Sustainability_Report.pdf, accessed 24 March 2021).

References

Benn, S., & Baker, E. (2009). Advancing sustainability Through change and innovation: A Co-evolutionary perspective. *Journal of Change Management*, *9*(4), 383–397. https://doi.org/10.1080/14697010903360574

Bøje, D. M. (2012). Reflections: What does quantum physics of storytelling mean for change management? *Journal of Change Management*, *12*(3), 253–271. https://doi.org/10.1080/14697017.2011.609330

Bøje, D. M. (2005b). Epilogue: Critical spirituality. *Journal of Management, Spirituality & Religion*, *2*(3), 399–405. https://doi.org/10.1080/14766080509518600

Bøje, D. M. (2005a). Wilda. *Journal of Management, Spirituality & Religion*, *2*(3), 342–364. https://doi.org/10.1080/14766080509518592

Bøje, D. M., Burnes, B., & Hassard, J. (Eds.). (2012). *The Routledge Companion to Organizational Change* (0 ed.). Routledge. https://doi.org/10.4324/9780203810279

Bucci, J. J. 2018. Change Management: Considering a Peniel Approach for Managing Change in Organizations. In The Palgrave Handbook of Workplace Spirituality and Fulfillment (pp. 943–968). Palgrave Macmillan. https://doi.org/10.1007/978-3-319-62163-0

Bruckner, D. W. (2020). Small-scale animal agriculture. In B. Fischer (Ed.), *The Routledge Handbook of Animal Ethics* (pp. 198–210). Routledge.

Burchard, M. J. (2018). Cultivating a garden of beauty and meaning: Organizational spirituality's restorative mission from a theological, scientific, and aesthetic perspective. In G. E. Roberts & J. E. Crossman (Eds.), *The Palgrave Handbook of Workplace Spirituality and Fulfillment* (pp. 345–365). Palgrave Macmillan. https://doi.org/10.1007/978-3-319-62163-0_13

Burton, O., Jeong, S., & Saini, K. M. (2018). Dark spirituality: Its impact on the strategic and operational efficiency of organizations. In G. E. Roberts & J. E. Crossman (Eds.), *The Palgrave Handbook of Workplace Spirituality and Fulfillment* (pp. 969–987). Palgrave Macmillan. https://doi.org/10.1007/978-3-319-62163-0_36

Bushe, G. R. (2012). Appreciative inquiry: Theory and critique. In D. M. Freidenreich, B. Burnes, & J. Hassard (Eds.), *The Routledge Companion To Organizational Change* (pp. 87–103). Routledge.

Case, P., & Gosling, J. (2010). The spiritual organization: Critical reflections on the instrumentality of workplace spirituality. *Journal of Management, Spirituality & Religion*, *7*(4), 257–282. https://doi.org/10.1080/14766086.2010.524727

Dehler, G. E., & Welsh, M. A. (1994). Spirituality and Organizational Transformation: Implications for the New Management Paradigm. *Journal of Managerial Psychology*, *9*(6), 17–26. https://doi.org/10.1108/02683949410070179

Dent, E. B., Higgins, M. E., & Wharff, D. M. (2005). Spirituality and leadership: An empirical review of definitions, distinctions, and embedded assumptions. *The Leadership Quarterly*, *16*(5), 625–653. https://doi.org/10.1016/j.leaqua.2005.07.002

Dhiman, S., & Kriger, M. (2018). Eastern approaches to organizational well-being: Ontological levels of leadership in Hinduism, Buddhism, and Taoism. In S. Dhiman, G. E. Roberts, & J. E. Crossman (Eds.), *The Palgrave Handbook of Workplace Spirituality and Fulfillment*. Palgrave Macmillan. https://doi.org/10.1007/978-3-319-61929-3_2-1

Dhiman, S., Roberts, G. E., & Crossman, J. E. (2018). *The Palgrave Handbook of Workplace Spirituality and Fulfillment*. Palgrave Macmillan.

du Plessis, E. M., & Just, S. N. (2021). Mindfulness – it's not what you think: Toward critical reconciliation with progressive self-development practices. *Organization*, 13. https://doi.org/10.1177/1350508421995755

Elder, M. (2020). Cultured meat. In B. Fischer (Ed.), *The Routledge Handbook of Animal Ethics*. Routledge.

Etchanchu, H., de Bakker, F., & Delmestri, G. (2021). Social movement organizations' agency for sustainable organizing. In S. Teerikangas, T. Onkila, K. Koistinen, & M. Mäkelä (Eds.), *Research Handbook of Sustainability Agency* (pp. 194–210). Edward Elgar.

Fischer, B. (2020). *The Ethics of Eating Animals: Usually Bad, Sometimes Wrong, Often Permissible*. Routledge.

Fowler, J. W. (1981). *Stages of Faith: The Psychology of Human Development and the Quest for Meaning* (1st ed). Harper & Row.

Geh, E. Z., & Tan, G. (2009). Spirituality at work in a changing world: Managerial and research implications. *Journal of Management, Spirituality & Religion*, *6*(4), 287–300. https://doi.org/10.1080/14766080903290093

Gill, R. (2002). Change management – Or change leadership? *Journal of Change Management*, *3*(4), 307–318. https://doi.org/10.1080/714023845

Goltz, S. M. (2018). Organizational change: Insights from Buddhism and Acceptance and Commitment Therapy(ACT). *Journal of Management, Spirituality & Religion*, *15*(5), 424–449. https://doi.org/10.1080/14766086.2018.1513857

Goodhart, C., & Pradhan, M. (2017). *Demographics will reverse three multi-decade global trends* (BIS Working Paper No. 656 No. 656). Bank for International Settlements. https://ssrn.com/abstract=3015065

Gosling, J., & Case, P. (2013). Social dreaming and ecocentric ethics: Sources of non-rational insight in the face of climate change catastrophe. *Organization*, *20*(5), 705–721. https://doi.org/10.1177/1350508413489814

Groen, J. (2007). Spirituality within a religious workplace: Is it so different? *Journal of Management, Spirituality & Religion*, *4*(3), 310–325. https://doi.org/10.1080/14766080709518667

Hawken, P. (2007). *Blessed Unrest: How the Largest Social Movement in History Is Restoring* Grace, *Justice, and Beauty to the World*. Viking Press.

Hayes, T. (2018, January 29). *Why we are investing in alternative proteins*. https://thefeed.blog/2018/01/29/why-we-are-investing-in-alternative-proteins/

Jairath, G., Mal, G., Gopinath, D., & Singh, B. (2021). A holistic approach to access the viability of cultured meat: A review. *Trends in Food Science & Technology*, *110*, 700–710. https://doi.org/10.1016/j.tifs.2021.02.024

John, T., & MacAskill, W. (forthcoming). Longtermist institutional reform. In N. Cargill & T. M. John (Eds.), *The Long View*. FIRST.

Kawall, J. (2003). Reverence for life as a viable environmental virtue. *Environmental Ethics*, *25*(4), 339–358. https://doi.org/10.5840/enviroethics20032542

Kühl, S. (2020). The blind spots in theory U: The reconstruction of a (change-) management fashion. *Journal of Change Management*, *20*(4), 314–321. https://doi.org/10.1080/14697017.2020.1744883

Lever, J., & Evans, A. (2017). Corporate social responsibility and farm animal welfare: Towards sustainable development in the food industry? In S. O. Idowu & S. Vertigans (Eds.), *Stages of Corporate Social Responsibility* (pp. 205–222). Springer International Publishing. https://doi.org/10.1007/978-3-319-43536-7_10

Long, B. S., & Mills, H. J. (2010). Workplace spirituality, contested meaning, and the culture of organization: A critical sensemaking account. *Journal of Organizational Change Management*, *23*(3), 325–341. https://doi.org/10.1108/09534811011049635

Lurie, A. (2013). Faith and spirituality in the workplace: A Jewish perspective. In J. Neal (Ed.), *Handbook of Faith and Spirituality in the Workplace. Emerging Research and Practice* (pp. 85–101). Springer. https://doi.org/10.1007/978-1-4614-5233-1_6

Mabey, C., & Mayrhofer, W. (2015). What Kind of Leader Are You Becoming? In C. Mabey & W. Mayrhofer (Eds.), *Developing Leadeship. Questions Business Schools Don't Ask* (pp. 1–28). Sage.

Maheshwari, A. K., & Gupta, R. K. (2018). Vedic leadership: Theory and practice of operating from natural law. In G. E. Roberts & J. E. Crossman (Eds.), *The Palgrave Handbook of Workplace Spirituality and Fulfillment* (pp. 491–511). Palgrave Macmillan. https://doi.org/10.1007/978-3-319-62163-0_57

Major, R. (2013). Workplace spirituality as an aggregate construct of organizational theory concepts: Shutting down Hewlett-Packard's volume systems division. In J. Neal (Ed.), *Handbook of Faith and Spirituality in the Workplace* (pp. 519–534). Springer. https://doi.org/10.1007/978-1-4614-5233-1_30

Mitroff, I. I., & Denton, E. A. (1999). A study of spirituality in the workplace. *MIT Sloan Management Review, 40*(4), 83–92.

MSR Division. (2018). *Annotated list of workplace spirituality organizations*. Management, Spirituality & Religion Division, Academy of Management. https://msr.aom.org/ourlibrary/workplacespirituality

Munir, K., Ansari, S. (Shaz), & Brown, D. (2021). From Patañjali to the "gospel of sweat": Yoga's remarkable transformation from a sacred movement into a thriving global market. *Administrative Science Quarterly*, 1–46. https://doi.org/10.1177/0001839221993475

Neal, J. (2018). Overview of workplace spirituality research. In S. Dhiman, G. E. Roberts, & J. E. Crossman (Eds.), *The Palgrave Handbook of Workplace Spirituality and Fulfillment* (pp. 1–56). Palgrave Macmillan. https://doi.org/10.1007/978-3-319-61929-3_45-1

Neal, J. (2013a). Epilogue: Where do we go from here? In J. Neal (Ed.), *Handbook of Faith and Spirituality in the Workplace* (pp. 733–739). Springer. https://doi.org/10.1007/978-1-4614-5233-1_44

Neal, J. (2013b). Faith and spirituality in the workplace: Emerging research and practice. In J. Neal (Ed.), *Handbook of Faith and Spirituality in the Workplace: Emerging Research and Practice* (pp. 3–18). Springer. https://doi.org/10.1007/978-1-4614-5233-1_1

Neal, J. (Ed.). (2013c). *Handbook of Faith and Spirituality in the Workplace: Emerging Research and Practice*. Springer.

Pandey, A., & Navare, A. V. (2018). Paths of yoga: Perspective for workplace spirituality. In G. E. Roberts & J. E. Crossman (Eds.), *The Palgrave Handbook of Workplace Spirituality and Fulfillment* (pp. 101–126). Palgrave Macmillan. https://doi.org/10.1007/978-3-319-62163-0_4

Pavlovich, K. (2020). Quantum empathy: An alternative narrative for global transcendence. *Journal of Management, Spirituality & Religion, 17*(4), 333–347. https://doi.org/10.1080/14766086.2019.1706626

Poole, M. S., & Van de Ven, A. H. (2004). *Handbook of Organizational Change and Innovation*. Oxford University Press. https://books.google.at/books?id=Pu-vw387jmkC

Porras, J. I., & Silvers, R. C. (1991). Organization development and transformation. *Annual Review of Psychology, 42*(1), 51–78. https://doi.org/10.1146/annurev.ps.42.020191.000411

Pruzan, P., & Zsolnai, L. (2019). An interview with Peter Pruzan on spiritual transformation in management. *Journal of Management, Spirituality & Religion, 16*(2), 221–230. https://doi.org/10.1080/14766086.2018.1548972

Robbins, J. (2001). *The Food Revolution: How Your Diet Can Help Save Your Life and Our World*. Conari Press.

Roberts, G. E., Crossman, J. E., & Bucci, J. J. (Eds.). (2018). Change management: Considering a peniel approach for managing change in organizations. In *The Palgrave Handbook of Workplace Spirituality and Fulfillment* (pp. 943–968). Palgrave Macmillan. https://doi.org/10.1007/978-3-319-62163-0

Russell, M. L. (2013). The secret of leadership success. In J. Neal (Ed.), *Handbook of Faith and Spirituality in the Workplace: Emerging* Research *and* Practice (pp. 237–254). Springer. https://doi.org/10.1007/978-1-4614-5233-1_15

Scharmer, O. (2020). Social systems as if people mattered response to the Kühl critique of theory U. *Journal of Change Management, 20*(4), 322–332. https://doi.org/10.1080/14697017.2020.1744884

Schweitzer, A. (1947). *The Spiritual Life: Selected Writings of Albert Schweitzer; Edited by Charles R.* Joy; *Introduction by Robert Coles & Bob Kerrey.*

Singer, P. (2011). *The Expanding Circle: Ethics, Evolution, and Moral Progress*. Princeton University Press. https://books.google.at/books?id=Yve7lgvtLcsC

Smith, A. F. (2016). *A Critique of the Moral Defense of Vegetarianism*. Palgrave Macmillan. https://books.google.at/books?id=du0YDAAAQBAJ

Stead, W. E., & Stead, J. G. (2013). Green man rising: Spirituality and sustainable strategic management. In J. Neal (Ed.), *Handbook of Faith and Spirituality in the Workplace* (pp. 271–283). Springer. https://doi.org/10.1007/978-1-4614-5233-1_17

Stoner, J. A. F. (2013). Creating a spiritually friendly company. In J. Neal (Ed.), *Handbook of Faith and Spirituality in the Workplace: Emerging Research and Practice* (pp. 491–517). Springer. https://doi.org/10.1007/978-1-4614-5233-1_29

Taylor, S., & Bell, E. (2012). The promise of re-enchantment. Organizational culture and the spirituality at work movement. In D. M. Bøje, B. Burnes, & J. Hassard (Eds.), *The Routledge Companion to Organizational Change* (0 ed., pp. 568–579). Routledge. https://doi.org/10.4324/9780203810279

Tyson Sustainability Report 2019. (2019). https://www.tysonsustainability.com/downloads/Tyson_2019_Sustainability_Report.pdf

Waddock, S. (2015). *Intellectual Shamans: Management Academics Making a Difference*. Cambridge University Press. https://books.google.at/books?id=a8WTBQAAQBAJ

Waddock, S., & Steckler, E. (2013). Wisdom, spirituality, social entrepreneurs, and self-sustaining practices: What can we learn from difference makers? In J. Neal (Ed.), *Handbook of Faith and Spirituality in the Workplace: Emerging Research and Practice* (pp. 285–301). Springer. https://doi.org/10.1007/978-1-4614-5233-1_18

Whitney, D. (2010). Appreciative inquiry: Creating spiritual resonance in the workplace. *Journal of Management, Spirituality & Religion, 7*(1), 73–88. https://doi.org/10.1080/14766080903497656

Willett, W., Rockström, J., Loken, B., Springmann, M., Lang, T., Vermeulen, S., Garnett, T., Tilman, D., DeClerck, F., Wood, A., Jonell, M., Clark, M., Gordon, L. J., Fanzo, J., Hawkes, C., Zurayk, R., Rivera, J. A., De Vries, W., Majele Sibanda, L., . . . Murray, C. J. L. (2019). Food in the anthropocene: The EAT–Lancet Commission on healthy diets from sustainable food systems. *The Lancet, 393*(10170), 447–492. https://doi.org/10.1016/S0140-6736(18)31788-4

Zohar, D., & Marshall, I. N. (2004). *Spiritual Capital: Wealth We Can Live by*. Bloomsbury. https://books.google.at/books?id=205pPwAACAAJ

Zsolnai, L. (2006). Extended stakeholder theory. *Society and Business Review, 1*(1), 37–44. https://doi.org/10.1108/17465680610643337

Richard Oxarart, Jeffery D. Houghton, Christopher P. Neck

7 Organizational Behavior and Workplace Spirituality

Organizational behavior (OB) has been defined as a field of research on human behavior focused on understanding, explaining, and improving attitudes within organizational and workplace contexts (Neck et al., 2020). OB is both interdisciplinary in its focus (e.g., psychology, sociology, etc.) and multi-level (i.e., individual, group, and organization). Interestingly, OB scholars often examine the interface between these various levels, drawing on theories created both by OB scholars and from scholars in underlying disciplines. For instance, it is not uncommon for OB scholars to study *individual* perceptions of the *organizational* environment within the workplace, facilitating research on a wide range of organizational issues and outcomes.

Spirituality in the workplace, both at a micro and macro level, should be of great interest to OB scholars because of its potential to serve as an effective framework for understanding and shaping workplace attitudes and behaviors in positive ways. Although there is growing interest in spirituality in the workplace among OB scholars (Geigle, 2012; Gotsis & Kortezi, 2008; Houghton et al., 2016; Krishnakumar & Neck, 2002), much of the work to date has been conceptual in nature and is therefore somewhat lacking in empirical support. This relative lack of empirical evidence affords OB researchers with an excellent opportunity to explore the relationships between workplace spirituality and a host of OB outcomes. Indeed, given their interests in examining individual perceptions within organizational contexts, OB scholars are especially well-positioned to study spirituality in organizations to help fill this gap in the literature.

This chapter examines workplace spirituality as it has been studied by OB scholars. Therefore, a particular focus of this chapter is on outcomes frequently studied in the OB literature. We begin by summarizing some of the more important findings in the OB literature regarding how spirituality functions in the workplace and how it relates to various outcomes. This first part of the chapter focuses on OB areas where a substantial amount of research has been done and is followed by a section outlining less explored areas that may provide interesting avenues for future research. After reviewing a sampling of studies from each of these areas, we continue by discussing some of the methods used to study workplace spirituality in OB. Finally, the chapter probes some of the shortcomings in the extant literature before suggesting possible future directions for OB researchers interested in understanding how spiritualty can affect employees at both the individual and organizational levels.

https://doi.org/10.1515/9783110711349-007

OB and Workplace Spirituality: Principal Research Findings

Organizational Citizenship Behaviors and Counterproductive Work Behaviors

Organizational citizenship behaviors (OCBs) and counterproductive work behaviors (CWBs) are of great interest to management scholars for their ability to predict various multilevel outcomes in the workplace. Unsurprisingly, workplace spirituality has been examined both conceptually and empirically in an effort to increase our understanding of these important OB constructs. OCBs, which are extra-role behaviors that go beyond basic job duties (Organ, 1988), have been found to have a significant positive relationship to workplace spirituality (Ahmadi et al., 2014; Pawar, 2009). For instance, Belwalkar, Vohra and Pandey (2018) using a sample of 613 banking employees, found that workplace spirituality was significantly and positively related to OCBs as mediated by job satisfaction. Similarly, study of 305 registered nurses linked workplace spirituality to both OCBs and affective organizational commitment (Kazemipour et al., 2012). Furthermore, Nasurdin, Nejati and Mai (2013) were able to show empirically a positive relationship between workplace spirituality and OCBs in a sample of academic staff employees, while Nur and Organ (2006) found greater OCBs for companies using Management-by-Virtues, which can be likened to workplace spirituality. Some researchers have even suggested a bidirectional relationship wherein OCBs could serve as both an antecedent and outcome of workplace spirituality (Pawar, 2009).

Other researchers have examined the possibility that workplace spirituality may influence employee counterproductive work behaviors (CWBs; Gruys & Sackett, 2003). For example, Ahmad and Omar (2014) argued that job satisfaction is positively related to workplace spirituality and negatively related to deviant work behaviors (or CWBs). Subsequently, using a sample of 641 employees working in the hospitality industry, Haldorai, Kim, Chang and Li (2020) found that workplace spirituality mediated the relationship between organizational justice climate and CWBs. The findings to date suggest that workplace spirituality may be an important variable in our understanding of both positive and negative employee behaviors.

Job Satisfaction

Job satisfaction is one of the most studied relationships at the intersection of workplace spirituality and organizational behavior. Job satisfaction, which may be described as an affective or emotional reaction to one's work (e.g. Weiss, 2002), has been found empirically to be related to workplace spirituality in many studies. For instance, Gupta, Kumar and Singh (2014) found a significant and positive correlation between spirituality in the workplace and job satisfaction using a sample of 100 payroll employees in the insurance industry. Furthermore, Noor and Arif (2011) through the analysis of qualitative data gathered on medical doctors in Pakistan concluded that organizational and personal spirituality was strongly related to a person's satisfaction with their job.

Van Der Walt and De Klerk (2014) claimed that the spiritual dimension of understanding work behaviors has been understudied and were able to empirically show, using a large sample of 600 white-collar workers, that workplace spirituality is positively related to job satisfaction. This positive relationship between workplace spirituality has been found using a variety of samples in various contexts, giving us some confidence that this relationship does hold in the work environment (e.g. Altaf & Awan, 2011; Belwalkar et al., 2018; Fanggidae, 2017; Garg, 2017; Hassan et al., 2016).

Organizational Commitment

Another important outcome of interest for OB scholars is organizational commitment, which may be defined as the extent to which a person identifies with their organization (e.g. Meyer & Alien, 1991; Porter & Steers, 1977). Here again, workplace spirituality has been found to have a positive impact on an employee's organizational commitment. Vandenberghe (2011) proposed a model of spiritual leadership in which organizational commitment mediates the relationship between a spiritual leadership style and a variety of positive work outcome including OCBs, turnover, performance. The model further suggests that the climate for spirituality and personal spirituality would moderate these relationships. Researchers have also empirically explored this relationship. In one example, Fanggidae (2017), using structural equation modeling, was able to show a positive linkage between spirituality in the workplace and organizational commitment. Likewise, Rego and colleagues (2007) employing two samples (one from Brazil and the other from Portugal) found that workplace spirituality was positively related to organizational commitment. In a later study (Rego & Pina E Cunha, 2008), these researchers reported that workplace spirituality had a positive effect on affective, normative, and continuance commitment using cluster analyses.

Beyond these findings supporting a direct relationship between workplace spirituality and organizational commitment, oftentimes commitment is positioned as a mediator between workplace spirituality and other important OB outcomes. Kazemipour et al. (2012), for instance, found that affective organizational commitment mediates the relationship between workplace spirituality and OCBs. Whether used as an outcome variable of interest or as a mediator, a growing body of evidence suggests that workplace spirituality may have a positive effect on organizational commitment.

Creativity and Innovation

In their seminal review of the workplace spirituality literature, Krishnakumar and Neck (2002) explained that spirituality is useful in part because it can allow people to think beyond the normal or physical boundaries of our world. This type of expanded consciousness can be important for fostering creative thinking and problem-solving in the workplace environment. Creativity has been defined in terms of the generation of novel and useful ideas, while innovation, in contrast, may be described as a process aimed toward developing, expanding, modifying, and applying creative ideas (e.g. DiLiello & Houghton, 2006). Some researchers have begun to explore empirically the possible relationship between workplace spirituality and creativity and innovation. For instance, Zsolnai and Illes (2017) examined a few spiritually inspired businesses in operation (e.g., Organic India, The Economy of Communion, & Triodos Bank) and concluded that these businesses flourish due to the creativity of their founders and because of their spiritual-focused vision and missions. Along similar lines, Ranasinghe and Samarasinghe (2019) have proposed a model wherein workplace spirituality increases innovative work behaviors as mediated by intrinsic motivation. Likewise, Fawcett and colleagues (2008) posit that creativity in the workplace stems from various elements within the work culture, some of which include elements in the spiritual domain, such as belongingness and affirmation. Still, much of the research that explores the relationship between spirituality and creativity and innovation is conceptual in nature, making this area is ripe for future research.

Employee Engagement

Employee engagement, which involves fulfilling and positive work related frames of mind as demonstrated by an employee's vigor, dedication, and absorption (e.g. Schaufeli et al., 2002), is yet another key outcome of interest for OB scholars. Engagement has been found to be increased by a variety of dispositional and situational variables, but how does spirituality in the workplace affect employee engagement? In a notable attempt to answer this question, Saks (2011) proposed a framework that modeled spirituality in relation to important psychological outcomes, such as finding meaningfulness in work, meaningfulness at work, psychological safety, and availability. Saks (2011) maintains that these psychological outcomes increase employee engagement in both their tasks and their work environment. For instance, if employees feel psychological safety that allows them to express themselves freely in the workplace, they are more likely to be fully engaged in the workplace.

More recently, Milliman, Gatling and Kim (2018) set out to examine the direct effect of workplace spirituality on workplace engagement. These researchers advanced that spirituality in the workplace would result in higher levels of intrinsic motivation, thereby increasing engagement. Their empirical research based on this assertion included 292 employees in the hospitality industry. Their findings provided support for a direct effect of workplace spirituality on work engagement and further suggested that this workplace engagement translates into increased employee service effectiveness. Similarly, Petchsawang and McLean (2017)

examined the relationship between mindful meditation and work engagement, with spiritualty as a mediator between these two potentially important work constructs. They reported that workplace spirituality fully mediated the relationship between meditation and work engagement in their sample. These empirical studies lend some confidence to the supposition that workplace spirituality is a useful tool for enhancing employee engagement.

Work Performance

Although overall organizational performance is often considered a rather distal outcome relative to the individual processes studied in OB, it is still considered among the most important to understand, especially in terms of OB's practical value. A few researchers have attempted to make more direct linkages between workplace spirituality and work performance at the individual and work unit levels. For example, Petchsawang and Duchon (2012) examined spirituality, meditation, and work performance in two different studies. In the first study, they found a relationship between meditation and spirituality scores, lending support to the idea that the practice of mediation can lead to higher levels of workplace spirituality. In their second study, they showed a positive relationship between spirituality and work performance, as partially meditated by meditation.

In an effort to elucidate the nature of the relationship between workplace spirituality and work performance, Tischler, Biberman and Mc Keage (2002) proposed a number of possible explanatory models. Notably, these researchers proposed a connection between emotional intelligence and workplace spirituality, positing that the two may interact to explain various gains or losses in an individual's job performance.

Another interesting study was performed by Duchon and Plowman (2005), who examined the amount of measured spirituality in various high- and low-performing work units within an organization. Their findings reflected higher measured levels of spirituality in higher performing units. Taken together, these studies bolster confidence in the assertion that workplace spirituality positively affects work performance.

OB and Workplace Spirituality: Additional Research Areas

The OB constructs and outcomes above have garnered substantial attention by researchers interested in understanding spirituality in the workplace, yet there is still much to be learned and done. Some additional constructs of interest have been studied by a relatively smaller number of OB researchers thus far. These areas, therefore, are ripe for scholars who wish to extend the research on workplace spirituality in OB contexts.

Employee Well-being

Employee well-being has been studied in OB for its effects on both work and home life for individuals (e.g. Baptiste, 2008). Notably, Pawar (2016) examined employee well-being, in terms of emotional, psychological, social, and spiritual aspects of life. This researcher was able to empirically show that each of these four types of employee well-being was positively affected by workplace spirituality. Similarly, Walia (2018) examined four dimensions of workplace spirituality, including compassion, mindfulness, meaningful work, and transcendence, and found each to be predictive of employee well-being. Interestingly, Garg (2017) found that workplace spirituality was a necessary condition to a variety of positive workplace outcomes, including job satisfaction, employee commitment, and work-life balance satisfaction. These studies furnish support to the idea that workplace spirituality is useful in terms of increasing employee well-being.

Trust and Honesty

Trust, which may be defined as the dependence on the honesty and reliability of another, has a rich history in the OB literature (e.g. Colquitt et al., 2007). In the workplace spirituality domain, Jurkiewicz and Giacalone (2004) cited trust as one of the most important factors in their framework on values and workplace spirituality. Similarly, Daniel (2010) used both honesty and trust in their conceptualization of spirituality in the workplace. Still, very few studies have empirically examined the proposed relationship between these constructs. In a notable exception, trust was examined as a mediator between workplace spirituality and job satisfaction (Hassan et al., 2016). These researchers found that trust functioned as a mechanism to explain the impact of workplace spirituality on job satisfaction, with positive relationships reported between each of these variables in their study (Hassan et al., 2016).

Stress, Work Overload, and Aggression

Work stress and work overload have been widely studied in the OB literature (e.g. Ganster & Schaubroeck, 1991), but one topic that has gone nearly untouched is how spirituality might affect stress or perceived levels of stress and work overload. One study by Daniel (2015) found in two samples, one in the United States and the other in Mexico, that meaningful work and spirituality had a negative relationship with perceived stress in the workplace. Kim and Seidlitz (2002) found that spirituality had a positive effect on emotional and physical adjustment to daily stress. Furthermore, Altaf and Awan (2011) examined job overload and its effects on job satisfaction and found that workplace spirituality was able to significantly moderate the negative effect of job overload on job satisfaction. Interestingly, Sprung, Sliter and Jex (2012) found that aggression might serve as a powerful moderator to some of the positive outcomes of spirituality. These researchers found, in a sample of 854 participants, that high levels of spirituality in workers caused them to be more vulnerable to negative outcomes in the presence of workplace aggression. Still, work remains to enhance our understanding of precisely how spirituality relates to stress and work overload in the workforce and what part aggression may play in this context.

Emotional Labor

Emotional labor occurs when employees are asked to display certain emotions regardless of their true underlying feelings at the time (e.g. Brotheridge & Grandey, 2002). Researchers have suggested that workplace spirituality may serve as a buffer to the potential negative effects of emotional labor in the workplace (Zou & Dahling, 2017). For instance, Byrne, Morton and Dahling (2011), posed several research questions focused on the possible role of spirituality and religious beliefs in shaping employees' emotional displays and in buffering the potential negative effects of emotional labor. Similarly, Lee, Lovelace and Manz (2014) advanced an integrative model of workplace spirituality in service organizations, which suggested that key values including respect, integrity, and ethics would buffer the negative effects of emotional labor as mediated by organizational commitment and job satisfaction. Although empirical studies examining these proposed relationships are scarce, Zou and his colleagues (Zou, Houghton, et al., 2020) recently explored a model in which workplace spirituality influenced the emotional labor strategy choice and ultimately the subjective well-being of service employees. More specifically, their results showed that greater workplace spirituality was related to more deep acting (i.e., changing perceptions of work behaviors and reappraising work situation so as to actually experience the required emotions accompanying emotional displays) and less surface acting (i.e., suppressing inappropriate feelings by faking the required emotional expression) thereby enhancing employee well-being. Interestingly, gender moderated the effects of workplace spirituality on emotional labor strategy choice, with stronger relationships noted for women than for men (Zou, Houghton, et al., 2020).

Leadership

Leadership, which may be described as a process of influence toward the accomplishment of goals, is yet another key research stream within the larger field of OB (Antonakis & Day, 2017). Although leadership and workplace spirituality is examined in greater depth elsewhere in this volume, we provide a brief overview here. Whereas most of the OB constructs reviewed above have been advanced as outcomes of workplace spirituality, leadership has primarily been portrayed as a key antecedent of spirituality at work. Notably, Houghton and his colleagues (2016) expanded Krishnakumar and Neck´s (2002) "spiritual freedom" model to include leadership as a primary mechanism for encouraging workplace spirituality in organizations. They go on to detail how various types of leadership, including servant leadership, authentic leadership, and ethical leadership, may lead to increased spirituality among followers (Houghton et al., 2016). They further note that a relatively new leadership approach called spiritual leadership (Fry, 2003) may hold the greatest potential for shaping spiritual diversity in the workplace because it actively incorporates various aspects of spirituality into the leadership process (Houghton et al., 2016). Spiritual leadership involves a number of leadership qualities that are very different than most other leadership styles studied in management and OB (e.g. forgiveness, humility, encouraging hope/faith, empathy) and has a strong focus on maximizing intrinsic motivation in their followership. Although Fry (2003)

suggested that spiritual leadership would increase OB outcomes such as organizational commitment, relatively few empirical studies have been advanced to date. In a notable exception, Zou and his colleagues (2020) found that workplace spirituality mediated the relationship between spiritual leadership and subjective well-being as moderated by power distance orientation in a sample of Chinese registered nurses.

Common Methodological Approaches

Samples

When studying spirituality in the workplace, most OB scholars have used either student samples (e.g. Milliman et al., 2003) or organizational members and employees (e.g. Rego & Pina E Cunha, 2008). A variety of organizations and industries have been examined empirically in the OB-workplace spirituality research, including education (Hassan et al., 2016), food (Petchsawang & McLean, 2017), hospitality (Haldorai et al., 2020), and healthcare (Zou, Zeng, et al., 2020), to name a few. Furthermore, this research has sampled internationally using participants from China, Thailand, USA, India, and a great many others. Still, there is a clear focus in this literature on sampling from working adults engaged with their various organizations.

Methods

Geigle (2012) discusses many of the methodological tools used to empirically examine spirituality in the workplace. Though some researchers examine qualitative data in this area of research, most seem to examine quantitative data. Furthermore, cross-sectional data collection methods, such as surveys seem to be the commonly used form of data collection for OB scholars in this sub-field.

To measure spirituality in the workplace, most OB researchers use self-report scales often based on Ashmos and Duchon´s (2000) measure of this construct. This measure examines four dimensions that include, meaningful work, sense of community, alignment between individual and organizational values, and one's inner life (Ashmos & Duchon, 2000). It was not uncommon to see adaptations of this scale for use in a particular context of interest. For instance, Pawar (2016) used the meaningful work and sense of community aspects only in his study of workplace spirituality and employee well-being. Some have also used Ellison´s (1983) measure of spiritual well-being in their research or have used it as a starting point to develop their own measures of such constructs. Finally, the faith at work scale (FWS: Lynn et al., 2009) has seen increased development and use in this literature.

These data have then been analyzed using correlation, regression, structural equation modelling (SEM), necessary condition analysis (NCA; e.g. Garg, 2017), and cluster analyses, as well as other analytic methods. Because reliability and validity of scales are important and, at times, difficult to assess in the social sciences, most researchers have used some form of factor analysis to validate their tools (see Pawar, 2016, as an example). Still, the literature in the sub-field is riddled with correlational studies, when more advanced and robust data analytic tools, such as SEM, are available.

Future Directions

Throughout this chapter, we have discussed some of the opportunities for researchers to continue to develop this literature and grow our knowledge about spirituality in the workplace using OB outcomes and theories. We suggest that the OB-related literature and research of spirituality in the workplace is still pre-paradigm but is quickly developing.

As we have seen in many of the studies sampled here in this chapter, workplace and individual spirituality is often studied as an antecedent to other OB outcomes. Still, sometimes it is used as a mediator or a moderator in other important relationships (see Petchsawang & McLean, 2017, as an example). Interestingly, Pawar (2009) positioned workplace spirituality as an outcome variable to a variety of OB concepts, including transformational leadership, OCBs, organizational support, and procedural justice. This raises important questions about bidirectionality in this research. Does workplace spirituality lead to OCBs or are OCBs a sign of employees' "transcendence of self-interests" (Pawar, 2009, p. 252)? Although this may seem to muddy the water in terms of our conceptual understanding of these constructs, it provides great opportunities for development in this research. Studies can be done to investigate the causal direction and flow of these important constructs.

Furthermore, Kolodinsky, Giacalone and Jurkiewicz (2008) suggested possible interaction effects between personal and organizational spirituality. Whilst they found little evidence of such interactions on the outcomes they studied in their research (i.e., job involvement, organizational identification, organizational frustration, and work reward satisfaction), there remain a great number of other employee consequences that could be studied. It is possible that a construct like OCBs could be affected differently than those examined by the researchers. Furthermore, researchers could test an adult sample of employees instead of students, to see if their proposed relationship might hold in a different context with different people.

Sheep (2006) discussed another important issue within the literature on workplace spirituality, that of the, "co-existence of multiple ethical work climates either within or between stakeholder sub-groups" (Sheep, 2006, p. 358). This author explains that there is a disconnect between the goals for studying workplace spirituality. One goal is simply instrumental in its value (e.g. promoting workplace spirituality leads to increased performance) and the other has more individual value or societal-level value (e.g. personal development leads to a more fulfilled life). Sheep (2006) suggests that we proceed with our research on workplace spirituality in a multi-paradigmatic way. He explains that different assumptions and measurement tools must be used to investigate these issues. Therefore, future research on workplace spirituality should proceed using both quantitative and qualitative research. Most of the studies discussed in this chapter have been based on quantitative data, whereas this author would seem to encourage more qualitative data depending on a researcher's goals and paradigmatic alignment (Sheep, 2006).

Lastly, Houghton et al. (2016), as an update to Krishnakumar and Neck (2002), offer additional guidance by suggesting other OB outcomes that could be useful for future researchers to explore. For instance, turnover and intention to quit seem to have a negative relationship with workplace spirituality (e.g. Milliman et al., 2003), but more still needs to be done clarify how workplace spirituality functions in this context. Do only certain aspects of workplace spirituality drive this intended behavior? This is an empirical question that has not yet been answered in the research. In short, there are myriad other relationships within OB that could be tested using workplace and individual spirituality as antecedents, mediators, moderators, or as outcomes to important variables.

Conclusion

The study of spirituality in the field of OB is still in its early stages, providing ample opportunities for scholars to investigate, develop, and theory-build within this subfield. Methodologically, future researchers are encouraged to employ both quantitative and qualitative methods. The relationships found in the extant literature as reviewed in the current chapter suggest using OB to investigate workplace spirituality is both warranted and important. As the future unfolds, OB researchers should continue to engage workplace spirituality as a key framework for understanding, explaining, and shaping employee attitudes and behaviors in organizations.

References

Ahmad, A., & Omar, Z. (2014). Reducing deviant behavior through workplace spirituality and job satisfaction. *Asian Social Science*, *10*(19), 107–112. https://doi.org/10.5539/ass.v10n19p107

Ahmadi, S., Nami, Y., & Barvarz, R. (2014). The relationship between spirituality in the workplace and organizational citizenship behavior. *Procedia – Social and Behavioral Sciences*, *114*, 262–264. https://doi.org/10.1016/j.sbspro.2013.12.695

Altaf, A., & Awan, M. A. (2011). Moderating affect of workplace spirituality on the relationship of job overload and job satisfaction. *Journal of Business Ethics*, *104*(1), 93–99. https://doi.org/10.1007/s10551-011-0891-0

Antonakis, J., & Day, D. V. (2017). Leadership: Past, present, and future. In J. Antonakis & D. V. Day (Eds.), *The Nature of Leadership* (3rd ed., pp. 3–26). Sage.

Ashmos, D. P., & Duchon, D. (2000). Spirituality at work: A conceptualization and measure. *Journal of Management Inquiry*. https://doi.org/10.1177/105649260092008

Baptiste, N. R. (2008). Tightening the link between employee wellbeing at work and performance: A new dimension for HRM. *Management Decision*. https://doi.org/10.1108/00251740810854168

Belwalkar, S., Vohra, V., & Pandey, A. (2018). The relationship between workplace spirituality, job satisfaction and organizational citizenship behaviors – an empirical study. *Social Responsibility Journal*, *14*(2), 410–430. https://doi.org/10.1108/SRJ-05-2016-0096

Brotheridge, C. M., & Grandey, A. A. (2002). Emotional labor and burnout: Comparing two perspectives of "people work." *Journal of Vocational Behavior*. https://doi.org/10.1006/jvbe.2001.1815

Byrne, C. J., Morton, D. M., & Dahling, J. J. (2011). Spirituality, Religion, and Emotional Labor in the Workplace. In *Journal of Management, Spirituality and Religion*. https://doi.org/10.1080/14766086.2011.630169

Colquitt, J. A., Scott, B. A., & LePine, J. A. (2007). Trust, trustworthiness, and trust propensity: A meta-analytic test of their unique relationships with risk taking and job performance. *Journal of Applied Psychology*. https://doi.org/10.1037/0021-9010.92.4.909

Daniel, J. L. (2010). The effect of workplace spirituality on team effectiveness. *Journal of Management Development*, *29*(5), 442–456. https://doi.org/10.1108/02621711011039213

Daniel, J. L. (2015). Workplace spirituality and stress: Evidence from mexico and US. *Management Research Review*, *38*(1), 29–43. https://doi.org/10.1108/MRR-07-2013-0169

DiLiello, T. C., & Houghton, J. D. (2006). Maximizing organizational leadership capacity for the future: Toward a model of self-leadership, innovation and creativity. *Journal of Managerial Psychology*. https://doi.org/10.1108/02683940610663114

Duchon, D., & Plowman, D. A. (2005). Nurturing the spirit at work: Impact on work unit performance. *Leadership Quarterly*. https://doi.org/10.1016/j.leaqua.2005.07.008

Ellison, C. W. (1983). Spiritual well-being: Conceptualization and measurement. *Journal of Psychology and Theology*. https://doi.org/10.1177/009164718301100406

Fanggidae, R. (2017). The influence of spirituality workplace to motivation, job satisfaction and organizational commitment. *Global Journal of Business and Social Science Review*, *5*(3), 170–176.

Fawcett, S. E., Brau, J. C., Rhoads, G. K., Whitlark, D., & Fawcett, A. M. (2008). Spirituality and organizational culture: Cultivating the ABCs of an inspiring workplace. *International Journal of Public Administration*, *31*(4), 420–438. https://doi.org/10.1080/01900690701590819

Fry, L. W. (2003). Toward a theory of spiritual leadership. *Leadership Quarterly*. https://doi.org/10.1016/j.leaqua.2003.09.001

Ganster, D. C., & Schaubroeck, J. (1991). Work stress and employee health. *Journal of Management*, *17*(2), 235–271.

Garg, N. (2017). Workplace spirituality and employee well-being: An empirical exploration. *Journal of Human Values*, *23*(2), 129–147. https://doi.org/10.1177/0971685816689741

Geigle, D. (2012). Workplace spirituality empirical research: A literature review. *Business and Management Review*, *2*(10).

Gotsis, G., & Kortezi, Z. (2008). Philosophical foundations of workplace spirituality: A critical approach. *Journal of Business Ethics*, *78*(4), 575–600. https://doi.org/10.1007/s10551-007-9369-5

Gruys, M. L., & Sackett, P. R. (2003). Investigating the dimensionality of counterproductive work behavior. *International Journal of Selection and Assessment*, *11*(1), 30–42. https://doi.org/10.1111/1468-2389.00224

Gupta, M., Kumar, V., & Singh, M. (2014). Creating satisfied employees through workplace spirituality: A study of the private insurance sector in Punjab (India). *Journal of Business Ethics*, *122*(1), 79–88. https://doi.org/10.1007/s10551-013-1756-5

Haldorai, K., Kim, W. G., Chang, H. (Sean), & Li, J. (Justin). (2020). Workplace spirituality as a mediator between ethical climate and workplace deviant behavior. *International Journal of Hospitality Management*, *86*, 102372. https://doi.org/10.1016/j.ijhm.2019.102372

Hassan, M., Bin Nadeem, A., & Akhter, A. (2016). Impact of workplace spirituality on job satisfaction: Mediating effect of trust. *Cogent Business and Management*, *3*(1). https://doi.org/10.1080/23311975.2016.1189808

Houghton, J. D., Neck, C. P., & Krishnakumar, S. (2016). The what, why, and how of spirituality in the workplace revisited: A 14-year update and extension. *Journal of Management, Spirituality and Religion*, *13*(3), 177–205. https://doi.org/10.1080/14766086.2016.1185292

Jurkiewicz, C. L., & Giacalone, R. A. (2004). A values framework for measuring the impact of workplace spirituality on organizational performance. *Journal of Business Ethics*, *49*(2), 129–142. https://doi.org/10.1023/B:BUSI.0000015843.22195.b9

Kazemipour, F., Amin, S. M., & Pourseidi, B. (2012). Relationship between workplace spirituality and organizational behavior among nurses through mediation of affective organizational commitment. *Journal of Nursing Scholarship*, *44*(3), 302.

Kim, Y., & Seidlitz, L. (2002). Spirituality moderates the effect of stress on emotional and physical adjustment. *Personality and Individual Differences*. https://doi.org/10.1016/S0191-8869(01)00128-3

Kolodinsky, R. W., Giacalone, R. A., & Jurkiewicz, C. L. (2008). Workplace values and outcomes: Exploring personal, organizational, and interactive workplace spirituality. *Journal of Business Ethics*, *81*(2), 465–480. https://doi.org/10.1007/s10551-007-9507-0

Krishnakumar, S., & Neck, C. P. (2002). The "what", "why" and "how" of spirituality in the workplace. *Journal of Managerial Psychology*, *17*(3), 153–164. https://doi.org/10.1108/02683940210423060

Lee, S., Lovelace, K. J., & Manz, C. C. (2014). Serving with spirit: An integrative model of workplace spirituality within service organizations. *Journal of Management, Spirituality and Religion*. https://doi.org/10.1080/14766086.2013.801023

Lynn, M. L., Naughton, M. J., & VanderVeen, S. (2009). Faith at Work Scale (FWS): Justification, development, and validation of a measure of Judaeo-Christian religion in the workplace. *Journal of Business Ethics*, *85*(2), 227–243. https://doi.org/10.1007/s10551-008-9767-3

Meyer, J. P., & Alien, N. J. (1991). A three-component conceptualization of organizational commitment. *Human Resource Management Review*. https://doi.org/10.1016/1053-4822(91)90011-Z

Milliman, J., Czaplewski, A. J., & Ferguson, J. (2003). Workplace spirituality and employee work attitudes: An exploratory empirical assessment. *Journal of Organizational Change Management*, *16*(4), 426–447. https://doi.org/10.1108/09534810310484172

Milliman, J., Gatling, A., & Kim, J. (Sunny). (2018). The effect of workplace spirituality on hospitality employee engagement, intention to stay, and service delivery. *Journal of Hospitality and Tourism Management*, *35*, 56–65. https://doi.org/10.1016/j.jhtm.2018.03.002

Nasurdin, A. M., Nejati, M., & Mei, Y. K. (2013). Workplace spirituality and organizational citizenship behaviour: Exploring gender as a moderator. *South African Journal of Business Management*. https://doi.org/10.4102/sajbm.v44i1.148

Neck, C. P., Houghton, J. D., & Murray, E. L. (2020). *Management* (3rd ed.). Sage.

Noor, S., & Arif, S. (2011). Achieving job satisfaction VIA workplace spirituality: Pakistani doctors in focus. *European Journal of Social Sciences*, *19*(4), 507–515.

Nur, Y. A., & Organ, D. W. (2006). Selected organizational outcome correlates of spirituality in the workplace. *Psychological Reports*. https://doi.org/10.2466/PR0.98.1.111-120

Organ, D. W. (1988). *Organizational Citizenship Behaior: The Good Soldier Syndrome*. Lexington Books.

Pawar, B. S. (2009). Some of the recent organizational behavior concepts as precursors to workplace spirituality. *Journal of Business Ethics*, *88*(2), 245–261. https://doi.org/10.1007/s10551-008-9961-3

Pawar, B. S. (2016). Workplace spirituality and employee well-being: An empirical examination. *Employee Relations*, *38*(6), 975–994. https://doi.org/10.1108/ER-11-2015-0215

Petchsawang, P., & Duchon, D. (2012). Workplace spirituality, meditation, and work performance. *Journal of Management, Spirituality and Religion*, *9*(2), 189–208. https://doi.org/10.1080/14766086.2012.688623

Petchsawang, P., & McLean, G. N. (2017). Workplace spirituality, mindfulness meditation, and work engagement. *Journal of Management, Spirituality & Religion*, *14*(3), 216–244. https://doi.org/10.1080/14766086.2017.1291360

Porter, L. W., & Steers, R. M. (1977). Antecedents and outcomes of organizations' commitment. *Administrative Science Quarterly*, *22*(1), 46–56.

Ranasinghe, V. R., & Samarasinghe, S. M. (2019). The effect of workplace spirituality on innovative work behavior. *International Business Research*, *12*(12), 29. https://doi.org/10.5539/ibr.v12n12p29

Rego, A., & Pina E Cunha, M. (2008). Workplace spirituality and organizational commitment: An empirical study. *Journal of Organizational Change Management*, *21*(1), 53–75. https://doi.org/10.1108/09534810810847039

Rego, A., & Pina E Cunha, M., & Souto, S. (2007). Workplace spirituality, commitment, and self-reported individual performance: An Empirical Study. *Management Research*, *5*(3), 163–183. https://doi.org/10.2753/JMR1536-5433050303

Saks, A. M. (2011). Workplace spirituality and employee engagement. *Journal of Management, Spirituality & Religion*, *8*(4), 317–340. https://doi.org/10.1080/14766086.2011.630170

Schaufeli, W., Salanova, M., González-romá, V., & Bakker, A. (2002). The measurement of engagement and burnout: A two sample confirmatory factor analytic approach. *Journal of Happiness Studies*. https://doi.org/10.1023/A:1015630930326

Sheep, M. L. (2006). Nurturing the whole person: The ethics of workplace spirituality in a society of organizations. *Journal of Business Ethics*, *66*(4), 357–375. https://doi.org/10.1007/s10551-006-0014-5

Sprung, J. M., Sliter, M. T., & Jex, S. M. (2012). Spirituality as a moderator of the relationship between workplace aggression and employee outcomes. *Personality and Individual Differences*, *53*(7), 930–934. https://doi.org/10.1016/j.paid.2012.06.011

Tischler, L., Biberman, J., & Mckeage, R. (2002). Linking emotional intelligence, spirituality and workplace performance: Definitions, models and ideas for research. *Journal of Managerial Psychology*, *17*(3), 203–218. https://doi.org/10.1108/02683940210423114

van der Walt, F., & de Klerk, J. J. (2014). Workplace spirituality and job satisfaction. *International Review of Psychiatry*, *26*(3), 379–389. https://doi.org/10.3109/09540261.2014.908826

Vandenberghe, C. (2011). Workplace spirituality and organizational commitment: An integrative model. *Journal of Management, Spirituality & Religion*, *8*(3), 211–232. https://doi.org/10.1080/14766086.2011.599146

Walia, K. (2018). The relationship between employee wellbeing and spirituality at workplace. *The IUP Journal of Organizational Behavior, XVII*(3), 28.

Weiss, H. M. (2002). Deconstructing job satisfaction. Separating evaluations, beliefs and affective experiences. *Human Resource Management Review*. https://doi.org/10.1016/S1053-4822(02)00045-1

Zou, W. C., & Dahling, J. (2017). Workplace spirituality buffers the effects of emotional labour on employee well-being. *European Journal of Work and Organizational Psychology*. https://doi.org/10.1080/1359432X.2017.1358164

Zou, W. C., Houghton, J. D., & Li, J. J. (2020). Workplace spirituality as a means of enhancing service employee well-being through emotional labor strategy choice. *Current Psychology*. https://doi.org/10.1007/s12144-020-01069-5

Zou, W. C., Zeng, Y., Peng, Q., Xin, Y., Chen, J., & Houghton, J. D. (2020). The influence of spiritual leadership on the subjective well-being of Chinese registered nurses. *Journal of Nursing Management*. https://doi.org/10.1111/jonm.13106

Zsolnai, L., & Illes, K. (2017). Spiritually inspired creativity in business. *International Journal of Social Economics*, *44*(2), 195–205. https://doi.org/10.1108/IJSE-06-2015-0172

Dorothea Alewell

8 Spirituality at Work and Human Resource Management

Introduction

As most of the topics in this book are related to HRM in some way, the task to write this chapter on Spirituality at Work and HRM in general, but with limited length and without producing a lot of overlapping with other chapters of this book, poses some kind of a dilemma. I deal with this dilemma by concentrating on the employers' perspective and stances on spirituality at work – and thus opt for discussion of a narrow section of HRM only.

I start with some thoughts on definitions and conceptions of spirituality at work, and highlight the difference between individual spirituality at work and employer stances. I then go on with the categorisation of employers' stances and ask why and where spirituality at work is (or could be) relevant for managing human resources, thus asking for the conceptualization of spirituality at work within HRM. The next step is to discuss some neglected aspects on the path of impact between spirituality and HRM outcomes, and finish with some summarising thoughts on what would be nice to see in research on spirituality at work and HRM in 10 years.

Definitions and Conceptual Levels of Spirituality at Work

Up to now, there still are intensive and ongoing debates – "with no end in sight" (Miller & Ewest, 2015) – about the definition of workplace spirituality or – as I prefer to term it – spirituality at work and the related levels and fields (Hill et al., 2000; Miller & Ewest, 2015; Loo, 2017; Heliot et al., 2020; Pfaltzgraff-Carlson, 2020). Ongoing debates on terms, definitions and conceptualizations imply that we still do not agree on what to look for and at what levels and fields in spirituality at work. To get a clear view on the relationship between HRM and spirituality at work, three aspects have to be clarified: first the relation between religion and spirituality, second the definition of spirituality *at work* in relation to spirituality in general, and third the relation between individual spirituality and employers' stances.

I define spirituality on the individual level, as individual needs and traits, attitudes and behaviours related to (McGhee & Grant, 2017; Mitroff et al., 1999; Sheep, 2006)

https://doi.org/10.1515/9783110711349-008

- (the search for) transcendence and connectedness with a power higher than the self and/or a greater whole,
- connectedness with other human beings,
- meaning in life and
- personal development of the human being between birth and death as existential poles of life.

The attitudes and behaviours may or may not anchor in a specific religion, for example in defining the higher power as God (as in Christianity and Jewry) or as Allah (as in Islam). If so, spirituality is religious spirituality – and may be alternatively termed as religiosity. Religious spirituality unfolds on religion as a collective, often heavily institutionalised basis. However, there are other, nonreligious forms of spirituality without a specific religion as a basis. Thus, in this definition, spirituality is a generic term and covers a broad spectrum of forms – from purely religious spirituality to purely nonreligious spirituality and many mixed forms in between. A related definition of spirituality as a generic term – including irreligious, mixed and religious forms – is used by several authors (e.g. Hill et al., 2000; Krishnakumar & Neck, 2002; Miller & Ewest, 2015).

However, this definition of spirituality as a generic term including religious and nonreligious spirituality is not unanimously shared (Miller & Ewest, 2015), as many other authors sharply delineate spirituality and religiosity (Duffy, 2006; Joelle & Coelho, 2019; Mitroff et al., 1999; Petchsawang & Duchon, 2009; Zinnbauer & Pargament, 2005). So why use the term as a generic term in the context of HRM? Delineating spirituality and religiosity in analysing, describing and understanding the effects and antecedents of spirituality in theoretical and empirical research and in HRM in practice poses some severe – and in my view unsolvable – difficulties (Hill et al., 2000): Individuals may follow a specific religion in some but not in all aspects of their spirituality. For example, they may apply prayers of their specific religion and attend services of their church, but have normative ideas about living together with other persons that deviate strongly from official doctrine, and attend spiritual meditation classes without reference to religion, too. In the same vein, religious and spiritual behaviour and practices cannot be excised clearly, for example prayer as a religious practice and meditation as a spiritual practice: How would we, for instance, assign the Christian prayer of the heart, which is a form of religious meditation, to either spirituality or religiosity? How do we know what kind of spiritual meditation is performed during a prayer? Probably even religious individuals themselves will often not know exactly whether their attitudes and behaviour conform to official religious doctrine of a specific religious convention – and/or whether their subjective interpretation is already outside official doctrine or contains a broad mixture of elements from different traditions. And even within religious communities, there often are more than one official interpretations and strands of argumentation on questions of faith – so that even official personnel of the religious community will sometimes not be able to clearly separate spirituality (including all individual differences) and religiosity (with its strong collective and normative focus). If all this together is spiritual life, then a sharp separation between religious and spiritual practices, attitudes and behaviours applied by researchers, and put into practice in empirical research, is not possible.

Turning to the definition of *workplace* spirituality or spirituality *at work*, one may on the one hand ask whether and how individual spirituality gains importance at work and for work, and on the other hand, what stances employers develop with regard to individual spirituality at the workplace and within the organisation.

We should first note that individuals, and not the organisation, may have spiritual traits and spiritual needs and express their spirituality in many different attitudes and behaviours at work, at the workplace and within the organisation. For example, individuals can express their spirituality in meditation, yoga or prayer, in eating and drinking behaviour during fasten seasons or in general, in wearing religious clothes or jewellery, or in communications with colleagues, supervisors and clients that express spiritual or religious attitudes and convictions. Employees may interpret their work as individual calling or as important part of their search for meaning and community with other human beings. They may derive decisions in a transcendent context, develop their own personality in the work context as part of their personal spiritual journey or try to persuade and proselyte others with regard to their faith (Gebert et al., 2013; Loo, 2017; McGhee & Grant, 2017). In this perspective, I speak of spirituality at work when individuals bring their individual spirituality to work.

An aspect often not analysed is that even highly spiritual individuals may or may not bring spiritual needs to the workplace, deploy their spiritual traits at work or not, express their spirituality at the workplace or solely in other fields of life. I elaborate on this aspect later on.

Turning to employer stances on spirituality at work, let me first note that employees (with their individual spiritual traits and needs, and their desires and decisions to express spirituality at work in specific attitudes and behaviours) work in differing organisational frameworks and under differing stances and personnel policies of their employers – in general and with regard to spirituality, too. Some authors define workplace spirituality at this organisational level. For example, Ashmos and Duchon define spirituality at work as the recognition of the employer or decision makers in the firm that employees have an inner life of the soul and the spirit which is nourished by meaningful work and community with other persons (Ashmos & Duchon, 2000, p. 137). Krahnke et al. describe workplace spirituality as a framework of organisational values which are anchored in the culture of the firm and which support and facilitate experiences of transcendence and feelings of community with others resulting in wholeness and joy at work (Krahnke et al., 2003). Both teams of authors define spirituality at work on the side of the employer or firm, and as a positive stance with regard to religion. However, there is a wide array of possible employer stances with regard to spirituality at work – not only a positive or pro-spirituality one. Defining spirituality at the individual level and employer's stances with regard to individual spirituality or frameworks at the organisational level helps to clarify the levels of definition and to differentiate employer's stances.

Researchers have, to our best knowledge, not analysed the stances of employee representatives (as works councils or unions) with regard to workplace spirituality yet. However, there are already some conceptual approaches to classify employers' stances (Giacalone & Jurkiewicz, 2010; Mazumdar & Mazumdar, 2005; Mitroff et al., 1999; Ashfort & Pratt, 2010; Miller & Ewest, 2015; Tabesh & Jolly, 2019). These classifications are based on partially different criteria, some use more than one criterion at the same time and/or mix these together, sometimes in an unsystematic manner (Miller & Ewest, 2015; Alewell & Moll, 2021b). One of the newer classifications, developed out of a critique and advancement of the former classifications, is that by Miller and Ewest (2015). Using faith as generic term with the two sub-dimensions of religiosity (or religious spirituality) and spirituality (nonreligious spirituality), they classify employers as faith-avoiding, faith-safe, faith-friendly und faith-based (Miller & Ewest, 2015). Faith-based organisations have been founded with a spiritual goal or aim or in a specific faith tradition, often that of their founder. Faith-avoiding organisations try to keep the topic of faith out of their business as far as possible and stay neutral as much as possible. Faith-safe organisations concentrate on compliance with the law. They accommodate faith-based requests by employees as far as they have to according to law and jurisdiction, but not any further. Faith-friendly organisations secure compliance with the law and fair accommodation of requests, too, but moreover, they support and welcome free expression of individual spirituality at work. While this classification is the most advanced typology we know of and an important contribution to research on spirituality at work, there are still some problems – food for thought during the next ten years of research:

- An important focus of the classification is how positive (or embracing) or negative (or rejecting) the employer's stance with regard to faith (spirituality in our terms) is (Miller & Ewest, 2015). However, the classification does not allow an unambiguous classification of the degree of negativity or positivity of the employer's stance. For example, employers can be faith-safe and faith-avoiding at the same time. If the law of a country grants some right of religious freedom at work, employers can possibly not completely avoid the topic of spirituality at work. And even if their attitude is in essence faith-avoiding, employees may request religious freedom and force employers to deal with the topic, if not voluntarily, then by juridical pressure, and become eventually faith-safe in their decisions and practices, because courts may force them to. Alternatively, to take another example, faith-based organisations may also be faith-friendly, encouraging expression of spirituality by members of all faith traditions, but still being founded and imprinted in a specific tradition and employing a majority of employees following this tradition.

- The employer's stance with regard to religious spirituality and to nonreligious spirituality may be very different (Alewell & Moll, 2021b; Heliot et al., 2020) – potentially as a reaction to laws that regulate and protect aspects of religious freedom, but do often not refer to nonreligious spirituality.
- The antecedents and effects of the specific employers' stances and the related contextualisation in different fields of HRM are not a systematic part of the conceptualization yet. Decision makers in organisations may expect positive and/or negative effects of spirituality in different realms – for example, effects of nonreligious spirituality on health, stress management, creativity and innovation, or effects of religious spirituality on conflict, discrimination, diversity, and retention management. While Miller and Ewest explicitly integrate anti-discrimination and compliance with the law into their analysis (Miller & Ewest, 2015), the dominant contextualisation of employer's stances with regard to religious or non-religious faith in different HRM sub-functions still needs to be discussed. Alewell and Moll differentiate between three employers' perspectives focused on spiritual diversity, on spiritual needs and their satisfaction, and/or on spirituality as a capability enhancing performance, creativity and stress resilience. (Alewell & Moll, 2021b). Depending on the dominant perspective(s) and contextualisations, employers will expect different HRM effects and take on different stances. Overall, for empirical research, we need to enrich the classifications of employer stances.

Our own small-scale-qualitative-study for Germany hints – in accordance with expectations of researchers for the United States of America (Mitroff et al., 1999; Miller & Ewest, 2015) – at widespread faith-avoiding and faith-safe stances for religious spirituality, and much more positive stances for nonreligious spirituality (Alewell & Moll, 2019a, 2021a). However, up to now, our empirical knowledge about employers' stances with regard to spirituality at work, about antecedents of these attitudes and employers expectations on effects of spirituality at work is very small – and there is a lot research to do during the next ten years. Neither do we know in which HR fields (for example diversity management, recruiting, retention management, personnel development) employers expect effects and under which perspective they contextualise spirituality at work, nor do we know how positive or negative these specific expectations are. And finally, research is necessary if and how far these expectations coin the employer's stances – or if some other factors, for example cultural aspects in different countries, dominantly influence these. Summarising, to gain a viable and sound basis for quantitative empirical investigations, existing typologies on employers' (and works councils' and unions') stances with regard to spirituality at work and related instruments of measurement have to be developed (further), complemented by the differing perspectives and taking into account potential differences between religious and nonreligious spirituality.

Relevance of Spirituality for Different Fields of HRM

There has been and there still is a discussion on the relevance of spirituality at work for Human Resource Management or for organisations in general. At first sight, the impartial observer of practice may – in spite of the many research contributions – ask what spirituality and work have to do with each other – even more so in the face of a lively discussion on secularisation for many developed and industrialised societies (Pickel, 2011) his first blush impression may intensify if one perceives the near non-existence of this topic at an explicit level in many large firms. Spirituality and work may thus appear as two completely unrelated fields (Wicks, 2014; Mitroff et al., 1999; Gebert et al., 2013) where neutral or negative employer and employee stances on spirituality at work are to be expected for the majority of organisations and persons.

However, at second blush and from the perspective of the informed observer, the picture is much richer and more colourful, and there are good reasons to concern HRM and/or management in general with spirituality at work (Miller & Ewest, 2015). Neal states that there is a trend in modern HRM concepts to utilise more and more of employees' resources: First, there was an increasing utilisation of physical resources, then of mental-cognitive resources, and eventually psychic and emotional resources were deployed at work. Nowadays, the next and final step is to focus on spiritual resources, on the soul of employees (Neal, 2013). And some authors (Miller & Ewest, 2013, 2015; Alewell & Moll, 2019b) show that (and how) a stronger focus of HRM on spirituality connects smoothly to recent strands of discussion, for example to

- discussions on holistic work-life-balance, where up to now the "life" aspect was strongly defined by family and leisure time in a reductionist way, but may in future be supplemented by spirituality issues, too,
- discussions on diversity and anti-discrimination, with a strong focus on age, gender, nationality, ethnicity as criteria up to now, with a deeper focus on religion and spirituality yet to come into focus (Alewell & Rastetter, 2019),
- debates with regard to differences between preferences and needs of persons belonging to different generations, with typical spiritual needs for meaning and community being hypothesised as more important for younger generation cohorts (see Alewell & Brinck, 2017, with a critical stance to such hypotheses),
- ideas and thoughts regarding state of the art leadership, centring in theory around transformational and charismatic leadership styles – with the central concepts of charisma and visions being intensely linked to essentially spiritual topics (Oh & Wang, 2020), a tendency that some managers seek counselling and help in religious institutions (Alewell & Müller, 2019); and discussions on radical uncertainty and "*unverfügbarkeit*" as a linking pin between theology and management (Huppenbauer, 2008; Huppenbauer & Grand, 2007);
- compliance efforts of organisations which are up to now often concerned with data protection, corruption, labour and social security law and basic human

rights, but which could be focused on freedom of religious expression and protection against discrimination in all fields of HRM, too (Miller & Ewest, 2015; Meyer, 2020; Hoppe & Groffy, 2019),
- values, ethical behaviour and responsibility are discussed in the contexts of corporate governance, compliance and ethical leadership. Religion is one important source of such values and behaviours.
- Moreover, very topical, there is a new influence with the COVID-19 pandemic. Topics of illness, danger to life, death and dying with all the related deep emotions and existential importance to human beings sweep into the organisational context. And wherever existential questions come to the foreground, individual spiritual – and especially religious – resources may become more important than in the past to cope with such challenges.

Research and discussion of the past decades, thus, show that a deeper focus on employees' spirituality is already more or less implicitly prepared in many HRM strands of discussion and could tie in there, but has yet to unfold and become more explicit. And if so, spirituality at work may get into focus under very different topics, HRM themes and terms, for example, in the context of compliance, anti-discrimination and diversity, the context of performance, creativity and stress management, or of recruitment and retention management, in the context of leadership values, or of health management. It may also be contextualised and promoted under very different terms, aims and goals and with very different instruments and policies. Right now, our theoretical and empirical research and existing classifications of employer stances do not mirror this broad spectrum of HRM relevance, and for many countries, for example for Germany, there are no specific results yet, if, and how, with what aims and goals, expectations and contextualisation employers handle spirituality at work.

However, researchers already discuss some of these issues in separated strands of research, for example discrimination and diversity.

Religion and Spirituality, Discrimination and Diversity

In a partially separated strand of discussion, religion is discussed as a potential criterion of discrimination and diversity management (Bennett, 2008; Ghumman et al., 2013; Benefiel et al., 2014); for Germany (Hoevels, 2015), for France (Hennekam et al., 2018)). However, for example in Germany, religion is only seldom used as diversity criterion (for a conceptual overview, Alewell & Rastetter, 2019; for reasons, Gebert et al., 2013). Our knowledge on the situation in different countries is still small, and the call of (Benefiel et al., 2014, p. 184) for more research on religion as diversity criterion is still topical.

For example, in Germany, the freedom of (expression of) religion is guaranteed in the constitution, but so is the property right of the employer. Because both rights may conflict, courts have developed guidelines in their jurisdiction how to balance the employer's rights and the employee's right, which help to decide under which conditions the employer is allowed to forbid or restrict expressions of religion at work (Alewell & Rastetter, 2019; Meyer, 2020). There are juridical conflicts with regard to religious garment at work, religious signs as decoration in office rooms and the terms of use of rooms of silence (for an overview of German jurisdiction, Meyer, 2020; Hoppe & Groffy, 2019) but we do not know how often such conflicts arise outside juridical conflicts. Moreover, religious and nonreligious spirituality may show strong differences with regard to diversity and discrimination – as it is only religious spirituality that is protected by the constitution and the General Law on equality (AGG, Allgemeines Gleichstellungsgesetz).

In research, discrimination as a potential negative effect is contrasted with diversity which is often interpreted as positive due to resulting higher creativity and capability to innovate (Hanappi-Egger, 2015; Rastetter & Dreas, 2016). However, there are multiple diversity criteria, for example age, gender, nationality or ethnicity, and religion, and how organisations design their diversity management with regard to religion and spirituality and the combination of diversity criteria including religion is more or less open. As far as we know, for example in Germany, religion is a diversity criteria used only very seldom. There are a number of potential reasons (Alewell & Rastetter, 2019): Fear of conflict, of discrimination, and of division of employees into subgroups; lack of a sound data basis, and the assessment that religion may hamper organisational rationality and performance calculus (Alewell & Rastetter, 2019; Gebert et al., 2013). Which of these reasons are empirically valid and important remains to be analysed in the future.

In ten years, it would be nice to see a more thorough integration between the strands of discussion on discrimination and diversity and discrimination on the one hand and on spirituality at work on the other hand. This would help to better integrate the discussion on potential benefits and dangers, on positive and negative effects of spirituality at work, and give a better basis to look at the effects of both religious and nonreligious spirituality. Additionally, the longstanding research traditions and results of the sociology of religion could help to better understand the positive and negative effects religion may have in institutions and organisations (Alewell & Moll, 2021b).

Spirituality's Path to Impact

As already shown, spirituality can be conceptualised as an important individual resource or trait, or as an individual need. There is much research that analyses whether and how using the resource (or satisfying the need) affects individual and organisational HRM outcomes. For instance, researchers analyse the relation with performance (Garcia-Zamor, 2003; Duchon & Plowman, 2005; Houghton et al., 2016), job satisfaction (King & Williamson, 2005; Milliman et al., 2003; Garg, 2017; Mensah et al., 2019), social behavior (Pawar, 2009; Houghton et al., 2016), creativity (Krishnakumar & Neck, 2002; Ashmos & Duchon, 2000; Mitroff et al., 1999), initiative and engagement (Whitaker & Westerman, 2014), well-being of employees (Fry & SLOCUM, 2008), and further aspects as general life satisfaction, burn-out (Yang & Fry, 2018; Kolodinsky et al., 2008) or ethical behavior (Cavanagh, 1999; Garcia-Zamor, 2003; McGhee & Grant, 2017). Yet, effects are sometimes ambivalent and instable, (with regard to job satisfaction, see, for example, King & Williamson, 2005; Gupta et al., 2014; Milliman et al., 2003; Garg, 2017; Mensah et al., 2019; for ethical behaviour McGhee & Grant, 2017) and much more research on moderators and mediators of effects and other reasons for ambivalence of results is needed.

One important aspect could be, that many research studies on effects of individual spirituality at work (for an exception see (King & Williamson, 2005; Alewell et al., 2020) do not explicitly differentiate between spirituality as an attitude or need, between the desire of the employees to express spirituality at work and between the factual expression of spirituality at work in attitudes and behaviour. Often, authors (implicitly or explicitly) analyse spirituality as a personal trait or characteristic, which may have positive effects more or less irrespective of context.

However, individuals may have the wish or desire to satisfy their spiritual needs at the workplace or live this need in other fields of their life. If they have the wish to express spirituality at work, they may nevertheless decide against it or feel unable to do so, for example because they fear discrimination or perceive their working context as hostile against spiritual expression. In short, we need to differentiate between

- traits and/or needs,
- the desire to express their (religious or nonreligious) spirituality or satisfy their needs in the specific context of work, and
- the actual expression of their (religious or nonreligious) spirituality at work

(King & Williamson, 2005; Alewell et al., 2020; Heliot et al., 2020; Gebert et al., 2013 with reference to activation of religious identities).

These specific aspects of individual spirituality are important for different functions of HRM: For example, traits and needs may become especially relevant in recruiting and retention management, but the desire to express spiritual needs at work and the resulting behaviour and communication may be more important for developing and leading employees and for cooperation in diverse teams and conflict management. The actual expression may be especially relevant for teamwork as well as in diversity and conflict management. As a result, we need much more research on the full path – employees' spiritual needs or traits, their desire to express their religious and/or nonreligious spirituality in different contexts, their actual expression of spirituality at the workplace and the relationship between these individual-level-concepts, and on factors influencing them. For example, individual perceptions of employer stances or organisational culture with regard to individual spirituality at the workplace may influence the desire to express individual spirituality at the workplace or its factual expression. Perceived religious discrimination or cultural elements as the degree of laicism may influence these elements, coining the degree of publicity or privacy with regard to the expression of religion in a country. Additionally, the tasks and the structure of the workplace may be important – high autonomy and a high degree of decision latitude may open up a field of opportunities and responsibility in which individual spirituality unfolds as a need, or is perceived as especially useful resource. A related perspective is that in "weak situations" individuals may use their spirituality as an important resource, while in a "strong situation" with low autonomy and low discretion the effects of spirituality may be of much less relevance. It would be nice to see more results on these topics in ten years.

Future Development of the Field and Open Research Questions

Summarising some of the arguments with regard to the general development of the field into the future, I develop my personal "bucket list" of what progress to welcome in the near future based on the previous considerations:

- A quick development to more clarity in central terms as a basis for sound empirical research (see also section on terms and definitions above): more clarity in terms and definitions, and levels of analysis with regard to spirituality, religion and religiosity, with an integrative view on religious and nonreligious spirituality and a clear distinction between employer-sided and employee-sided concepts;
- a clear separation between individual spirituality as a trait and/or as a need, the desire to satisfy this need in the specific context of work and the actual expression of spirituality at work, and research on the path between these variables,
- a much more realistic view on spirituality at work in firms which takes spirituality seriously as a productive element with relevance for HRM in research and practice on the one hand – but does not close the eyes to the darker sides connected with spirituality on the other hand, for example, conflict and discrimination and related fears, negative stereotypes, potentials to invade the privacy of the employees, or the danger to exploit individual resources of the soul for purely economic reasons,
- a closer tying in with the sociology of religion, lifting up the treasures of these long standing research traditions to more intensive attention within the workplace spirituality movement, especially on positive and negative effects of religion

and religiosity in collectives and institutions (Pickel, 2011; Alewell & Moll, 2021a) – ideas and results that may be transferable to firms and organisations.
- Much more large-scale empirical research on spirituality at work for the different regions, countries or cultural spheres, and for all aspects and facets of the topic (see below for a list of more specific research questions).

Concretising these aspects in more detail and with higher specificity, there are some bundles of open research questions:
1. How frequent and how strong are individual religious and nonreligious spirituality in employees? Do specific groups of employees differ with respect to this question? Do employees desire to bring and express their individual (religious and/or nonreligious) spirituality to/at work? How frequent and how strong is this desire? Do employees prefer to keep their spirituality a private matter? Why or why not? Do we find more of a trait relation or more of a need-satisfaction relation? Is spirituality at work "relevant" with regard to the frequency employees bring and express their spirituality to/at work?
2. Does the desire to bring and/or express spirituality at work depend on the employees' experience of religious or spiritual discrimination? How frequent and intense and in which fields or for which groups of employees do such experiences exist? How do employers and works councils react, what do they do to prevent such discrimination?
3. How can we classify and conceptualise employers' stances with regard to spirituality at work in richer classifications? How can we classify and conceptualise employee representatives' (as works councils' or unions') stances with regard to spirituality at work? Which stances of employers, work councils and unions are prevalent under which conditions?
4. Which spirituality-at-work-related policies and instruments do employers implement, and what do they expect with regard to the effects of these instruments and policies? Do these policies and instruments differ between religious and nonreligious spirituality?
5. How do employers contextualise their stances and activities on spirituality at work and does this differ between religious and nonreligious spirituality – as a distinct HRM function, or integrated in other HRM sub-functions, for example, in diversity management, in organisational health management, in recruiting or retention management or as part of compliance activities? When and why (not) do employers deploy religious and/or nonreligious spirituality as a criterion of diversity management? What is the attitude of works councils?
6. Which relations between (religious and nonreligious) spirituality and HRM outcome variables exist in which countries and cultural spheres? Which moderators and mediators are active in these relations? Do these relations depend on the tasks performed and/or the level or autonomy of the employee?

References

Alewell, D., & Brinck, K. L. (2017). Generationsunterschiede in den Vorstellungen über „gute Arbeit" – Fakt oder Fiktion? In H. Surrey & V. Tiberius (Eds.), *Die Zukunft des Personalmanagements.Herausforderungen, Lösungsansätze und Gestaltungsoptionen* (1st ed., pp. 79–91). vdf Hochschulverlag AG an der ETH Zürich.

Alewell, D., Brinck, K. L., & Moll, T. (2020). (How) does religiousness impact on job satisfaction? *Unpublished Manuscript, Submitted for Review.*

Alewell, D., & Moll, T. (2019a). Religion, Religiosität und Spiritualität am Arbeitsplatz in deutschen Unternehmen. In D. Alewell & W. Matiaske (Eds.), *Standards guter Arbeit.Disziplinäre Positionen und interdisziplinäre Perspektiven* (1. Auflage, pp. 107–138). Nomos. https://doi.org/10.5771/9783845299310-107

Alewell, D., & Moll, T. (2019b). Religiosität und Spiritualität am Arbeitsplatz in deutschen Unternehmen. In D. Alewell & W. Matiaske (Eds.), *Standards guter Arbeit.Disziplinäre Positionen und interdisziplinäre Perspektiven* (1. Auflage, pp. 107–137). Nomos.

Alewell, D., & Moll, T. (2021a). An exploratory study of spirituality in German enterprises. *Management Revue. Socio Economic Studies, 1.*

Alewell, D., & Moll, T. (2021b). Employers' strategies on faith and spirituality at work: Conceptual thoughts for Germany. In E. Pio, R. Kilpatrick, & T. Pratt (Eds.), *Reimagining faith and management.The impact of faith in the workplace.*

Alewell, D., & Müller, B. (2019). Was suchen Führungskräfte im Kloster? In B. Feldbauer-Durstmüller, T. Wolf, & M. Neulinger OSB (Eds.), *Unternehmen und Klöster* (pp. 265–289). Springer Fachmedien Wiesbaden.

Alewell, D., & Rastetter, D. (2019). On the (ir)relevance of religion for human resource management and diversity management: A German perspective. *German Journal of Human Resource Management: Zeitschrift Für Personalforschung, 34*(1), 9–31. https://doi.org/10.1177/2397002219882399

Ashfort, B. E., & Pratt, M. G. (2010). Institutional spirituality: An oxymoron? In R. A. Giacalone & C. L. Jurkiewicz (Eds.), *Handbook of Workplace Spirituality and Organizational Performance* (2nd ed., pp. 44–58). Taylor and Francis Routledge.

Ashmos, D. P., & Duchon, D. (2000). Spirituality at work: A conceptualization and measure. *Journal of Management Inquiry, 9*(2), 134–145. https://doi.org/10.1177/105649260092008

Benefiel, M., Fry, L. W., & Geigle, D. (2014). Spirituality and religion in the workplace: History, theory, and research. *Psychology of Religion and Spirituality, 6*(3), 175–187.

Bennett, M. F. (2008). Religious and spiritual diversity in the workplace. In M. A. Moodian (Ed.), *Contemporary Leadership and Intercultural Competence: Exploring the Cross-Cultural Dynamics Within Organizations* (pp. 45–60). SAGE PUBN.

Cavanagh, G. F. (1999). Spirituality for managers: Context and critique. *Journal of Organizational Change Management, 12*(3), 186–199. https://doi.org/10.1108/09534819910273793

Duchon, D., & Plowman, D. A. (2005). Nurturing the spirit at work: Impact on work unit performance. *The Leadership Quarterly, 16*(5), 807–833. https://doi.org/10.1016/j.leaqua.2005.07.008

Duffy, R. D. (2006). Spirituality, religion, and career development: Current status and future directions. *The Career Development Quarterly, 55*(1), 52–63. https://doi.org/10.1002/j.2161-0045.2006.tb00004.x

Fry, L. W., & SLOCUM, J. W. (2008). Maximizing the triple bottom line through spiritual leadership. *Organizational Dynamics, 37*(1), 86–96. https://doi.org/10.1016/j.orgdyn.2007.11.004

Garcia-Zamor, J.-C. (2003). Workplace spirituality and organizational performance. *Public Administration Review, 63*(3), 355–363. https://doi.org/10.1111/1540-6210.00295

Garg, N. (2017). Workplace spirituality and employee well-being: An empirical exploration. *Journal of Human Values*, *23*(2), 129–147. https://doi.org/10.1177/0971685816689741

Gebert, D., Boerner, S., Kearney, E., King, J., Zhang, K., & Song, L. J. (2013). Expressing religious identities in the workplace. Analyzing a neglected diversity dimension. *Human Relations*, *67*(5), 543–563.

Ghumman, S., Ryan, A. M., Barclay, L. A., & Markel, K. S. (2013). Religious discrimination in the workplace: A review and examination of current and future trends. *Journal of Business and Psychology*, *28*(4), 439–454. https://doi.org/10.1007/s10869-013-9290-0

Giacalone, R. A., & Jurkiewicz, C. L. (2010). The science of workplace spirituality. In R. A. Giacalone & C. L. Jurkiewicz (Eds.), *Handbook of Workplace Spirituality and Organizational Performance* (2nd ed., pp. 3–26). Taylor and Francis Routledge.

Gupta, M., Kumar, V., & Singh, M. (2014). Creating Satisfied Employees Through Workplace Spirituality: A Study of the Private Insurance Sector in Punjab (India). *Journal of Business Ethics*, *122*(1), 79–88. https://doi.org/10.1007/s10551-013-1756-5

Hanappi-Egger, E. (2015). *Diversität, Diversifizierung und (Ent)Solidarisierung. Eine Standortbestimmung der Diversitätsforschung im deutschen Sprachraum*. Springer VS.

Heliot, Y., Gleibs, I. H., Coyle, Adrian, Rousseau, D. M., & Rojon, Celine. (2020). Religious identity in the workplace: A systematic review, research agenda, and practical implications. *Human Resource Management*, *59*, 153–173.

Hennekam, S., Peterson, J., Tahssain-Gay, L., & Dumazert, J.-P. (2018). Managing religious diversity in secular organizations in France. *Employee Relations*, *40*(5), 746–761. https://doi.org/10.1108/ER-06-2017-0142

Hill, P. C., Pargament, K. I., Hood, R. W. Jr., MCullough, M. E., Swyers, J. P., Larson, D. B., & Zinnbauer, B. J. (2000). Conceptualizing religion and spirituality: Points of commonality, points of departure. *Journal for the Theory of Social Behaviour*, *30*(1), 51–77.

Hoevels, N. (2015). Muslime in der aktuellen Rechtsprechung zum Arbeitsrecht. In M. Khalfaoui & M. Möhring-Hesse (Eds.), *Eine Arbeitsgesellschaft – Auch für Muslime.Interdisziplinäre und interreligiöse Beiträge zur Ewerbsarbeit* (pp. 83–93). Waxmann Verlag.

Hoppe, C., & Groffy, G. (2019). "Solange IV"? Religiöse Symbole am Arbeitsplatz im Spiegel der deutschen Rechtsprechung und des EuGH. *Arbeitsrecht Aktuell*, 211–213.

Houghton, J. D., Neck, C. P., & Krishnakumar, S. (2016). The what, why, and how of spirituality in the workplace revisited: A 14-year update and extension. *Journal of Management, Spirituality & Religion*, *13*(3), 177–205. https://doi.org/10.1080/14766086.2016.1185292

Huppenbauer, M. (2008). *Handeln im Kontext von Unverfügbarkeit. Probleme des Wissenstransfers zwischen Management und Theologie.*

Huppenbauer, M., & Grand, S. (2007). Managementforschung und theologische Ethik im Diskurs: Beobachtungen und Reflexionen aus der "Trading Zone" von Management und Religion. *Zeitschrift Für Evangelische Ethik*, *51*(2), 129–145.

Joelle, M., & Coelho, A. M. (2019). The impact of spirituality at work on workers' attitudes and individual performance. *The International Journal of Human Resource Management*, *30*(7), 1111–1135. https://doi.org/10.1080/09585192.2017.1314312

King, J. E., & Williamson, I. O. (2005). Workplace Religious Expression, Religiosity and Job Satisfaction: Clarifying a Relationship. *Journal of Management, Spirituality & Religion*, *2*(2), 173–198. https://doi.org/10.1080/14766080509518579

Kolodinsky, R. W., Giacalone, R. A., & Jurkiewicz, C. L. (2008). Workplace values and outcomes: Exploring personal, organizational, and interactive workplace spirituality. *Journal of Business Ethics*, *81*(2), 465–480. https://doi.org/10.1007/s10551-007-9507-0

Krahnke, K., Giacalone, R. A., & Jurkiewicz, C. L. (2003). Point-counterpoint: Measuring workplace spirituality. *Journal of Organizational Change Management, 16*(4), 396–405. https://doi.org/10.1108/09534810310484154

Krishnakumar, S., & Neck, C. P. (2002). The "what", "why" and "how" of spirituality in the workplace. *Journal of Managerial Psychology, 17*(3), 153–164. https://doi.org/10.1108/02683940210423060

Loo, M. K. L. (2017). Spirituality in the workplace: Practices, challenges, and recommendations. *Journal of Psychology and Theology, 45*(3), 182–204. https://doi.org/10.1177/009164711704500303

Mazumdar, S., & Mazumdar, S. (2005). How Organizations Interface with Religion: A Typology. *Journal of Management, Spirituality & Religion, 2*(2), 199–220. https://doi.org/10.1080/14766080509518580

McGhee, P., & Grant, P. (2017). The transcendent influence of spirituality on ethical action in organizations. *Journal of Management, Spirituality & Religion, 14*(2), 160–178. https://doi.org/10.1080/14766086.2016.1268539

Mensah, H. K., Asiamah, N., & Azinga, S. A. (2019). The association between nurses' religiousness and job satisfaction. *International Journal of Ethics and Systems, 35*(3), 426–443. https://doi.org/10.1108/IJOES-04-2018-0061

Meyer, C. (2020). Das Kopftuch am Arbeitsplatz und unternehmerische Neutralitätskonzepte: Wie verändert europäisches Gleichbehandlungsrecht den Umgang mit der Religionsfreiheit in Arbeitsverhältnissen zwischen Privaten? *Europäische Zeitschrift Für Arbeitsrecht*, 206–223.

Miller, D. W., & Ewest, T. (2013). The Present State of Workplace Spirituality: A Literature Review Considering Context, Theory, and Measurement/Assessment. *Journal of Religious & Theological Information, 12*(1–2), 29–54. https://doi.org/10.1080/10477845.2013.800776

Miller, D. W., & Ewest, T. (2015). A new framework for analyzing organizational workplace religion and spirituality. *Journal of Management, Spirituality & Religion, 12*(4), 305–328. https://doi.org/10.1080/14766086.2015.1054864

Milliman, J., Czaplewski, A. J., & Ferguson, J. %J J. of organizational change management. (2003). *Workplace spirituality and employee work attitudes: An exploratory empirical assessment. 16*(4), 426–447.

Mitroff, I. I., Mitroff, I., & Denton, E. A. (1999). *A spiritual audit of corporate America: A hard look at spirituality, religion, and values in the workplace* (First Edition, Vol. 140). Jossey-Bass.

Neal, J. (2013). Introduction. In J. Neal (Ed.), *Handbook of Faith and Spirituality in the Workplace. Emerging Research and Practice* (pp. 3–18). Springer.

Oh, J., & Wang, J. (2020). Spiritual leadership: Current status and Agenda for future research and practice. *Journal of Management, Spirituality & Religion, 17*(3), 223–248. https://doi.org/10.1080/14766086.2020.1728568

Pawar, B. S. (2009). Individual spirituality, workplace spirituality and work attitudes: An empirical test of direct and interaction effects. *Leadership & Organization Development Journal, 30*(8), 759–777. https://doi.org/10.1108/01437730911003911

Petchsawang, P., & Duchon, D. (2009). Measuring workplace spirituality in an Asian context. *Human Resource Development International, 12*(4), 459–468. https://doi.org/10.1080/13678860903135912

Pfaltzgraff-Carlson, R. (2020). Reconceptualizing organizational spirituality: Theological roots for scientific and practical fruits. *Journal of Management, Spirituality & Religion, 17*(3), 249–269. https://doi.org/10.1080/14766086.2020.1762712

Pickel, V. (2011). *Religionssoziologie. Eine Einführung*. Springer VS.

Rastetter, D., & Dreas, S. A. (2016). Diversity Management als eine betriebliche Strategie. In K. Fereidooni & A. P. Zeoli (Eds.), *Managing Diversity. Die diversitätsbewusste Ausrichtung des Bildungs- und Kulturwesens, der Wirtschaft und Verwaltung* (pp. 319–339). Springer VS (Research).

Sheep, M. L. (2006). Nurturing the Whole Person: The Ethics of Workplace Spirituality in a Society of Organizations. *Journal of Business Ethics*, *66*(4), 357–375. https://doi.org/10.1007/s10551-006-0014-5

Tabesh, P., & Jolly, P. M. (2019). Beyond the law: Processes underlying religious accommodation decisions. *Management Decision*, *57*(5), 1254–1266. https://doi.org/10.1108/MD-11-2017-1087

Whitaker, B. G., & Westerman, J. W. (2014). Linking spirituality and values to personal initiative through psychological empowerment. *Journal of Management, Spirituality & Religion*, *11*(3), 269–291. https://doi.org/10.1080/14766086.2014.905221

Wicks, A. (2014). Stakeholder theory and spirituality. *Journal of Management, Spirituality & Religion*, *11*(4), 294–306. https://doi.org/10.1080/14766086.2014.917984

Yang, M., & Fry, L. W. (2018). The role of spiritual leadership in reducing healthcare worker burnout. *Journal of Management, Spirituality & Religion*, *15*(4), 305–324. https://doi.org/10.1080/14766086.2018.1482562

Zinnbauer, B. J., & Pargament, K. I. (2005). Religiousness and Spirituality. In R. F. Paloutzian & C. L. Park (Eds.), *Handbook of the psychology of religion and spirituality* (pp. 21–42). Guilford Press.

John James Cater, Veland Ramadani, Leo-Paul Dana

9 Family Business and Work Spirituality and Religion

Introduction

The purpose of this chapter is to review the influences of spirituality and religious values within the field of family business studies. We reviewed 26 articles, exploring the exemplary contributions that exist within this emerging research area. We noted outstanding achievements in this sub-field from 2007 to 2020. Then, we discuss the current standing of the research area and provide a foundation for further research.

Family businesses are the most common form of business organization throughout the world today (Astrachan & Shanker, 2003; Kellermanns, 2013). In most countries worldwide, family businesses produce over half of the GDP, provide over half of the private sector jobs, and comprise over 70 percent of all business entities (European Family Businesses, 2020). The field of spirituality and religion has experienced tremendous growth in interest among management scholars since the 1980s (Tracey, 2012). Entrepreneurship scholars have long recognized the significance of religious values as drivers of new venture creation (Balog et al., 2014; Dana, 2009). Within the narrower field of family business studies, only recently have scholars noted the close connection between family business and the development of spirituality and religion in the work-place (Neal & Vallejo, 2008). The purpose of this chapter is to review the influence of spirituality and religion within the field of family business studies.

Spirituality and religious values contribute to the building of ethical values within family firms (Astrachan et al., 2020). To provide clarity for this review, we offer definitions for the terms: "spirituality," "religion," and "family business." The management literature has offered many definitions of spirituality. Still, the following is succinct: spirituality refers to a relationship with a higher power or being that affects the intentions and actions we take in this world and is individualized (Fry, 2003). In this sense, spirituality transcends the tenets and principles of any one religion; moreover, religion is institutionalized and is associated with specific doctrine, shared beliefs, and agreed-upon practices (Madison & Kellermanns, 2013). The founders of family firms may seek to instill values embedded in their religion (Abdelgawad & Zahra, 2020; Kidwell et al., 2012). In a broader sense, religion may be viewed as a depository of values. The values disseminated by a religion may influence beliefs that affect business practices throughout a society, even among those who may not adhere to the religion (Dana, 2009). A working definition of family firm is a "business governed and managed to shape and pursue the vision of the

https://doi.org/10.1515/9783110711349-009

business held by a dominant coalition controlled by members of the same family or a small number of families in a manner that is potentially sustainable across generations of the family or families" (Chua et al., 1999, p. 25).

Review Method

This review focused on relevant empirical articles that examined the interrelationships of family business, spirituality, and religious values from 2007 to 2020. We begin the review with seminal works by Dana (2007) on religious values in family firms and Neal and Vallejo(2008)

on spirituality in family businesses and to continue the review to the present. We searched extensively across the literature with numerous targeted searches for "family firm" or "family business" and "religion" and "spirituality." Notably, we found that the three journals exclusively dedicated to family business studies (*Family Business Review, Journal of Family Business Strategy,* and *Journal of Family Business Management*) were just beginning to recognize the importance of spirituality and religion to the study of family business. These journals yielded only two articles for this review. Two special issues dedicated to spirituality and religion in family firms, one by the *Journal of Management, Spirituality & Religion* in 2013, and the other by the *Journal of Business Ethics* in 2020, provided many of the articles in this review. In total, eleven articles on family business and spirituality or religion appeared in the *Journal of Business Ethics*, seven in the *Journal of Management, Spirituality & Religion*, one in *Enterprises et Histoire*, one in *Family Busines Review*, one in the *Journal of Family Business Management*, one in the *Journal of Corporate Finance*, one in the *Journal of Enterprising Communities: People and Places in the Global Economy*, one in the *Journal of Biblical Integration in Business*, and one in *Quality and Quantity*. In Table 9.1, we display some key descriptive characteristics of the studies included in the review. We specify three major article types, half a dozen investigative methods, and various sample sizes. The leading construct examined was religious values, with studies of spirituality representing the second construct. All of the major religions in the world were included either in single denomination or multiple religion studies. Articles focused on the effect of religious values in family firms on philanthropic activities, firm performance, leadership, and commitment to the organization. Studies of spiritual values in family firms considered forms of firm commitment and business performance.

In Table 9.2, we provide a summary of each selected article and include the authors' names and year of publication. We explain the research focus, study design, and key findings for each of the 26 articles included in the study. In the remainder of this chapter, we study the five articles on spirituality in family firms, analyze the 21 articles on religion in family firms, and then provide insights for future research.

Table 9.1: Key characteristics of studies.

Article type	Qualitative	13
	Quantitative	8
	Conceptual	5
Investigative method	Survey	5
	Archival/Database	3
	Interview	1
	Case study	11
	Ethnography	1
	Conceptual	5
Sample size	Less than 100	13
	Greater than 100	8
	Not specified	5
Construct examined	Religion	21
	Spirituality	5
Specific denomination	Not specified	8
	Multiple religions identified	6
	Christian	8
	Muslim	3
	Hindu	1
Research focus	Spiritual values	-> FF commitment, OCBs, trust, performance
	Religious values	-> F.F. performance, business outcomes (profit)
	Religious values	-> F.F. values, leadership, political involvement, strategic renewal, goals
	Religious values	-> FF commitment
	Religious values	-> FF CSR, philanthropy, stewardship

Table 9.2: Summary of the research on family business and spirituality and family business and religion (in chronological order).

Article	Research Focus	Study Design	Key Findings
Neal & Vallejo (2008)	Family firm values > Spiritual values	Qualitative – Two case studies of family firms, one in Spain, one in Canada, becoming Spiritual firms Religion was not specified	Family firms possess cultural characteristics that stimulate the development of spirituality in the work-place more than those of non-family firms.
Madison & Kellermanns (2013)	Spiritual values > Organizational citizenship behaviors	Quantitative – Survey of 139 US family firm leaders (69 dyads) Religion was not specified	Strong support for the relationship between spiritual leadership and OCB. This relationship becomes stronger when the follower is a family member
Mitchell, Robinson, Marin, Lee, & Randolph (2013)	Spiritual values > Firm governance and performance	Conceptual – U.S. family firms Religion was not specified	The extent to which a firm develops and maintains work-place spirituality can have both positive and negative consequences on firm governance and performance.
Dede & Ayranci (2014)	Spiritual values > altruism and trust	Quantitative – 250 surveys in family firms in Turkey (Muslim)	Spiritual leadership is suitable for family businesses because intra-family altruism and trust can be related to spiritual leadership.
Tabor, Madison, Marler, & Kellermanns (2020)	Spiritual values > organizational commitment	Quantitative – A Survey of 231 US respondents matched within 77 family firms; religion was not specified.	Organizational commitment is enhanced by spiritual leadership. While spiritual leadership positively affects family employees, it negatively affects non-family employees experiencing high work-family conflict.
Dana (2007)	Religious values > Family business performance	Qualitative – Ethnography of Amish family farm in Lancaster County, PA in the U.S. A Protestant Christian Sect	The primary motive of family firm self-employment among the Amish is neither profit nor prestige, but rather the maintenance of cultural values, separately from mainstream society, to emphasize humility over pride.

Table 9.2 (continued)

Article	Research Focus	Study Design	Key Findings
Discua Cruz (2013)	Religious values > Firm performance	Conceptual – United Kingdom, Christian	Agency problems are more likely to be minimized when principal (owners) and agents (managers, employees) share the Christian faith. Compared to secular counterparts, stewardship principles in Christian family businesses are more likely to be reflected in communal activity.
Fang, Randolph, Chrisman, & Barnett (2013)	Religious values > Firm performance	Conceptual – US family firms, religion not specified	Religiosity may influence a family firm's relationship with its stakeholders and its economic and non-economic performance.
Litz (2013)	Family firm values < Religious values	Qualitative – One case study of a U.S. family firm (Nominal Catholic) in organized crime	Family organizations can possess specific characteristics that discourage religious values. Religious (Christian)conversion can lead to an organizational exit for a family member.
Paterson, Specht, & Duchon (2013)	Religious values > Family values in the family business	Qualitative – 12 interviews with U.S. family firms (5 different religious affiliations)	Religious beliefs are an essential factor in determining family values, which are reflected in the family business.
Sorenson (2013)	Religious values > Family business values	Qualitative – One case study of a U.S. family firm	A theoretical model on how moral and social values based on Catholic beliefs become embedded in the family business.
Yusof, Nor, & Hoopes (2014)	Religious values > CSR	Qualitative-One case study of an Islamic Malaysian family firm	By maintaining virtuous habits based on Islamic principles, the family business has avoided the equally unrealistic notions that CSR must be entirely selfless or entirely strategic to be legitimate.

Table 9.2 (continued)

Article	Research Focus	Study Design	Key Findings
Jiang, Jiang, Kim, & Zhang (2015)	Religious values > Lower risk-taking	Quantitative- 4159 surveys of database Chinese family firms, including Buddhists, Taoists, Christians, Muslims, and those with "no beliefs."	Firms with religious founders have lower leverage. Religious entrepreneurs have less risk than other firms. Firms founded by adherents of Western religions have low risk.
Ramadani, Dana, Ratten, & Tahiri (2015)	Religious values > Firm performance	Conceptual-Islamic business success	Islamic principles encourage entrepreneurship and business and ethics
Du (2017)	Religious values > Political involvement, but are moderated by corporate philanthropy	Quantitative – 2779 surveys of database Chinese family firms. Buddhists, Taoists, Protestants, Catholics, and Muslims	Religious belief is significantly positively associated with the likelihood of political involvement. Corporate philanthropy attenuates the positive association between religious belief and political involvement.
Wong, Smith, & Popp (2018)	Religious values > Firm performance	Qualitative – One case study of a British Christian family firm	Evangelical Protestant faith allowed the family firm founded in 1858 to engage successfully in international trade in the British Empire until 2016.
Abdelgawad & Zahra (2020)	Religious values > Strategic renewal	Conceptual – Religion is not specified.	Religious identity, insular or pluralistic, determines family firms' spiritual capital, influencing strategic renewal activities such as conflict resolution and resource allocation.
Barbera, Shi, Agarwal, & Edwards (2020)	Religious values > family cohesion and positive business outcomes	Qualitative – One case study of a U.S. Catholic family firm	Religious values facilitated a closer, more cohesive family unit and were manifested in the leadership style, which led to positive outcomes for the business.

Table 9.2 (continued)

Article	Research Focus	Study Design	Key Findings
Bhatnagar, Sharma, & Ramachandran (2020)	Religious values > family firm philanthropy	Qualitative – 14 case studies of Indian Hindu family firms	Two fundamental spiritual beliefs of dharma (duty towards society) and karma (right to action without expectation of rewards) instill a duty-bound giving culture in Hindus. However, the strength of each belief varies in controlling families.
Carradus, Zozimo, & Discua Cruz (2020)	Religious values > organizational stewardship	Qualitative – Six autobiographies of US Christian family business leaders.	Stewardship originates from the founder/leader's relationship with God, shaping the development and diffusion of stewardship based on faith-led organizational practices in family businesses.
Dieleman & Koning (2020)	Religious values > Ethical values -the identity of the family firm	Qualitative – One case study of a Malaysian Christian family business leader	Family business leaders can instill new religious values in family firms, which were not part of the founding principles. The values underpinning identity work arise from multiple sources, including religion.
Fathallah, Sidani, & Khalil (2020)	Religious values > Ethical behaviors	Qualitative – 13 case studies of Lebanese family firms (six Muslim and seven Christian;	Recognizes the influence of religious beliefs on the ethical behaviors of family firms. CFF and MFF drew differently on religion and family logic. CFF drew relatively more strongly on the family logic, while MFF drew more strongly on religion.

Table 9.2 (continued)

Article	Research Focus	Study Design	Key Findings
Kavas, Jarzabkowski, & Nigam (2020)	Religious values > Business activities	Qualitative – Two case studies of Turkish Muslim family firms	Religious values influence business activities through three mechanisms: (1) the family imports religious practices as business practices; (2) the family adheres to religious values as a rationale for business actions; and (3) religious values define business taboos (the evil eye) to avoid violating them.
Maung, Miller, Tang, & Xu (2020)	Religious values > CSR Charitable donations	Quantitative – Archival Survey data of 269 US family firm CEOs, Primarily Protestant Christians, some Jewish and some Hindu CEOs	Financial markets react more positively to charitable initiatives from firms with religion-declared CEOs, but only if these are family businesses.
Pieper, Williams, Manley, & Matthews (2020)	Religious values > family business goals	Quantitative – Survey of 105 private US family firms, religion not specified	Religiosity has a stronger positive effect on long-term goal orientation than on short-term. Religiosity has a positive impact on short-term and long-term goal orientation, but the relationship is stronger for long-term goal orientation.
Von Bieberstein, Crede, Essl, & Hack (2020)	Family membership and religious affiliation > stakeholder honesty	Quantitative – Experimental approach with a lying game and e survey of 600 Swiss respondents, religion was not specified	Stakeholders behave more honestly toward family managers compared to non-family managers. This effect is reinforced if the family manager is presented as religious.

Review of Research on Family Business and Work Spirituality

In their seminal article on work-place spirituality in family firms, Neal and Vallejo (2008) described eight internal characteristics of spiritual businesses, including work is a calling, enlightened leaders, spiritual teams, virtues and values-driven, accountability for values, creative, sense of family/community, focus on service, and long-term orientation. Thus, the authors practically identify the appearance of spirituality in family firms. In the second of the two exemplary case studies provided by Neal and Vallejo (2008), the owners sanctioned prayer before management and board meetings. Therefore, religious activity is present, but not just in one dominant faith, and all faiths are tolerated. The starting point for the concept of work-place spirituality is that family firms are an ideal setting, and the qualities that set family firms apart from other businesses match the eight internal characteristics of spiritual companies.

Spiritual leadership is considered a sub-field of study within the broader context of work-place spirituality. Fry (2003) defined spiritual leadership as the values, attitudes, and behaviors needed to motivate oneself and others to gain a sense of spiritual survival through calling and membership. Further, Fry (2003) identified transcendence through a vocational calling and a need for social connection or membership as essential to work-place spirituality.

In a conceptual article, Mitchell et al. (2013) developed a model describing how spirituality within family firms may affect stakeholder salience. The remaining three articles included in this study on family business and work spirituality quantitatively examined different aspects of spiritual leadership and outcomes for family members and employees. In a survey study of 77 dyads of leaders and employees within U.S. family firms, Madison and Kellermanns (2013) linked spiritual leadership with organizational citizenship behavior. Spiritual leadership was found to be effective for family member employees, but not for non-family employees. Dede and Ayranci (2014) conducted a survey study of 250 respondent family firms in Turkey and found support for a relationship between top managers' spiritual leadership and intra-family altruism and trust. In a survey of U.S. family firms, Tabor et al. (2020) found that spiritual leadership enhances employee commitment to the family firm and alleviates the negative effect of work-family conflict. To date, the literature confirms the efficacy of spiritual leadership in family firms.

Review of Research on Family Business and Religion

A common thread of altruistic love and regard for the interests of others joins workplace spirituality and religious values within family businesses (Fry, 2003). We now examine studies focused on religious values and family firms. In this review of the first 13 years of family business studies featuring religious values, we include 12 qualitative studies, five quantitative studies, and four conceptual articles. Scholars have largely turned to qualitative methods, often employing single case studies (Barbera et al., 2020; Dana, 2007; Dieleman & Koning, 2020; Litz, 2013; Sorenson,

2013; Wong et al., 2018; Yusof et al., 2014) in an attempt to understand the rich complexity of the combination of religion and family firms.

Dana (2007) produced a groundbreaking ethnographic study on the religious values of the Amish people in Lancaster County, Pennsylvania, U.S., and their effect on their family businesses. The Amish are a Protestant Christian sect that holds the values of ascetism, frugality, thrift, hard work, humility, and a desire for separation from mainstream society. Because of their strongly held religious values, the Amish reject modernization and technological developments, such as electricity and automobiles. However, because of their tremendous Protestant work ethic (Weber, 1904, 1958), Amish family farms are very productive, and their family businesses profitable. Thus, religious values provided the basis for family business values and family business success.

Following Dana (2007), most studies in this review reported that religious values supplied the moral principles of the family business. In a qualitative study of two Islamic family businesses in Turkey, Kavas et al. (2020) found that religious values provided a dominant meaning system in conducting business activities. In a qualitative comparison of religious groups, Fathallah et al. (2020) found that Christian family firms relied more on family logic. In contrast, Muslim family firms drew more on religious logic in forming ethical beliefs.

In further qualitative studies, Paterson et al. (2013) and Sorenson (2013) reported that Christian religious values held by family leaders formed the basis for family business values and that these values led to family cohesion (Barbera et al., 2020). Wong et al. (2018) reported the case of a British Christian family firm that engaged in international trade for over 150 years, crediting its success to the continued evangelical faith of the family throughout the generations of ownership. In the case of a Malaysian family firm, Dieleman and Koning (2020) found that successors may instill new religious values that were not held by the founder. Here, the founder, Yeoh Tiong Lay, was not religious and subscribed to Confucian cultural values, but the son, Francis Yeoh, credited the tremendous success of the company to the blessings of God and viewed Jesus Christ as his advisor.

Several articles noted positive associations of religious values with philanthropy, corporate social responsibility (CSR), and positive outcomes for family firms. In a Malaysian study, Yusof et al. (2014) found that family businesses that maintain virtuous Islamic religious values will be correctly perceived in their CSR initiatives as neither selfish nor purely strategic. In a study of 14 Indian Hindu family firms, Bhatnagar et al. (2020) reported two fundamental spiritual beliefs of dharma (duty towards society) and karma (right to action without expectation of rewards) instill a duty-bound giving culture. Carradus et al. (2020) traced the development of organizational stewardship to the Christian religious values of U.S. family business leaders.

In this review, there was one notable exception to the supply of religious values to the moral principles of the family business. In one study, family values opposed religious values. Illustrating the power of religious values, Litz (2013) provides an engaging and poignant story of the Christian conversion of Michael Franzese of the Colombo Family of organized crime. In this situation, if we accept the reported facts, Michael translated the nominal Christian values of the family into a deep conviction symbolized by believer's baptism, which resulted in his exit from the family business.

Quantitative Studies

While less prevalent in the literature than qualitative research, scholars have produced quantitative studies, finding religious values as a positive and beneficial variable for family firms. In two studies based in China, involving Buddhist, Taoist, Christian, and Muslim family firms, religious values have been associated with positive external engagement in political activity (Jiang et al., 2015) and positive internal benefits, such as lower leverage (Du, 2017). In two studies based on U.S. family firms, religious values also produced positive effects. When family firm CEOs expressed religious values, financial markets reacted positively to the family business' charitable initiatives (Maung et al., 2020). Then, religious values were found to positively affect long-term goal orientation for family firms (Pieper et al., 2020). Finally, in a Swiss study, the behavior of stakeholders was most honest towards family managers, who were also presented as religious (von Bieberstein et al., 2020).

Conceptual Studies

Two articles present the beliefs of the two largest religions globally, Christianity and Islam, respectively. Discua Cruz (2013) explored the principles of Christianity and their application to family firms. The author described Biblical values regarding responsibility towards the family, conflict resolution, and the significance of succession, which is a constant theme from Genesis to Jesus Christ in scripture. Overall, Discua Cruz (2013) laid a foundation for Christian leadership in family firms. Ramadani et al. (2015) describe the influence of Islam on business ownership and management, drawing on the tenets of the Qur'an. The five pillars of Islam (The Creed, Prayer, Charity, Fasting, and Pilgrimage) articulate how Muslim businesspeople should behave, not only in the marketplace but in all aspects of their lives. Overall, Islam encourages entrepreneurship and business activity. There were conceptual two articles in this review that do not specify a particular religion. However, these authors assert that religious values will positively affect firm performance (Fang et al., 2013) and that religious values may lead to strategic renewal through conflict resolution and proper resource allocation (Abdelgawad & Zahra, 2020).

Directions for Future Research

The nascent fields of work-place spirituality and religious values in family firms are open for additional work of all types – qualitative, quantitative, and conceptual. Future research may further examine the relationship between work-place spirituality and family values. Studies focusing on the effects of different cultures on spirituality and family firms are lacking. Researchers could examine spiritual leadership and various dependent variables, such as firm performance and follower satisfaction. We noted a scarcity of comparative religion studies with only such study extant (Fathallah et al., 2020). While for many years, studies based on Christianity dominated the management and entrepreneurship literature (Dana, 2009), we report on some diversity of religious articles, including Islamic, Hindu, and multi-religion studies. However, in this review, articles on Jewish family business were noticeably lacking. Further research could investigate the relationships between spiritual and religious family values on processes such as succession, communication, and conflict management.

In closing, this chapter aimed to review the existing literature on work-place spirituality and religious values in family firms. In reviewing 26 articles on this topic, we have described the status of the sub-field and laid a foundation for future research. There is an open door for scholars to contribute to this new and growing research area.

References

Abdelgawad, S. G., & Zahra, S. A. (2020). Family firms' religious identity and strategic renewal. *Journal of Business Ethics*, *163*(4), 775–787. https://doi.org/10.1007/s10551-019-04385-4

Astrachan, J. H., Binz Astrachan, C., Campopiano, G., & Baù, M. (2020). Values, spirituality and religion: Family business and the roots of sustainable ethical behavior. *Journal of Business Ethics*, *163*(4), 637–645. https://doi.org/10.1007/s10551-019-04392-5

Astrachan, J. H., & Shanker, M. C. (2003). Family businesses' contribution to the U.S. economy: A closer look. *Family Business Review*, *16*(3), 211–219. https://doi.org/10.1177/08944865030160030601

Balog, A. M., Baker, L. T., & Walker, A. G. (2014). Religiosity and spirituality in entrepreneurship: A review and research agenda. *Journal of Management, Spirituality & Religion*, *11*(2), 159–186. https://doi.org/10.1080/14766086.2013.836127

Barbera, F., Shi, H. X., Agarwal, A., & Edwards, M. (2020). The family that prays together stays together: Toward a process model of religious value transmission in family firms. *Journal of Business Ethics*, *163*(4), 661–673. https://doi.org/10.1007/s10551-019-04382-7

Bhatnagar, N., Sharma, P., & Ramachandran, K. (2020). Spirituality and corporate philanthropy in Indian family firms: An exploratory study. *Journal of Business Ethics*, *163*(4), 715–728. https://doi.org/10.1007/s10551-019-04394-3

Carradus, A., Zozimo, R., & Discua Cruz, A. (2020). Exploring a faith-led open-systems perspective of stewardship in family businesses. *Journal of Business Ethics, 163*(4), 701–714. https://doi.org/10.1007/s10551-019-04387-2

Chua, J. H., Chrisman, J. J., & Sharma, P. (1999). Defining the family business by behavior. *Entrepreneurship Theory and Practice, 23*(4), 19–39. https://doi.org/10.1177/104225879902300402

Dana, L. P. (2007). A humility-based enterprising community: The Amish people in Lancaster County. *Journal of Enterprising Communities: People and Places in the Global Economy, 1*(2), 142–154. https://doi.org/10.1108/17506200710752566

Dana, L. P. (2009). Religion as an explanatory variable for entrepreneurship. *The International Journal of Entrepreneurship and Innovation, 10*(2), 87–99. https://doi.org/10.5367/000000009788161280

Dede, N. P., & Ayranci, E. (2014). Exploring the connections among spiritual leadership, altruism, and trust in family businesses. *Quality & Quantity, 48*(6), 3373–3400. https://doi.org/10.1007/s11135-013-9962-x

Dieleman, M., & Koning, J. (2020). Articulating values through identity work: Advancing family business ethics research. *Journal of Business Ethics, 163*(4), 675–687. https://doi.org/10.1007/s10551-019-04380-9

Discua Cruz, A. (2013). Christian family businesses: Opportunities for future research. *Journal of Biblical Integration in Business, 16*(2), 7–28.

Du, X. (2017). Religious belief, corporate philanthropy, and political involvement of entrepreneurs in chinese family firms. *Journal of Business Ethics, 142*(2), 385–406. https://doi.org/10.1007/s10551-015-2705-2

European Family Businesses. (2020). *Family business statistics*. http://www.europeanfamilybusinesses.eu/uploads/Modules/Publications/family-business-statistics.pdf

Fang, H., an de Graaff Randolph, R., Chrisman, J. J., & Barnett, T. (2013). Firm religiosity, bounded stakeholder salience, and stakeholder relationships in family firms. *Journal of Management, Spirituality & Religion, 10*(3), 253–270. https://doi.org/10.1080/14766086.2012.758055

Fathallah, R., Sidani, Y., & Khalil, S. (2020). How religion shapes family business ethical behaviors: An institutional logics perspective. *Journal of Business Ethics, 163*(4), 647–659. https://doi.org/10.1007/s10551-019-04383-6

Fry, L. W. (2003). Toward a theory of spiritual leadership. *The Leadership Quarterly, 14*(6), 693–727. https://doi.org/10.1016/j.leaqua.2003.09.001

Jiang, F., Jiang, Z., Kim, K. A., & Zhang, M. (2015). Family-firm risk-taking: Does religion matter? *Journal of Corporate Finance, 33*, 260–278. https://doi.org/10.1016/j.jcorpfin.2015.01.007

Kavas, M., Jarzabkowski, P., & Nigam, A. (2020). Islamic family business: The constitutive role of religion in business. *Journal of Business Ethics, 163*(4), 689–700. https://doi.org/10.1007/s10551-019-04384-5

Kellermanns, F. W. (2013). Spirituality and religion in family firms. *Journal of Management, Spirituality & Religion, 10*(2), 112–115. https://doi.org/10.1080/14766086.2013.807688

Kidwell, R. E., Kellermanns, F. W., & Eddleston, K. A. (2012). Harmony, justice, confusion, and conflict in family firms: Implications for ethical climate and the "Fredo Effect." *Journal of Business Ethics, 106*(4), 503–517. https://doi.org/10.1007/s10551-011-1014-7

Litz, R. A. (2013). Leaving the godfather to follow God the father: Successor generation conversion in a mob family. *Journal of Management, Spirituality & Religion, 10*(2), 183–211. https://doi.org/10.1080/14766086.2012.758053

Madison, K., & Kellermanns, F. W. (2013). Is the spiritual bond bound by blood? An exploratory study of spiritual leadership in family firms. *Journal of Management, Spirituality & Religion, 10*(2), 159–182. https://doi.org/10.1080/14766086.2012.758052

Maung, M., Miller, D., Tang, Z., & Xu, X. (2020). Value-enhancing social responsibility: Market reaction to donations by family vs. non-family firms with religious CEOs. *Journal of Business Ethics*, *163*(4), 745–758. https://doi.org/10.1007/s10551-019-04381-8

Mitchell, R. K., Robinson, R. E., Marin, A., Lee, J. H., & Randolph, A. F. (2013). Spiritual identity, stakeholder attributes, and family business workplace spirituality stakeholder salience. *Journal of Management, Spirituality & Religion*, *10*(3), 215–252. https://doi.org/10.1080/14766086.2012.758054

Neal, J., & Vallejo, M. C. (2008). Family firms as incubators for spirituality in the workplace: Factors that nurture spiritual businesses. *Journal of Management, Spirituality & Religion*, *5*(2), 115–159. https://doi.org/10.1080/14766080809518697

Paterson, T. A., Specht, D., & Duchon, D. (2013). Exploring costs and consequences of religious expression in family businesses. *Journal of Management, Spirituality & Religion*, *10*(2), 138–158. https://doi.org/10.1080/14766086.2012.758051

Pieper, T. M., Williams, R. I., Manley, S. C., & Matthews, L. M. (2020). What time may tell: An exploratory study of the relationship between religiosity, temporal orientation, and goals in family business. *Journal of Business Ethics*, *163*(4), 759–773. https://doi.org/10.1007/s10551-019-04386-3

Ramadani, V., Dana, L. P., Ratten, V., & Tahiri, S. (2015). The context of Islamic entrepreneurship and business: Concept, principles and perspectives. *International Journal of Business and Globalisation*, *15*(3), 244–261. https://doi.org/10.1504/IJBG.2015.071906

Sorenson, R. L. (2013). How moral and social values become embedded in family firms. *Journal of Management, Spirituality & Religion*, *10*(2), 116–137. https://doi.org/10.1080/14766086.2012.758050

Tabor, W., Madison, K., Marler, L. E., & Kellermanns, F. W. (2020). The effects of spiritual leadership in family firms: A conservation of resources perspective. *Journal of Business Ethics*, *163*(4), 729–743. https://doi.org/10.1007/s10551-019-04379-2

Tracey, P. (2012). Religion and organization: A critical review of current trends and future directions. *Academy of Management Annals*, *6*(1), 87–134. https://doi.org/10.5465/19416520.2012.660761

von Bieberstein, F., Crede, A.-K., Essl, A., & Hack, A. (2020). Signaling and stakeholder honesty: On the individual and combined effects of owner family membership and religious affiliation. *Family Business Review*, *33*(3), 265–283. https://doi.org/10.1177/0894486520924301

Weber, M. (1904). *The Protestant Ethic and the Spirit of Capitalism, trans. Talcott*. Scribner.

Weber, M. (1958). *The City*. The Free Press.

Wong, N. D., Smith, A., & Popp, A. (2018). Religiosity, emotional states, and strategy in the family firm: Edm. Schluter & Co Ltd., 1953-1980. *Entreprises et Histoire*, *91*(2), 98–125. Cairn.info. https://doi.org/10.3917/eh.091.0098

Yusof, M., Mohd Nor, L., & Edward Hoopes, J. (2014). Virtuous CSR: An Islamic family business in Malaysia. *Journal of Family Business Management*, *4*(2), 133–148. https://doi.org/10.1108/JFBM-07-2013-0016

Edwina Pio, Guillermo Merelo

10 Gender and Diversity: Intersections of Faith, Religion, and Spirituality

Introduction

> Only the bird understands the textbook of the rose. . .
> For not every reader knows the inner meaning of the page. . .
> (Hafiz – quoted in Shah Idries (1968, p. 245))

Religion and its associated dimensions of spirituality and faith have long been at the centre of intellectual and academic critical movements, despite often being eschewed from management and organisations. From the secular and modernisation perspectives, religion was mostly seen as a burden impeding countries –and their women– to move forward in an imagined path to real modernisation based on economic and political freedoms (Bruce, 2002; Norris & Inglehart, 2011). On the opposite side of the theoretical spectrum, Marxist Feminist proponents saw religion as an instrument to perpetuate patriarchal values preventing women to fully enter the polity as equal players. Women were positioned as vulnerable and oppressed within the limiting structures of faith. Yet, the world faith developments dialogue and many organisations in the current century seek to affect a worldview transformation, to check unlimited and unsustainable growth and corporate greed through various faith initiatives (Pio et al., 2021).

This chapter discusses some approaches, empirical findings, new theorisations, and future challenges for individuals and organisations in understanding of gender, diversity and their intersections with faith, religion and spirituality.

From Marxist Feminism to Post-Secularism

Karl Marx's propositions that "religion is the opium of the people" (Marx, 1978, p. 54) has been historically considered to be the dogmatic crystallisation of myriad forms of injustice and oppression. Religion from this perspective, inscribes and reinforces the causes and effects that produce suffering humanity through articulating structures upon which injustice is reproduced, validated and entrenched (Hewitt, 1999). In her account of Marxist Feminism, Luxton (2014) observes how such views were influential

Acknowledgements: We are deeply grateful to our families, especially Isaac and Oscar and to the editors of this book for their inspiring work.

https://doi.org/10.1515/9783110711349-010

to the development of scathing critiques of "the system" and the recognition that this posited immense structural barriers to women's self-determination. The place of religion in this "system" becomes not just obvious but fundamental since dogmatic assumptions of womanhood entailed the perpetuation of traditional gender roles upon which women had been historically subjugated.

Trends incorporated into the realm of modernisation through secularisation theory, seem to be the aftermath of World War II, wherein demographic analyses Illustrated how, in different parts of the West, religious beliefs and practices started to decline significantly (Ashford & Timms, 1992; Davie, 1994). Secularization theory assumes that the processes of modernization have an ultimately negative effect on the significance of religion in society and its acceptance (Pollack, 2015). Although some proponents have argued that secularisation theory is probabilistic rather than deterministic (e.g. Norris & Inglehart, 2011), some of its proponents are forthright in declaring *God is dead* (Bruce, 2002). From this perspective, secularisation is not just a "prediction" but an "imperative need" derived from sociological and political anxieties about religion promoting the de-incorporation of visible religious traits from the public realm in order to promote a privatisation of the religious. Such privatisation was -and in many ways, still is- a fundamental feature of the dominant liberal model of modernity, encompassing the role of women in progressive societies. As argued by Deo (2018) the assumptions of religion incorporated in secularization theory touch not only on its functions, practices and characteristics, but also on its "dangers" from a positivist perspective, according to which, pure scientific reality is blinded by faith. But as she also argues, religion is not just beliefs and science is not just facts.

Following this line, at the turn of the century, secularization theory increasingly became the centre of strong critical analyses describing it not only as short-sighted but also as central to new understandings of colonialism upon which novel forms of exclusion in general and gender exclusion in particular were to be strategically articulated in societal discourses (Anidjar, 2006; Asad, 2003; Butler, 2008; Smith & Whistler, 2010; C. Taylor, 2007). A post-secular theoretical proposal therefore arises, as an epistemological turn (Smith & Whistler, 2010), questioning the divide between reason and faith as a location of knowledge in modernity (Vasilaki, 2016). In feminism, such a post-secular turn echoes earlier debates around how respect for group identity is essential in diverse democracies, while locating a novel movement and a manifesto of its theoretical interventions.

We identify two distinctive elements underpinning this turn. First is the understanding of the neo-colonialist legacies of secularism as a vehicle for orientalist portrayals of womanhood from a modernisation perspective. Taylor (2007) makes the case of secularism not being simply the absence of belief but itself a historical construction, which creates the conditions for a multiplication of options including belief and unbelief. Similarly, Smith & Whistler (2010) refer to secularism not as a neutral form of human interaction but as a new form of ideological colonisation and an imperialist weapon, that ignores the diversity and complexity of human nature and its endless negotiations between culture and the self. This understanding of secularism has resulted in a "hermeneutics of suspicion" between the West and the rest of the globe (Arora, 2018) with the consequent devaluation of religious identity held by non-Western women. It is in this context that post-secular propositions of feminism promise to unwrap what lies inside the Western scientific paradigm.

A second distinctive element refers to the notion of female agency. Behind secularist theory lie numerous Occidental assumptions of Oriental otherness deeply engraved in an alleged quest for modernisation. Thus, gender roles are positioned in an imaginary cartography of oppression resulting in romantic and/or condescending notions of a Western sisterhood in constant need of liberating their uneducated sisters from the pernicious effects of dogma, ignorance and bigotry perpetuated by savage cultures.

Saba Mahmood's influential work, the *Politics of piety* (2005) argues against Occidental simplistic understandings of Orientalist agency, for religious manifestations are regularly used to assert women's value Individually and collectively. In this regard, embodied performativity of religious practices is a means of resisting and setting limits to domination. This intricate examination of oppression and resistance leads to a second challenge: is it all possible to recognise the existence of a universal category of acts –such as those of resistance- outside the ethical and political contexts within which such acts obtain their particular meaning and within which their connotations are experienced? Mahmood draws attention to myriad and more nuanced contextual forms of resistance and structures of power than those encapsulated in the Western narrative of subversion and resistance (pp:9). A final, and more controversial challenge touches on the core notion of humankind and its assumed relentless search for freedom and autonomy. Mahmood's proposition provides alternatives to understand more nuanced arrangements of communal life through the lens of faith. In this regard, Mahmood's feminist proposition can be described as both a way of seeing the world and a way of acting upon it (Deo, 2018). In a similar vein, other scholars (Braidotti, 2008; Deo, 2018; Vasilaki, 2016) challenge European feminism by arguing that religious piety is not antithetical to agency.

Such heterogenous understandings now reach beyond feminist theorists and include post-structuralist scholars, ethnographers and theologists aiming to decode the intricate negotiations behind embodied religious practices among migrant communities (e.g. Jouili, 2015; Mirza, 2013; Scharff, 2011; Siraj, 2011) among women in their own countries (e.g. Jamjoom, 2010; Kato, 2015; Pandya, 2017; Rasmussen, 2010; Rinaldo, 2013; Zion-Waldoks, 2015), as well as myriad theoretical analyses on agency, religion and gender in the broadest possible sense (e.g. Avishai et al., 2015; Bangstad, 2011; Burke, 2012).

New Intersections and Ossified Tropes

In the post-secular, post-structuralist, post-modernist world, women are not simply women, they include Indigenous women, professional women, poor women or migrant women, heterosexual women, and the intersections of religion beyond dominant categories of 'womanhood' such as gay women, transgender women. Like the development of secularism, the exploration of gender in the post-secular era has been informed by parallel and sometimes even opposing theoretical streams, through complex non-linear progressions. Religious expectations of gender, with a few exceptions, are predicated upon genitalia across most religions. Performativity of gender is therefore ingrained in dogmatic views of the body and how this was allegedly created and consequently expected to perform. In the post-modern context, such views result in myriad tensions and convoluted negotiations of theory and praxis more evident in the case of gay and transgender women.

Judith Butler's seminal work on gender performativity (1990) is commonly acknowledged as a point of departure in analyses of queerness and religion (e.g. Armour, 2010; Jenzen & Munt, 2016). In her analyses, gender is a term rooted in cultural prescriptions of genitalia that result in expected markers of performativity based on historically constructed categories. Such presumptions posit markers and signifiers through which females are expected to act feminine and desire males, while males are expected to act masculine and desire females. Doing otherwise calls into question one's gender and consequently, one's sex (Armour, 2010).

Yet, an increasing body of literature (Crawley & Willman, 2018; Elwood & Leszczynski, 2018; Marchia & Sommer, 2019) indicates how the expected cohesion of constructed heteronormativity moves beyond assumed binaries to a richer tapestry of options emerging from the endless tensions in the dominant social script. Two major obstacles to our subject of analysis appear in the exploration of this tapestry. First religion is not normally a primary area of concern in the analysis of such tensions and, second, the study of new forms of womanhood in queer studies is concealed using overarching categories such as gay, queer, LGBTQ+. These factors have practically and theoretically influenced current understandings of religion, faith, and spirituality among gay and transgender women. Gender and religion from the lens of sexual identity illustrate the intricate, endless, and highly contextual negotiations between faith, community, and the self. Although different in their contextuality, narratives of this kind are bounded by a sense of semiotic cohesiveness flowing from myriad tensions in different social and religious scripts.

The negotiation of conflict at the communal and individual levels is an overarching theme in the scarce empirical literature on this subject. If the question of agency and religious performativity within historically constructed discourses underlies post-secular analyses of cisgender and heterosexual women, the same question does not necessarily apply outside such a circle of culturally given intelligibility. The question shifts to: can lesbian and transgender women live harmonious and self-fulfilling religious, faithful, and spiritual lives within their communities of practice? This shift is not minor if we consider that the type of performed sexuality involved in the question is in open opposition with core elements of religious dogmatic prescription.

For instance, McQueeney's (2007) analysis of two lesbian and gay affirming Protestant churches in Southeast USA reveals how renegotiating gender and sexual identity is a complex multi-layered process lived differently across groups. Clear differences between white and African American lesbians seem to lead to different hermeneutics of self-reassurance based on different contextualities of communal life. Such contextualities are widely influenced by several individual and group intersections based on race and class. Analysis of Buddhist queerness follows a similar pattern demonstrating how multiple axes of difference intersect and create tensions that force members of the LGBTQ+ community (women included) to negotiate and re-examine multiple facets of the self through performativity of gender roles; but also how religious interpretations can be used as means to foster acceptance and inclusion (e.g. Cheng, 2018; Gleig, 2012).

The ways in which lesbian and transgender women engineer distinctive hermeneutics of self-reassurance across locations and faiths has been the major topic of analysis in the past decade or so. To this end, exploring the lives, negotiations, and reconciliations of religions and second-generation migrant gay and transgender women in Western societies has been a major lens (Siraj, 2011; Y. Taylor & Snowdon, 2014a, 2014b) showing myriad ways in which women reconfigure their religious identity to incorporate discordant facets of the self and reclaim a place constructed upon their religious identity.

A common theme in how such hermeneutics of self-reassurance inform new rationales of religious performativity is widely given by the strategic use of the notion of God as the creator of diverse forms of gender and sexual orientations. "God made me this way" is thus a recurring topic in numerous narratives of this kind. This recurrent topic is even more evident in the explored narratives of transgender women, a sparsely researched area. Somewhat unsurprisingly, much of the existing literature on it is informed either by samples drawn from advocacy groups, mental health or counselling studies or other psychologically oriented pieces. From this perspective individuals who identify as transgender or gender variant and religious can face a unique set of challenges in attempting to integrate their faith and gender identity (Kidd & Witten, 2008, 2008; Levy & Lo, 2013). For instance, transgender Christians face myriad forms discrimination in their churches, experience periods of denial and struggle, face depression, disconnection and dissatisfaction with religion, but more importantly, find ways to build an individualised relationship with God and a sense of self that feels integral and true (Kennedy, 2008; Sheridan, 2001; Tanis, 2003).

Yarhouse & Carrs (2012) indicate that transgender Christian women engaged in religious coping strategies such as prayer, progressive readings of sacred texts and personal faith relationships with God and Jesus to overcome more negative religious experiences with congregations and clergy. Benson, Westerfield & van Eeden-

Moorefield (2018) found that Christian transgender individuals have opposing experiences of support and rejection in faith communities but maintain their faith beliefs even in the face of open rejection. Crasnow's (2017) ethnographic theological study of Jewish transgender religious experiences outlined the meaningful and affirming *mikveh* (religious purification bathing) rituals developed by and for transgender Jews to help celebrate their gender transitions within otherwise gender-normative religious frameworks. Levi & Lo (2013) found that transgender participants in their study use religious beliefs and practices as means to pave better relationships with their communities but also as a source of enlightenment to reconcile numerous elements of their own gender identity. Clearly, there is interest in academic research to address such transgender challenges, nonetheless this novel field has not yet been able to provide us with a rich tapestry of experiences. Furthermore, the limited picture we have so far, seems to be highly orientated to Western constructs of gender ambiguity from a Judeo-Christian perspective.

This situation has mostly excluded the experiences of non-dominant forms of gender ambiguity in other parts of the world. There are indeed other expressions of womanhood that do not quite fit the Western model of transgender. Most of these have been broadly studied from the sociological and anthropological perspective therefore, the links between religion and gender are only residually addressed. Recent examples of such literature include works on the Zapotecan Muxe in Mexico (Mendoza-Álvarez, 2018), the Fakaleti, Fa'afafine and other female gender constructs in the South Pacific (Besnier & Alexeyeff, 2014), and the Hihjras in India and Pakistan (Saeed et al., 2018).

When considering the diaspora, including migrant women, research indicates that Western tropes generally follow that of the subjugated individual, though some research focuses on their agency and how they decentre otherness (Essers et al., 2020; Pio & Essers, 2013; Pio & Syed, 2018). Regarding Indigenous women and faith, for centuries, Indigenous religions have been labelled "primitive", "primal" and "animistic" and their expressions, manifestations and symbols as superstitious or irrational (Marcos, 2010). But in the rich mosaic of gender expressions, Indigenous women and their relationships with religion are neither simple nor straightforward but circumscribed by myriad historical and contextual elements. A vast body of research depicts the struggles of Indigenous women to use spirituality as means to reaffirm and consolidate fragmented parts of their identity through contemporary discourses (e.g. Díaz, 2011; Honkasalo, 2015; Pio, 2020; Stephen, 2005; Utriainen & Salmesvuori, 2014; Valkonen & Wallenius-Korkalo, 2016; Yakushko, 2018).

The Organisational Level: New Times, New Questions

Contemporary workplaces must contend with complex intricacies regarding gender, diversity and faith. Historically there has been a divide between private and public forms of workplace identity. For over a century the Western workplace has been a relatively stable social constructs where symbols, meanings, roles, codes of honours and expectations have been articulated from a dominant white, masculine, Christian perspective. From a cultural semiotic proposition, one can regard such construct as a circle of shared intelligibility, a complex system of signification, where role performativity is not just expected but enforced through formal and informal mechanisms (Merelo, 2019; Sewell, 2005).

Early responses to more culturally diverse workforces resulted in the creation of an artificial neutral ground, a third space, neither fully private nor fully public, built upon an alleged principle of neutrality. In the case of religious identity this generally resulted in an imagined secular place. An employee that does not see religious life as separate and apart from daily life in such space will not fare well in such workplaces (Alexis, 2012). Beyond religion, such neutral space was relatively successful at amalgamating historical categories of social alterity into the workplace. Here workplace identity is thus conceived as a neutral ground where people "do not make a fuss" about "who" or "what" they are.

This concept of neutrality has just started to change as Western societies move towards cosmopolitan understandings of concepts such as diversity, equity and inclusion. Mere tolerance of "the other" in the workplace is slowly evolving to the construction of relational bridges between in and out groups and accommodations for diverse employees. However, this new system of signification is far from being seamless and straightforward, but a complex arena of numerous and sometimes opposing interpretations. In that regard, interpretations of "who" accommodates "what" is a polysemic construal with multiple points of entry.

Among all possible intersections, those associated with religion and gender are probably the most challenging. This is hardly surprising if one considers the multiple effects that both Western feminism and secularisation discourses trigger when assorted categories of exclusion combine and are to be perceived from a dominant Western lens. From this perspective, women are not just women and men are not just men; they are products of historical and cultural circumstances interpreted differently to the eye of the beholder. This is exemplified in the case of Muslims living in allegedly secular societies. Studies have illustrated that members of mainstream cultural groups in the West tend to hold more negative attitudes towards Muslim men than Muslim women (Dana et al., 2019; Pedersen & Hartley, 2012). As observed by Al-Saji, "the Muslim man can be denounced and described as medieval and barbaric, [and] the family defined as the place of women's seclusion and repression" (Al-Saji, 2010, p. 887).

Such notions of gender oppression have shaped Orientalist interpretations that religious women -especially Muslim women- in Western societies need to be rescued by members of educated, industrialised, rich democracies (Abdelhadi, 2019; Syed & Pio, 2010). The ban of public use of certain religious garments in countries such as Austria, Belgium, Canada, Denmark, France and Switzerland have mostly targeted Muslim women. These stances fuel discourses of otherness regarding Muslim women as composed of subjugated bodies waiting to be rescued and creating a sense of humiliation and exclusion (Karimi, 2018). Moreover, many Muslim women in the west pay ethno-religious penalties in organisations with market disadvantage and pay gaps (Pio, 2018, 2018; Syed & Pio, 2010). But as extensively demonstrated by post secular and transnational feminists, there are numerous shades and nuances that such broad interpretations choose to ignore. The most salient one being, that it is also the ultimate right of Muslim women to wear religious signifiers if they choose to do so.

Workplaces are not immune of such interpretations resulting in countless, often radically opposing approaches to diversity, equity and inclusion management (Fowler-Hermes & Gierbolini, 2014; Scheitle & Ecklund, 2017). While some workplaces may adopt a pragmatic approach through the alleged notion of secular neutrality resulting in forms of workplace assimilation, others may create support programmes targeting religious groups of workers from a condescending-educational perspective, and some may avoid recruiting members of "visible" religious groups to prevent conflict. Yet, a more comprehensive wholistic view requires organisations to understand employees to be as diverse as the circumstances surrounding them and faith as an intricate often visceral area of interpretation.

Conceived in this way, religion is similarly aligned with other diversity dimensions that can be used as tools for both inclusion and exclusion, sometimes simultaneously. Evidently, more empirical research is needed in this area but based on the preceding analysis, some hypothesis and research questions are pertinent: How exactly do notions of secularism affect organisations' practices? How do they affect the design of workplace interventions for religious groups in general and for women in particular? How are religious female employees affected by notions of modernisation rooted in secular understandings of the workplace? What new forms of resistance are being created from within religion and how do they affect the economic role of women?

Questions and hypotheses are likely to increase in complexity as further identities intersect with religion. The theoretical analysis we present provides grounds to expect novel forms of interpretation by employees and employers as societal complexity makes some of these intersections more evident. One such challenge, leading to rights conflicts in the workplace (Brown & Scott, 2019; Feldblum, 2002; Whitman, 2012) involves troubling relationships between what is conceived as historically opposed categories such as being religious and being a gay, transgender or gender fluid employee. The previous sections depict new forms of identity ownership and negotiation with social environments articulated at the many axes between religion and sexual identity. This can be likened to how distinctive strategies are built and negotiated by religious gay and transgender women to reclaim a place within their congregations, similar phenomena may occur at the workplace level. How do religious gay and transgender women perform this reclaiming in the workplace? How do non-religious members of the LGBTQ+ community in the workplace respond to this? How can organisations prevent exclusion based on secularist assumptions and expectations?

Many questions remain unanswered regarding the intersections of gender, religious and Indigenous peoples in the workplace. Religious Indigenous women (cisgender and transgender) around the world face extraordinary challenges both in their original communities and as migrants to advanced democracies. This is a significant area for future research.

Conclusion

Through a broad swathe of literature and analysis, we have sought to present some facets of gender and diversity pertaining to individuals and organisations, and how they intersect with faith, religion and spirituality, noting that there are reams that have been written in this area from various perspectives, that we have not touched upon. These include the dark side of religion such as terrorism, genital mutilation, child brides and human trafficking often girded by fundamentalist interpretations of sacred texts. Viewpoints from religions such as Buddhism, Sikhism and Zoroastrianism are further areas for investigation. There are also many positive experiences on the continuum and spiral of this broad domain that have inspired, bewitched, bothered, bewildered and transformed individuals, communities, organisations and societies with multiple perspectives.

A seeker asked the Sufi Jalaluddin Rumi if the Koran was a good book to read. He replied: "You should rather ask yourself if you are in a state to profit from it." A Christian mystic used to say of the Bible, "However useful a menu, it is not good for eating." (De Mello, 1993, p. 84).

References

Abdelhadi, E. (2019). The Hijab and Muslim women's employment in the United States. *Research in Social Stratification and Mobility*, *61*, 26–37. https://doi.org/10.1016/j.rssm.2019.01.006

Alexis, G. Y. (2012). Not Christian, but nonetheless qualified: The secular workplace-whose hardship? *Journal of Religion and Business Ethics*, *3*(1), 1.

Al-Saji, A. (2010). The racialization of Muslim veils: A philosophical analysis. *Philosophy & Social Criticism*, *36*(8), 875–902. https://doi.org/10.1177/0191453710375589

Anidjar, G. (2006). Secularism. *Critical Inquiry*, *33*(1), 52–77.
Armour, E. T. (2010). Blinding me with (queer) science: Religion, sexuality, and (post?) modernity. *International Journal for Philosophy of Religion*, *68*(1–3), 107–119. https://doi.org/10.1007/s11153-010-9246-5
Arora, A. (2018). Re-enchanting feminism: Challenging religious and secular patriarchies. *Postsecular Feminisms: Religion and Gender in Transnational Context*, 32–51.
Asad, T. (2003). *Formations of the Secular: Christianity, Islam, Modernity, 1 Stanford University Press*. University Press.
Ashford, S., & Timms, N. (1992). *What Europe Thinks: A Study of European Values*. Dartmouth.
Avishai, O., Jafar, A., & Rinaldo, R. (2015). A gender lens on religion. *Gender & Society*, *29*(1), 5–25. https://doi.org/10.1177/0891243214548920
Bangstad, S. (2011). Saba Mahmood and anthropological feminism after virtue. *Theory, Culture & Society*, *28*(3), 28–54. https://doi.org/10.1177/0263276410396914
Benson, K., Westerfield, E., & van Eeden-Moorefield, B. (2018). Transgender people's reflections on identity, faith, and Christian faith communities in the U.S. *Sexual and Relationship Therapy*, *33*(4), 395–420. https://doi.org/10.1080/14681994.2018.1472375
Besnier, N., & Alexeyeff, K. (Eds.). (2014). *Gender on the Edge: Transgender, Gay, and Other Pacific Islanders*. University of Hawaii Press. https://doi.org/10.1515/9780824840198
Braidotti, R. (2008). In spite of the times: The postsecular turn in feminism. *Theory, Culture & Society*, *25*(6), 1–24. https://doi.org/10.1177/0263276408095542
Brown, E., & Scott, I. (2019). Belief v. belief: Resolving LGBTQ rights conflicts in the religious workplace: Belief v. belief. *American Business Law Journal*, *56*(1), 55–113. https://doi.org/10.1111/ablj.12135
Bruce, S. (2002). *God is Dead: Secularization in the West* (Vol. 3). Blackwell.
Burke, K. C. (2012). Women's agency in gender-traditional religions: A review of four approaches: Women's agency in gender-traditional religions. *Sociology Compass*, *6*(2), 122–133. https://doi.org/10.1111/j.1751-9020.2011.00439.x
Butler, J. (1990). *1990 Gender Trouble: Feminism and the Subversion of Identity*. Routledge.
Butler, J. (2008). Sexual politics, torture, and secular time. *The British Journal of Sociology*, *59*(1), 1–23.
Cheng, F. K. (2018). Being different with dignity: Buddhist inclusiveness of homosexuality. *Social Sciences*, *7*(4), 51. https://doi.org/10.3390/socsci7040051
Crasnow, S. J. (2017). On transition: Normative Judaism and trans innovation. *Journal of Contemporary Religion*, *32*(3), 403–415. https://doi.org/10.1080/13537903.2017.1362880
Crawley, S. L., & Willman, R. K. (2018). Heteronormativity made me lesbian: Femme, butch and the production of sexual embodiment projects. *Sexualities*, *21*(1–2), 156–173. https://doi.org/10.1177/1363460716677484
Dana, K., Lajevardi, N., Oskooii, K. A., & Walker, H. L. (2019). Veiled politics: Experiences with discrimination among Muslim Americans. *Politics & Religion*, *12*(4), 629–677.
Davie, G. (1994). *Religion in Britain Since 1945: Believing Without Belonging*. Blackwell.
De Mello, A. (1993). *The Prayer of the Frog*. Gujarat Sahitya Prakash.
Deo, N. (2018). *Postsecular Feminisms: Religion and Gender in Transnational Context*. Bloomsbury Publishing.
Díaz, M. (2011). Native American women and religion in the American colonies: Textual and visual traces of an imagined community. *Legacy*, *28*(2), 205–231. https://doi.org/10.5250/legacy.28.2.0205
Elwood, S., & Leszczynski, A. (2018). Feminist digital geographies. *Gender, Place & Culture*, *25*(5), 629–644. https://doi.org/10.1080/0966369X.2018.1465396

Essers, C., Pio, E., Verduijn, K., & Bensliman, N. (2020). Navigating belonging as a Muslim Moroccan female entrepreneur. *Journal of Small Business Management*, 1–29. https://doi.org/10.1080/00472778.2020.1769989

Feldblum, C. R. (2002). Rectifying the tilt: Equality lessons from religion, disability, sexual orientation, and transgender. *Maine Law Review*, *54*(2), 160–194.

Fowler-Hermes, J., & Gierbolini, L. (2014). Religious accommodation in the workplace: The Devil is in the detail. *Labour and Employment Law*, *88*(5), 34.

Gleig, A. (2012). Queering Buddhism or Buddhist de-queering?: Reflecting on differences amongst western LGBTQI Buddhists and the limits of liberal convert Buddhism. *Theology & Sexuality*, *18*(3), 198–214. https://doi.org/10.1179/1355835813Z.00000000015

Hewitt, M. A. (1999). Ideology critique, feminism, and the study of religion. *Method & Theory in the Study of Religion*, *11*(1), 47–63. https://doi.org/10.1163/157006899X00384

Honkasalo, M. L. (2015). If the mother of god does not listen: Women's contested agency and the lived meaning of the Orthodox religion in North Karelia. *The Journal of American Folklore*, *128* (507), 64–92. https://doi.org/10.5406/jamerfolk.128.507.0065

Jamjoom, M. I. (2010). Female Islamic studies teachers in Saudi Arabia: A phenomenological study. *Teaching and Teacher Education*, *26*(3), 547–558. https://doi.org/10.1016/j.tate.2009.06.019

Jenzen, O., & Munt, S. R. (2016). Queer theory, sexuality and religion. In *The Ashgate Research Companion to Contemporary Regligion and Sexuality* (pp. 61–74). Routledge.

Jouili, J. S. (2015). *Pious Practice and Secular Constraints: Women in the Islamic Revival in Europe*. Stanford University Press. https://doi.org/10.1515/9780804794893

Karimi, H. (2018). The Hijab and work: Female entrepreneurship in response to Islamophobia. *International Journal of Politics, Culture, and Society*, *31*(4), 421–435. https://doi.org/10.1007/s10767-018-9290-1

Kato, A. (2015). *Weaving Women's Spheres in Vietnam: The Agency of Women in Family, Religion and Community*. Brill.

Kennedy, J. (2008). The transgender movement. *Christianity Today*, *52*(2), 54–58.

Kidd, J. D., & Witten, T. M. (2008). Understanding spirituality and religiosity in the transgender community: Implications for aging. *Journal of Religion, Spirituality & Aging*, *20*(1–2), 29–62. https://doi.org/10.1080/15528030801922004

Levy, D. L., & Lo, J. R. (2013). Transgender, transsexual, and gender queer individuals with a Christian upbringing: The process of resolving conflict between gender identity and faith. *Journal of Religion & Spirituality in Social Work: Social Thought*, *32*(1), 60–83. https://doi.org/10.1080/15426432.2013.749079

Luxton, M. (2014). Marxist feminism and anticapitalism: Reclaiming our history, reanimating our politics. *Studies in Political Economy*, *94*(1), 137–160. https://doi.org/10.1080/19187033.2014.11674957

Mahmood, S. (2005). *Politics of Piety: The Islamic Revival and the Feminist Subject*. Princeton University Press.

Marchia, J., & Sommer, J. M. (2019). (Re)defining heteronormativity. *Sexualities*, *22*(3), 267–295. https://doi.org/10.1177/1363460717741801

Marcos, S. (2010). *Women and Indigenous Religions*. Greenwood.

Marx, K. (1978). Contribution to the critique of Hegel´s philosophy of right. Introduction. In R. C. Tucker (Ed.), *The Marx-Engels Reader* (Vol. 474, pp. 412–413). Norton.

McQueeney, K. (2007). Multiple identities: Race, class, and gender in lesbian and gay affirming Protestant congregations. In *Handbook of the New Sexuality Studies* (pp. 201–208). Routledge.

Mendoza-Álvarez, C. (2018). A critical approach to gender identities in the "Muxe" case. *Humanities and Social Sciences*, *6*(4), 130. https://doi.org/10.11648/j.hss.20180604.16

Merelo, G. (2019). Imagining the other: The symbolic construction of political entitlement and exclusion among Mexican migrants in Sweden. In *Challenging the Political Across Borders: Migrants and Solidarity Struggles* (pp. 223–245). Central European University.
Mirza, H. S. (2013). 'A second skin': Embodied intersectionality, transnationalism and narratives of identity and belonging among Muslim women in Britain. *Women's Studies International Forum*, *36*, 5–15. https://doi.org/10.1016/j.wsif.2012.10.012
Norris, P., & Inglehart, R. (2011). *Sacred and Secular: Religion and Politics Worldwide*. Cambridge University Press.
Pandya, S. P. (2017). Renunciation, feminism, and social service: Hindu women in religious orders. *Affilia*, *32*(4), 504–516. https://doi.org/10.1177/0886109917718326
Pedersen, A., & Hartley, L. K. (2012). Prejudice against Muslim Australians: The role of values, gender and consensus: Anti-prejudice regarding Muslim Australians. *Journal of Community & Applied Social Psychology*, *22*(3), 239–255. https://doi.org/10.1002/casp.1110
Pio, E. (2018). Muslim women and careers. In S. Fielden & A. Broadridge (Eds.), *Research Handbook of Diversity and Careers* (pp. 357–374). Edward Elgar.
Pio, E. (2020). Gender and indigenous education and practice. In E. Pio, *Oxford Research Encyclopedia of Education*. Oxford University Press. https://doi.org/10.1093/acrefore/9780190264093.013.1326
Pio, E., & Essers, C. (2013). Professional migrant women decentring otherness: A transnational perspective: professional migrant women decentring otherness. *British Journal of Management*, *25*(2), 252–265. https://doi.org/10.1111/1467-8551.12003
Pio, E., Kilpatrick, R., & Pratt, T. (2021). *Reimagining Faith and Management: The Impact of Faith in the Workplace*. Routledge.
Pio, E., & Syed, J. (2018). To include or not to include? A poetics perspective on the Muslim workforce in the West. *Human Relations*, *71*(8), 1072–1095. https://doi.org/10.1177/0018726717733529
Pollack, D. (2015). Varieties of secularization theories and their indispensable core. *The Germanic Review: Literature, Culture, Theory*, *90*(1), 60–79. https://doi.org/10.1080/00168890.2015.1002361
Rasmussen, A. (2010). *Women, the Recited Qur'an, and Islamic Music in Indonesia*. Univ of California Press.
Rinaldo, R. (2013). *Mobilizing Piety: Islam and Feminism in Indonesia*. Oxford University Press.
Saeed, A., Mughal, U., & Farooq, S. (2018). It's complicated: Sociocultural factors and the disclosure decision of transgender individuals in Pakistan. *Journal of Homosexuality*, *65*(8), 1051–1070. https://doi.org/10.1080/00918369.2017.1368766
Scharff, C. (2011). Disarticulating feminism: Individualization, neoliberalism and the othering of 'Muslim women.' *European Journal of Women's Studies*, *18*(2), 119–134. https://doi.org/10.1177/1350506810394613
Scheitle, C. P., & Ecklund, E. H. (2017). Examining the effects of exposure to religion in the workplace on perceptions of religious discrimination. *Review of Religious Research*, *59*(1), 1–20. https://doi.org/10.1007/s13644-016-0278-x
Sewell, W. H. Jr. (2005). The concept(s) of culture. In G. M. Spiegel (Ed.), *Practicing History: New Directions in Historical Writing After the Linguistic Turn* (pp. 76–95). Routledge.
Shah, I. (1968). *The Way of the Sufi*. Penguin.
Sheridan, V. (2001). *Crossing Over: Liberating the Transgendered Christian*. Pilgrim Press.
Siraj, A. (2011). Meanings of modesty and the hijab amongst Muslim women in Glasgow, Scotland. *Gender, Place & Culture*, *18*(6), 716–731. https://doi.org/10.1080/0966369X.2011.617907
Smith, A. P., & Whistler, D. (2010). *After the Post-Secular and the Postmodern: New Essays in Continental Philosophy of Religion*. Cambridge Scholars Publishing.

Stephen, L. (2005). *Zapotec Women: Gender, Class, and Ethnicity in Globalized Oaxaca*. Duke University Press.
Syed, J., & Pio, E. (2010). Veiled diversity? Workplace experiences of Muslim women in Australia. *Asia Pacific Journal of Management*, *27*(1), 115–137. https://doi.org/10.1007/s10490-009-9168-x
Tanis, J. (2003). *Trans-Gender: Theology, Ministry, and Communities of Faith*. The Pilgrim Press.
Taylor, C. (2007). *A Secular Age*. Belknap Press of Harvard University Press.
Taylor, Y., & Snowdon, R. (2014a). Making space for young lesbians in church? Intersectional sites, scripts, and sticking points. *Journal of Lesbian Studies*, *18*(4), 393–414.
Taylor, Y., & Snowdon, R. (2014b). *Queering Religion, Religious Queers*. Routledge.
Utriainen, T., & Salmesvuori, P. (2014). *Finnish Women Making Religion: Between Ancestors and Angels*. Palgrave Macmillan.
Valkonen, S., & Wallenius-Korkalo, S. (2016). Practising postcolonial intersectionality: Gender, religion and indigeneity in Sámi social work. *International Social Work*, *59*(5), 614–626. https://doi.org/10.1177/0020872816646816
Vasilaki, R. (2016). The politics of postsecular feminism. *Theory, Culture & Society*, *33*(2), 103–123. https://doi.org/10.1177/0263276415590235
Whitman, M. E. (2012). The intersection of religion and sexual orientation in the workplace: Unequal protections, equal employees. *Equal Employees*, *65*(3), 713–740.
Yakushko, O. (2018). Witches, charlatans, and old wives: Critical perspectives on history of women's indigenous knowledge. *Women & Therapy*, *41*(1–2), 18–29. https://doi.org/10.1080/02703149.2017.1323474
Yarhouse, M. A., & Carrs, T. L. (2012). MTF transgender Christians' experiences: A qualitative study. *Journal of LGBT Issues in Counseling*, *6*(1), 18–33. https://doi.org/10.1080/15538605.2012.649405
Zion-Waldoks, T. (2015). Politics of devoted resistance: Agency, feminism, and religion among orthodox agunah activists in Israel. *Gender & Society*, *29*(1), 73–97. https://doi.org/10.1177/0891243214549353

Sectors

James Campbell Quick

11 Health and Wellbeing in the Context of Workplace Spirituality

Introduction

Workplace spirituality has continued to advance during the 12 years of the International Association of Management Spirituality and Religion conference series started in Austria at WU Vienna in 2010. The broad concept of workplace spirituality stretches further back into the twentieth century. The *Handbook of Workplace Spirituality and Organizational Performance, Second Edition* (Giacalone & Jurkiewicz, 2010) placed the emphasis in the domain on performance. Taking a difference approach, this chapter places the emphasis, rather, on the constructs of health and wellbeing within the context of workplace spirituality.

The chapter has five sections. The first section explores the context of workplace spirituality and the current state of affairs relevant to the constructs of health and wellbeing, concluding with an emphasis on spiritual vitality. The second section examines advances and foci during the decade of the 2010s. The third section looks ahead to the challenges of the 2020s. The fourth section examines the methods of inquiry into health and wellbeing within the context of workplace spirituality. Finally, the fifth major section identifies key publications relevant to health, wellbeing, and spiritual vitality.

The chapter distinguishes spirituality from religion, the latter being an organized system of beliefs, rituals, and practices established by a church, synagogue, mosque, or other specific organizational religious form (Quick et al., 2008). Hartshorne (1963) makes an important distinction between religion and Biblical faith, the latter falling within the domain of spirituality. The concerns of spirituality are peace, harmony, and transcendence, which means an acceptance of a life centered on others. General conclusions and universal guidelines about spirituality may be difficult to form given its subjective nature (Krishnakumar & Neck, 2002).

Workplace Spirituality: Context and State of the Art

We examine three questions as a way of understanding the context of workplace spirituality and the state of the art as a backdrop for the current chapter. These questions are: What is workplace spirituality? What is the basis for justified knowledge and beliefs? How are we to understand health and wellbeing?

https://doi.org/10.1515/9783110711349-011

What is Workplace Spirituality?

Mitroff and Denton (1999) set forth five models of spirituality for the workplace, specifically for corporate organizations. These models are: Religious-based organization; Evolutionary organization, one step removed from a religious-based organization; Revolutionary organization, a more extreme form often led by recovering addicts; Value-based organization, one that has an underlying, implicit dimension of spirituality; and Socially responsible organization, one that appears the most secular. An examination of these five models suggest that there is an underlying continuum of spirituality running from religious to secular organization along which these five models may be arrayed. This approach decouples religion and spirituality, which Quick et al. (2008) explicitly do in discussing spiritual vitality.

Krishnakumar and Neck (2002) explore exactly what is meant by "spirituality" in the workplace. Their thesis is that spirituality is a highly personal, as well as charged, construct that can have positive effects in organizations if allowed to flourish in both its variety and diversity. The authors consider religious views, existential views, and the intrinsic-origin view (i.e., it originates from inside the individual) of spirituality. There is not a uniform agreement nor widely accepted definition of spirituality. Setting aside the organizational performance issue as has been done above, the authors see potential benefits of spirituality in the workplace, including: intuition and creativity, honesty and trust, personal fulfillment, and commitment.

Leadership is a key construct in the study of organizational behaviour (Nelson & Quick, 2019). Related to workplace spirituality, Fry (2003) sets forth a theory of spiritual leadership that has bearing on health and wellbeing in this context. Fry's model of spiritual leadership incorporates vision, hope/faith, and altruistic love for the purpose of creating vision and value congruence across the leadership spectrum of organizational levels: strategic, team, and individual. Eden (In Press) argues that the science of leadership at its best rests on field experiments that provide actionable cause-and-effect results. While there is much validity in Eden's line of argument, there is a counterpoint to it within the domain of workplace spirituality.

What is the Basis for Justified Knowledge and Beliefs?

Justified knowledge and beliefs that rest on experimental design as the basis for knowing cause-and-effect relationships is valid within the natural sciences, or the Germanic Naturwissenschaften. The alternative domain is the Geisteswissenschaften, or the spiritual sciences. Within English these may be thought of as the humanities. The spiritual sciences are subjective, interpretative, and rely on history and experience as the basis for justified knowledge and beliefs. Martin Luther argued that he was justified by faith, and faith alone (Metaxas, 2017). While Bowlby (1988) argued that authority had no place in science, this is only true for the natural sciences. As Eden (in press) rightly points out, knowledge and beliefs in this domain are justified by experimentation, debate, and empirical evidence.

The same rules of evidence do not necessary apply in the spiritual domain. There is a place in spiritual for authority, depending on the person's individual spiritual beliefs. The ancient scriptures of the Holy Bible, the Koran, the Buddhist texts, and Hindu Vedas are among those authoritative sources. The spiritual person may not have a God or deity as a primary authority figure, though many do. These sources of authority stand in contrast to the authority of the organization and workplace, the latter being manifest in the leaders of the organization. One of the challenges of spirituality in the workplace is that of addressing this issue of dual authority. Lynch (2017, p. x) illustrates this in his discussion of "The Faith of the Centurion" (Matthew 8: 5–13). The centurion has a paralyzed servant who is suffering terribly. The centurion has also heard that Jesus Christ has the power to heal and so he defers to this authority in seeking help for his servant, without violating his own chain of command within the Roman Legion. The faith of the centurion is reported to account for the healing.

How Can We Understand Health and Wellbeing?

Such faith healings are often met with skepticism and doubts or questions are always legitimate in the pursuit of knowledge and the truth. Health and wellbeing are not exact sciences but their protection and enhancement should not be left to chance or faith alone. Within the context of workplace spirituality, health and wellbeing can be understood along four dimensions (Quick et al., 2008). These are: physical health, psychological wellbeing, spiritual vitality, and ethical character. Leadership has a joint responsibility with the individual members of the workplace to enhance these four dimensions of health and wellbeing. Much of physical health and even psychological wellbeing may fall under the authority of modern medical science, which can work in concert with the spiritual sciences. For example, a young physician attending the Choctaw in an Oklahoma Indian Hospital was mistaken for a chaplain when a patient mistook his black diagnostic book for a Holy Bible. The patient asked the physician to pray for him. Choosing not to clarify or debate, the young physician simply sat down with the man, then prayed for his healing and recovery. The physician later marveled at the man's healing, recovery, and release, all of which came more quickly than the medical prognosis had indicated.

Advances and Foci during the 2010s

What have been the advances and foci in health and wellbeing during the 2010s? The emphasis here is on psychological wellbeing, spiritual vitality, and ethical character, which are three key dimensions of health and wellbeing. The five advances discussed are: positivity (Fredrickson, 2013), gratitude and forgiveness (Cameron, 2007), inner peace and spiritual fitness (Lynch, 2017), coaching with compassion (Boyatzis & Jack, 2018), and developing leaders with character and emotional competence (Wasylyshyn & Gupta, 2021).

Positivity

Fredrickson (2013) revised her 3-to-1 positivity ratio and wisely concluded that positivity is not an exact science. However, positive thoughts and emotions impact physiology and behavior. A key aspect of her approach is the balance between the positive and the negative. Individuals who experience a roughly 1-to-1 ratio of positive to negative thoughts and emotions are difficult to spend time with due to the heavy dose of negativity; these people drain energy from others. The positive extreme are individuals who experience ratios of something like 11-to-1 positive to negative thoughts and emotions. These hyper-positive people are very difficult to engage and have a real challenge engaging life's real difficulties and challenges. Those individuals who have a ratio between these extremes have enough negativity to anchor them to reality yet sufficient positivity to give them lift and optimism. Positivity can be contagious in a good way just as infectious diseases can be contagious in a bad way.

Gratitude and Forgiveness

The expression of gratitude is a source of energy and renewal for a person that draws attention to the positive without denying the negative (Quick et al., 2013). In the workplace, the negative often takes the form of harm, injury, or damage, be that intentional or unintentional. For this reason, Cameron (2007) recommends forgiveness as a process through which the harm, injury, or damage can be repaired and healing can result. Forgiveness does not deny the harm nor absolve a person of responsibility in causing harm, injury, or damage. Forgiveness does not include forgetting, but rather encourages remembering so that learning may occur and repeat incidents do not occur. Forgiveness rituals are among the spiritual disciplines and practices that lead to healing and recovery from trauma and tragedy.

Inner Peace and Spiritual Fitness

Spiritual vitality can lead to inner peace and spiritual fitness. Lynch (2017) began his search for inner peace because of the chaos factor in the world around him. A modern day centurion as a US Army combat officer, he was physically healthy, psychologically well, and of sound ethical character but in spiritual need. As he searched for inner peace, he discovered a personal pathway anchored in Biblical faith. The pathway was not without twists, turns, and potholes, but it proved a reliable path. Spiritual vitality rests on spiritual fitness, the personal daily habits, rituals, and disciplines that turn life's chaos into an inner peace and order. Lynch's (2017) daily habits for spiritual fitness included prayer, to include confession, lifestyle evangelism, and strong marital bond with his wife. Inner peace and spiritual fitness did not interfere with Lynch's career commitments as he ascended to one of the top 50 commissioned officers in the U.S. Army as a lieutenant general before retiring.

Coaching with Compassion

Boyatzis and Jack (2018) draw on recent advances in neuroscience that reveals the underlying mechanisms of coaching, leading to coaching with compassion (i.e., coaching to the positive emotional attractor – PEA). They show how neuroscience explains different forms of empathy, drawing on brain regions that are essential to social–emotional connections with others, understanding ethical issues, and being open to new ideas and learning. Their work is very resonant with a value-based organization (Mitroff & Denton, 1999). Coaching with compassion is as deeply personal as Krishnakumar and Neck (2002) argue spirituality is deeply personal. The person coached with compassion benefits from the experience and so too does the coach or leader who is coaching with compassion. Further, as Boyatzis and Jack (2018) point out, coaching with compassion is more mutually beneficial than coaching for compliance (i.e., coaching to the negative emotional attractor – NEA). Bringing neuroscientific advances into the workplace offers real potential to enhance health and wellbeing.

Character and Emotional Competence

The character and emotional competence of an organization's leadership can have significant, positive impact of health and wellbeing in the workplace. The leadership of the USAF's largest logistics depot with 13,000 personnel implemented a six year (1995–2001) intervention that prevented all fatalities and saved $33 million in grievances and conflicts (Quick et al., 2013, p. 118). In another case the commanding general of the US Army's Fort Hood implemented a soldier-focused, family-oriented set of policies that, after one year, resulted in significant improvements in health and wellbeing indicators throughout the installation (Lynch & Dagostino, 2013, pp. 15–16). These included significant drops in incidences of domestic violence, divorce, and failed relationships. Hence, morale and wellbeing improved with enhanced work-life balance.

More consequentially, the suicide rate dropped precipitously, taking Fort Hood from the top of the Army list with most suicides to the bottom of the list with the lowest suicide rate. Traffic accidents on this massive installation nearly disappeared. Before, going from a traffic fatality every 15 or 20 days to, at one point, 245 days without a fatality.

Wasylyshyn and Gupta (2021) set out Leadership 3000 model for long-term leadership development that is highly consistent with the value-based organization (Mitroff & Denton, 1999) and focused on developing leaders of character and emotional competence. In Phase 1 of their four phase model, intensive assessments come from an in-depth life history, an extensive battery of psychometric testing, and targeted organizational interviews. From a health and wellbeing perspective, the key leader behaviors sought include emotional fortitude, courageous leadership, and pragmatic optimism. The leader's ability to use self-awareness, self-management, and relationship-building skills are crucial as is emotional resilience. Emotional competent leaders of good character serve both preventive and therapeutic functions in workplace health and wellbeing.

Challenges for the 2020s

There are four challenges to extending physical health, psychological wellbeing, spiritual vitality, and ethical character in workplaces around the world. These four challenges are: to validate the subjective, to study the variance or array of human spiritual experience, overcome totalitarianism and tyranny of the majority in the workplace, and manage effectively a dual authority system.

Validate the Subjective

Krishnakumar and Neck (2002) advance the case that workplace spirituality is highly personalized, which also means that it is not highly generalizable. Spiritual vitality cannot be imposed upon the person but rather can be invited from within the person. This rests on the authors intrinsic-origin view of spirituality. For workplace spirituality to flourish thus requires that the organization validate or affirm, without necessarily agreeing with or endorsing, the subjective human experience of spirituality. The standardization of processes and of objects within a workplace can have significant economic value. The attempt to standardize human beings in the workplace works against their basic nature, especially in the spiritual and ethical realms.

Study the Variance or Array of Spirituality

William James (1902) delivered a classic series of twenty Gifford Lectures at Edinburgh, Scotland from 1901 to 1902 that explored the varieties of religious experience, starting with attention to religion and neurology. Now over a century later and in the context of workplace spirituality would be a time to use James' earlier exploration as a touchstone for studying the variance and array of spiritual experience in the workplace. While the *Handbook of Workplace Spirituality and Organizational Performance, Second Edition* aims somewhat in that direction, it comes from an organizational and performance point of view. What is required here is a study with primary concern for health and wellbeing in the workplace, and particular attention to spiritual vitality and ethical character. While physical health and psychological wellbeing may be well addressed, spiritual vitality and ethical character are not always so (cf. Quick et al., 2008).

Overcome Totalitarianism and Tyranny of the Majority

Schwartz (1990) focuses attention on how totalitarianism and narcissistic process, as manifest in the organizational ideal, are toxic and lead to corporate decay. These are just the antithesis of spiritual vitality and ethical character in the workplace. There are limits to the legitimate authority and power of leadership in any organization and when that becomes overbearing and uncaring, it stifles workplace spirituality. However, followers have a responsibility in this dynamic as well (see Chapter 12 "Leadership and Followership" in Nelson & Quick, 2019). Effective followers are neither passive nor dependent. Rather, they are active, engaged, and accepting of responsibility. Like spirituality, good leadership is invitational. Totalitarianism and tyranny have no place in healthy corporate organizations and to the extent that they exist, spiritual vitality and ethical character are suppressed (Schwartz, 1990).

Accept and Manage the Dual Authorities

As Martin Luther rediscovered, the authority of scripture transcends and is separate from human authority (Metaxas, 2017). This principle of scriptural authority is applicable to a wide range of spiritual beliefs. Hence, in a spiritual vital organization, individuals with spiritual vitality will have dual authorities to consider, and manage. By the same token, organizational leadership has a challenge in acknowledging this dual authority arrangement, if they want to maintain the spiritual vitality of the workplace. The risk here is the classic person-role conflict to which Robert Kahn and his colleagues (1964) referred in their seminal organizational stress studies in role conflict and ambiguity. The spiritual person has an autonomy and integrity of character aligned with her/his spiritual beliefs, disciplines, and practices. A central question for the person and the organization is whether these dual authorities can co-exist and be managed for mutual benefit. Acknowledging that in some cases they cannot means that the person-organization relationship should be dissolved.

Methods of Inquiry in Health and Wellbeing

In contrast to the natural sciences that are reductionist in nature, the sciences of the spirit are holistic in nature; inclusive, not exclusive. The works cited in the advances and foci of the 2010s earlier in the chapter do not have a common method for considering health and wellbeing in the context of workplace spirituality. The methods varied from neurological measures, to psychometric assessments, to biographical inquiry, and finally organizational archival data. The methods and standards for top level psychological research vary depending upon whether the research is quantitative or qualitative, or mixed method (American Psychological Association, 2020: Chapter 3). Health and wellbeing in occupational settings and workplaces is interdisciplinary in nature, drawing on epidemiology, psychology, engineering, as well as spirituality and religion (Macik-Frey et al., 2007; Quick et al., 2013). Therefore, diversity of methods of inquiry adds value and texture to the domain of health and wellbeing.

To really get at the health and wellbeing of American workers, Pfeffer and his colleagues engaged a multi-year epidemiological study to examine morbidity and mortality as well as health care costs (Goh et al., 2016). At the organizational level, the two best indicators of health and wellbeing have been absenteeism and voluntary turnover (Cascio & Boudreau, 2011). While spirituality may be highly personal and spiritual vitality may be an abstract concept, theory and practice suggest that metaphysical constructs do have consequences in the real world (cf. Kant, 1956).

Key Publications for Health and Wellbeing

In addition to the various contemporary articles cited earlier in the chapter, there are two key publications to consider for health and wellbeing in the context of workplace spirituality. These are the *Handbook of Religion and Health, Second Edition* (Koenig et al., 2012) and *The SAGE Handbook of Organizational Wellbeing* (Wall et al., 2021). The spiritual connections between the mind (psyche) and body (soma) have been explored for decades (cf. Siegel, 1985). Koenig, King, and Carson (2012) provide a comprehensive collection of 29 chapters centered on physical health and mental health (psychological wellbeing). This is a rigorous treatment with connections to religion and spiritual practices. While Siegel (1985) showed what may appear to some miracles, those of faith accept the healing power of gratitude, forgiveness, and love. However, Koenig, King, and

Carson (2012) also confront the dark side of religious practices that stand in conflict with modern medicine and psychology, leading to harm and even premature death. This work is for the discerning reader and scholar to explore the connections across these important domains of knowledge.

The Wall, Cooper, and Brough (2021) comprehensive handbook of organizational wellbeing is also for the discerning reader and scholar. Organized into four major sections with 40 chapters on a host of dimensions of health, wellbeing, and spirituality in organizations, this puts a direct focus on the organization, the workplace, and occupational settings as the context. However, the chapters on grief, suicide prevention, and spiritual wellbeing are not just constrained to the workplace.

Concluding Comment

Workplace health and wellbeing may be conceived along four dimensions, which are physical health, psychological wellbeing, spiritual vitality, and ethical character. Health and wellbeing in the context of workplace spirituality is best studied through the spiritual sciences as well as the natural sciences. The latter is nomothetic by nature while the former is idiographic in nature. The idiographic framework is particularly suitable given the highly personalized nature of spirituality in the workplace.

References

American Psychological Association. (2020). *Publication Manual of the American Psychological Association* (7th ed.). American Psychological Assocoation. https://books.google.at/books?id=48MkEAAAQBAJ

Bowlby, J. (1988). *A Secure Base: Clinical Applications of Attachment Theory*. Routledge.

Boyatzis, R. E., & Jack, A. I. (2018). The neuroscience of coaching. *Consulting Psychology Journal: Practice and Research*, *70*(1), 11–27. https://doi.org/10.1037/cpb0000095

Cameron, K. (2007). Forgiveness in organizations. In D. Nelson & C. L. Cooper (Eds.), *Positive Organizational Behavior*. Sage. https://books.google.at/books?id=4AF5nnJMPQQC

Cascio, W. F., & Boudreau, J. W. (2011). *Investing in People: Financial Impact of Human Resource Initiatives* (2nd ed.). Pearson Education/FT Press. https://books.google.at/books?id=1ZlhBAAAQBAJ

Eden, D. (In Press). The science of leadership: A journey from survey research to field experimentation. *The Leadership Quarterly*. https://doi.org/10.1016/j.leaqua.2020.101472

Fredrickson, B. L. (2013). Updated thinking on positivity ratios. *American Psychologist*, *68*(9), 814–822. https://doi.org/10.1037/a0033584

Fry, L. W. (2003). Toward a theory of spiritual leadership. *The Leadership Quarterly*, *14*(6), 693–727. https://doi.org/10.1016/j.leaqua.2003.09.001

Giacalone, R. A., & Jurkiewicz, C. L. (Eds.). (2010). *Handbook of Workplace Spirituality and Organizational Performance* (2nd ed.). Taylor & Francis.

Goh, J., Pfeffer, J., & Zenios, S. A. (2016). The relationship between workplace stressors and mortality and health costs in the United States. *Management Science, 62*(2), 608–628. https://doi.org/10.1287/mnsc.2014.2115

Hartshorne, M. H. (1963). *The Faith to Doubt: A Protestant Response to Criticisms of Religion.* Prentice-Hall.

James, W. (1902). *The Varieties of Religious Experience: A Study in Human Nature.* The Modern Library.

Kahn, R. L., Wolfe, D. M., Quinn, R. P., Snoek, J. D., & Rosenthal, R. A. (1964). *Organizational Stress: Studies in Role Conflict and Ambiguity.* John Wiley & Sons.

Kant, I. (1956). *Groundwork of the Metaphysics of Morals.* Harper Torchbooks/The Academy Library. [Translated and analyzed by H.G. Paton].

Koenig, H. G., King, D., & Carson, V. B. (Eds.). (2012). *Handbook of Religion and Health* (2nd ed.). Oxford University Press. https://books.google.at/books?id=NiRZcCVbkZ4C

Krishnakumar, S., & Neck, C. P. (2002). The "what", "why" and "how" of spirituality in the workplace. *Journal of Managerial Psychology, 17*(3), 153–164. https://doi.org/10.1108/02683940210423060

Lynch, R. (2017). *Work Hard, Pray Hard: The Power of Faith in Action.* Simon & Schuster.

Lynch, R., & Dagostino, M. (2013). *Adapt or Die: Leadership Principles from an American General.* BakerBooks. http://public.ebookcentral.proquest.com/choice/publicfullrecord.aspx?p=3117406

Macik-Frey, M., Quick, J. C., & Nelson, D. L. (2007). Advances in occupational health: From a stressful beginning to a positive future. *Journal of Management, 33*(6), 809–840. https://doi.org/10.1177/0149206307307634

Metaxas, E. (2017). *Martin Luther: The Man Who Rediscovered God and Changed the World.* Viking.

Mitroff, I. I., & Denton, E. A. (1999). *A Spiritual Audit of Corporate America: A Hard Look at Spirituality, Religion, and Values in the Workplace* (1st ed.). Jossey-Bass Publishers (Warren Bennis signature series).

Nelson, D. L., & Quick, J. C. (2019). *ORGB6: Organizational Behavior.* Cengage/South-Western.

Quick, J. C., Cooper, C. L., Gavin, J. H., & Quick, J. D. (2008). *Managing Executive Health: Personal and Corporate Strategies for Sustained Success.* Cambride University Press.

Quick, J. C., Wright, T. A., Adkins, J. A., Nelson, D. L., & Quick, J. D. (2013). *Preventive Stress Management in Organizations* (2nd ed.). American Psychological Association. https://doi.org/10.1037/13942-000

Schwartz, H. S. (1990). *Narcissistic Process and Corporate Decay: The Theory of the Organization Ideal.* NYU Press.

Siegel, B. S. (1985). *Love, Medicine & Miracles.* Harper & Row Publishers.

Wall, T., Cooper, C. L., & Brough, P. (Eds.). (2021). *The SAGE Handbook of Organizational Wellbeing* (1st ed). SAGE Publications Ltd.

Wasylyshyn, K. M., & Gupta, R. K. (2021). Leadership development: A psychologically-informed process that spawned a generation of CEO's. *Management and Business Review, 1*(1), 71–78.

Payal Kumar, Kasturirangan Sudarshan

12 Workplace Spirituality and Policing

Introduction

Workplace spirituality as a phenomenon in the field of management has been a revelation. Scholars and practitioners have indicated that spirituality at the workplace has produced positive outcomes both for the organization and for the employee. Research suggests that such firms have greater efficiencies, generate a better rate of returns (Jurkiewicz & Giacalone, 2004; Fry, 2003), and can solve human resource challenges (Garg, 2017).

From an employee standpoint, empirical studies suggest that workplace spirituality (WS) can result in the following positive outcomes:

- intrinsic job satisfaction (Moore & Casper, 2006)
- enhanced employee engagement and grit (Singh & Chopra, 2016)
- improved employee well-being and an increase in positive attitude amongst employees (Kolodinsky et al., 2008)
- development of employees' inner life at the workplace (Sheep, 2004)
- more interconnectedness and a sense of purpose to create a more meaningful world (Karakas, 2010; Milliman et al., 1999)
- enhanced creativity (Freshman, 1999; Shinde & Fleck, 2015), which is the cornerstone for innovation and which paves the way for holistic organizational growth (Wong, 2003).

Apart from the various positive outcomes, spirituality is recognized as a prominent means to manage stress (Behera & Dash, 2015). Work-related stress has had a severe impact on the modern workforce due to hyper-competition, high aspirations, and societal pressures (Mujtaba et al., 2020). The unfortunate black swan event – the Covid-19 pandemic – has also exacerbated stress levels, with many people who work from home feeling claustrophobic and mentally drained (NUHS, 2020). In fact, work-related stress is one of the most common causes of mental illness and withdrawal of organizational support by the employee. As Stinchcomb says, "Illnesses related to stress have now replaced infectious diseases as the leading cause of death (2004, p. 259)."

If there is one occupation that is more susceptible and vulnerable to job-related stress and burnout, it is policing (Farr-Wharton et al., 2016). Occupational stress is intrinsic to police work, given that the police often encounter stressful situations on a daily basis (Campbell & Nobel, 2009). Women officers seem to be more susceptible to workplace stress than their male counterparts (Violanti et al., 2016).

There are various reasons attributable to the innate presence of stress in the police force, including a demanding work schedule and the constant threat of being

https://doi.org/10.1515/9783110711349-012

attacked (S. G. Brown & Daus, 2016). Policing is regarded as a thankless profession as the police face constant verbal abuse and public scrutiny (Chopko et al., 2015; Kumar & Kamalanabhan, 2014).

Apart from the occupational stress, there is also the inevitable organizational stress common to any organization. Police culture inculcates a militaristic and monolithic structure as part of the behavioural norms for police officers, which leads to a certain amount of cynicism and hostility amongst them. Stress accumulates especially as police officers lack a platform to vent their frustration (Braithwaite & Gohar, 2014).

The handling of stress in the police organization is imperative and of the utmost significance, as a law enforcement agency is pivotal to a state's peaceful existence. People's high expectations of police officers to maintain peace and to ensure that the community is crime-free also add more job pressure and stress. Therefore, the impact of work-related stress on police officers has a deleterious impact not only on the police organization and the employee, but also on society (Collins & Gibbs, 2003).

As Kuo puts it, the success of a law enforcement agency like the police, is dependent on how inherent stress is handled (2015). Many scholars have analyzed the impact of spirituality as a stress-prevention mechanism. Having seen the positive impact of WS on employee well-being and job performance in non-police organizations, the practice of WS in police organizations has been the subject of keen interest of various management scholars.

In the next sections, the literature has been surveyed in the context of the following themes:- 1. Policing 2. Stress and fatigue amongst the police 3. Outcomes of WS on the police. The chapter ends with a discussion section.

Policing: Functions and Features

One of the major responsibilities of a government is law enforcement. Failure of law enforcement is tantamount to failure of a state, and the corollary is that effective law enforcement is a hallmark of a well-functioning state (Kelkar & Shah, 2019). The law enforcement agency's core objective in a state is to prevent persons from inflicting harm on others and to provide overall security to its people (Sullivan, 2004).

One of the major protagonists in law enforcement is the police force. The police force as a law enforcement agency is instrumental in ensuring peace and harmony in the state through effective implementation of law and order. Therefore, police officers act as 'peace officers' in ensuring the state remains crime and violence-free (Elliott, 2003). The policing process has evolved significantly with more autonomous status given to police organizations to function independently without any political interference, and that too with more sophisticated training and rigorous selection processes (Mawby, 2008).

While policing is meant to embrace societal welfare responsibilities with community policing at its essence, over time through different policing models, the welfare responsibilities of a 'peace officer' have shifted towards more militaristic control-based processes. The militaristic police, euphemistically known as the 'New Police' has met severe criticism for meting out high-handed treatment, brought to the fore in recent times with the brutality exhibited in the George Floyd case, further intensifying the Black Lives Matter movement. Cases of high-handedness and excessive force by police officers has led to the public losing trust and respect for police officers. When asked about the police, Sir Robert Peel said that *"the police are the people and the people are the police"* (Hurd, 2007). This seems far removed from the reality of the police force today.

In this backdrop, modern-day policing in the 21st century has a myriad of challenges. From maintaining peace to managing modern, sophisticated crimes, there is an increasing need for more community policing with softer approaches (Millie & Das, 2008). To add to the stress, due to the proliferation of the internet in recent times, there is constant public scrutiny of policing processes. The traditional militaristic approach will not work in the social media era. As such, the constant scrutiny by the general public, as well as activists questioning the actions of police officers has significant adverse effects in the discharge of 'peace officer' duties (Schultz, 2019).

Policing: Fatigue & Stress

Amidst this evolution and the challenges that the police fraternity has witnessed, there is a noticeably higher level of stress and job burnout. Stress in the police force has become an occupational status symbol (Stinchcomb, 1987), and it is considered to be an inheritance in the occupation (Anshel, 2000). In other words, stress for police officers is inevitable.

Stress in the workplace is often due to handling demands beyond an individual's capacity or bandwidth, especially when it is not possible to avoid, alter, or control these demands (Stinchcomb, 1987). Fatigue, which results from stress, is widely prevalent, and the police profession is no exception. In professions where welfare activity is a major ingredient – like in the police force – stress is more palpable than in other professions (Stinchcomb, 2004). Various studies have indicated the significant amount of stress that the police force encounters (Chopko et al., 2016; Karunanidhi & Chitra, 2015). The severe stress and fatigue that police officers encounter at work has even led down the path of suicide. The National Police Suicide Foundation said that almost 98 per cent of the officers they surveyed had contemplated committing suicide on account of stress (Smith & Charles, 2010). The policing profession is rated as one of the top jobs in the context of illness and on-the-job injuries (Pearsall, 2012).

Causes of Stress

Stress for police officers is majorly on account of the profession's intrinsic nature and on account of organizational stress in handling administrative hassles (Pandya, 2017). The innate nature of the work, which requires police officers to be on their toes and be vigilant, requiring utmost commitment, is also a cause of concern leading to stress at work. The constant threat to lives is an indicator of inherent stress (Sigler & Wilson, 1988). As the former President of the USA, Barack Obama (Obama, 2021) puts it, "Understand, our police officers put their lives on the line for us every day. They've got a tough job to do to maintain public safety and hold accountable those who break the law." The intrinsic nature of the work, or in other words, the sociological stress on account of the nature of responsibilities that the police officer is entrusted with, also leads to episodic stress due to certain gruesome events and incidents (J. M. Brown & Campbell, 1994).

While organizational stress is common to any organization, it is more prevalent in the police organization due to the criminal justice system that is provoked by autocratic bureaucrats and politicians (Hart et al., 1994). Organizational stress has been more common and pervasive than sociological stress for police personnel (Ayres & Flanagan, 1990). Apart from the long working hours, the police organization, similar to other organizations, succumbs to hierarchical pitfalls. The top-down hierarchy and the pleasing of senior officers to get a promotion is a regular feature even for police professionals (Webster, 2014). Independent decision making is curtailed in the administrative process leading to an organizational dilemma. Lack of employee engagement and guidance, lack of interpersonal relationships within the organization, archaic management philosophies etc., are some of the other pitfalls that police officers fall into, leading to organizational stress.

A study by the Bureau of Police Research and Development, New Delhi (2015) identifies the causes of fatigue for India's police officers, which are indicated in Table 12.1. Even though the study is of Indian police officers, one can reasonably assume that this is fairly generalizable to other police officers too.

Outcomes of Fatigue and Stress

One wonders how much stress impacts police officers, given that stress is an inevitable part of their work. Furthermore, as part of their rigorous police academy training, trainees undergo training in a stressful environment to combat the anticipated stress and fatigue (Patterson, 2016). Police officers get trained in a highly intense,

Table 12.1: Major causes of fatigue and stress amongst police officers.

Intrinsic – Sociological Stress	Organizational Stress
– Life threat & violence – Anytime emergency – High expectations from the public – Dramatic events (episodic stress) – Work away from family & friends	– Erratic duty hours, lack of family time – Lack of proper/good sleep – Poor and untimely food – Work environment lacking adequate facilities – Hostile behaviour of superiors & colleagues – Frequent court attendance – Centralized management with top to bottom hierarchy causing friction and internal politics

Source: Authors' own.

military-style environment to create a perception of being strong physically and mentally. This ensures that police officers will never be made to look fragile and vulnerable (Rose & Unnithan, 2015). Despite this, various studies indicate significant impact is caused on account of stress on police officers (see Table 12.2).

The efforts to counter stress in academy training are concentrated more on the physical element, i.e., in making police officers physically strong with little to no emphasis on the mental fitness element (DeNysschen et al., 2018), leading police officers to succumb to fatigue and stress. Police officers are prone to anxiety and depression at twice the rate of the general population (Mumford et al., 2015). Chronic stress eventually separates and dents the zeal/passion towards policing (Stinchcomb, 2004).

Table 12.2: Outcomes of job-related stress.

Theme	Outcomes of stress	Citations
Organizational Impact	Loss of morale to perform at work Premature retirement and increase in sickness-related absence	Leitner, Posner, & Lester (1983) Frank, Lambert, & Qureshi, (2017); Brown & Campbell (1994)
	Organizational alienation and cynical attitude	Buck (1972); Graves (1996)
	Emotional fluctuation leading to job-related violence	Kop, Euwema, & Schaufeli (1999)
	Frustrated cop syndrome – leading to anger, victimization, and feeling helpless to render effective criminal justice, especially on account of organizational stress.	Cebulak (2001)
	Committing suicide	Mumford, Taylor, & Kubu (2015)

Table 12.2 (continued)

Theme	Outcomes of stress	Citations
Personal impact	Emotional burnout, frustration, anxiety disorders	NIMHANS (1996)
	Domestic violence and increase in divorce rate amongst police officers	Waters & Ussery (2007)
	Deterioration in health and well-being of police officers	Paoli & Merllie (2001)
	Drug abuse; addiction to alcohol and smoking	Terry (1981); Violanti et al. (2016)
	Increased risk of illness and other health issues, including coronary heart diseases, diabetes, cancers and cardiovascular diseases	Guralnick (1963); Milham (1983)
	Premature death	Richard & Fell (1976)
	Post-traumatic stress disorders leading to demoralization and brutalization	Spragg (1992)

Source: Authors' own

As seen in Table 12.2, the deleterious consequences of stress are hindrances to the effective functioning of law enforcement. It is imperative that the well-being of the police force is considered for the effective functioning of the state, with prevention being better than cure. Stress prevention enables police officers to thrive in the system for a longer period, the benefits of which can percolate to the people (Frank et al., 2017).

Outcomes of Workplace Spirituality on Policing

The relevance of spirituality in real life as well as from a research perspective has increased immensely, more so during the uncertain times of the pandemic, where people took recourse to spirituality as an immunity measure (Roman et al., 2020). Many scholars have defined spirituality, but there does not seem to be any identifiable common definition.

Spirituality represents a perennial search for life's purpose and meaning in the various definitions (Krishnakumar & Neck, 2002). Also, as Piedmont (Piedmont, 1999) puts it, spirituality views life holistically in interconnection with others. With increasing relevance and the positive impact that spirituality has fostered on personal life, it was introduced into the workplace to improve employees' well-being. Workplace spirituality is the process of applying spirituality through labour (Baldacchino, 2017). The increased interest in workplace spirituality has been described as a spiritual movement (Ashmos & Duchon, 2000), with more firms embracing WS.

In terms of outcome variables, several studies have identified a positive influence of workplace spirituality (WS) on both organizations and the people working in them. Spirituality in the workplace promotes employee motivation, enhances positive behaviour, and increases productivity (Olufemi-Ayoola & Ogunyemi, 2018). Furthermore, WS is said to lead to greater job satisfaction and organizational commitment (Pawar, 2014). Kinjerski and Skrypnek use the term 'spirit at work' to describe WS (2004). In another study of long-term caregivers, it was found that a spirit at work program at the workplace is a cost-effective way to improve employee job satisfaction, boost employee organizational commitment, and reduce attrition, ultimately leading to better patient care (Kinjerski & Skrypnek, 2008).

Further, firms incorporating WS have greater efficiencies, generate a better rate of returns (Jurkiewicz & Giacalone, 2004; Fry, 2003), and can solve human resource challenges (Garg, 2017). Workplace spirituality enhances morale, resulting in fewer absences at work (Gupta & Singh, 2016). Therefore, a considerable number of studies have shown the positive impact that WS can have on organizations and their workforce. On the other hand, some scholars say that WS is a mere management fad or just a tool to control employees (Fernando, 2005). Others, such as Gibbons (2000), say that WS is another failed management concept, such as Total Quality Management. Still others have criticized the use of spirituality for organizational gains, arguing that spirituality is intimate and personal to one's own life and cannot be a doctrine for mass consumption.

With stress being inherent and rife in the policing profession, an effective prevention tool is imperative for all the stakeholders concerned, including the general public. Various organizational remedies, including clinical intervention, can alleviate stress and fatigue amongst police officers. Despite some policing agencies offering chaplains volunteering to support police officers with spiritual care to combat stress and mental trauma (Gouse, 2016), they have not been effective due to a lack of knowledge amongst the police officers in recognizing stress and mental illness (Donnelly et al., 2015).

Further, these facilities are more in the form of cure and not as prevention. It is similar to the way in which vaccination is essential when the possibility of infection from a virus is high. In these situations, the primary focus should be on prevention. Therefore, implementing workplace spirituality as a prevention tool can be an option, especially for police officers. Dåderman and Colli (2014) stressed the need for spirituality in police officers and the police organization, considering the holistic impact spirituality has on mental well-being in order to combat acute stress (Dåderman & Colli, 2014). See Table 12.3 for the summary of positive outcomes of WS in the police force.

The key themes that emerge from these positive outcomes are:
- Meaningful existence
- Positive commitment towards work
- Increase in faith
- Mindfulness

- Virtuous leadership
- Compassionate worldview
- Happiness
- Calmness and resilience
- Values and ethics-based living
- Integrity
- Stress relief

Table 12.3: Positive outcomes of WS on police.

Citations	Findings
Charles, Travis & Smith (2014); Hesketh, Ivy, & Smith (2014)	Spirituality fosters lower stress levels, well-being and optimism. Spirituality also builds resilience.
Waters & Ussery (2007)	Spirituality builds resilience and offers a generous worldview imperative for police officers while dealing with criminal justice.
Pandya (2017)	Spiritual programmes for police officers provide a more social constructivist view of crime. Criminals are seen in a more compassionate manner with potential to reform. Spiritual training provides an option for the restitution of criminals over punishment.
Feemster (2009)	Spirituality assists in the effective management of emotional intelligence, ethics and stress in law enforcement.
Carlier (1999)	Spiritual awareness influences police officers' vitality and longevity.
Charles (2009)	Prayer and meditation practices increase the quality of work performed and commitment.
Iyer & Deshmukh (2018); Shinde & Fleck (2015)	Spirituality diminishes stress and improves performance at work.
Willetts (2009)	Faith-based spirituality makes inner life reflective, thereby enabling people to recognize good and evil, justice and injustice, hope and peace
Naidoo (2014)	WS drives values-based virtuous leadership and assists in effective leadership through integrity.
Reave (2005)	Spiritual leadership fosters trust, integrity and respect amongst co-workers. Virtuous leadership leads to a positive work environment with strong ethics.
Daniel (2015)	Meaningful activities by police officers will reduce occupational stress

Source: Authors' own

Furthermore, in a recent study by Robinson (2019), the participating police officers found peace and calmness while practicing spirituality. The study also revealed the necessity of incorporating spiritual training in the police academies by police tutors to influence better health, well-being and job satisfaction among the police officers.

In another study by Pandya (2017) on the impact of spirituality on police officers from 15 different countries, two sets of officers were studied, with one set receiving spiritual training. This study suggests that the police officers provided with spiritual treatment and training indicated more humane qualities such as a compassionate outlook, constructivist and transformative approach towards prisoners, etc.

In light of the overall positive impact that WS harnesses at the ground level, there are various workplace spirituality programmes being conducted that are targeted at police officers. For instance in India, the National Institute of Mental Health and Neurosciences (NIMHANS), a premier public institute for mental health and neuroscience has tied up with the state of Tamil Nadu in the southern part of India for the *Police Wellbeing Programme (PWB)*, wherein NIMHANS will train around 500 police officers on mental well-being and handling stress. The programme includes amongst other things, training on meditation, yoga, mental counselling, etc. These trained officers will in turn act as trainers; the programme objective is to improve the mental health and efficiency of the workforce, from top-level officers to the last rung in the hierarchy. The PWB also focuses on capacity building and frequent follow-up with police officers to gauge the efficiency and success of the programme (NIMHANS, 2019).

Dr Nataraj, a prominent retired Indian senior police officer, who is currently an active politician, in an interview conducted by the authors, said that "spirituality which is beyond caste, community and religion is a major driving force for police officers to render their tasks in a calm equipoise state of mind, amidst severe work pressure & stress". Attributing spirituality as a strong force in his decision making, Dr. Nataraj has been instrumental in initiating many social outreach programmes while in the police force, including prisoner rehabilitation, and environmental protection.

Dr Nataraj also shared from his experiences that the spiritual training for police officers also removed the gender disparity between men and women police officers, resulting in male officers acknowledging that women are often more balanced when it came to solving disputes and maintaining peace in society. This has led to the setting up of numerous all-woman police stations across the state of Tamil Nadu in South India, and this in turn has been emulated by other South Asian countries.

Similarly, one can also see such well-being programmes in other parts of the world. For instance, in the UK, as part of its National Police Wellbeing Programme, the Blue Light Wellbeing Framework was devised to collate a database of best practices and areas of improvement in the wellbeing of police officers (College of Policing, 2017). Also, as a common trend, one can notice the incorporation of yoga and mindful training to police officers for mitigating the impact of mental stress, for instance, the Yoga and Mindful Program by the City of Falls Church Police Department in the USA (Elliot & Lauttamus, 2014).

Discussion

Despite the positive impact that WS brings for the police, there has been resistance by police organizations to embrace this and to inculcate spirituality in police officers (Moran, 2017). For a long period, police culture reflected a militaristic attitude, where cynicism, criticism, and hostility were handled resolutely. Displaying an act of weakness was a strict no-no, as police officers often tried to conceal their stress and trauma (Bent-Goodley & Smith, 2017). Another factor for resisting WS in police organizations is the lack of understanding of the concept of spirituality. Many police officers related spirituality with religion, and therefore spirituality was not entertained at a very basic level.

To sum up, policing is one of the most stressful professions, with the stress being noticeable not just in terms of physical tiredness and injuries, but also in terms of mental well-being and balance. Literature, specifically with regard to the police, indicates that WS has a positive impact on stress alleviation, apart from other positive outcomes, and yet there are several barriers to WS to be fully imbibed in the police force.

We would encourage future research on WS and policing to delve into the impact of WS in ensuring police officers continue as peace officers, relegating unfortunate incidents like that of George Floyd as exceptions rather than the rule. Furthermore, insightful research can be conducted on how young police officers – millennials and generation Z – understand WS, and whether baby boomers can mentor them in workplace spirituality.

References

Anshel, M. H. (2000). A conceptual model and implications for coping with stressful events in police work. *Criminal Justice and Behavior*, *27*(3), 375–400. https://doi.org/10.1177/0093854800027003006

Ashmos, D. P., & Duchon, D. (2000). Spirituality at work: A conceptualization and measure. *Journal of Management Inquiry*, *9*(2), 134–145. https://doi.org/10.1177/105649260092008

Ayres, R. M., & Flanagan, G. S. (1990). *Preventing Law Enforcement Stress: The Organization's Role*. US Department of Justice. https://www.ojp.gov/ncjrs/virtual-library/abstracts/preventing-law-enforcement-stress-organizations-role

Baldacchino, D. (2017). Spirituality in the healthcare workplace. *Religions*, *8*(12), 1–10. https://doi.org/10.3390/rel8120260

Behera, S., & Dash, M. (2015). Stress and spirituality among school teachers. *Indian Journal of Health and Wellbeing*, *6*(3), 305.

Bent-Goodley, T., & Smith, C. M. (2017). An African-centered approach to community policing. *Journal of Human Behavior in the Social Environment*, *27*(1–2), 92–99. https://doi.org/10.1080/10911359.2016.1266856

Braithwaite, J., & Gohar, A. (2014). Restorative justice, policing and insurgency: Learning from Pakistan. *Law & Society Review*, *48*(3), 531–561. https://doi.org/10.1111/lasr.12091

Brown, J. M., & Campbell, E. A. (1994). *Stress and Policing: Sources and Strategies*. John Wiley & Sons.

Brown, S. G., & Daus, C. S. (2016). Avoidant but not avoiding: The mediational role of anticipated regret in police decision-making. *Journal of Police and Criminal Psychology*, *31*(4), 238–249. https://doi.org/10.1007/s11896-015-9185-2

Buck, V. E. (1972). *Working Under Pressure*. Crane Russak.

Bureau of Police Research and Development. (2015). *Study of fatigue in police personnel: Causes and remedies*. BPRD.

Campbell, D. J., & Nobel, O. B.-Y. (2009). Occupational stressors in military service: A review and framework. *Military Psychology*, *21* (sup2),S47–S67. https://doi.org/10.1080/08995600903249149

Carlier, I. V. E. (1999). Finding meaning in police traumas. In J. M. Violanti & D. Paton (Eds.), *Police Trauma: Psychological Aftermath of Civilian Combat* (pp. 227–240). Charles C. Thomas Publisher, Ltd. https://books.google.at/books?id=3YqsCQAAQBAJ

Cebulak, W. (2001). Fairness, job frustration, and moral dilemmas in policing that impact police effectiveness. *Journal of Police and Criminal Psychology*, *16*(2), 48–57. https://doi.org/10.1007/BF02805180

Charles, G. L. (2009). How spirituality is incorporated in law enforcement. *FBI Law Enforcement Bulletin*, *78*(5), 22–25.

Charles, G. L., Travis, F., & Smith, J. (2014). Policing and spirituality: Their impact on brain integration and consciousness. *Journal of Management, Spirituality & Religion*, *11*(3), 230–244. https://doi.org/10.1080/14766086.2014.887479

Chopko, B. A., Facemire, V. C., Palmieri, P. A., & Schwartz, R. C. (2016). Spirituality and health outcomes among police officers: Empirical evidence supporting a paradigm shift. *Criminal Justice Studies: A Critical Journal of Crime, Law and Society*, *29*(4), 363–377. https://doi.org/10.1080/1478601X.2016.1216412

Chopko, B. A., Palmieri, P. A., & Adams, R. E. (2015). Critical incident history questionnaire replication: Frequency and severity of trauma exposure among officers from small and midsize police agencies. *Journal of Traumatic Stress*, *28*(2), 157–161. https://doi.org/10.1002/jts.21996

College of Policing. (2017). *Blue light wellbeing framework*. (https://oscarkilo.org.uk/app/uploads/2017/06/Blue-Light-Wellbeing-Framework.pdf)

Collins, P. A., & Gibbs, A. C. C. (2003). Stress in police officers: A study of the origins, prevalence and severity of stress-related symptoms within a county police force. *Occupational Medicine*, *53*(4), 256–264. https://doi.org/10.1093/occmed/kqg061

Dåderman, A., & Colli, D. (2014). The significance of the sense of coherence for various coping resources in stress situations used by police officers in on-the-beat service. *International Journal of Occupational Medicine and Environmental Health*, *27*(1), 3–15. https://doi.org/10.2478/s13382-014-0227-2

Daniel, J. L. (2015). Workplace spirituality and stress: Evidence from Mexico and US. *Management Research Review*, *38*(1), 29–43. https://doi.org/10.1108/MRR-07-2013-0169

DeNysschen, C. A., Cardina, C., Sobol, J. J., Zimmerman, B., & Gavronsky, A. (2018). Health, wellness, and fitness training: A pilot study on preparing physically fit and police academy-ready graduates. *International Journal of Police Science & Management*, *20*(1), 66–79. https://doi.org/10.1177/1461355718756412

Donnelly, E., Valentine, C., & Oehme, K. (2015). Law enforcement officers and employee assistance programs. *Policing: An International Journal of Police Strategies & Management*, *38*(2), 206–220. https://doi.org/10.1108/PIJPSM-11-2014-0116

Elliot, J., & Lauttamus, M. P. (2014). Yoga and mindfulness program: City of falls church police department, officer safety corner. *The Police Chief*, *81*, 12–13.

Elliott, L. (2003). When justice means restoring the moral bond of community. *The Vancouver Sun*.

Farr-Wharton, B., Azzopardi, J., Brunetto, Y., Farr-Wharton, R., Herold, N., & Shriberg, A. (2016). Comparing Malta and USA police officers' individual and organizational support on outcomes. *Public Money & Management*, *36*(5), 333–340. https://doi.org/10.1080/09540962.2016.1194078

Feemster, S. L. (2009). Wellness and spirituality. Beyond survival practices for wounded warriors. *FBI Law Enforcement Bulletin*, *78*(5), 2–8. Washington DC: FBI.

Fernando, M. (2005). *Workplace spirituality: Another management fad?* Research Online, UoW. https://ro.uow.edu.au/cgi/viewcontent.cgi?article=1163&context=commpapers

Frank, J., Lambert, E. G., & Qureshi, H. (2017). Examining police officer work stress using the job demands–resources model. *Journal of Contemporary Criminal Justice*, *33*(4), 348–367. https://doi.org/10.1177/1043986217724248

Freshman, B. (1999). An exploratory analysis of definitions and applications of spirituality in the workplace. *Journal of Organizational Change Management*, *12*(4), 318–329. https://doi.org/10.1108/09534819910282153

Fry, L. W. (2003). Toward a theory of spiritual leadership. *The Leadership Quarterly*, *14*(6), 693–727. https://doi.org/10.1016/j.leaqua.2003.09.001

Garg, N. (2017). Workplace spirituality and employee well-being: An empirical exploration. *Journal of Human Values*, *23*(2), 129–147. https://doi.org/10.1177/0971685816689741

Gibbons, P. (2000). Spirituality at work: Definitions, measures, assumptions, and validity claims. In J. Biberman & M. Whitty (Eds.), *Work and Spirit: A Reader of New Spiritual Paradigms for Organizations* (pp. 111–131). University of Scranton Press.

Gouse, V. (2016). An investigation of an expanded police chaplaincy model: Police chaplains' communications with local citizens in crisis. *Journal of Pastoral Care & Counseling*, *70*(3), 195–202. https://doi.org/10.1177/1542305016666554

Graves, W. (1996). Police cynicism: Causes and cures. *FBI Law Enforcement Bulletin*, *65*, 16–21.

Gupta, V. K., & Singh, A. P. (2016). Conceptualization and organizational outcome correlates of spirituality at workplace. *Indian Journal of Community Psychology*, *12*(2), 391–403.

Guralnick, L. (1963). *Mortality by Occupation and Cause of Death Among Men 20 to 64 Years of Age: United States, 1950*. US Department of Health, Education, and Welfare. https://books.google.at/books?id=Kf0PAQAAIAAJ

Hart, P. M., Wearing, A. J., & Headey, B. (1994). Perceived quality of life, personality, and work experiences: Construct validation of the police daily hassles and uplifts scales. *Criminal Justice and Behavior*, *21*(3), 283–311. https://doi.org/10.1177/0093854894021003001

Hesketh, I., Ivy, J., & Smith, J. (2014). Keeping the Peelian spirit: Resilience and spirituality in policing. *The Police Journal: Theory, Practice and Principles*, *87*(3), 154–166. https://doi.org/10.1350/pojo.2014.87.3.672

Hurd, D. (2007). *Robert Peel: A Biography*. Weidenfeld & Nicolson.

Iyer, R. D., & Deshmukh, M. (2018). Moderating effect of workplace spirituality on role stressors and job satisfaction among Indian nurses. *Journal of Management and Public Policy*, *9*(2), 15–30. https://doi.org/10.5958/0976-0148.2018.00002.1

Jurkiewicz, C. L., & Giacalone, R. A. (2004). A values framework for measuring the impact of workplace spirituality on organizational performance. *Journal of Business Ethics*, *49*(2), 129–142. https://doi.org/10.1023/B:BUSI.0000015843.22195.b9

Karakas, F. (2010). Spirituality and performance in organizations: A literature review. *Journal of Business Ethics*, *94*(1), 89–106. https://doi.org/10.1007/s10551-009-0251-5

Karunanidhi, S., & Chitra, T. (2015). Job attitude in relation to perceived occupational stress, interrole-conflict and psychological well-being of women police. *Indian Journal of Positive Psychology*, *6*(1), 19.

Kelkar, V. L., & Shah, A. (2019). *In Service of the Republic: The Art and Science of Economic Policy*. Penguin Random House.

Kinjerski, V. M., & Skrypnek, B. J. (2004). Defining spirit at work: Finding common ground. *Journal of Organizational Change Management*, *17*(1), 26–42. https://doi.org/10.1108/09534810410511288

Kinjerski, V. M., & Skrypnek, B. J. (2008). The promise of spirit at workIncreasing job satisfaction and organizational commitment and reducing turnover and absenteeism in long-term care. *Journal of Gerontological Nursing*, *34*(10), 17–25. https://doi.org/10.3928/00989134-20081001-03

Kolodinsky, R. W., Giacalone, R. A., & Jurkiewicz, C. L. (2008). Workplace values and outcomes: Exploring personal, organizational, and interactive workplace spirituality. *Journal of Business Ethics*, *81*(2), 465–480. https://doi.org/10.1007/s10551-007-9507-0

Kop, N., Euwema, M., & Schaufeli, W. (1999). Burnout, job stress and violent behaviour among Dutch police officers. *Work & Stress*, *13*(4), 326–340. https://doi.org/10.1080/02678379950019789

Krishnakumar, S., & Neck, C. P. (2002). The "what", "why" and "how" of spirituality in the workplace. *Journal of Managerial Psychology*, *17*(3), 153–164. https://doi.org/10.1108/02683940210423060

Kumar, V., & Kamalanabhan, T. J. (2014). Sources of stress among police officials: A qualitative investigation. *Indore Management Journal*, *6*(1), 79–88.

Kuo, S.-Y. (2015). Occupational stress, job satisfaction, and affective commitment to policing among Taiwanese police officers. *Police Quarterly*, *18*(1), 27–54. https://doi.org/10.1177/1098611114559039

Leitner, L. A., Posner, I., & Lester, D. (1983). Stress, mood and job satisfaction in police chiefs. *The Police Chief*, *50*(1), 54–55.

Mawby, R. I. (2008). The police organization. In T. Newburn (Ed.), *Handbook of Policing* (2nd ed.). Willan Publishing.

Milham, S. (1983). *Occupational mortality in Washington State* (DHHS (NIOSH) Publication Number 83-116). US Government Printing Office.

Millie, Ph.D., Andrew, & Das, D. K. (Eds.). (2008). *Contemporary Issues in Law Enforcement and Policing* (1st ed.). CRC Press. https://doi.org/10.1201/9781420072327

Milliman, J., Ferguson, J., Trickett, D., & Condemi, B. (1999). Spirit and community at Southwest Airlines: An investigation of a spiritual values-based model. *Journal of Organizational Change Management*, *12*(3), 221–233. https://doi.org/10.1108/09534819910273928

Moore, T. W., & Casper, W. J. (2006). An examination of proxy measures of workplace spirituality: A profile model of multidimensional constructs. *Journal of Leadership & Organizational Studies*, *12*(4), 109–118. https://doi.org/10.1177/107179190601200407

Moran, R. (2017). Workplace spirituality in law enforcement: A content analysis of the literature. *Journal of Management, Spirituality & Religion*, *14*(4), 343–364. https://doi.org/10.1080/14766086.2017.1376287

Mujtaba, B. G., Cavico, F. J., & Senathip, T. (2020). Strategies for personal, organizational and professional leadership success. *Scientific Journal of Research & Reviews*, *2*(3), 1–10. https://doi.org/10.33552/SJRR.2020.02.000538

Mumford, E. A., Taylor, B. G., & Kubu, B. (2015). Law enforcement officer safety and wellness. *Police Quarterly*, *18*(2), 111–133. https://doi.org/10.1177/1098611114559037

Naidoo, M. (2014). The potential of spiritual leadership in workplace spirituality. *Koers – Bulletin for Christian Scholarship*, *79*(2), 1–8. https://doi.org/10.4102/koers.v79i2.2124

NIMHANS. (1996). *Occupational stress and mental health of police personnel in India*. Nimhans Publication, Bangalore.

NIMHANS. (2019). *Annual Report 2019-20*. (https://nimhans.ac.in/wp-content/uploads/2020/12/NIMHANS-ANNUAL-REPORT-2018-19-English.pdf)

NUHS. (2020). *Workplace resilience survey*. retrieved from www.iamaccb.sg

Obama, B. (2021). *BrainyQuote.com*. Retrieved April 10, 2021, from BrainyQuote.com Web site: https://www.brainyquote.com/quotes/barack_obama_677273

Olufemi-Ayoola, F., & Ogunyemi, K. (2018). Genesis and growth of workplace spirituality. In S. Dhiman, G. E. Roberts, & J. E. Crossman (Eds.), *The Palgrave Handbook of Workplace Spirituality and Fulfillment* (pp. 901–922). Springer International Publishing. https://doi.org/10.1007/978-3-319-62163-0_51

Pandya, S. P. (2017). Dealing with crime, criminals and the criminal justice system through spirituality: A cross-national experimental study with police officers. *The Police Journal*, *90*(4), 348–377. https://doi.org/10.1177/0032258X16681024

Paoli, P., & Merllié, D. (2001). *Third European survey on working conditions 2000*. European Foundation for the Improvement of Living and Working Conditions.

Patterson, G. T. (2016). A brief exploratory report of Coping strategies among police recruits during academy training. *Psychological Reports*, *119*(2), 557–567. https://doi.org/10.1177/0033294116662685

Pawar, B. S. (2014). Leadership spiritual behaviors toward subordinates: An empirical examination of the effects of a leader's individual spirituality and organizational spirituality. *Journal of Business Ethics*, *122*(3), 439–452. https://doi.org/10.1007/s10551-013-1772-5

Pearsall, B. (2012). Sleep disorders, work shifts and officer wellness. *NIJ Journal*, *270*, 36–39.

Piedmont, R. L. (1999). Does spirituality represent the sixth factor of personality? Spiritual transcendence and the five-factor model. *Journal of Personality*, *67*(6), 985–1013. https://doi.org/10.1111/1467-6494.00080

Reave, L. (2005). Spiritual values and practices related to leadership effectiveness. *The Leadership Quarterly*, *16*(5), 655–687. https://doi.org/10.1016/j.leaqua.2005.07.003

Richard, W., & Fell, R. (1976). Health factors in police job stress. In W. H. Kroes & J. J. Hurrell (Eds.), *Job Stress and the Police Officer: Identifying Stress Reduction Techniques* (pp. 73–84). US Department of Health, Education, and Welfare.

Robinson, L. (2019). *Police officers' perceptions of spirituality for managing occupational stress and job performance* [Walden Dissertations and Doctoral Studies]. Walden University.

Roman, N. V., Mthembu, T. G., & Hoosen, M. (2020). Spiritual care – 'A deeper immunity' – A response to Covid-19 pandemic. *African Journal of Primary Health Care & Family Medicine*, *12*(1), 2456. https://doi.org/10.4102/phcfm.v12i1.2456

Rose, T., & Unnithan, P. (2015). In or out of the group? Police subculture and occupational stress. *Policing*, *38*(2), 279–294. https://doi.org/10.1108/PIJPSM-10-2014-0111

Schultz, J. (2019). *Media coverage of law enforcement and effects of the image created* [Senior Thesis. 127]. Dominican University of California. https://doi.org/10.33015/dominican.edu/2019.CMS.ST.01

Sheep, M. L. (2004). Nailing down gossamer: A valid measure of the person-organization fit of workplace spirituality. *Academy of Management Proceedings, 2004*(1), B1–B6. https://doi.org/10.5465/ambpp.2004.13862520

Shinde, U., & Fleck, E. (2015). What spirituality can bring to leaders and managers: Enabling creativity, empathy and a stress free workplace. *Journal of Organizational Psychology, 15*(1), 101–110.

Sigler, R. T., & Wilson, C. N. (1988). Stress in the work place: Comparing police stress with teacher stress. *Journal of Police Science and Administration, 16*(3), 151–162.

Singh, J., & Chopra, V. G. (2016). Relationship among workplace spirituality, work engagement and grit. *IOSR Journal of Business and Management, 18*(11), 21–27. https://doi.org/0.9790/487X-1811032127

Smith, J., & Charles, G. L. (2010). The relevance of spirituality in policing: A dual analysis. *International Journal of Police Science & Management, 12*(3), 320–338. https://doi.org/10.1350/ijps.2010.12.3.179

Spragg, G. S. (1992). Post-traumatic stress disorder. *Medical Journal of Australia, 156*(10), 731–733. https://doi.org/10.5694/j.1326-5377.1992.tb121519.x

Stinchcomb, J. B. (1987). *Redesigning stress reduction training: Has stress become a status symbol?* International Conference on Corrections and Law Enforcement Training, Miami, FL.

Stinchcomb, J. B. (2004). Searching for stress in all the Wrong places: Combating chronic organizational stressors in policing. *Police Practice and Research, 5*(3), 259–277. https://doi.org/10.1080/156142604200227594

Sullivan, L. E. (2004). *Encyclopedia of Law Enforcement.* Sage Publications. http://public.ebookcentral.proquest.com/choice/publicfullrecord.aspx?p=996907

Terry, W. C. (1981). Police stress: The empirical evidence. *Journal of Police Science and Administration, 9*(1), 61–75.

Violanti, J. M., Fekedulegn, D., Hartley, T. A., Charles, L. E., Andrew, M. E., Ma, C. C., & Burchfiel, C. M. (2016). Highly rated and most frequent stressors among police officers: Gender differences. *American Journal of Criminal Justice, 41*(4), 645–662. https://doi.org/10.1007/s12103-016-9342-x

Waters, J. A., & Ussery, W. (2007). Police stress: History, contributing factors, symptoms, and interventions. *Policing, 30*(2), 169–188. https://doi.org/10.1108/13639510710753199

Webster, J. H. (2014). Perceived stress among police officers: An integrative model of stress and coping. *Policing, 37*(4), 839–857. https://doi.org/10.1108/PIJPSM-06-2014-0064

Willetts, J. (2009). A brief introduction to the language of spirit and law enforcement. *FBI Law Enforcement Bulletin, May, 78*(5), 3.

Wong, P. T. P. (2003). *Spirituality and meaning at work.* Retrieved from: http://www.meaning.ca/archives/presidents_columns/pres_col_sep_2003_meaning-at-work.htm

Payal Kumar, Kasturirangan Sudarshan

13 Workplace Spirituality and Creative Industries

Introduction

Spirituality, once considered to be personal, individual-centric and intimate, has evolved into a phenomenon which today is broadly discussed in boardrooms, town-hall meetings and conferences. Increasing discussion and research work centres around the spiritual workplace – a workplace that supports and develops the spirit and well-being of its employees, and where the firm's stakeholders are seen to be as important as the shareholders (Walsh et al., 2003). So much so, that this increased interest in workplace spirituality (WS) has even been described to be a spiritual movement (Ashmos & Duchon, 2000).

Spiritually-inclined organizations are said to exhibit both extrinsic and intrinsic value. Research suggests that such firms have greater efficiencies, generate a better rate of returns (Jurkiewicz & Giacalone, 2004; Fry, 2003) and can solve human resource challenges (Garg, 2017). Various empirical studies also suggest that workplace spirituality provides intrinsic job satisfaction (Moore & Casper, 2006), enhances employee engagement and grit (Singh & Chopra, 2016), promotes employee wellbeing and shapes a positive attitude amongst employees(Kolodinsky et al., 2008), while helping the employee to develop their inner life at the workplace (Sheep, 2004). WS not only provides employees with meaning at work at the personal level, but often goes beyond the individual due to a sense of interconnectedness with others in the organisation and a desire to create a more meaningful world (Karakas, 2010; Milliman et al., 1999).

Apart from wellbeing of the employee, WS is also said to boost creativity (Freshman, 1999; Shinde & Fleck, 2015), which is the cornerstone for innovation and which paves the way for holistic, organisational growth (Wong, 2003). Creativity is the bedrock for employees in the creative industries, also known as the cultural industries. Creative industries include film and video, music, advertising, fashion designing as well as the performing arts, television and radio, and software (DCMS, 1998). An individual's creative skills and imagination combined with the economic value of their innovation, is the foundation of creative industries (DCMS, 2001). From an economic perspective, global creative industries are estimated at around US $2250 billion and account for more than 30 million jobs worldwide, with major employers in this domain from the visual arts, books and music (UNESCO & EY, 2015).

In the next sections, we survey the literature with reference to 1. Workplace Spirituality 2. Creativity in the Workplace and 3. Creative Industries, and then end the chapter with a discussion section. The literature review is interspersed with quotations from interviews of thought leaders in this field.

https://doi.org/10.1515/9783110711349-013

Workplace Spirituality

Many scholars have defined spirituality, but there does not seem to be any identifiable common definition. While there are hundreds of articles, papers and books on this topic, Brown says the more she reads, the more she realizes that the concept is opaque (2003). For some spirituality represents a perennial search for the purpose and meaning of life (Krishnakumar & Neck, 2002). Others say it is a disposition of the mind or one's outlook (Covey, 2004), and still others that it represents inner consciousness (Sisk & Torrance, 2001) or even morality (Kohlberg & Ryncarz, 1990). Olufemi-Ayoola & Ogunyemi (2018) have tabulated various definitions of WS, including inner-life, wellbeing, feeling connected and compassionate towards co-workers, etc.

There are very few studies on the antecedents of WS. In one such study, Badrinarayanan & Madhavaram (2008) have listed supervisory behaviour, organisational values, ethical climate, and wellness lifestyle as antecedents. In other studies, supervisory and senior management behaviour are said to impact the psychological health and spiritual wellbeing of the employee (Dent et al., 2005; Gilbreath & Benson, 2004). At the firm level, WS is said to be best fostered in those firms with ethical climates (Parboteeah & Cullen, 2003) and best implemented through a person-organisation fit (Afsar & Badir, 2017).

In terms of outcome variables, several studies have identified a positive influence of WS on both organisations and the people working in them. WS is said to promote employee motivation, enhance positive behaviour and increased productivity (Olufemi-Ayoola & Ogunyemi, 2018). Furthermore, WS is said to lead to greater job satisfaction and also organisational commitment (Pawar, 2009). Kinjerski & Skrypnek use the term 'spirit at work' to describe WS (Kinjerski & Skrypnek, 2004). In a 2008 study of long-term care givers, they found that a spirit at work program at the workplace is a cost-effective way to improve employee job satisfaction, boost employee organizational commitment, and reduce attrition, ultimately leading to better patient care. Earlier, Moxley (2000) pointed out that harnessing the inner spirit at the workplace enables an employee approach work with a heightened sense of purpose and satisfaction. According to Fry (2003), when employees deem the organisations that they work with as spiritual, they, in turn, become more ethical and committed, and less fearful.

However, not all scholars believe that WS leads to positive outcomes. Some say that WS is a mere management fad or just a tool to control employees (Fernando, 2005). Others, such as Gibbons (2000) say that WS is another failed management concept such Total Quality Management. Still others suggest that employees in spiritual organisations feel unappreciated, unconnected, and lost (Meyer et al., 1993). Furthermore, the jury remains out on an increase in productivity and the company bottom line, with Poole (2009) questioning the business case for WS (see Table 13.1).

Table 13.1: Antecedents and outcomes of WS.

Title	Theme	Findings
(Parboteeah & Cullen, 2003)	Antecedents of WS	WS is best fostered in those firms with ethical climates
(Gilbreath & Benson, 2004; Dent et al., 2005)		Supervisory and senior management behavior impact the psychological health and spiritual wellbeing of the employee
(Badrinarayanan & Madhavaram, 2008)		Supervisory behavior, organizational values, ethical climate, and wellness lifestyle are antecedents of workplace spirituality (WS)
(Afsar & Badir, 2017)		WS is best implemented through a person-organization fit.
(Milliman et al., 1999; Karakas, 2010)	Positive outcomes of WS	Provides employees with meaning at work, goes beyond the individual due to a sense of interconnectedness with others in the organization and a desire to create a more meaningful world
(Fry, 2003)		When employees deem the organizations that work with as spiritual, they, in turn, become more ethical and committed, and less fearful.
(Sheep, 2004)		Helps the employee to develop their inner life at the workplace
(Moore & Casper, 2006)		Workplace spirituality provides intrinsic job satisfaction.
(Kolodinsky et al., 2008)		Promotes employee wellbeing and shapes a positive attitude amongst employees
(Pawar, 2009)		Leads to greater job satisfaction and organizational commitment
(Singh & Chopra, 2016)		WS enhances employee engagement and grit.
(Olufemi-Ayoola & Ogunyemi, 2018)		Promotes employee motivation, enhances positive behavior and increased productivity
(Meyer et al., 1993)	Studies questioning positive outcomes of WS	Employees in spiritual organizations feel unappreciated, unconnected, and lost.
(Gibbons, 2000)		WS is another failed management concept such Total Quality Management.
(Fernando, 2005)		WS is a mere management fad or just a tool to control employees
(Poole, 2009)		The business case for WS is questionable.

Source: Author's own.

Workplace and Creativity

Organisations have, for a very long period, emphasised and focused on creativity as a fundamental value proposition that provides a distinct advantage over competitors. Creativity is said to be linked to effectiveness, productivity and innovation amongst employees (Runco, 2004), thanks to ideas being generated and also due to existing ideas being reshaped (Nonaka, 1991). A creative mind can lead to immense transformation – culturally and societally (Harman & Hormann, 1990). A study commissioned by Adobe (State of Create, 2016) suggests that 70% of people believe being creative is valuable to society and 65% believe this adds value to the economy.

Artists, musicians, designers and architects have described being creative as akin to being spiritual (Howkins, 2007). However, it is noteworthy that workplace creativity as a phenomenon in the creative industries is not all a rosy picture, given that creative persons can be subject to high mood disorders (Mayo, 2009). In a study undertaken by Ulster University in 2018 (Ulster University, 2018), more than 500 people employed in the creative industries in Ireland were surveyed for their mental health and wellbeing. Some of the key findings that emerged include that the pressure to reach high standards and irregular work lead to severe stress and depression, and that there was a high suicidal tendency amongst the participants. Another study in Australia, Mentally Healthy (2018), suggests that the workforce in media, marketing and creative industries is more vulnerable to mental illnesses, with many employees showing high symptoms of depression and anxiety.

Both intrinsic and extrinsic factors are said to boost employee creativity. Amabile (1996) suggests that for employees, intrinsic motivation is a crucial facilitator for creativity and so too is a stimulating work environment. Also, a quality relationship with supervisors promotes the generation of more creative ideas from employees (Zhao et al., 2014). Personal characteristics conducive to creativity include openness and broad-mindedness (Dollinger et al., 2004). Marques & Dhiman (2014) say that demography is also an important variable of study, as the younger generation in the workforce seem to be more open to explore things that the older generations were not: "In recent years, we have seen a growing number of intellectual and practice based gatherings on spirituality, motivation, alternative learning, and right-brain thinking, and an increasing legion of scholars looking for ways that have not yet widely been introduced." (2014, p. x). See Table 13.2 for a datewise overview of some of the workplace and creativity literature.

Table 13.2: Studies on workplace and creativity.

(Wong, 2003)	In the context of work, creativity is one of the attributes of workplace spirituality.
(Dollinger et al., 2004)	Personal characteristics conducive to creativity include openness and broad-mindedness
(Runco, 2004)	Organizations focus on creativity as this is linked to effectiveness, productivity and innovation amongst employees.
(Howkins, 2007)	When creativity translates into a tradeable product or service, it gives rise to the creative economy.
(Rego & Pina e Cunha, 2008)	WS is said to have a positive spillover effect on employees' job satisfaction and organizational commitment, that can further enhance creativity, and lead to individual and professional growth.
(Mayo, 2009)	Creative people are subject to high mood disorders.
(Marques & Dhiman, 2014)	Demography is an important variable, as the younger generation in the workforce seem to be more open to explore things that the older generations were not.
(Zhao et al., 2014)	A quality relationship with supervisors facilitates the generation of more creative ideas from employees
(Olalere, 2018)	WS leads to creativity and innovation amongst employees
(Bhawuk, 2019)	Creativity can be said to be a gift of spirituality

Source: Author's own

Workplace Spirituality and Creative Industries

The significance of a creative economy from a global standpoint can be reckoned from the fact that 2021 has been declared as the International Year of Creative Economy for Sustainable Development by the United Nations (UN). The UN acknowledges that "creative industries can help to foster positive externalities while preserving and promoting cultural heritages and diversity, as well as enhance developing countries' participation in and benefit from new and dynamic growth opportunities in world trade" (UN, 2019, p. 2).

Various global organisations have defined creative industries, as per Table 13.3: Table 13.4 lists some examples of creative industries:

From the definitions and classifications, one can infer that when creativity translates into a tradeable product or service, it gives rise to the creative economy (Howkins, 2007). Furthermore, the industries are a concoction of creative and cultural industries, with an intrinsic manifestation of human qualities (Peris-Ortiz et al., 2019). Says Father Oswald A J Mascarenhas, S J., JRD Tata Chair in Business Ethics, XLRI,

Table 13.3: Defining creative industries.

Defined by	Definition
(Creative Industries Mapping Documents, 2001, Department of Digital, Culture, Media & Sports, United Kingdom)	". . . those industries which have their origin in individual creativity, skill and talent and which have a potential for wealth and job creation through the generation and exploitation of intellectual property."
(United Nations Council for Trade and Development (UNCTAD) Creative Economy Report, 2008, p. 13)	The creative industries: – are the cycles of creation, production and distribution of goods and services that use creativity and intellectual capital as primary inputs; – constitute a set of knowledge-based activities, focused on but not limited to arts, potentially generating revenues from trade and intellectual property rights; – comprise tangible products and intangible intellectual or artistic services with creative content, economic value and market objectives; – constitute a new dynamic sector in world trade.
(United Nations General Assembly Seventy-Fourth Session, 2019, p. 2)	the creative economy is called the 'Orange Economy' and defined as "knowledge-based economic activities and the interplay between human creativity and ideas, knowledge and technology, as well as cultural values or artistic, cultural heritage and other individual or collective creative expressions."

Source: Author's own

India, "Real work is the impression of one's personality on matter – specifically exemplified in pottery, sculpture, painting, embroidery, gardening and parenting. Work defined thus frees creativity, imagination, character, commitment and humanity."

According to Wong (2003), in the context of work, creativity is one of the attributes of workplace spirituality. For some employees engaged in the creative industries such as arts and music, spirituality plays a decisive role. Artists, musicians, designers and architects have described being creative as akin to being spiritual (Howkins, 2007). They believe they undergo a transcendental experience during the creative process which takes them to a different plane when they get immersed in their creative work (Mayo, 2009). Frida Kahlo, "found the language that would eventually impel her to tell her story, unflinchingly, charting her personal and spiritual quest and suffering" (Rummel, 2000, p. 18).

While creativity can lead to a spiritual experience, there are studies that suggest reversal causality, in other words, WS leads to creativity and innovation amongst employees (Olalere, 2018), and problem-solving capabilities (Tischler et al., 2002). This connection between a spiritual experience and ensuing creativity, however, is not exclusive to those working in the creative industries. Take the case of Srinivasa

Table 13.4: Classification of creative industries.

Classification by	Creative Industries
(Creative Industries Mapping Documents, 2001, Department of Digital, Culture, Media & Sports, United Kingdom)	– Crafts – Designer Fashion – Film and Video – Advertising – Architecture – Arts and Antiques – Markets – Television and Radio – Software and Computer Services
(UNESCO, Measuring the Economic Contribution of Cultural Industries, 2009)	– Audio-visual and Interactive Media – Architecture – Tourism – Books and Press – Cultural and Natural Heritage – Performance and Celebration – Visual Arts and Crafts – Design and Creative Services
(United Nations Council for Trade and Development (UNCTAD) Creative Economy Report, 2010, p. 8)	– Heritage – Arts – Media – Functional creation (advertising, architecture, design goods, recreational services etc.)

Source: Author's own

Ramanujan, the mathematical genius who rose from a humble background to be the first Indian to be elected as a Fellow of Trinity College, Cambridge. He ascribed his work to divine inspiration, in which he said that complex mathematical solutions would come to him after he had vision of the mother Goddess (India Today, 2017: https://www.indiatoday.in/education-today/gk-current-affairs/story/srinivasa-ramanujan-life-story-973662-2017-04-26, downloaded on 13/11/2020). In this context, creativity can be said to be a gift of spirituality (Bhawuk, 2019).

Organisations would do well to provide space for spirituality and creativity, which can lead to spiritual wellbeing. While wellness is defined as "the integration of social, mental, emotional, spiritual, and physical health at any level of health or illness" (Greenberg, 1985, p. 404), spiritual wellness is seen to be "a balanced openness to or pursuit of spiritual development" (Chandler et al., 1992, p. 170).

How can organisations foster spirituality and wellbeing? Space can be created for leisure and also for prayer and reflection. In an interview by the authors of this chapter, Dr Mrinalini Kochupillai, faculty at Munich Intellectual Property Law Center; formerly Senior Research Fellow, Chair of Business Ethics and Global Governance, Germany, she said:

> Expanding the adoption of spiritual practice within workplaces does not take away from the very personal or community based nature of religious preferences. While several public places (such as international airports) have started providing for 'prayer rooms' catering to needs of various religious communities, workplaces can either adopt similar models to support individual spiritual or religious practices, or support collective secular spiritual practices at specific times in the workplace, such as starting every meeting with a 2 minute mindfulness silence. As is evidenced by a growing body of scientific research, such practices enhance employee well-being, (team) connectedness, and support overall work productivity, which, in turn, can enhance workplace creativity and innovation. (Kochupillai, 2020)

Discussion

The creative economy is growing significantly year on year, hand-in-hand with technological advancements, with greater coverage being afforded to this in the print and electronic media. In an interview of Chris Frost, Professor Emeritus of Journalism, Liverpool John Moores University, UK, (2020) he said: "Journalism plays a pivotal role in the creative industries. By writing about and criticizing creative arts and production, journalists stimulate interest in and consumption of a wide range of creative outputs that are a major part of the commercial life of any civilized country. Creativity adds magic to our lives and the journalism of creativity helps spread that stardust far and wide."

The increasing importance of WS, creative industries and innovation can be seen from a unique conference on Ethics in Innovation in 2017, which saw an interplay of ethics, science and Industry 4.0, on the same platform. Organized by the World Forum for Ethics in Business and the Max Planck Institute for Innovation and Competition in Munich, the conference dwelt on the multiple stakeholder lens to seek answers to ethical questions in innovation.

Furthermore, the Center for Management in the Creative Industries (CMCI) has been formed as a collaboration between Sotheby's Institute of Art and Claremont Graduate University's Drucker School of Management, School of Arts and Humanities, and Getty Leadership Institute. It is aimed at students who aspire to work in the creative industries, such as in film production. Said Larry Crosby, former Dean of the Drucker School of Management, "The creation of the CMCI marks the next phase of the Drucker School's focus on management challenges and opportunities that are specific to the creative industries and the creative economy more generally," (Claremont Graduate University, 2015: https://www.cgu.edu/news/2015/03/claremont-graduate-university-announces-creation-of-new-center-for-management-in-the-creative-industries-3/ downloaded on 05/11-2020).

To summarise, various studies have focused on the positive impact WS has on organisations and its stakeholders. In fact there are some organisations that prefer to be labelled as 'spiritual organisations' owing to the benefit this brings to all the stakeholders concerned, including enhanced creativity and innovation amongst employees and clients. The Times of India Group, India, is one such example. The group comprises of businesses spanning print media, internet, music and multimedia. At one time the group had an employee training programme called "Self Mastery," with the aim to controlling ego and unleashing individual potential. More recently, the Times of India has formed the "Times Foundation" with the twin aim of encouraging sustainability and transformation, which includes spiritual awareness as an important pillar. Also, the media outlet publishes a popular weekly column known as The Speaking Tree.

On the other hand, there are scholars who argue that WS has no real purpose or value. Finally, there are scholars who believe that what in fact ails many modern organizations today is a form of spiritual emptiness and impoverishment (Mitroff & Denton, 1999). This emptiness is exacerbated by toxic leaders full of self-seeking greed, lacking in spiritual maturity (Delbecq, 2009), and also by lean methodologies, which sacrifice creativity and meaning for the employee at the altar of hyper-efficiency (Mehri, 2006).

In an interview by the authors of this chapter with Father Oswald A J Mascarenhas, S J., JRD Tata Chair in Business Ethics, XLRI, India, he said, "To avoid spiritual emptiness, organizations need to cultivate WS. WS should bring joy, mindfulness and meaning to life and family. It is a humanization of the work and environment, which cultivates bonding, togetherness, harmony and human solidarity, national dedication and citizenship."

While there is a lot of work on workplace spirituality and also on creativity, there is very little work that synthesizes the two. Also, while existing literature suggests that spirituality and creativity are interlinked, this does not mean that all creative industries embrace WS. More work needs to be done on the antecedents and outcomes of WS in creative as well as other industries, preferably in the form of longitudinal studies.

Future research on WS and creative industries can also delve into gender in conflict and post-conflict economies. Charlotte Karam, associate professor at the Olayan School of Business, American University of Beirut, a section editor of Feminisms and Business Ethics, and an editorial board member of the Journal of Business Ethics, is known for her work as a leadership development consultant in the MENA region, particularly in Lebanon, Iraq and Libya. In a recent interview of her by the authors she said, "After suffering from civil war, man-made disasters, and an entrenched corrupt political class responsible for government failings, the workplace often serves as a bastion or conduit of hope and compassion. This is the case for all industries, but particularly the case of creative industries, where the increasingly disenfranchised and frustrated youth turn to information technology and art to channel their energies to the world outside their local conflicted spaces. Future research would do well to unpack the relationship between workplace spirituality and creative industries against the backdrop of failing states, and the interaction between the embedded oppressive structures and the intersectional identities of the populations trying to survive and have a liveable future within."

References

Adobe. (2016). *State of create.* Retrieved from: https://www.adobe.com/content/dam/acom/en/max/pdfs/AdobeStateofCreate_2016_Report_Final.pdf

Afsar, B., & Badir, Y. (2017). Workplace spirituality, perceived organizational support and innovative work behavior: The mediating effects of person-organization fit. *Journal of Workplace Learning, 29*(2), 95–109. https://doi.org/10.1108/JWL-11-2015-0086

Amabile, T. (1996). *Creativity in Context: Update to the Social Psychology of Creativity.* Westview Press.

Ashmos, D. P., & Duchon, D. (2000). Spirituality at Work. *Journal of Management Inquiry, 9*(2), 134–145. https://doi.org/10.1177/105649260092008

Badrinarayanan, V., & Madhavaram, S. (2008). Workplace spirituality and the selling organization: A conceptual framework and research propositions. *Journal of Personal Selling & Sales Management, 28*(4), 421–434. https://doi.org/10.2753/PSS0885-3134280406

Bhawuk, D. P. S. (2019). Toward a spirituality-based theory of creativity: Indigenous perspectives from India. In K. H. Yeh (Ed.), *Asian Indigenous Psychologies in the Global Context* (pp. 139–168). Palgrave Macmillan. https://doi.org/10.1007/978-3-319-96232-0_7

Brown, R. B. (2003). Organizational spirituality: The sceptic's version. *Organization, 10*(2), 393–400. https://doi.org/10.1177/1350508403010002013

Chandler, C. K., Holden, J. M., & Kolander, C. A. (1992). Counseling for spiritual wellness: Theory and practice. *Journal of Counseling & Development, 71*(2), 168–175. https://doi.org/10.1002/j.1556-6676.1992.tb02193.x

Claremont Graduate University. (2015). *Claremont Graduate University announces creation of new Center for Management in the Creative Industries.* Retrieved from: https://www.cgu.edu/news/2015/03/claremont-graduate-university-announces-creation-of-new-center-for-management-in-the-creative-industries-3/ (Downloaded on 05-11-2020).

Covey, S. (2004). *The Seven Habits of Highly Effective People: Restoring the Character Ethic.* Simon & Schuster.

Delbecq, A. L. (2009). Spirituality and business: One scholar's perspective. *Journal of Management, Spirituality & Religion, 6*(1), 3–13. https://doi.org/10.1080/14766080802648599

Dent, E. B., Higgins, M. E., & Wharff, D. M. (2005). Spirituality and leadership: An empirical review of definitions, distinctions, and embedded assumptions. *The Leadership Quarterly, 16*(5), 625–653. https://doi.org/10.1016/j.leaqua.2005.07.002

Department of Culture, Media & Sports, UK. (1998). *Creative Industries Mapping Documents.* Retrieved from: https://www.gov.uk/government/publications/creative-industries-mapping-documents-1998

Department of Culture, Media & Sports, UK. (2001). *Creative Industries Mapping Documents.* Retrieved from: https://www.gov.uk/government/publications/creative-industries-mapping-documents-2001

Dollinger, S. J., Urban, K. K., & James, T. A. (2004). Creativity and openness: Further validation of two creative product measures. *Creativity Research Journal, 16*(1), 35–47. https://doi.org/10.1207/s15326934crj1601_4

Fernando, M. (2005). *Workplace spirituality: Another management fad?* Research Online, UoW. https://ro.uow.edu.au/cgi/viewcontent.cgi?article=1163&context=commpapers

Freshman, B. (1999). An exploratory analysis of definitions and applications of spirituality in the workplace. *Journal of Organizational Change Management, 12*(4), 318–329. https://doi.org/10.1108/09534819910282153

Frost, C. (2020). *Personal interview.*

Fry, L. W. (2003). Toward a theory of spiritual leadership. *The Leadership Quarterly, 14*(6), 693–727. https://doi.org/10.1016/j.leaqua.2003.09.001

Garg, N. (2017). Workplace spirituality and employee well-being: An empirical exploration. *Journal of Human Values, 23*(2), 129–147. https://doi.org/10.1177/0971685816689741

Gibbons, P. (2000). Spirituality at work: Definitions, measures, assumptions, and validity claims. In J. Biberman & M. Whitty (Eds.), *Work and Spirit: A Reader of New Spiritual Paradigms for Organizations* (pp. 111–131). University of Scranton Press.

Gilbreath, B., & Benson, P. G. (2004). The contribution of supervisor behaviour to employee psychological well-being. *Work & Stress, 18*(3), 255–266. https://doi.org/10.1080/02678370412331317499

Greenberg, J. S. (1985). Health and wellness: A conceptual differentiation. *Journal of School Health, 55*(10), 403–406. https://doi.org/10.1111/j.1746-1561.1985.tb01164.x

Harman, W. W., & Hormann, J. (1990). *Creative Work: The Constructive Role of Business in a Transforming Society*. Institute of Noetic Sciences Publication.

Howkins, J. (2007). *The Creative Economy: How People Make Money from Ideas*. Penguin Books.

India Today. (2017). *Srinivasa Ramanujan: The mathematical genius who credited his 3900 formulae to visions from Goddess Mahalakshmi*. https://www.indiatoday.in/education-today/gk-current-affairs/story/srinivasa-ramanujan-life-story-973662-2017-04-26

Jurkiewicz, C. L., & Giacalone, R. A. (2004). A values framework for measuring the impact of workplace spirituality on organizational performance. *Journal of Business Ethics, 49*(2), 129–142. https://doi.org/10.1023/B:BUSI.0000015843.22195.b9

Karakas, F. (2010). Spirituality and performance in organizations: A literature review. *Journal of Business Ethics, 94*(1), 89–106. https://doi.org/10.1007/s10551-009-0251-5

Kinjerski, V. M., & Skrypnek, B. J. (2004). Defining spirit at work: Finding common ground. *Journal of Organizational Change Management, 17*(1), 26–42. https://doi.org/10.1108/09534810410511288

Kochupillai, M. (2020). *Personal interview.*

Kohlberg, L., & Ryncarz, R. A. (1990). Beyond justice reasoning: Moral development and consideration of a seventh stage. In C. N. Alexander & E. J. Langer (Eds.), *Higher Stages of Human Development: Perspectives on Adult Growth* (pp. 191–207). Oxford Univeristy Press.

Kolodinsky, R. W., Giacalone, R. A., & Jurkiewicz, C. L. (2008). Workplace values and outcomes: Exploring personal, organizational, and interactive workplace spirituality. *Journal of Business Ethics, 81*(2), 465–480. https://doi.org/10.1007/s10551-007-9507-0

Krishnakumar, S., & Neck, C. P. (2002). The "what", "why" and "how" of spirituality in the workplace. *Journal of Managerial Psychology, 17*(3), 153–164. https://doi.org/10.1108/02683940210423060

Marques, J., & Dhiman, S. (Eds.). (2014). *Leading Spiritually*. Palgrave Macmillan. https://doi.org/10.1057/9781137455635

Mayo, K. R. (2009). *Creativity, Spirituality, and Mental Health: Exploring Connections*. Ashgate Publications. https://books.google.at/books?id=yVvTjgEACAAJ

Mehri, D. (2006). The darker side of lean: An insider's perspective on the realities of the Toyota production system. *Academy of Management Perspectives, 20*(2), 21–42. https://doi.org/10.5465/amp.2006.20591003

Meyer, J. P., Allen, N. J., & Smith, C. A. (1993). Commitment to organizations and occupations: Extension and test of a three-component conceptualization. *Journal of Applied Psychology, 78*(4), 538–551. https://doi.org/10.1037/0021-9010.78.4.538

Milliman, J., Ferguson, J., Trickett, D., & Condemi, B. (1999). Spirit and community at Southwest Airlines: An investigation of a spiritual values-based model. *Journal of Organizational Change Management, 12*(3), 221–233. https://doi.org/10.1108/09534819910273928

Mitroff, I. I., & Denton, E. A. (1999). *A Spiritual Audit of Corporate America: A Hard Look at Spirituality, Religion, and Values in the Workplace* (1st ed.). Jossey-Bass Publishers.

Moore, T. W., & Casper, W. J. (2006). An examination of proxy measures of workplace spirituality: A profile model of multidimensional constructs. *Journal of Leadership & Organizational Studies, 12*(4), 109–118. https://doi.org/10.1177/107179190601200407

Moxley, R. S. (2000). *Leadership and Spirit: Breathing New Vitality and Energy into Individuals and Organizations* (1st ed). Jossey-Bassand Center for Creative Leadership.

Nonaka, I. (1991). The knowledge creating company. *Harvard Business Review, 69*(6), 96–104.

Olalere, A. A. (2018). Workplace spirituality and creativity. In G. E. Roberts & J. E. Crossman (Eds.), *The Palgrave Handbook of Workplace Spirituality and Fulfillment* (pp. 989–1010). Springer International Publishing. https://doi.org/10.1007/978-3-319-62163-0_58

Olufemi-Ayoola, F., & Ogunyemi, K. (2018). Genesis and growth of workplace spirituality. In S. Dhiman, G. E. Roberts, & J. E. Crossman (Eds.), *The Palgrave Handbook of Workplace Spirituality and Fulfillment* (pp. 901–922). Springer International Publishing. https://doi.org/10.1007/978-3-319-62163-0_51

Parboteeah, K. P., & Cullen, J. B. (2003). Ethical climates and spirituality: An exploratory examination of theoretical links. In R. A. Giacalone & C. L. Jurkiewicz (Eds.), *Handbook of Workplace Spirituality and Organizational Performance* (pp. 137–152). M.E. Sharpe.

Pawar, B. S. (2009). Individual spirituality, workplace spirituality and work attitudes: An empirical test of direct and interaction effects. *Leadership & Organization Development Journal, 30*(8), 759–777. https://doi.org/10.1108/01437730911003911

Peris-Ortiz, M., Cabrera-Flores, M. R., & Serrano-Santoyo, A. (Eds.) (2019). *Cultural and Creative Industries: A Path to Entrepreneurship and Innovation*. Springer. https://doi.org/10.1007/978-3-319-99590-8

Poole, E. (2009). Organisational spirituality – A literature review. *Journal of Business Ethics, 84*(4), 577–588. https://doi.org/10.1007/s10551-008-9726-z

Rego, A., & Pina e Cunha, M. (2008). Workplace spirituality and organizational commitment: An empirical study. *Journal of Organizational Change Management, 21*(1), 53–75. https://doi.org/10.1108/09534810810847039

Rummel, J. (2000). *Frida Kahlo: A Spiritual Biography*. Crossroad.

Runco, M. A. (2004). Creativity. *Annual Review of Psychology, 55*(1), 657–687. https://doi.org/10.1146/annurev.psych.55.090902.141502

Sheep, M. L. (2004). Nailing down gossamer: A valid measure of the person-organization fit of workplace spirituality. *Academy of Management Proceedings*, 2004(1), B1–B6. https://doi.org/10.5465/ambpp.2004.13862520

Shinde, U., & Fleck, E. (2015). What spirituality can bring to leaders and managers: Enabling creativity, empathy and a stress free workplace. *Journal of Organizational Psychology, 15*(1), 101–110.

Singh, J., & Chopra, V. G. (2016). Relationship among workplace spirituality, work engagement and grit. *IOSR Journal of Business and Management, 18*(11), 21–27. https://doi.org/0.9790/487X-1811032127

Sisk, D. A., & Torrance, E. P. (2001). *Spiritual Intelligence: Developing Higher Consciousness*. Creative Education Foundation Press.

Tischler, L., Biberman, J., & McKeage, R. (2002). Linking emotional intelligence, spirituality and workplace performance: Definitions, models and ideas for research. *Journal of Managerial Psychology*, *17*(3), 203–218. https://doi.org/10.1108/02683940210423114

Ulster University. (2018). *Changing arts and minds: A survey of health and wellbeing in the creative sector.* https://www.inspirewellbeing.org/media/9236/changing-arts-and-minds-creative-industries-report.pdf

United Nations Council for Trade and Development (UNCTAD). (2008). *Creative Economy Report, 2008.* Retrieved from: https://unctad.org/system/files/official-document/ditc20082cerover view_en.pdf

United Nations Council for Trade and Development (UNCTAD). (2010). *Creative Economy Report, 2010.* Retrieved from: https://unctad.org/system/files/official-document/ditctab20103_en.pdf

United Nations Economic, Social, and Cultural Organisation (UNESCO) & Ernst & Young (EY). (2015). *Cultural times: The first global map of cultural and creative industries*. Retrieved from: https://en.unesco.org/creativity/sites/creativity/files/cultural_times._the_first_global_map_of_cultural_and_creative_industries.pdf

United Nations Economic, Social, and Cultural Organization. (2009). *UNESCO framework for cultural statistics*. UNESCO Institute for Statistics. Retrieved from: http://www.uis.unesco.org/culture/Documents/framework-cultural-statistics-culture-2009-en.pdf.

United Nations General Assembly Seventy-Fourth Session. (2019). *International Year of Creative Economy for Sustainable Development.* Retrieved from: https://undocs.org/A/C.2/74/L.16/Rev.1

UnLtd, Everymind & Never Not Creative. (2018). *Mentally Healthy*. Retrieved from: https://www.adnews.com.au/news/mental-health-of-ad-industry-lower-than-national-average

Walsh, J., Weber, K., & Margolis, J. D. (2003). Social issues and management: Our lost cause found. *Journal of Management*, *29*(6), 859–881. https://doi.org/10.1016/S0149-2063(03)00082-5

Wong, P. T. P. (2003). *Spirituality and meaning at work.* Retrieved from: http://www.meaning.ca/archives/presidents_columns/pres_col_sep_2003_meaning-at-work.htm

Zhao, H., Kessel, M., & Kratzer, J. (2014). Supervisor-subordinate relationship, differentiation, and employee creativity: A self-categorization perspective. *The Journal of Creative Behavior*, *48*(3), 165–184. https://doi.org/10.1002/jocb.46

Key Issues

Nurit Zaidman

14 (Western) Self-Spirituality: Literature Review, Conceptual Framework and Research Agenda

Introduction

The emerging interest in "post-traditional spirituality" in the West has been documented by several scholars, showing its growth in France, Great Britain, the Netherlands, and Sweden (Houtman & Aupers, 2007; Woodhead, 2004). Charles Taylor, and other scholars, have related to this as a cultural revolution, denoting that it has "profoundly altered the conditions of belief in our societies", shaping the contours of society as a whole (Taylor, 2007, p. 473; Heelas, 2008). The focal point of this cultural revolution is the individual and personal experience. Within this, key aspirations are unity, integrity, and holism. The language of this new culture is replete with assertions of harmony, balance, flow, integration, and "being at one" (Taylor, 2007, pp. 506–513; Heelas, 1996; Houtman & Aupers, 2010).

Research into the cultural and sociological aspects of self-spirituality culture tends to focus on the debate regarding the market orientation of self-spirituality (Heelas, 2008; Houtman & Aupers, 2010; e.g. Redden, 2016), or on the positive and negative aspects of workplace spirituality (Watts, 2018a), with an over-emphasis on its discourse (e.g. Bell & Taylor, 2003; Gotsis & Kortezi, 2008). Despite the recognition in the growth of self-spirituality, (Houtman & Aupers, 2007; Woodhead, 2004; Taylor, 2007; Heelas, 2008), existing research does not present a comprehensive analysis of this culture as it is enacted in Western society institutions: For profit organizations, public health organizations, public schools, etc., and most importantly, adherents' homes. It also tends to portray a schematic view of the perceived value of self-spirituality as constructed in relation to these contexts by adherents.

Some knowledge, however, has been acquired about the incorporation of self-spirituality into organizations. Studies show that self-spirituality adherents are hesitant – or even afraid – to disclose their involvement with self-spirituality in their workplaces, and that self-spirituality has generally been excluded from the public domain (Islam & Holm, 2016; Mitroff & Denton, 1999; Tejeda, 2015; Zaidman & Goldstein-Gidoni, 2011; Zaidman, 2020). Research have pointed out to the factors explaining organizational rejection showing differences in the fundamental principles of knowing and organizing (Karjalainen et al., 2019; Zaidman, 2020). Tensions between self-spirituality and the organization have been conceptualized in relation to rationality, equality in relationships, and the perspective of the 'the whole person' including the premise that every aspect of an individual – including her or his

https://doi.org/10.1515/9783110711349-014

body, mind, and spirit – should be fully present at work (Zaidman, 2020). While existing research identifies these factors, there is a need for further theoretical development of these topics, especially on the later, in light of existing research that has denoted the limited legitimacy attributable to a person's body within an organization (Mumby & Putnam, 1992).

Occasionally, adherents, consultants and other actors may act out their beliefs or practices, with an impact on their patients, colleagues, and customers (Heelas, 2008; Hyland et al., 2015; Boyle & Healy, 2003; Lychnell, 2017). These efforts are often accompanied by some degree of translation (Islam et al., 2017; Zaidman et al., 2009).

Overall, existing research ignores considering contextual characteristics as factors explaining responses to self-spirituality such as the type of the practice (e.g., mindfulness is accepted but other practices are rejected) and the differences between workplaces and occupations in terms of the factors that enhance or inhibit the expressions of self-spirituality. Likewise, distinctions should be made between different workplaces and occupations in terms of adherents and practitioner's introduction, disclosure, negotiation, etc. of different self-spirituality practices; and in the general modes of enactment of self-spirituality practices within these contexts.

Furthermore, little is known about the incorporation of self-spirituality at home. This is an important aspect, given that the domestic scene constitutes a primary site for processes of socialization, and that it serves as an important socio-cultural setting within which identities are articulated and negotiated (Hirvi, 2016). Yet, we do not know if and how adherents disclose and express self-spirituality at home, and if and how it effects their interactions with family members. There is no conceptual grounding to asses this phenomenon and it is unclear if existing theorizing regarding self-spirituality incorporation into organizations can be applicable to the domestic domain.

Finally, we know little about adherents' perspectives and the value that they attribute to self-spirituality as lived experience in their workplace and at home. Several studies have shown that self-spirituality adherents perceive it as empowering; as a source of self-confidence, direction, and meaning; and as a useful outlook to adopt in the work domain (e.g. Boyle & Healy, 2003; Hedges & Beckford, 2000; Kabat-Zinn, 2003; Mitroff & Denton, 1999; Narayanasamy & Owens, 2001; Zaidman et al., 2018; Zaidman & Goldstein-Gidoni, 2011). However, in the main, these studies overlook the distinctions that should be made between these evaluations as constructed and experienced within contexts. For instance, the perceived value of self-spirituality in the context of adherents' interactions with their children.

This chapter proposes a conceptual framework that could provide a platform for future research to assess the scope of this cultural revolution in mainstream Western society institutions. The conceptual framework is based on the literature of lived religion (e.g. Ammerman, 2020; Edgell, 2012; Harvey, 2014; McDannell, 1995), and the qualitative field-based literature on self-spirituality. The focus here is on adherents who are not self-employed, and on those who live with family members who are not self-spirituality adherents.

What is Self-Spirituality?

Self-spirituality is a multifaceted cultural phenomenon, incorporating ideas, concepts and practices from a range of domains including esotericism, psychology, Eastern philosophy, complementary and alternative medicine, religion, feminism, the human potential movement, the ecology movement and neo-paganism (Hanegraaff, 1998). In spite of its diversity of perspectives, scholars have identified several common core and interrelated dimensions of self-spirituality. The first is the *transcendence of the self*, i.e. a belief that one is connected to other people, ideas, nature, or some kind of "higher power" (Ashforth & Pratt, 2003). Closely linked to this is an emphasis on authentic selfhood and inner wisdom, and on connecting with these inner depths (Sointu & Woodhead, 2008; Flere & Kirbiš, 2009; Houtman & Aupers, 2007). Secondly, people who embrace self-spirituality tend to be committed to a vision of authentic *selfhood-in-relation*. Such relationality is conceived as fundamentally small-scale and egalitarian in outlook (Sointu & Woodhead, 2008). The third overarching dimension is *holism and harmony*, i.e. the integration of different aspects of one's self into a coherent and symbiotic conception of the self (Ashforth & Pratt, 2003; Flere & Kirbiš, 2009). This dimension includes a focus on the body (Sointu & Woodhead, 2008). The fourth dimension is a belief in personal *growth:* a clear sense of what one seeks to become, and what one needs to do in order to achieve self-actualization (Ashforth & Pratt, 2003).

The Conceptual Framework

The framework is based on existing qualitative research focusing on the incorporation of self-spirituality to organizations, including theories of translation, organization wisdom, power in organization, ethics, and on aspects of gender relations in the workplace (as surveyed below). To this research, I propose adding insights from the lived religion research with its focus on people's practices as they are contextualized in space and time (Edgell, 2012; Harvey, 2014; Neitz, 2011).

The first part of the conceptual framework deals with understanding participants' perspectives on the value of self-spirituality. The second part presents several "social practices" based on which one can learn about the interactional aspects of self-spirituality in contexts, namely, relationships, embodiment, materiality, ethics (Ammerman, 2020; Edgell, 2012; Harvey, 2014), and language (Zaidman et al., 2018). The third part relates to the ways that adherents apply while attempting to exhibit self-spirituality, and to the modes of incorporation of self-spirituality in participants' workplaces and at home. It considers contextual characteristics dictating if and how self-spirituality aspects can be enacted, including issues of power and gender (Ammerman, 2020; Zaidman, 2020).

A. Adherents Subjective Experience of Self-Spirituality in Specific Contexts

The focus here is on the questions: How do adherents perceive self-spirituality and what is the meaning they attribute to it? How do they experience self-spirituality in the context of their work and home? While several studies have illuminated several functional aspects of self-spirituality to adherents (e.g. Boyle & Healy, 2003; Hedges & Beckford, 2000; Mitroff & Denton, 1999; Narayanasamy & Owens, 2001; Zaidman et al., 2018), there is a need to contextualize this knowledge and to be aware of its problematization (e.g. Watts, 2018b).

B. Aspects of Self-Spirituality Social Practice

Guided by Ammerman (2020), and based on lived religion and self-spirituality research, I present below five aspects of self-spirituality interactional social practice.

The Embodiment of Self-Spirituality

The focus on the body is understood as being the access point to unique selfhood and as an integrated part of the holistic view of the person (Ashforth & Pratt, 2003; Sointu & Woodhead, 2008). This perspective is reflected in numerous practices in which adherents and practitioners relate to the body including yoga, reiki and meditation. The latter has attracted much interest and there is a growing research about the workplace benefits of mindfulness (Hyland et al., 2015). However, scant research refers to the involvement of other body oriented self-spirituality practices in the workplace. An exception is Van Otterloo, Aupers, and Houtman (2012) study about professionals from the Netherlands that experienced feelings of stress, alienation and personal crises, evoked by the denial of self-spirituality practices in their welfare organizations, leading several of them to leave their organizations. Another example is Lychnell's (2017) study, which described how participants apply spiritual knowledge drawn from a Buddhism-based meditation program when facing difficult situations at work, contributing to the emergence of several perspectives to challenging workplace situations. It is suggested to further explore what practices of the body, or of the mind-body, adherents and practitioners experience, construct, apply, etc. within the context of their workplace and at home, and how. (The discussion about complementary or alternative medicine is excluded from this framework because it does not fully hold to self-spirituality principles as defined here).

The Materiality of Self-Spirituality: Spaces and Objects

The materiality of religious life exists both within officially religious contexts and beyond, in objects and in spaces. This observation has recently shifted the focus of research to examine how do ordinary people use material objects in their religious or spiritual life in the workplace, home, school, etc. (Ammerman, 2020; McDannell, 1995).

As for self-spirituality culture, Zaidman (2007) shows how New Age shops become a 'church' denoting the unique arrangement of space and objects including the creation of boundaries between the sacred and the profane. While this study describes the New Age shop as a shrine, we do not know much about the materiality of self-spirituality in adherents' workplaces. Research on personalizing space at the workplace, including aspects related to employee identification and attachment (Ashkanasy et al., 2014) can be applied to illuminate data about the use of material objects by self-spirituality adherents, or the absence of it.

To my knowledge, extant research overlooks studying the use of material objects by self-spirituality adherents at home. Research on the materiality of religion at home can be applied as a basis for an investigation on this topic. For instance, there are studies that focus on the home shrine describing its importance for the family and denoting gender differences in its maintenance (Andrews, 2019; Thanissaro, 2018). In another study, Eshaghi (2015) analyzes pilgrimage photographs arguing that they have the capacity to extend the sacred time experienced during the pilgrimage into the ordinary time of everyday life.

Relationships

According to Harvey (2014, p. 2) "Understanding religion as everyday life . . . is that religion has everything to do with the relationships that constitute, form and enliven people in everyday activities in this material world". Several studies illuminate equality and crossing boundaries in adherents' professional communication. It was found that egalitarian expressions of relationships promoted by consultants in for-profit organizations, and by spiritual care providers in public health organizations were perceived as a threat to the existing social order (Zaidman & Goldstein-Gidoni, 2011; Zaidman, 2017). The results of another study show that sellers in New Age shops take several roles that go beyond mere economic exchange such as being counselors (Zaidman, 2007). On the other hand, in a study conducted in public schools it was found that the enactment of self-spirituality programs involved acceptance of the social hierarchy between the instructor and the pupils in each class (Zaidman & Goldstein-Gidoni, 2021). These seemingly contradictory results need further exploration.

Self-Spirituality Ethics

We refer to ethics as the moral principles that govern a person's behavior or the conducting of an activity. At the organizational level, several studies reflect on practitioners' ethics while they introduce, translate or incorporate self-spirituality into organizations. Islam, Holm and Karjalainen (2017) argue that the mindfulness concept can be read as an "empty signifier" with regard to its capacity to encode and contain a range of social contradictions. They demonstrate how, in the course of mindfulness programs, these oppositions are framed in such a way as to align with dominant managerial perspectives. Similarly, Zaidman and Goldstein-Gidoni (2021) found that when introducing self-spirituality to public schools brokers use self-spirituality practices to evoke diverse (at times contradictory) meanings. Additionally, it was found that in public schools as well as in for-profit organizations, brokers apply specific incremental tactics, such as the progressive disclosure of certain self-spirituality contents (Karjalainen et al., 2019; Islam & Holm, 2016; Zaidman et al., 2009) camouflage (Zaidman et al., 2009) and concealment (Zaidman et al., 2009).

More research is needed in order to understand how self-spirituality ethics is lived by individuals. A rare example is Watts (2018b) study about self–spirituality ethics and the ways it is actually practiced by a Canadian who self-identifies as spiritual but not religious. Several ethical principles have been identified such as 'the ethic of self-responsibility', namely, the principle that individuals ought to take responsibility for themselves; the authority of the self, with a focus on accumulated experiences, feelings etc.; and the ethic of productivity, i.e., the engagement in a constant process of self-work aiming to achieve "growth."

Self-Spirituality Language

Language is the basis of our communication with others. Preliminary results of a pilot conducted for this chapter from this project' pilot show that the main practice that women apply at home is self-spirituality language, and that they are more open in communicating this language with their children compared to their spouse. Only one study examined the incorporation of self-spirituality language to organizations. It examined gender differences in the way adherents from two countries apply self-spirituality language in the workplace (Zaidman et al., 2018). Based on this research, it seems that rather than using self-spirituality surveys that are built upon etic categories, a survey that is built upon emic categories of self-spirituality language can be a useful research tool to assess who speaks this language, where, to whom and on what occasions. Such knowledge can serve as an indication of the enactment of this culture (Zaidman et al., 2018).

C. The Enactment of Self-Spirituality within Contexts

In the main (excluding mindfulness), extant research on the enactment of self-spirituality in the workplace indicates that self-spirituality is marginalized and rejected (Zaidman, 2020). Based on this data, three sub-sections are presented: Conditions that determine the disclosure of self-spirituality; The Process, namely, the actions that adherents take and the General modes of self-spirituality incorporation. As for the enactment of self-spirituality at home, since there is no research on this topic, several studies about religion at home are discussed as a possible conceptual platform.

Workplace

Conditions that Determine the Disclose of Self-Spirituality

One study shows that a paramedic's reliance on spiritual resources to balance their emotions during work often depended upon the quality of the relationship with a work partner and on the colleague's spiritual orientation (Boyle & Healy, 2003). More research is needed within this area.

The Process: The Actions that Individuals Take

In general, extant research identifies two main methods that individuals (practitioners and adherents) apply when they introduce, expose or implement self-spirituality practices in organizations. The first is translation. Existing research shows that in public schools and for-profit organizations, self-spirituality is often translated as a technique for achieving profit-oriented ends, as well as a tool for improving and increasing organizational competitiveness, effectiveness, and productivity (Islam & Holm, 2016; Islam et al., 2017; Karjalainen et al., 2019; Zaidman et al., 2009; Zaidman & Goldstein-Gidoni, 2021). The process often involves claiming a basis in empirical evidence and scientific theory as a form of expert authority (Karjalainen et al., 2019).

The second method is making calculated choices regarding what aspect of the self-spirituality practice to expose, when and to whom. It was found that women employed in various organizations attested to using spiritual language during coffee breaks (but not during official work hours); with their colleagues (but not with their superiors); with other women (but not with men); and with close friends at work (but not with other colleagues) (Zaidman et al., 2018).

In general, the discussion about the translation of self-spirituality in organizations is un-contextualized and the research about the actions that individuals take lacks reference to issues of power, political influence and gender.

Modes of Incorporation

Based on extant research Zaidman (2020) proposes a gender-based classification of three modes of self-spirituality incorporation into organization. The classification considers the value of self-spirituality at work, its translation, and its impact on the organization's public domain. The domesticated masculine mode of incorporation appears to align itself with the organization's public domain. The 'feminine-intrinsic' mode of self-spirituality incorporation describes a situation when self-spirituality is experienced as individual wisdom. The 'feminine-context-bounded' mode of self-spirituality incorporation relates to situations that demand walking the line between the concealment and the exposure of adherents' choices. One can examine if this classification, or a variation of it, can be applied to data related to the ways self-spirituality is incorporated by adherents at home.

Research also refers to the incorporation of self-spirituality in organizations while adherents and practitioners create time and place boundaries. For example, spiritual care providers met with patients in unconventional locations and timetables. They 'travel' with patients to imaged places and times. In this way they were able to work with patients by creating a 'bubble', detached from the external organizational culture (Zaidman, 2017). Another example is a manger of a cosmetic shop who created an isolated territory in which the workers accepted this language, but not her managers and her suppliers (Zaidman et al., 2018). Future research should consider self-spirituality modes of incorporation in relation to workplaces and occupations.

Home

The domestic space constitutes a primary site for the process of socialization. It provides an important socio-cultural setting in which identities are being articulated and negotiated in relation to and in an active dialogue with the surrounding cultural and material environment. At the same time, home is also one of the daily contexts in which people not only maintain but also challenge, negotiate and modify cultural, linguistic and religious traditions (Hirvi, 2016). Thus, according to Dollahite, Marks, Dalton (2018), the home is a place where religious practices could enhance harmony or tension. The authors refer to a number of core ideas and practices that, when experienced in families, result in inherent inconsistencies and tensions. For instance, if family members diverge on the relative importance of transcendent or mundane experience, conflict may ensue. This might be the case with self-spirituality adherents who might experience transcendence while their family members would not share the same experience. Likewise, choices that are made whether to allow into one's personal and family life various ideas, images, and practices that may divide or harmonize family members (Dollahite et al., 2018). One can study not only if these aspects of self-spirituality help or harm families (as do Dollahite et al., 2018), but also the variety of consequences on adherents and their family members daily lives.

Future research can examine if adherents need to negotiate, or to apply particular behaviors (such as translation) while attempting to practice self-spirituality at home.

Table 14.1: A grid of research focus – Workplace and home.

	Perceived value (in general)	**Actual practice: relationships, embodiment, materiality, ethics and language**	**Conditions what determines the disclosure of self-spirituality**	**Process: what actions do adherents take in order to disclose or apply self-spirituality**	**Modes of incorporation including parameters such as: public space, power,**
Workplace type	What value is attributed to self-spirituality in relation to adherents workplace	How each practice is expressed, performed, displayed in a specific workplace	What factors enhance or inhibit the expressions of self -spirituality practices in a specific workplace		Modes of incorporation in relation to workplace
Profession type	What value is attributed to self-spirituality in relation to adherents profession	How each practice is expressed, performed, displayed in a specific profession			Modes of incorporation in relation to profession
Home	What value is attributed to self-spirituality in the context of interaction with family members	How are self-spirituality practices expressed, displayed and performed at home	Do adherents disclose self spirituality? what determines the disclosure of self-spirituality?		The consequences of self-spirituality practices within the family in terms of tension, harmony, etc.; Time and space allocation; Gender and power

Table 14.2: Research focus – The individual in relation to different contexts.

	Participant 1	Participant 2	Participant 3	Participant 4	Participant 5
Subjective experience and actual practice in the workplace					
Subjective experience and actual practice at home					
1. Describe and analyze the subjective experiences of adherent in the workplace and at home 2. Detach [?] coherence or divergence in the ways each participant applies self-spirituality practices at home and in the workplace. 2. Classify patterns 3. Provide contextual explanations considering workplace and home characteristics, issues of power, gender, etc.					

References

Ammerman, N. T. (2020). Rethinking religion: Toward a practice approach. *American Journal of Sociology*, *126*(1), 6–51.

Andrews, A. N. (2019). 'Gopāl is my baby': Vulnerable deities and maternal love at Bengali home shrines. *The Journal of Hindu Studies*, *12*(2), 224–241. https://doi.org/10.1093/jhs/hiz011

Ashforth, B. E., & Pratt, M. G. (2003). Institutionalized spirituality: An oxymoron? In *Handbook of Workplace Spirituality and Organizational Performance* (pp. 93–107). M. E. Sharpe.

Ashkanasy, N. M., Ayoko, O. B., & Jehn, K. A. (2014). Understanding the physical environment of work and employee behavior: An affective events perspective: The physical work environment. *Journal of Organizational Behavior*, *35*(8), 1169–1184. https://doi.org/10.1002/job.1973

Bell, E., & Taylor, S. (2003). The elevation of work: Pastoral power and the new age work ethic. *Organization*, *10*(2), 329–349. https://doi.org/10.1177/1350508403010002009

Boyle, M. V., & Healy, J. (2003). Balancing mysterium and onus: Doing spiritual work within an emotion-laden organizational context. *Organization*, *10*(2), 351–373. https://doi.org/10.1177/1350508403010002010

Dollahite, D. C., Marks, L. D., & Dalton, H. (2018). Why religion helps and harms families: A conceptual model of a system of dualities at the nexus of faith and family life: Why religion helps and harms families. *Journal of Family Theory & Review*, *10*(1), 219–241. https://doi.org/10.1111/jftr.12242

Edgell, P. (2012). A cultural sociology of religion: New directions. *Annual Review of Sociology*, *38*(1), 247–265. https://doi.org/10.1146/annurev-soc-071811-145424

Eshaghi, P. (2015). To capture a cherished past. Pilgrimage photography at Imam Riza´s Shrine, Iran. *Middle East Journal of Culture and Communication*, *8*(2–3), 282–306. https://doi.org/10.1163/18739865-00802007

Flere, S., & Kirbiš, A. (2009). New age, religiosity, and traditionalism: A cross-cultural comparison. *Journal for the Scientific Study of Religion*, *48*(1), 161–169. https://doi.org/10.1111/j.1468-5906.2009.01435_1.x

Gotsis, G., & Kortezi, Z. (2008). Philosophical foundations of workplace spirituality: A critical approach. *Journal of Business Ethics*, *78*(4), 575–600. https://doi.org/10.1007/s10551-007-9369-5

Hanegraaff, W. J. (1998). *New Age Religion and Western Culture: Esotericism in the Mirror of Secular Thought*. State University of New York Press.

Harvey, G. (2014). *Food, Sex and Strangers: Understanding Religion as Everyday Life*. Routledge.

Hedges, E., & Beckford, J. (2000). Holism, healing and the new age. In S. Sutcliffe & M. Bowman (Eds.), *Beyond New Age: Exploring Alternative Spirituality* (pp. 167–187). Edinburgh University Press.

Heelas, P. (1996). *The New Age Movement: The Celebration of the Self and the Sacralization of Modernity*. Blackwell.

Heelas, P. (2008). *Spiritualities of Life: New Age Romanticism and Consumptive Capitalism*. Blackwell Publishing.

Hirvi, L. (2016). Exploring the domestic homes of Sikhs in Finland as a "cosmos of senses." *Home Cultures*, *13*(1), 23–37. https://doi.org/10.1080/17406315.2016.1122963

Houtman, D., & Aupers, S. (2007). The spiritual turn and the decline of tradition: The spread of post-christian spirituality in 14 western countries. *Journal for the Scientific Study of Religion*, *46*(3), 305–320. https://doi.org/10.1111/j.1468-5906.2007.00360.x

Houtman, D., & Aupers, S. (2010). Religions of modernity: Relocating the sacred to the self and the digital. In S. Aupers & D. Houtman (Eds.), *Religion of Modernity, Relocating the Sacred to the Self and the Digital* (Vol. 2, pp. 1–30). http://www.pdcnet.org/oom/service?url_ver=Z39.88-2004&rft_val_fmt=&rft.imuse_id=asrr_2011_0002_0001_0103_0106&svc_id=info:www.pdcnet.org/collection

Hyland, P. K., Lee, R. A., & Mills, M. J. (2015). Mindfulness at work: A new approach to improving individual and organizational performance. *Industrial and Organizational Psychology*, *8*(4), 576–602.

Islam, G., & Holm, M. (2016, 9.7). *Banking on mindfulness: Presence and performance in a financial risk office*. 32nd European Group for Organizational Studies (EGOS) Colloquium, Naples.

Islam, G., Holm, M., & Karjalainen, M. (2017). Sign of the times: Workplace mindfulness as an empty signifier. *Organization*, *3*(1), 9–27. https://doi.org/10.1177/1350508417740643

Kabat-Zinn, J. (2003). Mindfulness-based interventions in context: Past, present, and future. *Clinical Psychology: Science and Practice*, *10*(2), 144–156. https://doi.org/10.1093/clipsy.bpg016

Karjalainen, M., Islam, G., & Holm, M. (2019). Scientization, instrumentalization, and commodification of mindfulness in a professional services firm. *Organization*, *28*(3), 483–509. https://doi.org/10.1177/1350508419883388

Lychnell, L. (2017). When work becomes meditation: How managers use work as a tool for personal growth. *Journal of Management, Spirituality & Religion*, *14*(3), 255–275. https://doi.org/10.1080/14766086.2017.1307782

McDannell, C. (1995). *Material Christianity: Religion and Popular Culture in America*. Yale University Press.

Mitroff, I. I., & Denton, E. A. (1999). A Study of Spirituality in the Workplace. *Sloan Management Review*, *40*(4), 83–92.

Mumby, D. K., & Putnam, L. L. (1992). The politics of emotion: A feminist reading of bounded rationality. *Academy of Management Review*, *17*, 465–486.

Narayanasamy, A., & Owens, J. (2001). A critical incident study of nurses' responses to the spiritual needs of their patients. *Journal of Advanced Nursing*, *33*(4), 446–455. https://doi.org/10.1046/j.1365-2648.2001.01690.x

Neitz, M. J. (2011). Lived religion: Signposts of where we have been and where we can go from here. In G. Giordan & W. H. Swatos (Eds.), *Religion, Spirituality and Everyday Practice* (pp. 45–55). Springer Netherlands. https://doi.org/10.1007/978-94-007-1819-7_4

Redden, G. (2016). Revisiting the spiritual supermarket: Does the commodification of spirituality necessarily devalue it? *Culture and Religion*, *17*(2), 231–249. https://doi.org/10.1080/14755610.2016.1183690

Sointu, E., & Woodhead, L. (2008). Spirituality, gender, and expressive selfhood. *Journal for the Scientific Study of Religion*, *47*(2), 259–276. https://doi.org/10.1111/j.1468-5906.2008.00406.x

Taylor, C. (2007). *A Secular Age*. The Belknap Press of Harvard University Press. https://books.google.at/books?id=hWRXYY3HRFoC

Tejeda, M. J. (2015). Skeletons in the broom closet: Exploring the discrimination of Pagans in the workplace. *Journal of Management, Spirituality & Religion*, *12*(2), 88–110. https://doi.org/10.1080/14766086.2014.933710

Thanissaro, P. N. (2018). Buddhist shrines: Bringing sacred context and shared memory into the home. *Journal of Contemporary Religion*, *33*(2), 319–335. https://doi.org/10.1080/13537903.2018.1469277

van Otterloo, A., Aupers, S., & Houtman, D. (2012). Trajectories to the New Age. The spiritual turn of the first generation of Dutch New Age teachers. *Social Compass*, *59*(2), 239–256. https://doi.org/10.1177/0037768612440965

Watts, G. (2018a). Missing the forest for the trees: "Spiritual" religion in a secular age. *Toronto Journal of Theology*, *34*(2), 243–256. https://doi.org/10.3138/tjt.2018-0112

Watts, G. (2018b). On the politics of self-spirituality: A Canadian case study. *Studies in Religion*, *47*(3), 345–372. https://doi.org/10.1177/0008429818764114

Woodhead, L. (2004). *Christianity: A Very Short Introduction*. Oxford Univeristy Press.

Zaidman, N. (2007). The new age shop – Church or marketplace? *Journal of Contemporary Religion*, *22*(3), 361–374. https://doi.org/10.1080/13537900701637510

Zaidman, N. (2017). The incorporation of spiritual care into Israeli medical organizations. In S. Feraro & J. R. Lewis (Eds.), *Contemporary Alternative Spiritualities in Israel* (pp. 83–94). Palgrave Macmillan US. https://doi.org/10.1057/978-1-137-53913-7_5

Zaidman, N. (2020). The incorporation of self-spirituality into Western organizations: A gender-based critique. *Organization*, *27*(6), 858–881. https://doi.org/10.1177/1350508419876068

Zaidman, N., & Goldstein-Gidoni, O. (2011). Spirituality as a discarded form of organizational wisdom: Field-based analysis. *Group & Organization Management*, *36*(5), 630–653. https://doi.org/10.1177/1059601111416232

Zaidman, N., & Goldstein-Gidoni, O. (2021). The translation of self-spirituality into organizations. *Social Compass*, *68*(1), 130–147. https://doi.org/10.1177/0037768620962387

Zaidman, N., Goldstein-Gidoni, O., & Nehemya, I. (2009). From temples to organizations: The introduction and packaging of spirituality. *Organization*, *16*(4), 597–621. https://doi.org/10.1177/1350508409104510

Zaidman, N., Janson, A., & Keshet, Y. (2018). "Power from within" and masculine language: Does new age language work at work? *Journal of Management Inquiry*, *27*(4), 392–404. https://doi.org/10.1177/1056492617714893

Marie Holm

15 Mindfulness and More: Spiritual Forms of Meditation

In recent decades, we've seen a shift, especially in the western world, from traditional religions to a myriad of spiritual practices. Along this spiritual smörgåsbord are all varieties of yoga, meditation, mudras and mantras, to Spiritualism and Spiritism, and everything in between. Some of these spiritual practices piggyback quasi-scientific claims and others maintain themselves as faith-based, beyond what can be explained and deemed rational. Some are composed of disperse informal adherents, committed in heart and mind though not on paper, and others incorporate, enlisting supporters to proselytise, furthering their expansion.

A mainstay at this table of plenty has been mindfulness, which has been picked up by many for a plethora of purposes, ranging from enhanced awareness to dulling pain from the capitalistic plunders in our suffering world. Indeed, efforts to address stress and suffering have spawned a $4.5 trillion wellness economy (Global Wellness Institute, 2020). Contemplative practices have entered companies in the context of employee training programs, psycho-social interventions under the banner of self-development and stress management.

The most popular of these practices is mindfulness, which has been shown to improve well-being, productivity and other functional outcomes. While cultivating mindfulness brings benefits for individuals and society, other practices also merit consideration. So, mindfulness has become all the buzz, but what broader possibilities exist? How could alternative approaches also be beneficial for workplaces, for the workers within them, and society around them? Let's commence an attempt to answer these questions by explaining what mindfulness is.

Mindfulness, a Prominent Type of Spirituality

Mindfulness is variably defined, at the individual level, as actively noticing new things (Langer, 1990), purposefully paying attention to the present moment without making judgements (Williams & Kabat-Zinn, 2013), and a state of consciousness or "receptive attention" to present experience (Good et al., 2016). Whereas Langer (1990), amiably referred to as the 'mother of mindfulness' and her proponents see mindfulness as a state that can be cultivated during daily life, Kabat-Zinn, known as the 'father of mindfulness' and his following view mindfulness as a practice to be regularly out in the form of meditation (Williams & Kabat-Zinn, 2013). Alongside, mindfulness is also integrally viewed as a trait that can be built up in oneself through practice (Good et al., 2016) whether through meditation or other methods

https://doi.org/10.1515/9783110711349-015

such as yoga (Munir et al., 2021). In sum, mindfulness is considered as a state, a trait or a practice, and herein we focus on it primarily as a practice, alternately known as an intervention (Good et al., 2016), as our interest is in spiritual forms of meditation.

At the collective level, mindfulness is seen in regard to how various processes relate to each other to create organizational attention, such as group members acting in sync to surmount a crisis (Weick & Sutcliffe, 2006), or as collective minding, a way of making sense of what is happening (Barry & Meisiek, 2010; Sutcliffe et al., 2016), or as collective wisdom (E. King & Badham, 2020). Particularly this latter grouping of a collective notion of mindfulness, collective wisdom, garners attention toward improving socio-economic conditions and political governance (ibid) such that mindfulness transforms not only individuals but also society, for the better.

While many mindfulness practitioners maintain that it is unrelated to spirituality, as does Kabat-Zinn (Purser, 2019), if a broad definition of spirituality is taken, then it would be included. Many prominent definitions of workplace spirituality include notions of an inner life, meaningful work, and sense of community (Neal, 2018, p. 9). Following this stream of thinking, spirituality does not necessarily involve a deity, which one could alternatively call creative force, divine being or another term, and thus extends from humanism to the esoteric. Turning then to how one spiritual practise, that of mindfulness meditation, can help humankind, we proceed to an overview of what benefits research has shown on individual and collective levels.

Benefits of Mindfulness to Individuals and Society

Most studies about meditation have been done about mindfulness, showing how it can boost well-being, creativity and other factors (see the meta-reviews of Eby et al., 2019; Good et al., 2016; Badham & King, 2019 of corporate mindfulness studies). Compared to studies of other forms of meditation, such as transcendental meditation, mindfulness studies have had a more robust research methodology, so have made more headway into top-tier academic journals.

Over eighty percent of the 67 published studies on mindfulness-based corporate training that Eby and colleagues (2019) included in their review had an aim of reducing stress and/or strain, and the remaining minority incorporate other health and well-being outcomes. Among well-being outcomes are experience of positive emotions and improved attention. Many of these studies were in clinical settings, though, more and more, researchers are venturing into other organisations to garner impacts of mindfulness both on individual and collective aspects, namely, enhanced engagement and performance alongside diminished levels of stress (ibid).

To attempt to summarise documented benefits of mindfulness is an ambitious feat, as Good et al. (2016) note that more than 4,000 scholarly articles on this subject had already appeared by the time of their analysis. Nevertheless, they managed to categorise these findings into how mindfulness influences attention, and thereby affects cognition, emotion, behaviour, and physiology. In terms of workplace outcomes, they find support amongst these plentiful publications for how mindfulness raises levels of performance, builds relationships, and augments well-being.

Mindfulness literature could be broadly grouped into four categories as per Badham and King's (2019) perspective, according to the extent of focus on the instrumental goals versus substantive purpose of mindfulness. These scholars contrast individual and collective mindfulness with wisdom on those two levels; thereby not merely placing positivistic research as being at opposite ends of the spectrum as critical research on mindfulness, building a middle-ground, of integral perspectives. Wisdom herein denotes ethical and philosophical dimensions as well as their applications in practice.

In the organisational context, mindfulness has also been explored as way for actors to make sense of events and to adapt accordingly toward forming the best possible outcomes (Barry & Meisiek, 2010; Weick & Sutcliffe, 2006). They, and other researchers within the sense-making paradigm, have looked at how collective mindfulness enables teams to refine how they communicate and co-ordinate to solve dire situations. This research looks at mindfulness as a form of attention focus within organisations in regard to collaboration, and by doing so, adds a collective dimension to the otherwise individual-focused literature.

Mindfulness is perceived by many as a tool to improve oneself and society, though simply sitting in silence and watching one's thoughts as they roll by without grasping on. Undoubtedly, this modern tool does ease the suffering of many, plus brings purported benefits, to some extent. Until recently, mindfulness was largely unquestionably accepted as an ultimate solution to bolster well-being, unleash creativity, and solve all other woes of the world. While yes, it has merits in stress-reduction and can reap value in competitive corporate environments, prudence is needed to avoid aggrandised claims (van Dam et al., 2017) as the mindfulness movement surges on.

VanDam and colleagues (2017) put forth that mindfulness research has advanced tremendously since the advent of this concept around the 1970s, though there is still room for improvement in how studies are designed and carried out. They also caution that although mindfulness has desirable attributes in terms of well-being, stress reduction and other outcomes, for those who have post-traumatic stress disorder, depression or other risk factors caused by psychological conditions, care must be taken before and during meditation practice. When necessary, psychological support needs to be accessible to practitioners, to cope with painful memories that may arise, and understand what they are feeling as a result of mindfulness or other forms of meditation.

Mindfulness-Based Interventions at Work

In the context of organisations, spirituality has been limited essentially to applications of mindfulness. Numerous instructors lead mindfulness courses in corporations, either independently or as part of an organisation, such as the Potential Project and the Search Inside Yourself Institute that was launched by a former engineer of Google, that links mindfulness with emotional intelligence. For instance, the non-profit organisation Institute for Mindful Leadership provides various courses of corporate mindfulness, in high-profile companies including Proctor & Gamble and Target as well as the American Red Cross (LoRusso, 2020, p. 5). Many a multinational firm provide mindfulness meditation training to their employees, from Google to Nike to Apple, the list goes on.

The background and certifications of instructors vary, from having either the training to teach Mindfulness-Based Stress Reduction (MBSR) in the form that Kabat-Zinn (2003) designed (initially within a clinical setting and thereafter extended to non-medical contexts), or another completed accreditation; whereas other trainers teach based on an extension of their own personal contemplative practice. Corporate trainings take an array of forms and focuses, with one common standard being MBSR which runs weekly through a span of eight weeks plus a day retreat, however many other options of mindfulness training programs exist. Online versions continue to pop up too, further prompted by the Covid-19 pandemic, including that of mobile application Headspace.

Mindfulness training focuses on individuals, navel-gazing, intangibly tied to a remote utopian vision of saving society from its ills (Walsh, 2018). Acceptably secular and scientific, mindfulness moved from monasteries to medicine to the boardroom, toting benefits ranging from better control of one's emotions, to awakening creativity (Islam et al., 2017) and ameliorating psychological well-being (Badham & King, 2019; Eby et al., 2019).

This palatable practice, mindfulness, spans the sacred and the profane, thus is inevitably people-pleasing. That is, mindfulness is generally presented as a secular practice yet is thought to still extoll the virtues of the religion that once encompassed it. Further, whatever mindfulness was at its origins becomes molded to fit the desires of its consumer, to quell the stresses of modern life or optimise concentration and decision-making prowess.

Mindfulness is typically introduced into firms as an attempt to boost mental well-being, productivity and other functional outcomes (Islam et al., 2017; Karjalainen et al., 2019; LoRusso, 2020). Some implementations involve physical practices alongside mental aspects, such as yoga, which are postures and movements of Indian origin intertwined in a set of ethics and philosophy (Munir et al., 2021). These scholars describe a similar process of adaptation that has taken place for yoga as has been the case of mindfulness, to suit Western organsations.

Corporate mindfulness interventions are marketed as being capable of cultivating mindful awareness in participants (Eby et al., 2019; Reb et al., 2020). While mindful programs are mostly implemented in groups, the practise is predominantly individually-based (E. King & Badham, 2020). However, bridges to broader aims are appearing, such as Brummans, Hwang & Cheong (2013) who describe participants who thereafter lead others to adopt mindfulness, spreading the movement to assist others in overcoming burdens of stress and avoiding burnout. Proceeding to a next thought, the following section outlines possible additions and alternatives to corporate mindfulness within the span of spirituality.

Additional Spirituality-Based Interventions at Work

The Covid-19 pandemic has highlighted that our world continues to struggle with gross inequality, rampant injustice plus environmental challenges, pending possible disaster. Rather than aggravating these problems by propagating the status quo, with its neoliberal tendencies to enable privileged individuals to self-aggrandise and to hail economic growth at any cost, collective transformations are necessary to bring about a better world (Bell et al., 2020). Corporate mindfulness, at least in part, serves toward solving these grand challenges, through a changed mindset.

Yet, at least for the time being, the noble communal aims of spirituality are still largely at odds with capitalistic discourse (Karjalainen et al., 2019). While a multitude of spiritual perspectives have existed though the millennia, few visible inroads have been made as of yet into organisations other than mindfulness. For spirituality that is present at work, the original practices tend to be transformed to match the scientised, instrumentalised and commodified design that neoliberalism has imbued into organisational life (Heelas, 2009; Karjalainen et al., 2019).

Some practitioners seek to re-find and reclaim an original version of this contemplative practice, alternately based on Eastern mindfulness, right mindfulness or Engaged Buddhism (S. B. King, 2009), that has not been watered-down by the West. Such programs are sprouting up as social mindfulness, engaged mindfulness and with other terms, reflecting a return to the roots of ethically based, less capitalistically-constricted iterations of ancient religious traditions (see for example Walsh, 2018; Purser, 2019).

Unlike other forms of corporate mindfulness, these social forms keep the religious foundation intact, thus instructing about ethics and social aspects. In doing so, these interventions transcend individual-level focus to awaken collective-level change. Among these approaches are second-generation mindfulness programs, Buddhist-derived interventions that are overtly spiritual, combining meditative insight, ethical awareness, and wisdom insights and practices (E. King & Badham, 2020). These reintegrate a philosophical foundation, such as Patel and Holm (2018) describe, in re-instating values of non-materialism, openness to change and connection with nature, fostering responsible and benevolent behaviours from mindful managers toward the betterment of society.

Such is the case for emergences of paranormal, esoteric and new age spiritualities at work, in that they undergo a process of transformation as they cross into the business realm (Heelas, 2009). Terminology is covertly changed to avoid taboos, such as for psychics, mediums and channelers, that Zaidman (2015) likens to business consultants. Advice is doled out by these spiritual consultants as to which stocks to buy, which people to hire and so on, all without necessarily mentioning a belief system or ethical code of conduct.

Plus, for these practices, those involved often prefer anonymity and secrecy, to avoid being judged as lacking credibility. Religious affiliations and even spiritual connotations are often stripped from these forms of practices upon entering the pretences and premises of organisations. Simultaneously, such ironically often lucrative and sought-after spiritual practises are often sidelined from being even spoken of to others at work, relegated to the personal sphere.

For the time being then, organisational forms of spirituality are restricted mostly to mindfulness, though alternatives are arising, that could unfold more vast and diverse benefits. Inevitably, these alternatives also undergo a conversion process, to a greater or lesser extent, to take shape in an organisationally-friendly format. Now that mindfulness has paved a pathway for spiritual practises to assume a place in mainstream society, we might well see the advent of new movements. Among these could be the meditation practise of attunement from Spiritualism, for instance, a religion based on a set of guiding philosophical principles (Kirsebom, 2012). This type of meditation, attunement, cultivates awareness of one's own energy in a similar way as mindfulness does, by calming and quieting the mind, and then proceeds to extend awareness to a connection with all beings.

Additional philosophies and practices might well also find their way to become more commonplace, and find entry points into corporate life as well. This possibility is in part thanks to the mindfulness movement, as it opened and widened this window to spirituality at work. As of yet, research on forms of spiritual practices other than mindfulness meditation is sparse, albeit a growing stream of literature.

References

Badham, R., & King, E. (2019). Mindfulness at work: A critical re-view. *Organization*, 135050841988889. https://doi.org/10.1177/1350508419888897

Barry, D., & Meisiek, S. (2010). Seeing more and seeing differently: Sensemaking, mindfulness, and the workarts. *Organization Studies*, *31*(11), 1505–1530. https://doi.org/10.1177/0170840610380802

Bell, E., Gog, V., Sorin, Simionca, A., & Taylor, S. (Eds.). (2020). *Spirituality, Organization and Neoliberalism: Understanding Lived Experiences*. Edward Elgar.

Brummans, B. H. J. M., Hwang, J. M., & Cheong, P. H. (2013). Mindful authoring through invocation: Leaders' constitution of a spiritual organization. *Management Communication Quarterly, 27* (3), 346–372. https://doi.org/10.1177/0893318913479176

Eby, L. T., Allen, T. D., Conley, K. M., Williamson, R. L., Henderson, T. G., & Mancini, V. S. (2019). Mindfulness-based training interventions for employees: A qualitative review of the literature. *Human Resource Management Review, 29*(2), 156–178. https://doi.org/10.1016/j.hrmr.2017.03.004

Global Wellness Institute. (2020). *Defining the mental wellness economy*. GWI.

Good, D. J., Lyddy, C. J., Glomb, T. M., Bono, J. E., Brown, K. W., Duffy, M. K., Baer, R. A., Brewer, J. A., & Lazar, S. W. (2016). Contemplating mindfulness at work: An integrative review. *Journal of Management, 42*(1), 114–142. https://doi.org/10.1177/0149206315617003

Heelas, P. (2009). *Spiritualities of Life: New Age Romanticism and Consumptive Capitalism* (Vol. 3). Blackwell Publishing.

Islam, G., Holm, M., & Karjalainen, M. (2017). Sign of the times: Workplace mindfulness as an empty signifier. *Organization, 3*(1), 9–27. https://doi.org/10.1177/1350508417740643

Kabat-Zinn, J. (2003). Mindfulness-based interventions in context: Past, present, and future. *Clinical Psychology: Science and Practice, 10*(2), 144–156. https://doi.org/10.1093/clipsy.bpg016

Karjalainen, M., Islam, G., & Holm, M. (2019). Scientization, instrumentalization, and commodification of mindfulness in a professional services firm. *Organization, 28*(3), 483–509. https://doi.org/10.1177/1350508419883388

King, E., & Badham, R. (2020). The wheel of mindfulness: A generative framework for second-generation mindful leadership. *Mindfulness, 11*(1), 166–176. https://doi.org/10.1007/s12671-018-0890-7

King, S. B. (2009). *Socially Engaged Buddhism*. University of Hawaii Press.

Kirsebom, A. (2012). *Mediumskap og klarsyn: I teori og praksis*. Kolofon Forlag.

Langer, E. J. (1990). *Mindfulness*. Da Capo Press.

LoRusso, J. D. (2020). *Spirituality, Corporate Culture, and American Business: The Neoliberal Ethic and the Spirit of Global Capital*. Bloomsbury.

Munir, K., Ansari, S. (Shaz), & Brown, D. (2021). From Patañjali to the "gospel of sweat": Yoga's remarkable transformation from a sacred movement into a thriving global market. *Administrative Science Quarterly*, 1–46. https://doi.org/10.1177/0001839221993475

Neal, J. (2018). Overview of workplace spirituality research. In S. Dhiman, G. E. Roberts, & J. E. Crossman (Eds.), *The Palgrave Handbook of Workplace Spirituality and Fulfillment* (pp. 1–56). Palgrave Macmillan. https://doi.org/10.1007/978-3-319-61929-3_45-1

Patel, T., & Holm, M. (2018). Practicing mindfulness as a means for enhancing workplace pro-environmental behaviors among managers. *Journal of Environmental Planning and Management, 61*(13), 2231–2256. https://doi.org/10.1080/09640568.2017.1394819

Purser, R. (2019). *McMindfulness: How Mindfulness Became the New Capitalist Spirituality*. Watkins Media Ltd.

Reb, J., Allen, T., & Vogus, T. J. (2020). Mindfulness arrives at work: Deepening our understanding of mindfulness in organizations. *Organizational Behavior and Human Decision Processes, 159*, 1–7. https://doi.org/10.1016/j.obhdp.2020.04.001

Sutcliffe, M., Vogus, T. J., & Dane, E. (2016). Mindfulness in organizations: A cross-level review. *Annual Review of Organizational Psychology and Organizational Behavior, 3*(1), 9–27.

van Dam, N. T., van Vugt, M. K., Vago, D. R., Schmalzl, L., Saron, C. D., Olendzki, A., Meissner, T., Lazar, S. W., Kerr, C. E., Gorchov, J., Fox, K. C. R., Field, B. A., Britton, W. B., Brefczynski-Lewis,

J. A., & Meyer, D. E. (2017). Mind the hype: A critical evaluation and prescriptive agenda for research on mindfulness and meditation. *Perspectives on Psychological Science, 13*(1), 36–61. https://doi.org/10.1177/1745691617709589

Walsh, Z. (2018). Mindfulness under neoliberal governmentality: Critiquing the operation of biopower in corporate mindfulness and constructing queer alternatives. *Journal of Management, Spirituality & Religion, 15*(2), 109–122. https://doi.org/10.1080/14766086.2017.1423239

Weick, K. E., & Sutcliffe, K. M. (2006). Mindfulness and the quality of organizational attention. *Organization Science, 17*(4), 514–524. https://doi.org/10.1287/orsc.1060.0196

Williams, J. M., & Kabat-Zinn, J. (Eds.). (2013). *Mindfulness*. Taylor & Francis. https://doi.org/10.4324/9781315874586

Zaidman, N. (2015). Business consulting vs. channeling: What is the difference? *Journal of Contemporary Religion, 30*(1), 89–105. https://doi.org/10.1080/13537903.2015.986978

David M. Boje

16 Storytelling Nature-spirituality: An Autoethnographic Journey of Rediscovery

Introduction

What is the role of storytelling Nature-spirituality in sustainability of public land? Too often our spirituality detaches itself from the aliveness of Nature, how even the rocks, trees, and seedlings are spiritual. Too often I forget I am not in Nature, I am Nature. Nature is separate from us, and just de-spirited, becomes calculable material resource, a thing that is lifeless. It is not just organizations that abuse Nature. This is an autoethnographic journey of rediscovering my spiritual self, my living story (Bøje, 2005, 2012). It is easy to let ego take charge, and to just carry on. In this case, there are mobs of neighbors doing illegal dumping, setting fire to trees and shrubs, just to have a good ole time. As someone who loves nature, it's hard to offer love and forgiveness. This combination of de-spirited Nature by most government organizations and some (but not a majority of) neighbors who treat public land as a free dump site has led to the tragedy of the commons. The aliveness of Nature has been marginalized, its spirituality not treated seriously. How do I reconnect with the spiritual of Nature? My approach is a return to 'Indigenous Ways Of Knowing' (IWOK) that might inspire changes in 'Western Ways Of Knowing' (WWOK). In this way, the trees, rocks, water, the microbes invisible to the naked eye, have their living spiritual Nature. I want to find out if a spiritual approach to public land, its soil, water, vegetation, and ensemble-aliveness can make some kind of difference to mobs. This is a case study, an autoethnography of my spiritual encounters with public land abuse, and learning to hear Mother Nature's voice, her aliveness of spirit, and my ethical answerability to let her take care of her air, water, earth, and fire.

Prologue

Sometimes I listen but I don't hear. This makes it harder to hear Nature. For example, in 1995, Grace Ann Rosile took me to meet a Jain Monk. He gave me a Jain name, '*Arihant*' by the Gurudev Shree Chitrabhanu (1978, 1979a, 1979b, 1980). I asked, "what does it mean?" He replied, and I wrote it in my notebook this way, "You are conqueror of your inner enemies. Meditate on it daily." I did so for ten years, then came back, tired and exhausted, and asked for a new name. He asked what I was doing. I told him, "each morning I meditate on my inner enemies and how to conquer each of them. I have so many enemies, I want a new name." He

https://doi.org/10.1515/9783110711349-016

told me, "Arihant means you have no enemies, everyone is your friend." Why did this mishearing happen? I was programmed with an academic mind, a 'Western Way of Knowing' (WWOK) and was still in the grip of its programming. Each word-thought I grew up into has a thousand vibrant energies of WWOK culture, society, education, politics, media, and capitalism. Daily meditation was helping me to not just listen, but to actually hear a spiritual voice.

I keep learning the difference between my listening and my hearing. August 2020, after a Vision Quest in the Organ Mountains of New Mexico, Mike ThreeBears, (on Zoom due to the pandemic), gave me the name, *'Surrenders to Spirit.'* Again, I misheard my name, writing down *'Sacrifices to Spirit'* in my notebook. I am getting used to this new answer. To 'who I am?' 'Surrenders to Spirit' is who I am in my own living story, and in my shamanic drumming meditation daily practice sessions. I am only now hearing the name, seeking its meaning.

No Good Deed Goes Unpunished

I began noticing this year, after Vision Quest 2020, I was accused by local teens and some young adults of being this grumpy old man. All I was doing was picking up trash, trying to keep the ephemeral pond, located on public lands habitable to the aquatic life that was seasonal. I was picking up all the trash, the broken beer bottles, shotgun shells, and plastic water bottles, and even diapers and COVID-19 masks. A nasty mess, somewhat dangerous to even venture to the pond. The teens and some adults, with the pandemic, had escalated. They were burning tires, pallets and junked furniture. I photographed the mess on my morning walks. I wanted to help Mother Nature. You will see, as I unfold and unpack the case, perhaps Mother Nature, can take care of herself. I was shoveling the burn piles of trash. I thought the fires had gone out. But shovel full after shovel full, into the bed of our pickup truck, and sometimes it caught fire, and I'd put it out with shovel full of sand, again and again. What I learned is I had become a meddling enabler and not at all helping the teens do what I had done at their age, have a booze-fest in the wild. I always packed out, but that is how my dad taught me. As you shall see, I was not helping Mother Nature, and that to understand spirituality of Nature, I had to learn my role.

I found myself picking up the litter, hauling the illegally dumped mattresses, tire, and broken furniture to the landfill. I actually made an earthship greenhouse out of the tires, and some compost bins out of a few of the pallets. But, the amount of dumping week after week, was overwhelming. So I put it into the dump site. There were fires set in the pond, and several days each week scores of beer, wine, and liquor bottles, plus lots of plastic soda and water bottles. Burning tires, mattresses, and pallets leaves, a mess of melted glass chards, nails, radial wire, and springs. It's a nasty mess and takes days to clean up. I'd shovel it into the pickup bed, and use magnets to gather the nails and screws. Then off to the land fill, and pay the $4 fee to be able to shovel it into an ash bin, which would take me several hours.

The pickup I drive caught fire, when I loaded the burn pit, still smoldering and smoking, in the back. Then as I unloaded the ash pit into the dumpster at our ranch, it caught fire. Each time, I shoveled sand and put out the fire, only to have it catch fire again and again. So I ran to our barn, and began carrying buckets of water and throwing them at the flames in the dumpster. I finally managed to carry the fire from the burn pile to the dumpster on our ranch. I became like Mickey Mouse in Fantasia, carrying a pail of water in each hand, putting out the fire. And it kept reigniting. Even a day later it reignited and burned the lids off the dumpster and all the paint. So I stopped picking up teen's trash and went out to just enjoy the desert life.

On President Biden Inauguration Day the errant neighbors began pouring gasoline on the ground and just burning entire trees and shrubs where they stood. I suppose it was less work to rip branches off trees, or just ignite an entire tree, than to actually perform the labor of hauling the discarded material to the pond. I had done the usual storytelling things. I made reports of license plates and photos of the burn events, the illegal dumping, and so on to the Sheriff's Office. I contacted the codes enforcers of city and county government. All to no avail. With the COVID-19 pandemic, public agencies were overwhelmed, were working split-shifts, and were understaffed. I did manage to meet up with two codes officers. We wore our masks and toured the dump sites. They told me forensic stories. From the look of the trash, there is an underground business happening. The illegal trash looks like a business that removes junk from backyards and cleans up houses (or apartments) after someone has passed or moved, and everything of real value was sold off. Instead of paying a $4 landfill fee, and driving the three miles to the local transfer site, they just drive onto public land and dump it for free. I asked if they could catch them.

> It's hard. You have to catch them in the act. They post sentries and by the time there's a report, and you head out there, they've scattered. Even when you catch them, they say there's 'no signs' or 'did not know it was public land' or 'everyone does it. What's the big deal?'

I showed the codes officers jettisoned envelopes and receipts with names and addresses. "They just tell you, someone stole their trash, and they had no idea how it got there." As it turns out, it's all but impossible to catch illegal dumpers. I heard that the Bureau of Land Management (BLM) was installing motion-activated wildlife cameras in an effort to catch illegal dumpers in the act. BLM parcels are nearby, and most neighbors think its all BLM. So, I wrote letters to the editor, thanking BLM for putting the hidden camera on public land. This act of storytelling lowered the incidence rate for a month, but once no actual fines for levied and no arrests, the dumping returned with a vengeance. It actually got worse.

I organized several Zoom meetings with neighbors, and invited city and county officials. One official, from a neighboring district showed up. The sheriff's office told me to stop bothering them. It was not just trash, but neighbors (some of them, not many) head to the desert public land to do target practice. They shoot automatic and semi-automatic weapons of every descriptions. It gets noisy during hunting seasons. In and out of hunting season, any weekend, and some weekdays, there is a lot of gun fire. Sparkles (my dog) is very sensitive to gunfire, while Cuddle-bear (my other dog) couldn't care less. I am a Vietnatm War veteran, so I am used to gunfire. Sparkles stops at the sound of gun fire, freezes motionless in her tracks, and waits there till I head for home. When I am out running with the dogs, and the armed citizens assemble, sometimes we mingle. I used to just walk among them, and collect the trash. After a few encounters, some jeering, 'hey here's a diaper, pick it up, old man' I decided it was not a good idea.

My neighbors who had dads who taught them to respect Nature, to pack out, to obey the laws, and so on – said the pond was a lost cause. Since the COVID-19 pandemic, the mob had taken over its territory. There is just nothing to be be done. So I turned to spiritual intervention. Each day I go out too early for the gun slinger, drinking crowd to be awake, and do some shamanic drumming, alternating, one day at the pond, the next day, down in the Alameda Arroyo. So, one day I encounter the burned trees, the ash pit, the usual assemblage of broken bottles and trash, and the next day, I get some peaceful Nature, where there is still some liter but not so much it overwhelms you. A friend told me to do this experiment. Close your eyes, feel the energy around you, and point in the direction of the most energetic area. Odds are, you will be pointing to liter, because people without spiritual mooring, sense a spiritual place, and toss their garbage onto it. Could it be the most spiritual places of public land, have the biggest trash heaps?

How Do I Make Sense of all This?

What are the antenarrative processes constitutive of these multi-use public land and water narratives? (Bøje, 2012) I put a storyboard together to depict the underlying processes.

Swainson Hawks that nest in this place, all the trillions of biotic microcosm life beneath my feet, constitute life here. The quantum energy filed includes Grandfather and Grandmother Hackberry Trees, and their seeds. I began to eat the pulpy flesh of the seeds, as my *dieta* (Bøje & Henderson, 2014; Henderson & Bøje, 2016). Already a vegan, the fasting preparation was not difficult. *Dieta* involves ingesting the seed pulp, aligning with the plants vibrations and my inner body vibrations in

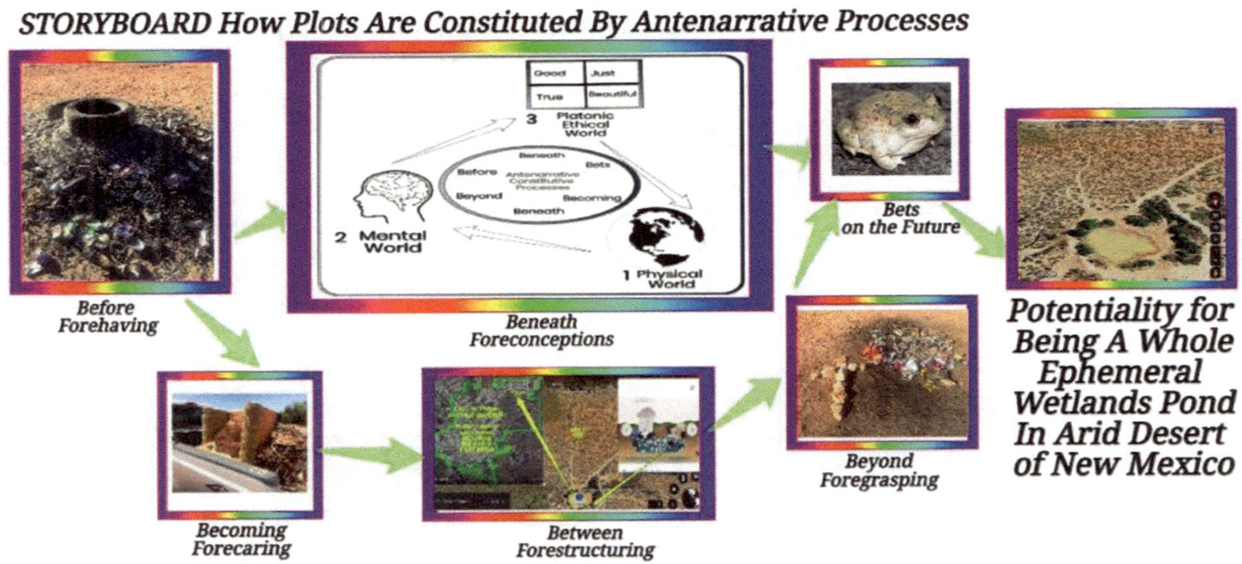

Figure 16.1: Presentation on antenarratives to true storytelling: Staging using storyboarding.

the "indisputable presence" (Gagliano, 2018) of our Beneath (pre-words, pre-language) and our Beyond (fore-grasping intuitive spiritual presence).

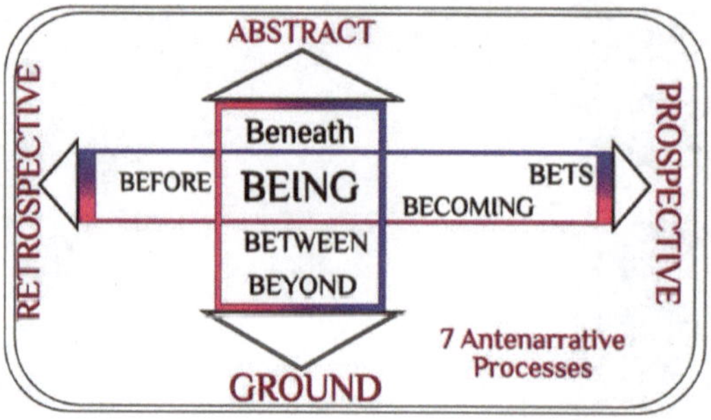

Figure 16.2: Seven antenarrative processes in-context.

I want to stress how important it is that we are all breathing the same air as the grandparent trees, nourished with the same water vapor atmosphere, the vibrations of life, the breathing in and out, during the shamanic drumming, it penetrates me.

> At each inhalation, free oxygen breathed out by plants enters into us in all it levity and allows us to convert what we eat into energy. At each exhalation, we let go of carbon dioxide and water, which plants ingeniously combine with a touch of sunlight to make their own food and, once again, more oxygen. (Gagliano, 2018, p. 15)

Tree and human partake of the same air, water, earth, and fire elements of life. With each breath, in and out, I reflect I am more plant-like, more aware of the community of plants, those ensemble colonies of trillions of living cells in my body, within my own Self, because I am an earthy being. I am in inseparable exchange of carbon, water, and nutrients with plant life. In my *dieta*, begun in June 2020, my daily meditative shamanic apprenticeship, my humble request to approach Grandfather and Grandmother Hackberry Trees in the Chihuahua Desert, I was engaged in antenarrative relational processes pre-constitutive of the story I now tell. I have begun learning hackberry tree. By August 2020 I was preparing for the Vision Quest, Michael ThreeBears offered to me. My *dieta* of consuming a few hackberry seed pulps (seed itself much to hard to eat), becomes a seed to plant. During the August Vision Quest, of course many spiritual encounters, the *dieta*, unfolded. In December 2020, I began planting fallen hackberry seeds, moving them to mulchy areas protected by the grandparent trees. I was growing four that sprouted and still grow in our home nursery. Antenarratively, this is about getting into Being, the Beyond, and the Beneath (the vertical energy work) of working with vibrant mattering energy waveforms. For Vision Quest, I collected a fallen Grandfather Hackberry Tree branch for a Talking Stick to use in the ceremony. This is my *dieta* relation of my 'I Am' with the Grandfather Hackberry Tree's 'I Am.'

I started to research the antenarratives, behind the narratives and stories being spun by various city, county, state, and federal agencies. The technical terms (Before, Beneath, Bets, Becoming, Being, Between and Beyond) are from my work on the science of storytelling (Larsen et al., 2020).

BEFORE – In the past burning tires, pallets, plastic bottles, aluminum cans, and mattresses leaves a toxic mess.

BENEATH – To tell this story, you need concepts (foreconceptions) and here I show the relation between concepts of Physical World, Mental Word (what story is in head of people dumping and burning, polluting and breaking laws) and the Mental World of the government, the residents looking as bystanders doing nothing.

BEING – In existentialism, particularly Heidegger, Being-There is an uncovering ways of BEING' in place/space we inhabit here-and-now. "To free oneself for a binding directedness is possible only by being free for what is opened up in an open region" (Heidegger, 2003, section on Ground of Correctness)

BETS ON THE FUTURE – What future do all the characters (government & business, universities, & environment organizations, and residents of New Mexico) want. The leases raises money for schools, However, currently the parcel is not leased for anything.

BECOMING – I haul out the burn pit each time it reappears, and haul out the daily litter. Good news, for last five days June 19 to June 23 2020, no more litter or burn pits. It's peaceful place with potential.

BETWEEN – The jurisdictions for governing the uses and care of the land fall in-between the infrastructure of City, County, and Federal – State Land Office. Most residents and many officials assume it is BLM that has jurisdiction. Not True at all.

BEYOND – means intuitive that is beyond the five senses, and here I am working with Shamanic Drumming Circle folks who came up with this idea to storyboard the situation.

More About Being-There. For example, a narrative is "never a presuppositionless apprehending of something presented to us" it's a "fore-given" (Heidegger, 1926, 1962). BEING is not the empirical (that is the ontic). Rather, BEING is something veiled, and we do an uncovering, by going to deeper levels. Being is not just the now, it is the place, the here-and-now of a Situation. Things in the here-now, are either present-at-hand (such as some broken tool that is unusable) or ready-to-hand in a process such as in blacksmithing, a hammer that works, and is accessible, is ready-to-hand.

Another Example: The Trees are already BEING-in-the-World. The trees are present-at-hand. Yet, if the concept of bonfire (BENEATH) changes to, burn trees 'ready-to-hand' in site, in the here-now, then BEING (fore-given) shifts. If trees are natural living systems of Nature, and if those trees have entanglements of many other microscopic species (fungi, microorganisms, bacteria), and many other species (birds, toads, rabbits) that are visible to us, then that presentment of bonfire-by-burning-live-trees is an existential shift.

Why had I become grumpy old man? What went wrong with all my organizing, and a score of YouTubes, and conference presentations? Teens and some misguided adults have been holding binge drinking parties, most weekends, burning tires, pallets, shooting beer bottles with pistols and rifles, and littering the place. For the past year, I collected broken and whole bottles, shoveled the burn and ash pits into my pickup, only to re-shovel the nasty mess into the dumpster on our farm. I took pictures of the vehicles, and the trash, and turned the reports into the 'No Throw' app on my cellphone. A student in one of my Ph.D. courses had developed the app. But nothing happened. It was COVID-19 epidemic of 2020, and Dona Ana County municipality was not doing anymore illegal dumping removal. On Dec. 15 2020, I watched as a young man unloaded more kindling and logs for the next bonfire at the pond.

I did my usual shamanic drumming, sitting on the pallets by the latest preparations for the bonfire. I noticed brand new tie down, yellow in color, with tag still on it. I pulled it from the soon to be burning pile of lumber, logs, and pallets. I drummed for my son Ray, and for clarity on what to do on the East Mesa. I faced Grandfather Hackberry Tree.

As I put my drum in its backpack, and get my two dogs, Sparkles and Cuddlebear, I heard the roar of the pickup with the American Flag on it. I walked right under the tree, and to the top of the berm on the other side. I had peace in my heart, and walked down into the pond to give the teen back his yellow tie-down rope. I did not judge, blame, or accuse. Just stayed in social distance, my mask in place, no mask on his face. We wished each other well.

Figure 16.3: Bird's nest in the trees being added to burn pile about to be lit, still ready to burn, Dec 16 2020, with Grandfather Hackberry Tree visible in the distance, on the pond brim.

As I looked at the bird's nest on December 15th, I was overwhelmed by the beauty of the scene, the little bird's nest, visible just beneath Grandfather Hackberry Tree, as he tends his new seedlings, waiting for better days.

With COVID-19, everything changed. The teens' drunken binging, and a fair number of adults, were generating more daily trash than I ever saw. It got to be more trash than I could manage to haul out, and overfilled our dumpster each week, so I hauled the excess to the landfill. I had become their enabler, picking up dirty diapers, COVID-masks, broken bottles. I had a change of heart. I am deciding this month, how to reach out to neighborhood teens, during this COVID-19 pandemic. I meditated daily, wrote in my notebooks, about water, and how it was inseparable from earth (the living soil under our feet), from fire (changes in heating of the planet), and from the air (getting more polluted). This insight of the inseparability of water, earth, fire, and air, had prompted me to abandon a 120,000 word book draft, and just start over. I was starting over a lot of drafts in 2020.

I meditated on how to have a heart of care for the ecosystem, and picked up trash and illegal dumping daily, to do the caring. I confronted teens and adults who carried guns, and picked up the trash in the midst of their drunken parties. I took pictures, and when I could get one of a license plate, I filled reports with county codes officers (via the 'No Throw' app) and made written reports with photos to Sheriff's Office. Nothing changed at all. I held a meeting, wearing COVID-19 masks with the manager of State Land Office (SLO), and a dozen neighbors, to discuss options for leasing the public land.

I was organizing neighbors, and talked to everyone in the Academy of Management. I let people know the laws of the matter. I looked into other regulations and ordinance. Again, all being violated with no enforcement whatsoever. I tried an appeal using social media. I began doing almost weekly videos (with Julia Haden and Duncan Pelly posted to YouTube) and making conference presentations. Many were about the onto-story the 'vibrant matter' of an assemblage of things. An onto-story is how the energy of an assemblage of things has a story to tell. Onto-story comes from the awesome work of Jane Bennett (2008 Vibrant Matter book). William James the pragmatist, says things tell a story. Here I find tires in the desert that are not yet burned, on a pile of already burned tires, beer cans and bottles, plastic of all types of bottled water, and other litter. It's a tragedy of the commons, the critical essence of living Earth, that nobody seems to care about, until the ground water is polluted by nano particles of plastic from what is being burned. Sure it's illegal, but what kind of education and parenting system raises its youth to not care. I pack out the tires, glass bottles, plastic battles, and so on.

In some videos, I make cob mix of horse manure (aka horse shit) to upcycle and make art of making walls and an Earthship? Greenhouse (See Appendix for videos). Again, this all had no positive result for the ecology and was not slowing down the teen-binge drinking (and quite a few adults). I was generating lots of videos, maps, pictures, and words, but not much has really changed. Rattling the governmental and enforcement cage, I managed to get one call back from a county worker, who looked up the history of the pond, and who had possible jurisdiction.

The ephemeral wetlands pond, might be over a century old, and redone in the public works program of the depression. It was possibly a stage coach stop, where the horses were watered, and before that a watering hole for the mining wagon horses to replenish their thirst. It had been a cattle grazing parcel, but not for some years. "Who owns this land?" I asked. "It's owned by the State Land Office". State Land Office (SLO) is one of two divisions of the Federal Department of the Interior, the other one is Bureau of Land Management (BLM). Everyone even the elected city and county officials think its all BLM, but where I live its mostly SLO.

I checked the SLO rules and regulations: There are no motorized vehicles (no ATVs, no Motorcylcles, no OHMs, and no UTVs, pickup trucks, or cars) allowed beyond the parking lot. The 'Friends of EMT' pay $35 a yeart to the New Mexico State Land Office for a recreational use permit. Target shooting is not allowed. Friends of EMT pack out everything they pack in. Here are 10 reasons why OHM, UTV, ATVs are destroying public lands, particularly on East Mesa.

Figure 16.4: Ten ways recreational vehicles destroy the soil.

I looked with my horizontal third eye. I am vigilant, knowing a soon to be burned pile, left by teens and a few adults, a drunken beer and whisky fest soon to be consummated. With my vertical third eye, I am Arihant, and 'Surrenders To Spirt' aware of the spirituality of the Whole of Life, where I Indwell. Grandfather Hackberry Tree will continue to care for his seedlings, inviting Sumac Tree and the fungal strands to send water, carbon, sulphur, phosphorous, and nutrients to the seedlings. I reflect on my teen years. How exciting to have a chance to create community with the teens today. I wonder if nature and commerce can find a balance. Is it possible for business modeling to take an ecological turn (Bøje & Jørgensen, 2020; Bøje & Rana, 2021; Sparre & Bøje, 2020).

Epilogue

In May 2021, I discovered a grove of Hackberry tress, a dozen, all in a circle. It is a place that gives me hope.t

References

Bennett, M. F. (2008). Religious and spiritual diversity in the workplace. In M. A. Moodian (Ed.), *Contemporary Leadership and Intercultural Competence: Exploring the Cross-Cultural Dynamics Within Organizations* (pp. 45–60). SAGE PUBN.

Bøje, D. M. (2005). Wilda. *Journal of Management, Spirituality & Religion*, *2*(3), 342–364.

Bøje, D. M. (2012). *The -of-care of the life-path of organizations' double-spiral-antenarrative choices through landscapes*. https://davidboje.com/Boje/index.htm

Bøje, D. M., & Henderson, T. L. (2014). *Being Quantum: Ontological Storytelling in the Age of Antenarrative*. Cambridge Scholars Publishing.

Bøje, D. M., & Jørgensen, K. M. (2020). A 'storytelling science' approach making the eco-business modeling turn. *Journal of Business Modeling*, *8*(4), 8–25.

Bøje, D. M., & Rana, M. B. (2021). Defining a sustainably-driven business modeling strategy with a 'storytelling science' approach. In *Handbook of Sustainability-Driven Business Strategies in Practice*. Edward Elgar Publishing.

Chitrabhanu, G. S. (1978). *Realized What You Are: The Dynamics of Jain Meditation*. Dodd, Mead, and Company.

Chitrabhanu, G. S. (1979a). *The Philosophy of Soul and Matter*. Dhanjibhai P. Shah.

Chitrabhanu, G. S. (1979b). *The Psychology of Enlightenment: Meditations on the Seven Energy Centers*. Dodd, Mead, and Company.

Chitrabhanu, G. S. (1980). *Twelve Facets of Reality: The Jain Path to Freedom*. Dodd, Mead, and Company.

Gagliano, M. (2018). *Thus Spoke the Plant: A Remarkable Journey of Groundbreaking Scientific Discoveries and Personal Encounters With Plants*. North Atlantic Books.

Heidegger, M. (1926). *Being and Time* (J. Stambaugh, Trans.) State University of New York Press.

Heidegger, M. (1962). *Being and Time* (J. Macquarrie & E. Robinson, Trans.) Blackwell. heidegger macquarrie robinson 1962 Being and time.

Henderson, T. L., & Bøje, D. M. (2016). *Managing Fractal Organizing Processes*. Routledge.

Larsen, J., Bøje, D. M., & Bruun, L. (2020). *True Storytelling: Seven Principles for an Ethical and Sustainable Change-Management Strategy*. Routledge.

Sparre, M., & Bøje, D. M. (2020). Utilizing participative action research with storytelling interventions to create sustainability in Danish farming. *Leadership & Organization Development Journal*, *38*(4), 41–54.

Appendix

Here are some of the videos we did on the East Mesa Ephemeral Pond Situation:

1. Take Care of Water and Water Takes Care of Us All Boje's Presentation to the Global Water Conference May 26 2020 https://youtu.be/X79a0q2cgn0
2. Videos is about Onto-Story https://youtu.be/6jhhJlky3zI An Onto-Story is the story that material Things like Spadefoot and Fairy Shrimp are telling to us. Ont-Story comes from the work of Jane Bennett (2008) and is a way to understand the vibrant mater of Things, and their relation to other things, such as the burned and about to be burned tires I am rescuing from the desert so that pollution does not further destroy Life On Desert Pond (pun intended).
3. PART I: Onto-Story of East Mesa Pond being Trashed at https://youtu.be/6jhhJlky3zI
4. PART II: Pack Out what Others Don't Pack Out to save Pond habitat. Video link https://youtu.be/S3XQUhAh6Ys
5. PART III: How to make Horse Manure Cob walls and Earthship Greenhouse to upcycle bottles and cans and plastic of Ephemeral Pond https://www.youtube.com/watch?v=xZ6VbM4N-Wo
6. PART IV: What would Henry Thoreau Say about Trashing Ephemeral Pond? Video link https://youtu.be/L5l8-LQ2Lcs
7. PART V: What onto-story the burned trash of party goers has to tell humanity? Video link https://youtu.be/GwSVtXtk3XU
8. PART VI: What onto-story has trash bags littering Ephemeral Pond to tell us all? Video link https://youtu.be/_bchK1F_4R0
9. PART VII: As My Dad Always Said, Don't Just tell the problem, what Solution to you have? Video link https://youtu.be/IrgFh_ZIzrM
10. PART VIII: The Angel of Truth looking back on the wreckage upon wreckage of western civilization, piling up. Video Link at https://youtu.be/cFlsZO5Hvtw PART IX: What is the VERITAS of a place? Video link https://youtu.be/knFURkkVo20
11. PART X: Why burning tires in Wetland Pond of East Mesa is ECOCIDE and your own SUICIDE? Video link https://youtu.be/vGAxl2AwVIs
12. PART XI: David Boje does Shamanic Drumming with Intention of Calling on Grandfather Tree of the Ephemeral Pond to enter SACRED SPACE and give thanks for this wetland place. Video link https://youtu.be/KhcCj2zTfaM
13. PART XII: How to dump your burn pit ashes in county landfill instead of in the East Mesa Wetlands Pond Video link https://youtu.be/sEgL_e4neao
14. PART XIII: Raving PartiersTrashing East Mesa Ephemeral in Las Cruces New Mexico Pond Sunday Jun 14 2020 at nooner-drunk-fest. Do they realize they are Polluting Jornada East Mesa Aquifer that feeds Mesilla Aquifer of Las Cruces Drinking Water for Everyone-, including themselves and the uniquely adapted aquatic creatures. Heck just inhaling the wood smoke with the nano-plastic

particles is enough to mess up their lungs for life. Video link https://youtu.be/L4dQIcLgBaA
15. Part XIV No Law on East Mesa of Las Cruces/County/BLM since COVID-19 and long Before David Boje, Video link https://youtu.be/tKwa48TZyfw
16. The D.r D and Princess Gaia interview with Boje about the importance of the Aliveness of Place https://youtu.be/zvPqyo5Gky8
17. Duncan and Julia is interview pond June 22 2020 https://youtu.be/uBU9ELxCW88.
18. ANTESTORY of Ephemeral Pond Fairy Shrimp and Spadefoot MICROCOSMOS David Boje Aug 2nd 2020 Video link https://youtu.be/JusLb78KPRg
19. Stardust Divination for Gathering of Circles – Shamanic journeying to Microcosmos Aug 1st 2020 Video link https://youtu.be/TpwWcYq439U
20. Why are there Carnivore and Omnivore New Mexico Spadefoot Toad Tadpoles 7 29 2020 Boje Video link https://youtu.be/ALL4z8ANyWE
21. Come out to see first spadefoot tadpoles of season EAST MESA EPHEMERAL POND July 27 2020 David Boje Video link https://youtu.be/oq1v_Hiihg0
22. Overstory and Understory of Walking with Wetlands Water to the Ephemeral Pond – David Boje interview July 24 2020 Video link https://youtu.be/7nXfzWtqIdU
23. Who says Temporary Water Does Not Exist? First Monsoon Rainstorm Fills East Mesa Wetlands Pond July 21 2020 Video link https://youtu.be/ECXlmwEy_3Q
24. Overstory and Understory of Walking with the Wetlands Waters to Ephemeral Pond Matters – David Boje July 14 2020 Video link https://youtu.be/Ggpy4ly-LbI
25. Storytime with David – We are all made of Stardust 200803 Storytime with David – We are all made of Stardust 200803 – YouTube link is https://youtu.be/toouEbkobf8
26. Storytime with David – A Call for Visionaries 140720 https://youtu.be/r55cO31vqQg?list=PLijSv3zeLzZ_ovs9d7n3HPK8JGW-z8kyy
27. Aliveness of Place https://youtu.be/zvPqyo5Gky8

Epistemologies/Methodologies

Sharda S. Nandram, Puneet K. Bindlish

17 Indigenous Studies with an Integrative Research Approach

Introduction

On the basis of the purpose of research, Management research can be characterized as either *fundamental or applied*. Here, fundamental research refers to a systematic study often undertaken to understand a phenomenon without specific application in mind (*Legal Information Institute*, 2021). Here the 'why' question is more dominant. Whereas, applied research is a form of systematic inquiry where the 'how' question is more dominant with the aim of gathering insights and knowledge towards directly realizing its *benefits to practice*.

Fundamental research is different in a way that it lays the foundation for further advancement in knowledge as modern scientific work is always a work in progress and scholars across the globe have conversations about fundamental features of a phenomenon through their publications. In applied research one tries to get access to accumulated theories, knowledge, methods, and techniques for specific management problems with a clear purpose to solve those problems (Roll-Hansen, 2009).

On the basis of the object of research, the process of knowing could be for a known thing or an unknown one. Consequently, fundamental research has two knowledge dimensions: *"Knowing the known" and "Knowing the unknown"*. The two differ in the sense that for the former knowledge dimension, a researcher would focus on definitions as a starting point. Whereas in the latter, one would not start with a definition as it may not be existing or inadequate in the literature. Therefore, a researcher in the latter case of knowing the unknown, takes a broad view on the epistemology. This further may involve incorporating experiences (one's own as well as others') and tapping into the subjective realms of our being. While letting respondents express their experiences, the researcher tries to sense what it is about and induce a pattern from these experiences. Quite often, during the process of knowing a concept through deciphering this pattern, the knower encounters a split between two apparently opposing perspectives – *Essentialism and Existentialism.* For a researcher, even to fall into a particular philosophical category it requires an understanding to uncover existing ontological understanding of the phenomenon alongside the researcher's personal experience of the same phenomenon. Essentialism proposes a view that, for any specific entity (such as an animal, a group of people, a physical object, a concept), there is a set of attributes which are necessary to its identity and function. Whereas, existentialism holds that philosophical thinking

https://doi.org/10.1515/9783110711349-017

begins with the human subject – not merely the thinking subject, but the acting, feeling, living human individual.

As a researcher with an integrative perspective as opposed to a dichotomous one, it may not be possible to position oneself completely into one of these philosophical categories. This is usually encountered during indigenous research in diverse contexts. In such a scenario, both a thinking perspective to define the attributes related to the topic as well as experiential perspective in the local context where the topic is being studied, are important (Panda & Gupta, 2007). However, a non-indigenous (or universalist) study aims at an understanding of a phenomenon, where the theological and philosophical concepts have been assumed to have universal application, regardless of the local context. Is there an integrative research approach possible for studies that allow us to incorporate the non-universalistic dimension too? This means that we focus on the local context, its dynamics based on different purposes and perspectives of the entities in that context while we also connect to the underlying common ground of that local group based on their view of the world. An example could be a worldview which assumes that everything and everyone is connected at a deeper spiritual ground. Assuming this may lead to a researcher's choices towards search for the interconnectedness, which can be labeled as integrativeness. This has been the reason behind writing this book chapter. The chapter suggests a few building blocks for what one may call an *integrative research approach* by taking the case of leadership research through analysis of potential research methodologies. Subsequently we conclude with a discussion on how this topic can benefit from an indigenous research approach.

Comparison of Research Methodologies

Researchers before looking for fresh paradigms, need to acknowledge that there has always been an influence of dominant philosophy or worldview on the ways researchers conduct their research (Bindlish & Nandram, 2019). This can be best shown by an example on the topic of leadership which has been studied for centuries now. There are various methodological issues raised in leadership research literature (Bindlish et al., 2019). Some of the approaches that had been attempted by leadership researchers can be broadly put under these categories namely: inductive, deductive and alternative ones.

1. *Inductive approach*: Bass and Stogdill (1981) studied 7500 references for his Handbook of Leadership, Rost (1991) studied 587 titles covering 221 definitions. There are plenty more definitions which still do not lead to a complete understanding, or which seems not broadly applicable or which may not hold for contemporary times (Walters, 2009). In a way, researchers seem to be looking for other newer approaches. As they are offering often the same perspective consequently leading to similar results.

2. *Deductive approach*: Availability of enormous, rather endless, empirical data also is not able to provide an integrated understanding (Stodgill & Bass, 1981). Researchers have expressed frustration over the growing amount of data which is not bringing us anywhere near to a detailed understanding of the concept of leadership. Empirical investigations for the last several decades of leadership research have not yielded an unequivocal conceptual understanding of leadership (Bennis & Nanus, 1985). Infact, this was the view shared in the 1980s. After almost two decades, Vroom and Jago (2007) commented "Although this assertion is over 20 years old, our position is that any serious review of recent literature would reveal that the quote is as relevant today as it was then". On one hand this shows that there is skewness towards applied empirical research rather than fundamental conceptual research. On the other hand, some researchers felt that the leadership research lacked the right measures and was quite weak in research designs (Yukl, 1981)
3. *Towards alternative approaches*: Taking the quest further from above lines of thought, researchers explored other approaches. Some suggested using life stories as a valid way to explore the complexities of leadership. It was further argued that life stories incorporate diversity and interdisciplinary analyses thus promoting critical new methods of conceptualizing and researching leadership (Shamir et al., 2005). However biographies were argued to be better than an autobiography for leadership research citing that it is more reliable and less prone to leader's personal bias (Gronn, 2005). The traditional ways of studying leadership through traits and situations, have also been criticised for inability to produce sound scientific evidence adequate enough to guide practice (Vroom & Jago, 2007). Although acknowledging that leadership understanding is problematic in various ways, many researchers expressed frustration over almost a century of non-yielding effort to find the holy grail of leadership. A few recent researchers have asked to introspect on whether we are searching for the right thing or not (Pye, 2005). To ascertain that, a few suggested that we step out of conventional western universalist mindset and explore leadership from eastern perspective, after setting aside our cherished conventional models for a moment altogether.

After studying the shortcomings of the existing approaches to leadership, the researcher encounters the following choices:
1. *Same paradigms again*: One may still get tempted to attempt the same way again, as the dominant worldview expressed in academic literature still welcomes research that follows the existing aspects of the dominant worldview and studies using new paradigms will not have many takers at places where it matters as they usually serve the same dominant worldviews.
2. *Integration of philosophies or synthetic integration*: One could attempt a moderate approach of proportionately mixing or assembling all approaches giving

appropriate weightage (in some cases, democratic) to conventional approaches. This approach is being referred to here as an "integration of philosophies" based approach. Similar to a chemical mixture which retains the properties of its constituents, this integration retains the fundamental shortcomings like "data cranking null hypothesis rituals" (Cohen, 1994; Gigerenzer et al., 2004; Sedlmeier, 2009), skewness towards applied research and research designs casted in same dominant worldview.

It may also lead to perceptual errors because the perceptual units as viewed by actors in a worldview may be quite different as viewed by observers in a different worldview. An example is someone living in a linear worldview versus someone living in a cyclic worldview with the understanding that life does not stop with the death of our body in this life. The ignoring of different worldviews may lead to a fundamental attribution error.

Researchers invariably may underestimate the degree to which a person's behaviour reflects situational demands, which may determine his actions more powerfully than his personality. Managing diversity of worldviews among actors and researchers, is one of the most fundamental issues. This could be addressed and explored through a different approach. Researchers have observed that the synthesized worldview, in its attempt to bridge various worldviews, brings compromise between different practices emanating from those worldviews. This compromise mostly happens at systemic or framework level (Graen & Wakabayashi, 1994). This option of the integration approach has become more dominant due to a reductionist view taken in social research design.

The growing usage of statistical tools (originally meant for material science such as physics) in social science and consequent usage of "hypothesis testing" increases this tendency. Although this has been criticised severely with strong evidence and arguments, labelling it as "null ritual", the practice is dominating the choices made by researchers for their scientific contributions. Although in contemporary models, not all studies require a hypothesis, Karl Popper's 'Theory of Empirical Falsification' (also known as 'Conjectures and Refutations') (Popper, 1963) is a popular example. Stacey's complexity theory (Stacey et al., 2000) and Karl Weick's sense-making theory (Weick et al., 2005) are some of the theories which philosophically seem to be going in that direction of an alternative research paradigm.

When one studies some characteristics of conventional methods of research derived from research methodology books of Cassell and Symon (2004); Huberman and Miles (2002); and Miles (1990) one can conclude that there are some shortcomings in these approaches: real life situations may not be explained, a lack of generalisability issues, and oversimplified views may be derived. Some aspects in reality might not be measurable as they occur over a long period of time. Sometimes theories may become leading while practice may be different. Furthermore the influence of the researcher in the research process may be taken into account as this may vary among researchers and therefore one may not find the same emerging patterns. Some researchers may rely too much on existing theories and therefore develop blind spots that are not seen during the research process leading to observation of the phenomenon partly. Even inductive methods such as grounded theory may show problems as theories that are built from scratch do not find opportunities to get validated, hypotheses are not developed to test at a later stage. This problem exists mainly because understanding the lived human experience is a time consuming activity and when a researcher has spent time studying this he may not have resources to do a follow up of validating outside the area of the substantive theory. This can happen in quasi experimental and single subject designs. Another problem is that in some types of methods such as historical and archival conflicting interpretations may be possible and generations may not exist to give the localized background information that may be required for a good interpretation of observations. Studies done in natural settings may have the weakness of having less control over the research. Action research may lead to biases and it may be a challenge to organize the administrative part which is required so that the researcher can play the role of facilitator and monitor the process. Content analysis and textual and hermeneutics may miss out the nonverbal information or the researcher may influence the choices that lead to emergence of meaning while other researchers may not agree with this meaning making process. Surveys, interviews and questionnaires may be superficial for some topics. Case studies and life stories are selections which may not be appreciated by other researchers. Most of these weaknesses can be mentioned if we intend to generalize or we want universalists' understanding. Seeing all such weaknesses it seems that transpersonal research approaches provide an alternative to cope with some of these. They acknowledge the researcher's experience and allow unique frameworks and experiences and do not intend generalizability.

Out of various research approaches available in social science and management, the transpersonal approaches are closer to addressing shortcomings in contemporary research. Some of the common transpersonal research approaches, conventional research approaches and disciplined methods of enquiry have been reviewed and presented in Table 17.1.

The dominant and non-dominant worldviews are not synthesizable and perhaps, non-integratable due to their natural differences like linear and nonlinear worldviews, cause-effect and effect-cause perspectives. Therefore, any integration of the above mentioned approaches would be synthetic in nature and may not even be possible. The paradigm leading to approaches of deduction of elements and summing up, would not lead to resolution to the research problem of for example leadership. Therefore an alternative approach is suggested by us labeled as integrative research approach.

Table 17.1: Common transpersonal research approaches.

Approach	Description	Strengths	Weaknesses
Integral Enquiry	research is multifaceted and pluralistic	Extensive and Intensive study; tolerance for ambiguity	quality may be compromised
Intuitive Enquiry	intuition backed by wide variety of data collection and analysis	scope for incorporating full dimensionality of human knowing	bias and prejudices of research need to be balanced by independent researchers
Organic Research	story from researcher's personal experience	exploration of topic in which researcher has interest; story telling and listening	may become indistinguishable from a novel !!
Phenomenological Enquiry	transpersonal awareness is noumenal (devoid of perception-as is)	unique, strong philosophical framework and well articulated methods	explanation is not the focus
Informed Exceptional Human Experience Enquiry	focus on human mystical, exceptional experiences like dreams	thorough involvement of researcher	fear of it becoming a dominant one !

Integrative Research Approach

As discussed above, artificial or synthetic integration or unification of worldviews is not the right direction, as it sacrifices the indigenous nature of reality. The sacrificed portion is lost or in other words "*digested*" by the dominant paradigm. Therefore, an integrative research paradigm would be worth exploring. For the indigenous context, in the literature some approaches for conducting research have been mentioned such as de-colonizing views (Ashcroft et al., 2006; Dharampal, 1983) and using indigenous narratives (Cole, 2017). For integrative research however these may not be enough.

Bindlish et al. (2018) suggest a new approach where researchers prepare themselves mentally and spiritually before starting indigenous research using various techniques of social re-engineering as part of an integrative research approach (Bindlish et al., 2019). Nandram (2015) mentions that any research which is about understanding a phenomenon may benefit from a mental and spiritual preparation of the researcher in order to be clear in the mind for data collection in the field. Nandram mentions the mindful inquiry as a way to prepare oneself for a lucid observation and interpretation of what is being seen in a particular context (Nandram, 2013b). Understanding the worldview of the interviewee is an important element for getting a holistic view of the study. Suppose a person believes in the karma theory then it is important for the researcher to be aware of this as some actions in the person's mind may be scheduled for the future including future lives (Nandram, 2013a). For example in a study on stress the lack of stress may not be related to an intervention given but due to a person's worldview that he may have another future life to live and achieve the goals which he cannot achieve now. By ignoring this information we may make fundamental attribution errors.

For establishing an integrative research paradigm one can derive perspectives from Indian research methods which is labelled here as ancient Indian research methodologies. These emanate from a Vedic or so called dharmic worldview and can guide in studies that intend to take an alternative to the conventional hypothesis testing. There are plenty of interesting features of such methodologies. Let's take an example from the syllogism process for instance, "*Phala-Hetu*", it is about 'effect – cause' in that order. It is a retrospective understanding of causation where one puts his effort first and then makes inferences of a possible cause (Malhotra, 2009).

Different from the universalistic paradigm, an integrative paradigm focuses on integral (not synthetic) unity without the nomothetic perspective of claiming generalizations at the manifest level (Nandram et al., 2019). Research following an integrative approach may ask for contemplations on fundamental aspects, thought experiments and inclusion of intuition, and indigenous explorations (Panda & Gupta, 2007). It may also involve a departure from a typical psychologist or behaviorist's questionnaire style and could be more towards an open ended observational interview approach, which in practice, is more experienced than interviewing. The ancient Indian models do not explicitly divide research into fundamental and applied. The research, in general, is inclined towards discovering the real nature of the named concept (*padārtha*) and the fundamental constituent nature of the concept (*tattva*).

The Process of Integrative Research

Every indigenous context has many possibilities to enrich integrative research approaches. Here are a few aspects from ancient Indian research background. Any integrative research process involves one or more of these aspects:

1. Conviction (*niścaya*) – Here in general conviction for knowledge in search of truth, precedes the research. In other words, it is the researcher's conviction on "what is to be known". The researcher's conviction to know is the leading factor. This aspect of the integrative research paradigm brings focus back on that which is worth knowing and encourages theoretical thinking from different perspectives and scenarios of the process of knowing. This process of knowing comes from the framework of knowledge trinity (knower, knowable, knowledge) derived from Vedic wisdom (Bindlish et al., 2017, 2018; Nandram, 2019).

A researcher who aims to study indigenous knowledge systems needs to have a conviction about it as it requires an open mind, engagement in that system, and participating in that system without knowing what he can expect regarding the quantity and quality of data sources and time that he has to spend to have a clear understanding. This part is inadequately addressed in the contemporary research paradigms.

2. Subject matter or object (*jñēya*) – This is the integral part of the conviction (*niścaya).* It is the end object, which is to be known or to be researched to know. This end object is also known as *pramēya*, an object to be known as per Nyāya philosophy, one of the six prominent Indian philosophical schools. This part resembles the process of defining one's research question where the researcher has chosen for a clear research focus after studying the extant literature. But in indigenous research using an integrative approach this studying of literature may not be always possible due to lack of sources in accessible ways and language. Like in many Indian scriptures there is no authorship and there are hundreds or even thousands of interpretations as they are localized due to context, living lineages, and languages.
3. Objective (*prayōjana*) – At a broad abstract level, the objective could be the attainment of worldly goals (*abhyudaya)* or liberation (*niḥśrēyasa)* or a combination of both. Other objectives emanate from them. This understanding comes from an Indian philosophy known as Vaiśeṣika philosophy. In further categorization, the objective could be one or more from the four life goals as per Hindu worldview: righteousness (*dharma*) means for prosperity (*artha*), worldly or material desires (*kama*), and emancipation or liberation (*mokṣa*). The first three are part of worldly goals (*abhyudaya)* and the last one is a spiritual goal (*niḥśrēyasa).* In contemporary research these broad categories of objectives are not thought about when conducting the research but for the theme of spirituality it is an important objective. In contemporary context this process can be equated with the problem statement and management problem that the researcher is trying to solve which will always be related to worldly goals.

   Every research is expected to be clear on the objective in this manner as the subject matter (*jñēya)* and objective *(prayōjana*) are integral parts of the conviction (*niścaya*) of the researcher who follows an integrative research paradigm. At a secondary level, the researcher may additionally develop curiosity (*jijñāsā)* or doubt *(saṁśaya).* The resolution of the curiosity or clarification of the doubt could be a secondary objective for research.
4. Thesis (*siddhānta*) – This is the final compilation or presentation of the knowledge of the subject matter (*jñēya).* Usually, it has statements established using one or more research methods (*yukti*). The thesis principles (*siddhānta)* may have three components: the aspect of the named concept which is to be known (*pakṣa*); the reasoning of syllogism used (*hētu*); and the evidence for used syllogism (*dr̥ṣṭānta*).

On the basis of the applicability, the principles (*siddhānta*) are categorized into either a principle applicable everywhere (*sarvatantra siddhānta*) or a principle applicable in a particular context (*pratitantra siddhānta*). This part of the process resembles the research design and generalizability in modern research paradigms. The interesting pattern here is that in modern paradigms we may talk about external validity but still we may be cautious about the context to which the validity is attributed to while the principle of *sarvatantra siddhānta* in the integrative paradigm is more conclusive. Another interesting pattern is that in an integrative research approach the applicability to a particular context *(pratitantra siddhānta)* is also appreciated as universal applicability which brings the balance which otherwise often is lacking in contemporary research designs.

5. Integrative review (*samanvaya*) – The research in a Indian model always ends up with a philosophical reconciliation process. The underlying assumption is the interconnectivity of all living and nonliving beings. During this process the thesis is therefore viewed from various perspectives and objections are removed in a manner that all have a common understanding of the subject matter *(jñēya).* This process of reconciliation may require a process of dialogue (*śāstrārtha)* which is sometimes misinterpreted as "debate" or "defense". This is a process that aims at arriving at an acceptable understanding of the description of object or reality. This process has three components: researcher's position on the subject matter (*pakṣa*); the reason (*hetu*); and the evidence or syllogism (*dr̥ṣṭānta*).

It is worth mentioning that the researcher's position often does not get a prominent place in contemporary research approaches. This part of the process is comparable with the conclusion and discussion aspect in contemporary approaches. However the intent to reconcile seems exclusive in the integrative approach. In other approaches critique is the driving force of developing new insights and comparison with the already dominating worldview is the way to conclude a research while here there is no dominant or less-dominant worldview, different perspectives and purposes of entities are intentionally included for a specified context as a major part of the research. Furthermore, this process of *samanvaya* invites for a reflection on the findings from the side of the researcher as his experiences are also given space in an integrative research approach.

Conclusion

The important research aspects for understanding indigenous phenomena can be found in an integrative paradigm, derived from ancient Indian research methods, which seemed to be missing or less highlighted in conventional approaches. Usually in dominant research paradigms there is less relevance given to conviction (*niścaya)* and the positioning of the researcher (*pakṣa*) while these are important contributions to experience the topic of research as an integrative approach gives spaces for inclusion of both objective realities and subjective experiences. Furthermore in conventional approaches, there is a limited subject matter (*jñēya)* and objectives (*prayōjana)* are not incorporated holistically by including worldly and spiritual goals. Another conclusion is that in conventional approaches there is a limited integrative review (*samanvaya).* Yet another conclusion is that the integrative approach gives space for both local (*pratitantra siddhānta*) and universal applicability (*sarvantantra siddhānta*). The whole research process should be followed by a complete review of several aspects, perspectives and purposes that are relevant for the subject matter in order to reconcile. If a research paradigm is able to integrate these aspects, then it can be called an integrative research approach which will be beneficial to both modern and indigenous phenomena in social context.

References

Ashcroft, B., Griffiths, G., & Tiffin, H. (2006). *The Post-Colonial Studies Reader*. Routledge.

Bass, B. M., & Stogdill, R. (1981). Handbook of leadership. *Theory, research, and managerial.* The Free Press. New York.

Bennis, W., & Nanus, B. (1985). The strategies for taking charge. *Leaders, New York: Harper. Row, 41.*

Bindlish, P. K., & Nandram, S. S. (2019). Manifestation of worldview in a metaphor. *International Journal of Business and Globalisation, 23*(3), 464474. https://doi.org/10.1504/IJBG.2019.102925

Bindlish, P. K., Nandram, S. S., & Gupta, R. K. (2019). Definition schema for redefining leadership: An integrative approach. *International Journal of Indian Culture and Business Management, 18* (1), 34–58. https://doi.org/10.1504/IJICBM.2019.096921

Bindlish, P. K., Nandram, S. S., Gupta, R. K., & Joshi, A. (2018). How to prepare the researcher for indigenous context: An integrative approach. *International Journal of Indian Culture and Business Management, 17*(2), 221–237. https://doi.org/10.1504/IJICBM.2018.094255

Bindlish, P. K., Nandram, S. S., & Joshi, A. (2017). Integrative intelligence as the path forward. In S. S. Nandram & P. K. Bindlish (Eds.), *Managing VUCA Through Integrative Self-Management* (pp. 263–287). Springer.

Cassell, C., & Symon, G. (2004). *Essential Guide to Qualitative Methods in Organizational Research*. Sage.

Cohen, J. (1994). The earth is round (p<. 05). *American Psychologist, 49*(12), 997–1003.

Cole, P. (2017). An Indigenous research narrative: Ethics and protocols over time and space. *Qualitative Inquiry, 23*(5), 343–351. https://doi.org/10.1177/1077800416659083

Dharampal. (1983). *The Beautiful Tree: Indigenous Education in the Eighteenth Century*. Biblia Impex.

Gigerenzer, G., Krauss, S., & Vitouch, O. (2004). The null ritual. What you always wanted to know about significance testing but were afraid to ask. In D. Kaplan (Ed.), *Sage Handbook of Quantitative Methodolgy for Social Sciences* (pp. 391–408).

Graen, G. B., & Wakabayashi, M. (1994). Cross-cultural leadership making: Bridging American and Japanese diversity for team advantage. In H. C. Triandis & L. M. Hough (Eds.), *Handbook of Industrial and Organizational Psychology* (Vol. 4, pp. 415–446). Consulting Psychologists Press Palo Alto, CA.

Gronn, P. (2005). Leading questions: Questions about autobiographical leadership. *Leadership, 1* (4), 481–490.

Huberman, M., & Miles, M. B. (2002). *The Qualitative Researcher's Companion*. Sage.

Legal Information Institute. (2021). Cornell Law School. http://www.law.cornell.edu/cfr/text/32/272.3

Malhotra, R. (2009). *Integral Unity and Synthetic Unity: Being Different*. Harper Collins.

Miles, M. B. (1990). New methods for qualitative data collection and analysis: Vignettes and pre-structured cases. *International Journal of Qualitative Studies in Education*, *3*(1), 37–51. https://doi.org/10.1080/0951839900030104

Nandram, S. S. (2013a). Karma theory. In D. Coghlan & M. Brydon-Miller (Eds.), *The Sage Encyclopedia of Action Research* (pp. 475–477). SAGE Publications.

Nandram, S. S. (2013b). Mindful inquiry. In D. Coghlan & M. Brydon-Miller (Eds.), *The Sage Encyclopedia of Action Research* (pp. 537–540). SAGE Publications.

Nandram, S. S. (2015). *Organizational Innovation by Integrating Simplification: Learning from Buurtzorg Nederland*. Springer International Publishing. https://doi.org/10.1007/978-3-319-11725-6

Nandram, S. S. (2019). *Integrative Spirituality in the Fourth Industrial Revolution: From How We Do Things to Why We Exist*. Vrije University Press. https://research.vu.nl/en/publications/integrative-spirituality-in-the-fourth-industrial-revolution-from

Nandram, S. S., Bindlish, P. K., Purohit, H., Joshi, A., & Hingorani, P. (2019). Foundations for social entrepreneurship: An integrative Indian perspective. In L. Bouckaert & S. C. van den Heuvel (Eds.), *Servant Leadership, Social Entrepreneurship and the Will to Serve* (pp. 161–186). Palgrave Macmillan.

Panda, A., & Gupta, R. K. (2007). Call for developing indigenous organisational theories in India: Setting agenda for future. *International Journal of Indian Culture and Business Management, 1* (1/2), 205–243. https://doi.org/10.1504/IJICBM.2007.014478

Popper, K. R. (1963). Science as falsification. *Conjectures and Refutations*, *1*(1963), 33–39.

Pye, A. (2005). Leadership and organizing: Sensemaking in action. *Leadership*, *1*(1), 31–49. https://doi.org/10.1177/1742715005049349

Roll-Hansen, N. (2009). *Why the Distinction Between Basic (Theoretical) and Applied (Practical) Research is Important in the Politics of Science*. London School of Economics and Political Science, Contingency and Dissent in Science Project.

Rost, J. C. (1991). *Leadership for the Twenty-First Century*. Greenwood Publishing Group.

Sedlmeier, P. (2009). Beyond the significance test ritual: What is there? *Zeitschrift für Psychologie/Journal of Psychology*, *217*(1), 1–5. https://doi.org/10.1027/0044-3409.217.1.1

Shamir, B., Dayan-Horesh, H., & Adler, D. (2005). Leading by biography: Towards a life-story approach to the study of leadership. *Leadership*, *1*(1), 13–29. https://doi.org/10.1177/1742715005049348

Stacey, R. D., Griffin, D., & Shaw, P. (2000). *Complexity and Management: Fad or Radical Challenge to Systems Thinking?* Psychology Press.

Stodgill, R. M., & Bass, B. M. (1981). *Stogdill's Handbook of Leadership. A Survey of Theory and Research*. Macmillan.

Vroom, V. H., & Jago, A. G. (2007). The role of the situation in leadership. *American Psychologist*, *62*(1), 17–24. https://doi.org/10.1037/0003-066X.62.1.17

Walters, D. C. (2009). Exploring a definition of leadership and the biography of Dr. Frank B. Wynn. *ProQuest Dissertations and Theses, Order No. 3360170, University of Montana*, 317.

Weick, K. E., Sutcliffe, K. M., & Obstfeld, D. (2005). *Organizing and the Process of Sensemaking* (5th ed., Vol. 16). Prentice Hall. http://pubsonline.informs.org/doi/abs/10.1287/orsc.1050.0133

Yukl, G. (1981). *Leadership in Organizations* (5th ed.). Prentice Hall.

Julia Storberg-Walker

18 Relating Differently: Exploring How a Relational Ontology Might Catalyze Transformative and Emancipatory Action-Oriented MSR Research

Abstract: The purpose of this chapter is to explore how enacting a *relational ontology* as a researcher might restore/repair the deep interconnection and interdependence between all life on the planet. While ontological matters might be considered too philosophical or far removed from the practical matters of research, this chapter seeks to illuminate the importance of adopting a relational ontological perspective, with the intention to continue to enhance the future-forming capacity of Management, Spirituality and Religion (MSR) researchers.

The term 'relational ontology' is used to describe various philosophies or ways of knowing that blur the distinction between subject and object; between researcher and the researched; and between human and nature. These philosophies/ways of knowing offer diverse ways to critically reflect on researcher subjectivity, competencies, and skills needed for meaningful MSR research. The preparation or development of the researcher and the practical research design decisions and actions are impacted by these ontologies, with significant consequences to the purpose, implementation, and potential impact of the studies. This chapter seeks to offer MSR researchers new ways to design and conduct transformative and emancipatory action-oriented research in this critical historical moment of tumultuous change and chaos.

Why Relational Ontologies?

This chapter is about what is real (ontology) and the implications of what is real for Management, Spirituality, and Religion (MSR) research. Quantum reality, as I understand and experience it, was best described by David Bohm (1980) as an unfolding co-emergence of energy into matter. The phrase *relational ontology* signifies this deep interdependence and co-creation of reality. Over time, I have learned that this way of understanding the world has been described in multiple and diverse ways – for example, actor network theory (Latour, 2005), agential realism (Barad, 2003), revolutionary critical pedagogy (Allman, 2001); autopoiesis (Maturana & Varela, 1980), relational being (Gergen, 2009), posthumanism (Braidotti, 2018), a quantum worldview (Tsao & Laszlo, 2019), and the implicit order in quantum theory (Bohm, 1980).

https://doi.org/10.1515/9783110711349-018

From these relational positions, a researcher's ideas and actions emerge within/from contexts, and context itself is a 'player' in the game of conducting research as much as the brain, intellect, cognition, and decision making. This stance is far from Newtonian separation and the paradigm of scientific reduction and cause-effect thinking. MSR scholarship has had to contend with this paradigm since its inception – the science of reduction to discover natural laws and generalizable results has been the gold standard for organizational and management scholars and researchers. MSR researchers have struggled to legitimize subjective ways of knowing and conducting research (Lin et al., 2016); they have had to find objective measures (MacDonald, 2011); and have been advised to operationalize and define terms (Tackney, Chappell, Harris, Pavlovich, Egel, Major, Finney, & Stoner (2017) in order to legitimize MSR research.

This chapter seeks to build on/from this scholarship to envision a new way of being a MSR researcher. This requires a shift in consciousness – from a consciousness of separation (e.g., typical for organization and management science research) – to a new way of being in the world that recognizes the interdependence and dependent origination (a Buddhist principle recognizing the mutuality of causation) of all of the material world. Rather than premised on separateness, this chapter suggests the future of MSR research should instead *get closer*. As described by Cuomo,

> . . . knowledge producers who aim to *get closer* abandon the dream of scientific progress which seeks absolute knowledge in the service of enlightened mastery and wealth, working instead for knowledge that acquaints us with the particulars of the world we affect. Arrogant inquiries accept a comfortable distance between knowledge and life, and hide their limits and inadequacies behind an epistemic (knowledge-making) posture that proclaims a unified route to knowing, a route that necessarily follows traditions of privilege and exclusion.
> (Cuomo, 2020, pp. 66–67; italics mine)

Getting closer is a metaphor, a pointer to what I argue is a relational approach to MSR research that is transformative, educative, and emancipatory. In this relational ontology, research has the potential to transform the researcher as much as the researched, because *getting closer* generates a moral obligation for care and a form of sacred reciprocity akin to Indigenous research methods (Kimmerer, 2013; Wilson, 2008). Modern science (starting with Galileo Galilei) does not *get closer* in a moral sense; indeed, as argued by Loizzo (2020), modern science has "undermined our faith in humanity and in the perfectibility of human society" and has fostered a "modern skepticism about our human potential for personal and social integration," (p. 72). *Getting closer* is a departure from the science of separation, objectification, and reduction, and it offers a compelling, relational route forward for impactful MSR research.

I believe relational ontologies and the intent to *get closer* are also a resistance to the assumptions and values associated with normal science. *Getting closer* is not widely recognized in the neo-liberal academy as a valid form of knowledge production, where competition, separation, rationality, and hierarchy are valued. Even the idea of *production* of knowledge itself would be resisted from a relational perspective, with the argument that the researcher is embedded within the production process and therefore a part of the results or findings. In the neo-liberalism of the academy, however, knowledge *can* be produced, consumed, and commodified. Because of these norms and values, researchers and educators teaching about relational ontologies and conducting research from this position often turn to non-Euro Western ideas, books, and articles for information and inspiration.

Likewise, over the years of teaching and research, I have found myself including more and more non-Euro-Western perspectives into my research projects and research design classes; the most recent addition has been to take a deep dive into relational ontologies – the focus of this chapter. For example, in a recent research design class one of the textbooks selected was authored by a feminist philosopher (Thayer-Bacon, 2017), and guest speakers and other assigned readings were from Indigenous scholars – as well as from diverse ethico-onto-epistemological perspectives. These readings and guest scholars, while positioned differently, all pointed to the critical idea of connection; of relation; of some sort of ethical responsibility grounded in reciprocity. They all pointed to the 'fact' that humans are part of nature; not objective observers of nature who stand apart from it.

On reflection, I now understand that by incorporating relational ontologies into the doctoral classroom was a strategy of resistance to the traditional view of a mechanized universe with separate cause and effect relationships – the paradigm that feminists suggest is a result of patriarchal ways of knowing and studying the world. At the same time, I continue to learn that both/and, yin/yang, and neither/nor might be a better way to understand how best to teach scholarly inquiry and do my own research. Most importantly, I believe that if one enacts a relational ontological perspective, they are given a powerful vantage point *from within* to design and execute any type of research design – be it quantitative or qualitative or mixed methods – that seeks to *get closer*. A relational ontological perspective dissolves the separation between researcher and researched, and instead invites the radical perspective of being infused by and emmeshed within an all-encompassing field of information and energy. Humans are *in* nature; *of* nature; not separate from it. Researchers are *infused by* and *in relationship* with the researched. This perspective, in my opinion, provides MSR researchers – because they are concerned with the spiritual, the sacred, and the meaningful – with the potential to conduct transformative, catalytic research for change.

So What Exactly Are Relational Ontologies?

I offer three different ways to begin to make sense of relational ontologies. First, I agree with noted educational scholar and feminist Barbara Thayer-Bacon's view that 'ontology' and 'spirituality' might be used interchangeably because both "help hold our worlds together and give meaning to our lives" (2017, p. 3). In this view, relational ontologies are nondualistic ways of understanding the world that "emphasize we are w/ holistically connected with our greater universe, materially and spiritually," (2017, p. 7). Thayer-Bacon offers the analogy of an ocean, a boat, and a fishing net to describe her idea of a relational ontology. In this view, all of the cosmos is represented as the vast ocean, representing all pure experience. We can't possibly know all of this vastness, so we create a net to help us make sense of it. Thayer-Bacon (2017) suggests:

> what we use to make these nets are our theories of knowing (epistemology) as well as our theories of being (our ontology). There are multiple kinds of epistemological and ontological nets we can design, maybe even an infinite variety, some more effective than others, in terms of the amount of Ocean life they are able to catch up . . . Whatever epistemological and ontological net we use, however fine the weaving, there is so much more in this vast Ocean of experience that our nets can catch. When we cast our nets, much will overflow the top of our nets as well as spill through it and escape back into the infinite Ocean. We cannot divorce ourselves from epistemological and ontological questions for they form the very weaving of the nets we use to catch up our everyday concerns and give them meaning. (p. 2)

In this metaphor, the net consists of warp and weft threads; the warp represents our ontological theories (e.g., being, or what is), and the weft our epistemological theories (e.g., how we know). While both threads of the weave are important, the weft thread generates the essence of our human experience. Thayer-Bacon suggests that ontology and spirituality are synonyms because the first being is "not tangible or material, and is primal to our survival" (2017, p. 3), and so the weft threads of the net substantially shape the meaning we give to our human experience. Thayer-Bacon goes on to describe how humans make their nets – first from inheriting the net from parents and family, then in school revising/repairing the net as learning and independence develop, then in adulthood through relationships. Our nets are not made in isolation, they are constantly created and re-created through experience and relationships, and unless the nets are made visible to us we run the risk of claiming that our experience is True. Once made visible (e.g., conscious) to us, we are more able to recognize the partiality, the limits to our knowing, and recognize the incredible vastness of All That Is.

This view of a relational ontology has profound implications for research and scholarship because it absolutely denies the existence of a separation between knower (the researcher) and the known (the researched). What we see, understand, and name is a function of our ontological and epistemological perspectives. A scholar/researcher in this view would be humble in all knowledge claims because they would recognize the 'vast Ocean of experience' that their research design did not catch up.

The second relational ontology I want to describe is from quantum theory. From this perspective, empirical scientific results combine with mathematical modeling to suggest the existence of what David Bohm calls an *implicate order* of energy and information. In this view, the implicate order is the basis of the universe; consciousness and matter co-emerge; and importantly for researchers – the implication is that there is no separation between researcher, the researched, and research instruments. Many scholars and philosophers have offered profound ideas about this interconnection, or 'consciousness of connectedness' (Tsao & Laszlo, 2019), and why it matters. For example, feminist/physicist/philosopher Karen Barad (2003) offers a perspective based on quantum theory called agential realism, which describes a reality in which every 'thing' is connected in a web of relations. In the agential realist view, a human has no more agency (think 'influence') over a collective experience (think workplace learning, or meaningful work) than do ideas, policies, culture/norms, technology, organizational structure, and so on. Agential realism, as I understand it, points to the co-creation of experience/meaning among human and non-human 'agents' and requires researchers to re-position themselves and their views of what is real. In agential realism, as with quantum theory, all material matter (e.g., what we see; what David Bohm calls the *explicate order*) co-emerges relationally. In this view, one cannot disconnect human experiencing from context; from practices; or from structure. This is a deep form of relational ontology – what *is*, comes into being *through relations*.

The third form of relational ontology I present in this chapter is from the Indigenous perspective. In describing Indigenous ideas, it is critically important to recognize how both individual and structural positions of power and advantage contribute to my research and scholarship (D'Arcangelis, 2018). As a White settler writing this chapter from my office on Massawomek and Manahoac land, I recognize the potential for me to further colonize the Natives of Turtle Island (North America) by appropriating Indigenous ontology, epistemology, and axiology. (Note: from what I understand, it is not possible to separate out reality (ontology) from knowing (epistemology) from responsibility (axiology) in Indigenous ways of knowing (IWOK). The separation of these concepts are offered here because that is how Western minds have been trained and developed – mine included).

As a White settler, I step into an impossible, liminal space when writing about, using, and describing Indigenous philosophies. Critical reflection about these matters is not sufficient, because it still assumes there is an "I" separate from others and separate from the structures of oppression within which I live and work. D'Arcangelis (2018) builds on Ahmed's (2004) reflexive double turn to propose a *radical reflexivity*, itself "a form of critical analysis, which would examine our subjectivities as windows into the operation and potential alteration of social structures in which *we are fully implicated*," (p. 12; italics mine). Radical reflexivity about Indigenous ideas is itself a characteristic of a relational ontology – a knowing that I as a researcher co-create the structures of oppression and privilege of *ideas* and *research values* that permeate the academy. In this view, I am *fully implicated* in the perpetuation of hierarchies of power and privilege – of knowledge, ideas, and research practices considered 'better' than others.

And, at the same time, I can honor and respect IWOK, philosophies, and research design practices. I have personally been told by multiple Indigenous scholars that with honor and respect and attribution, I can serve the sacred through teaching, research, and practices infused with IWOK. Consequently, I offer what I am learning in the classroom, through my research, and in my activism.

The next section are ideas drawn from Sean Wilson's *Research is Ceremony: Indigenous Research Methods* (2008); Robin Wall Kimmerer's (2013) *Braiding Sweetgrass: Indigenous Wisdom, Scientific Knowledge, and the Teaching of Plants*; and from Lyla June Johnston's Master's Thesis *Diné Bina'nitin Dóó O'hoo'aah/Education For Us, By Us: A Collective Journey in Diné Education Liberation.* These selections represent a diverse array of ideas and research practices that are grounded in an ethic of the inherent sovereignty and mindedness of all matter – human, animal, plant, cosmos; as well as responsibility, relations, and reciprocity. Human and non-human beings are integrally related in this relational ontology, and the dignity of all beings is a key principle. At once this ontological position places humans *with* nature, inseparable from it, and ethically and morally obligated to protect it, to ensure flourishing, and to work to correct/repair anything that diminishes dignity.

The three relational ontologies presented here – Thayer-Bacon's spirituality/ontology that gives integral meaning to existence; quantum theory findings suggesting energetic, co-emergent connection between all we see and do; and Indigenous ontologies demanding respect and reciprocity – all three shift the researcher/researched relationship in subtly different ways, and all three offer MSR researchers with a new grounding to conduct transformative and impactful research.

The next section presents research ideas from the three Indigenous scholars listed above to illuminate how profoundly coherent they are with the contemporary issues facing MSR and the world. It is as if the unfolding of human experience with the planet and all of its inhabitants has co-generated this light in our time of darkness; the light, to me, is the Indigenous way relating to all things as sacred, in a ceremonial sense, through the moral imperative of dignity and respect. Enacting this way of being in the world offers MSR researchers a powerful path towards generating meaningful and transformative research.

Indigenous Ways of Knowing (IWOK) and Research

I recently had an email exchange with an Indigenous scholar/activist about the difference between the words *spirituality* and *ceremony*. I was using the phrase 'Indigenous spirituality' to signify what I understood to be the multiple/diverse ways of being in unity with the sacred in my understanding of IWOK. My friend suggested that the phrase 'Indigenous ceremony' would be a better representation (thank you, Lyla June Johnston). The word shift had an immediate impact on me, and I saw the profound understanding of the sacredness of being human through understanding *life itself is ceremony*. Euro-western cultural norms have relegated ceremony and ritual far away from the center of what it means to be human. In contrast, traditional eastern wisdom has long emphasized the importance of ceremony and ritual (禮/lǐ), for example in Confucius' Analects Book I. And often, the word spirituality suggests a disembodied, 'higher' self that can transcend the material world.

But Indigenous *ceremony* pulls me back into my body; into my sweating, aching, breathing, stretching, bone and blood and muscle body. This is an experience of the sacred, if I choose to think and know that *my embodied life is ceremony.* My embodied life is an expression of the Source and of all that is sacred. Extending through to my embodied cognition and embodied mind, my ideas, writings, and research are also ceremony.

I should have known this months ago, through reading Shawn Wilson's book *Research is Ceremony: Indigenous Research Methods*. Despite the title telling me of the importance of the word ceremony, I didn't get it until my friend catalyzed a new, deeper, and more integrated understanding. I share this learning curve with you to illuminate the continual unfolding, the continual deepening, the continual sublime experiences of coming to know more about the sacred. I can be tuned in doing research, grocery shopping, walking my dog, going to faculty meetings. All can be ceremony if I choose to open to that potential.

Wilson's book is an exemplary contribution for sharing with the world an Indigenous relational ontology. For example, Wilson describes the inseparability of methodology and axiology when conducting research through IWOK:

> . . . we [researchers] are mediators in a growing relationship between the community and whatever it is that is being researched. And how we go about doing our work in that role is where we uphold relational accountability. We are accountable to ourselves, the community, our environment or cosmos as a whole, and also to the topics we are researching. We have all of these relationships that we need to uphold. (2008, p. 106)

Research as ceremony remains anchored in the body, infused by context completely. And, contextualizing knowledge demands integrity. An embodied, contextual understanding " . . . is necessary for that knowledge to become lived, become a part of our collective experience or part of our web of relationships," (Wilson, 2008, pp. 102–103). There is responsibility connected to knowledge and knowing that cannot be separated in IWOK; I understand this to be an ethical imperative because the lived knowledge that can be generated from research must enhance the sacredness of all life.

I invite all MSR researchers to consider reading Wilson's text, which offers substantive and powerful ideas for catalyzing the next generation of MSR research and scholarship. Here is one more quote from this powerful book that illuminates the deep adherence to a relational ontology:

> . . . if the researcher is separated from the research and it [the research] is taken away from its relationships, it will not be accepted within an Indigenous paradigm. The research will not show respect for the relationship between the research participants and topic . . . the research must accurately reflect and build upon the relationships between the ideas and the participants . . . (Wilson, 2008, p. 101)

Like Wilson (2008), Johnston (2017) and Wall Kimmerer (2013) are deeply grounded in a relational ontology, and each researcher offers examples of empirical research that bridges the material and subtle worlds through IWOK. The research is emancipatory, affirms the moral imperative of dignity of all, and is very embodied. These exemplars offer MSR researchers unique and powerful ways to see and sense how to *get closer* through IWOK. The invitation is open for readers to access this powerful wisdom.

The next section presents select details about *why* and *how* MSR research might be conceptualized and conducted through enacting a relational ontology. It is hoped with these new perspectives, MSR scholars can continue to build on the corpus of knowledge implicitly drawn at the intersection of IWOK, relational, and quantum ontology, and be catalysts for research that is deeply transformative.

Enacting/Generating Research from a Relational Ontology

This section offers answers to the questions: *Why* should MSR researchers enact a relational ontology? *How* might MSR researchers conduct research from this ontological perspective? Both types of questions have been debated by previous scholars, as will be described below, however with a subtle but important difference in focus.

Why Should MSR Researchers Enact a Relational Ontology?

Many scholars focus on changing a researcher's *paradigm* by creating arguments to validate subjective knowledge and reduce the distance between researcher and researched. These arguments often revolve around making the case for qualitative research as the 'best' way to understand meaning and spiritual phenomena, and the focus is on changing the paradigm or belief-system of the researcher from 'objective' science to 'subjective' experience.

The argument I am making here is different and perhaps more dis-locating in its impact. My argument does not attempt to legitimize subjective knowledge. My argument is an *ontological* argument about reality and it is centered on its epistemological correlates based on Indigenous, quantum, and relational ways of being in/with the material and subtle world. It is not about legitimizing qualitative research; in fact, as I mentioned earlier all forms of research (qualitative, quantitative, or mixed-methods) could be conducted from a relational ontological perspective.

Definitions are important, and there is a profound difference between *paradigm* and *ontology*. As described by Kuhn (1962), a paradigm represents a 'mature' science when there is consensus on theories, procedures, and models. Conversely, he labeled as 'immature' a science (historically, the domain of spirituality) that does not have theoretical or procedural consensus. In both categories of paradigm, the researcher is *outside* of the research project looking in as an objective, neutral observer. There is a separation between researcher and researched when one is talking about paradigm; this is completely different when one is talking about a relational ontology as I've described it earlier in the chapter.

Enacting a relational ontology involves *being* different as a researcher, and while some authors (for example Lin et al., 2016) describe practices for developing the 'inner landscape' of the researcher that enables *being* different, there are profound implications for designing research that remain unnamed in much of this previous work because, I think, the focus was on *paradigm* rather than *ontology*. The focus was on the *lens* or on the metaphor rather than *What Is*.

One of the seminal research textbooks relevant to this discussion is the book, *Toward a Spiritual Research Paradigm: Exploring New Ways of Knowing, Researching, and Being*. In this path-breaking work, authors Lin, Oxford, and Culham (2016) make a compelling case for the development of a spiritual research paradigm because "a large and vital part of human experience is excluded from the current research paradigms" (p. x). They also argue that "researchers need to embody what they research. This means researchers' spiritual cultivation and growth are part of the research endeavor" (p. xi). The book offers multiple and diverse ways to conceptualize and execute research through a spiritual research paradigm (SRP), and many of the chapters in this book offer substantive ideas, arguments, evidence, and applications of a SRP.

I appreciate the naming and distinguishing of a spiritual research paradigm because it is of critical importance to MSR, *and* I am making a different argument in this chapter. A SRP also means, at its core, that there are different paradigms from which a researcher can understand or make sense of the world. Naming and distinguishing different paradigms perpetuates separation (e.g., it is not aligned with a relational ontology) in these ways:

- It gives the researcher power to name and select one paradigm over the other;
- It leaves open the idea that the researcher is not in a co-emergent relationship with a chosen paradigm;
- It positions the researcher in the center of knowledge production;
- It assumes that reality is separated from our observation of it:
- It legitimizes/privileges paradigm (how to *look at* reality) over ontology (what *is* reality); and
- While it is a step forward to identify and start to legitimize different ways of knowing, it is limited to *how* researchers can know and does not address *what there is to know* (e.g., a relational reality).

A relational ontology, on the other hand, affirms that researchers literally co-generate reality as we go about designing and implementing research projects. This ontological position suggests that the cognitive ideas of a researcher literally co-emerge with the material conditions of the research. The researcher is embedded within the same relational web (Thayer-Bacon, 2017), the same quantum energetic field (Bohm, 1980), the same ceremonial space of reciprocity (Kimmerer, 2013) as the researched. The 'playing field' is leveled – the researcher is not like a coach directing the play of the game. The game is played *through* the researcher, not *by* the researcher.

Think about this for a moment. If the 'game' of research is played *through* the researcher, what might that mean to you? From an Indigenous ceremonial perspective, it means that there is no separation between knowledge and responsibility – all research is a moral and ethical act of reciprocity that recognizes the sovereignty and mindedness of all life. From a quantum perspective, it means that there exists an invisible, implicate order of unity between researcher and research that reflects continual emergence or *becoming*. From a Thayer-Bacon (2017) perspective, it means that ontology and spirituality are interchangeable and that all research can be considered manifestations of the sacred – if the researcher opens to the flow of what wants to emerge.

So, why should MSR researchers enact a relational ontology? The answer is perhaps controversial but it is clear: because through research we are given another opportunity to serve the source; the sacred; or in a different sense *What Wants To Emerge* from the implicate order (Bohm, 1980) or the consciousness of connectedness (Tsao & Laszlo, 2019). In alignment with Lin et al (2016), this means the inner landscape of the researcher needs to be cultivated and nurtured; but perhaps different from these authors, the knowing and the research comes from an ontological Unity that is impossible to name or classify.

The next section offers some practical ideas for implementing research through enacting a relational ontology.

How Might MSR Researchers ~~Conduct Research~~ Allow Research to Flow Through Them?

The reframing of the question above signals the profound shift when enacting a relational ontology. The egoic researcher shifts into a way of being in resonance with the unseen field of energy and information that Indigenous wisdom and the quantum theory point to. From this field, the purpose, implementation, and impact of the research can emerge. This section describes how MSR researchers might think about and then *not* think about conducting research through enacting a relational ontology.

The purpose of MSR research studies is usually related to some management topic connected to spirituality or religion – topics often under-researched in mainstream management and organization science. This research is focused on human experiences involving deep interconnectedness, transcendence, growth, transformation, mystery, or joy. These types of experiences often tap into a sense of flow (Csikszentmihalyi, 2008), Qi (Tsao & Laszlo, 2019), or what Gary Zukav (2014) calls authentic power: "the alignment of personality with the soul – and of multisensory perception: the expansion of human perception beyond the limitations of the five senses" (p. xxx). These deeply human/spiritual experiences are the topics of MSR research, which in the Newtonian perspective have been 'relegated' to non-scientific status.

Typically, we have been trained to craft a precise, well-defined, goal- and outcome-directed purpose statement for our research. The purpose is traditionally connected to a gap in knowledge, and the research intends to contribute towards filling that gap. Creswell (2016) argues that the purpose statement is the most important statement in a study, and that it should convey the essence of the project.

However, the *genesis* of the purpose is what is different when one enacts a relational ontology. Rather than beginning with a problem of practice to define the research problem, or anchoring a research problem in a gap in the literature, a researcher enacting a relational ontology will begin with mindfully looking inward/outward to sense or intuit what wants to emerge from the field of becoming. The moments of clarity or knowing may be brief, intermittent, or rare, but the researcher knows when they happen. Much has been written on this more subtle and inward knowing in research, for example, in the discipline of transpersonal psychology (Anderson & Braud, 2011; Braud & Anderson, 1998) and Jungian perspectives on research (Romanyshyn, 2013). Tsao and Laszlo (2019) point to existing research that suggests that "consciousness might in fact exist outside the brain rather than be generated by it" (6).

The challenge is how expand this capacity for accessing, surrendering, or opening to this larger field of potential. The next section offers suggestions from the discipline of transpersonal psychology. I have found that this discipline has generated dissertations, textbooks, and scholarly articles on practical and implementable ways to connect the material with the subtle world through research. There is a paradox in this that is important to recognize: naming and identifying steps to access is needed for many of us who are learning and developing competencies for this work. At the same time, we risk missing the ineffable if we don't let go of our rational/cognitive brain. The key is to hold both/and lightly.

Practices and Competencies for MSR Researchers

This section describes three ways that MSR researchers can deepen their abilities to enact relational ontology in their research. First, I describe different ways to access non-rational ways of knowing, following suggestions by transpersonal research scholars Anderson, Braud and Clements (Anderson, 2011; Braud & Anderson, 1998; Clements, 2011). Second, I argue for the importance of shadow work and synchronicities.

And third, I recommend using the language of metaphor for communicating research; Romanyshyn (2013) calls this a poetics of research.

Accessing Non-Rational Ways of Knowing. According to researchers Anderson and Braud (2011), researchers can access moments of clarity through four portals of understanding – thinking, sensing, feeling, and intuition. However, the researcher needs to cultivate ease and expertise in all four ways of knowing. Anderson and Braud's book *Transpersonal Research Methods for the Social Sciences: Honoring Human Experience* offers well-tested tools and steps for researchers to take to develop their fullest capacity in these multiple ways of knowing. They have identified three categories: 1) accessing usually unconscious processes (tacit knowing, active imagination, automatic writing, etc); 2) accessing direct knowing (intuition, sympathetic resonance, presencing); and 3) empathic identification (accurate, not emotional, identification with the phenomenon of study; for example: researchers Feynman identified as an electron and McClintock identified as a corn fungus chromosome) (Anderson & Braud, 2011, p. 250).

All three of these practices can facilitate our ability to have a direct/intuitive (Tsao & Laszlo, 2019) experience of surrendering to the cosmic purpose of our MSR research. At the same time, there are many challenges direct/intuitive knowing brings to a scholar/researcher. For example, direct intuitive experiences can challenge beliefs in normal science with its subject/object split. Direct intuitive experiences can challenge the belief that the world is made out of discrete entities. And for people who have not had direct/intuitive experiences, it is difficult to 'believe' in these ways of knowing because there is no shared meaning for shared comprehension. These non-rational ways of sensing or intuiting/knowing the world seem to *require* a personal subjective experience of direct knowing.

Interestingly, research on visual perception may offer an explanation and opportunity/hope for enhancing a shared understanding. Research is starting to understand the disjuncture between 'knowing' in an intellectual, analytical sense and 'knowing' that is direct/intuitive. These findings may explain some of the reasons why not everyone has 'seen' or 'sensed' a relational or quantum reality. For example, research has suggested that one cannot have a 'rational' scientific view and a direct/intuitive view at the same time (Mayer, 2007):

> The perceptions that characterize potentially anomalous experience [for example, a direct/intuitive experience] appear to emerge from a state of mind that is, in the moment of perception, radically incompatible with the state of mind in which perceptions characterizing rational thought are possible . . . That's a murderous proposition for most of us trained in a Western intellectual and scientific tradition . . . We're not accustomed to scientific investigation in which the phenomena we're attempting to study are themselves exclusive of the state of mind that lets us study them," (Mayer, 2007, p. 137)

This suggests that the state of mind associated with a relational ontology, including experiences with direct/intuitive knowing and other anomalous experiences (e.g., distance seeing), simply cannot be understood with the state of mind associated with Newtonian science. Ultimately, MSR researchers need to develop capacity to move between these two ways of experiencing the world to fully enact a relational ontology.

Doing Shadow Work. Romanyshyn (2013), also from the discipline of psychology as are Anderson, Braud, and Clements (Anderson, 2011; Braud & Anderson, 1998; Clements, 2011), is a Jungian psychologist/philosopher and has a different focus on what the researcher needs to do and what skills or competencies to develop. I believe the contributions in his book *The Wounded Researcher: Research with Soul in Mind* is critical when considering research from a relational ontology for many reasons. For example, the Jungian perspective expands the inner field within which the researcher works to include psyche (the unconscious) and its connection to synchronicity. This connection is important for epistemological and rhetorical reasons. Readers are urged to review the full book to get a broader understanding of the many potential contributions to MSR research a Jungian view offers.

Jung wrote about the intersection of quantum physics and psychology and found that both disciplines had an epistemological problem related to "the indissoluble bond that exists between the object to be investigated and the human investigator" (Romanyshyn, 2013, p. 31). To Jung, synchronicity (e.g., meaningful coincidences without apparent causal connection) in human experience is similar to the "form that light takes" (32) in relation to a researcher in a physics lab. Just like the property of light depends on the researcher observing it, so too the form of the material world (e.g., meaningful coincidences) depend on the unconscious state (e.g., psyche) of the observer. To Jung, "something about the unconscious state links psyche to matter," (p. 32).

Taking this idea into account as a MSR researcher would mean that the unconscious could influence the research process, and consequently any research claims or findings. This has huge implications for the potential value (or lack of value) of research. I sense that inner work, shadow work, and practices of connectedness (Tsao & Laszlo, 2019) would be critical elements of researcher preparation in order to be as clear a channel as possible for 'what wants to emerge' through the research process. Researchers would need to practice rigorous self-awareness and self-development strategies to prevent their research from becoming therapy (Anderson & Braud, 2011). This type of concern is not only found here; in many references to autoethnographic research there is a concern for narcissistic or therapeutic elements to potentially influence the research process (Chang, 2008). Rather than discount the autoethnographic research process as inherently flawed and of no value, autoethnographers have been mindful and diligent, and have produced many contributions to science (see, for example, The Qualitative Report at https://nsuworks.nova.edu/do/search/?q=autoethnography&start=0&context=6227772&facet=) There is no reason to believe that MSR researchers cannot do the same.

Writing Metaphorically. Jung also suggested that it is important for researchers to find language to communicate a neither/nor type of metaphoric sensibility rather than the usual both/and phrasing, and that both quantum physics and psychology have this challenge. " . . . Just as quantum physics has had to develop a language of probabilities, psychology needs to develop a language of potential and probable meanings, a language of approximations, a language that resists literalizing the visible and forgetting the invisible" (Jung, as cited in Romanyshyn, 2013, p. 35). Romanyshyn calls for researchers to consider metaphorical writing as a way to avoid objectification/freezing or reifying what is really always a potential – a fluid dynamic. Research findings or claims, if written in metaphor, would be "deliteralized, freed of their demand to be taken at face value, as the whole truth of the matter" (43).

I believe these three practices – accessing direct knowing, doing shadow work, and using metaphorical language (what Romanyshyn calls a 'poetics of research') are critical elements to consider in preparing for, implementing, and writing up MSR research through a relational ontology. Developing competency in accessing direct/intuitive awareness can aid MSR researchers to continually tap into the quantum/relational field while designing, conducting, and writing up research. This continued accessing can enhance the potential that the researcher is truly tapping into what wants to emerge, rather than merely filling a gap in the literature. Doing shadow work can provide a deep awareness of how the researcher's psyche may influence the research process. In addition, this work would seem to be another way for generating 'clear' and 'resonant' research findings free from ego. Finally, adopting a metaphorical view of the language of research could address the ineffable quality of human experiences relevant to quantum research.

Summary and Invoking Intention

The purpose of this chapter is to explore how MSR researchers might enact a *relational ontology* through research, and how this enactment might restore/repair the deep interconnection and interdependence between all life on the planet. The intention was to invite an expansion of the capacity of MSR researchers to conduct action-oriented, transformative, and emancipatory qualitative research.

Three different relational ontological views were presented, and specific ideas for enacting research from a relational ontological position were offered. The work of developing the inner capacities for this work involves non-linear, non-rational ways of knowing and being MSR researchers. From an IWOK perspective, the work is at once performative and normative, with the imperative to affirm and protect the sacredness of all life. The work is also healing and emancipatory, as illuminated through Johnston's (2017) Master's Thesis dedication: "To the colonized and to the colonizer. May we be free from the chains that keep us both from being what we are. Ayóóan..nishn." (p. iii).

May MSR researchers become fully what they are, through their research, and may this research catalyze transformation in body, mind, and spirit.

References

Ahmed, S. (2004). Declarations of whiteness: The non-performativity of anti-racism. *Borderlands, 3* (2).

Allman, P. (2001). *Critical Education Against Global Capitalism: Karl Marx and Critical Revolutionary Education*. Bergin & Garvey.

Anderson, R. (2011). Intuitive inquiry: The ways of the heart in human science research. In *Transforming Self and Others Through Research: Transpersonal Research Methods and Skills for the Human Sciences and Humanities* (pp. 15–70). State University of New York Press.

Anderson, R., & Braud, W. (2011). *Transforming Self and Others Through Research: Transpersonal Research Methods and Skills for the Human Sciences and Humanities*. State University of New York Press.

Barad, K. (2003). Posthumanist performativity: Toward an understanding of how matter comes to matter. *Signs: Journal of Women in Culture and Society, 28*(3), 801–831. https://doi.org/10.1086/345321

Bohm, D. (1980). *Wholeness and the Implicate Order*. Routledge.

Braidotti, R. (2018). Forword. In V. Bozalek, R. Braidotti, T. Shefer, & M. Zembylas (Eds.), *Socially Just Pedagogies: Posthumanist, Feminist and Materialist Perspectives in Higher Education*. Bloomsbury Acadamic.

Braud, W., & Anderson, R. (1998). *Transpersonal Research Methods for the Social Sciences: Honoring Human Experience*. Sage.

Chang, H. (2008). *Autoethnography as Method*. Routledge.

Clements, J. (2011). Organic inquiry: Research in partnership with spirit. In R. Anderson & W. Braud (Eds.), *Transforming Self and Others Through Research: Transpersonal Research Methods and Skills for the Human Sciences and Humanities* (pp. 131–161). State University of New York Press.

Creswell, J. W. (2016). *30 Essential Skills for the Qualitative Researcher*. SAGE.

Csikszentmihalyi, M. (2008). *Flow: The Psychology of Optimal Experience*. HarperCollins.

Cuomo, C. (2020). Knowledge and moral motivation: Getting closer. *Tarka, 0*, 62–67.

D'Arcangelis, C. L. (2018). Revelations of a white settler woman scholar-activist: The fraught promise of self-reflexivity. *Cultural Studies ↔ Critical Methodologies, 18*(5), 339–353. https://doi.org/10.1177/1532708617750675

Gergen, K. J. (2009). *Relational Being: Beyond Self and Community*. Oxford University Press.

Johnston, L. J. (2017). *Dinı Bina'nitin Dʊʊ O'hoo'aah/Education For Us, By Us: A Collective Journey in Dinı Education Liberation*. https://digitalrepository.unm.edu/educ_llss_etds/85/

Kimmerer, R. W. (2013). *Braiding Sweetgrass: Indigenous Wisdom, Scientific Knowledge and the Teachings of Plants*. Milkweed Editions.

Kuhn, T. S. (1962). *The Structure of Scientific Revolutions* (4th ed.). University of Chicago Press.

Latour, B. (2005). *Reassembling the Social: An Introduction to Actor-Network-Theory*. Oxford University press.

Lin, J., Oxford, R. L., & Culham, T. E. (2016). *Toward a Spiritual Research Paradigm: Exploring New Ways of Knowing, Researching and Being*. IAP.

Loizzo, J. J. (2020). Why we all must be scholar-practitioners: Towards a global renaissance of the science and practice of human awakening. *Tarka, 0*, 68–81.

MacDonald, D. A. (2011). Studying spirituality scientifically: Reflections, considerations, recommendations. *Journal of Management, Spirituality & Religion, 8*(3), 195–210. https://doi.org/10.1080/14766086.2011.599145

Maturana, H. R., & Varela, F. J. (1980). *Autopoiesis and Cognition: The Realization of the Living.* Springer Science & Business Media.

Mayer, E. L. (2007). *Extraordinary Knowing: Science, Skepticism, and the Inexplicable Powers of the Human Mind.* Bantam.

Romanyshyn, R. D. (2013). *The Wounded Researcher: Research With Soul in Mind.* Spring Journal Books.

Tackney, C. T., Chappell, S., Harris, D., Pavlovich, K., Egel, E., Major, R., Finney, M., & Stoner, J. (2017). Management, spirituality, and religion (MSR) ways and means: A paper to encourage quality research. *Journal of Management, Spirituality & Religion, 14*(3), 245–254. https://doi.org/10.1080/14766086.2017.1316764

Thayer-Bacon, B. J. (2017). *Relational Ontologies*. Peter Lang.

Tsao, F. C., & Laszlo, C. (2019). *Quantum Leadership: New Consciousness in Business*. Stanford University Press.

Wilson, S. (2008). *Research is Ceremony: Indigenous Research Methods*. Fernwood Publishing.

Zukav, G. (2014). *The Seat of the Soul* (25th ed.). Simon and Schuster.

Juliette Koning

19 Workplace Spirituality and the Ethnographic Gaze

Introduction

This chapter makes a case for the use of ethnography to come to a better understanding of spirituality in the workplace. In this chapter, workplace spirituality or spirituality in the workplace refers to research into faith/spiritual values and belief systems in the workplace and includes research within the wider MSR field (Management, Spirituality and Religion). It follows Fotaki, Altman & Koning (2020, p. 10) that "spiritual beliefs play a central role in the lives of religious adherents as well as the non-religious and atheists" and thus I place no restrictions to the labels as such. It is quite remarkable that the seemingly good fit between the two has not lead to a strong representation of ethnography in the study of workplace spirituality to date. It is not the intention to explore why this is the case but to present the wider family of ethnographic approaches (autoethnography, organizational ethnography, organizational autoethnography) and to highlight their potential contribution to the field of workplace spirituality. The chapter follows discussions in the workplace spiritualty domain to explore alternative ways of knowing and builds on my own ethnographic research experiences at the crossroads of religion and business as well as my writing on ethnography as a research approach.

Researching Workplace Spirituality

Scanning the field of Management, Spiritualty and Religion (MSR), a recurring theme is how this relatively young and emergirig field, should best study the "blank canvas" (Tackney et al., 2017, p. 245). Issues arise as to its ontology and epistemology and related research approaches (see for instance Lund Dean et al., 2003; Lund Dean & Fornaciari, 2007; Miller & Ewest, 2013; O. Burton et al., 2017; Tackney et al., 2017; Neal, 2018). These discussions revolve around developing effective measures and robust models in an attempt to position the field as scientific. As argued by Neal (2018) this more scientific drive, focused on the rigorous measurement of the construct spirituality, is due to the fields' association with classic management traditions. But as pointed out by Benefiel (2003a, 2003b, 2005), there might be a paradox between the objective, material, and quantifiable concerns of science (and by extension management and organization science) and the nonmaterialistic concerns of religiosity and spirituality. At the same time, Lin et al. (2016, p. x)

https://doi.org/10.1515/9783110711349-019

suggest the need for a research paradigm that integrates “soul and spirit” with “body and mind” and Tackney et al. (2017, p. 250) suggest “new sources of data (narratives, personal stories etc)” are required that allow research into “interconnected ways of being”. So what might be alternative methodologies and other ways of knowing; specifically those that allow to ask questions related to the “self” in the context of MSR (Neal, 2018, p. 48). The current discussions in the field of MSR and workplace spirituality, seem to culminate in a call for research approaches that are relational, intuitive, embodied, nonlinear and inclusive, and inquire about processes of meaning-making related to spirituality in the workplace. Ethnography, I will argue, comes a long way in addressing some of these concerns. Interestingly enough, a database search on ‘ethnography’ and ‘MSR’ or ‘workplace spirituality’ creates surprisingly few hits.

Ethnography

So, what can ethnography offer to the field of workplace spirituality and what examples are out there to help the interested scholar on their way? A short recap on the unique features of ethnography might be an important starting point.

As nicely put by Cunliffe (2010, p. 227), ethnography is “about understanding human experience – how a particular community lives by studying events, language, rituals, institutions, behaviours, artifacts and interactions”. Doing ethnography implies doing fieldwork (immersion in the field for some time) of which a large part consists of (participant) observation and exploring the phenomenon of interest in its ‘natural’ setting. Hence, ethnography is always context-sensitive approach, meaning that the interpretations the researcher arrives at are embedded in the setting (time and place) of the research. Because the researcher is the primary research tool, “their experiences and observations – as documented in a field journal and later processed – are a central source of data” (Zilber & Zanoni, 2020, p. 4; Hall, 2013). This requires reflexivity on the part of the researcher, a critical evaluation of how meaning and interpretation are constructed by the researcher (Cunliffe, 2003). This entails a level of awareness of how our positionality and experiences have an impact on what we ‘see’ and on the knowledge claims we arrive at (Ybema et al., 2009). For researching workplace spirituality, Lips-Wiersma (2003, p. 407) for instance argues that it is highly important to be open about “the dogmas, definitions, fears and desires we bring to the research and identify how these shape research questions, methodological choices, sampling and representation”.

Ethnography might in the eyes of those less familiar with it, consist of rather unorthodox ways of getting as close as possible to the life world of those researched. This often includes a mix of listening, observing, conversing, lurking, helping, reading, reflecting and so on with the aim to come to a better understanding of what is going on (in the community of focus) and why (van Maanen, 2001).

There is a drive to understand from within (which is not the same as 'going native', an often-heard claim) that includes the immersion of the researcher in the field for a significant amount of time, "exploring the microdynamics of social reality from the perspective of the people constructing and living it" (Zilber & Zanoni, 2020, p. 2). As stated by Azouz et al. (2021, p. 4), it is this behind the scene presence that allows the ethnographer to "capture religious and interpersonal subtleties". Many of today's ethnographic approaches seem to be underpinned by qualitative, interpretive, and critical paradigms that embrace subjectivity, emotionality, and an appreciation of the researcher's influence on the research. There is however, not just one tale ethnographers tell (another core ingredient of ethnography, the written outcome). Over time classic tales might become less popular, such as the realist tale (presenting the observations as the reality) while others arrive at the scene, such as the advocacy tale that addresses major injustices (van Maanen, 1988, 2010).

Some of the core characteristics of ethnography, such as immersion in a specific field (workplace, church, monastery) and through (participant) observation trying to capture a specific (culture) life world from close by, both the unique and the mundane, and to develop this into a piece of writing that challenges the reader to "question and re-examine their taken for granted beliefs" (Bate, 1997, p. 1153), makes ethnography quite suitable to capture the meaning of spirituality in the workplace. It allows the exploration of individual experiences of community/organizational members within its cultural context, as (Cullen, 2011) suggests in his study of a spiritualization program in a company.

An important feature of the ethnographic approach, is the experiential dimension. Elsewhere, I addressed that my participant observation and immersion in a Pentecostal-charismatic community "sensitised" me at a "personal level through vivid experiences" of the experiential dimensions of Pentecostal-charismatic Christianity (Koning & Waistell, 2012, p. 68). It relates to what Hall (2013, p. 132) sees as a unique feature of using ethnography in studying congregations, where "researchers may join in on the activities in the setting where they are conducting their research, and attempt to understand what those activities and actions mean to the people in the setting". Suspending judgement is an important consideration, specifically relevant when doing research in unfamiliar settings or on unknown practices (such as workplace spirituality). This is highly relevant and speaks to the idea of wanting to do justice to the experience of spirituality or religion, even more so if the researcher is not part of the community or culture. Reflexivity is a way to manage these experiences as ethnographer. Elsewhere (Koning & Ooi, 2013), I have written about moments of awkwardness I experienced while in the field (the earlier mentioned Pentecostal-charismatic community). But by unpacking these moments, I gained many insights into the religious community and their experiences, practices and behaviours. As argued by Davies (Davies, 2010, p. 13), reflexivity offers many analytical clues and is "epistemologically informative".

A recurring question, specifically as related to studying religious communities, is the insider/outsider query. As mentioned, ethnographic research is very much about trying to get as close as possible to the life worlds under study but it also requires some distance in order to 'see' the unique and mundane features of this life world and to be able to offer scientific insights. This process is always rife with emotions, positionality, relationship building and boundary questions. It is by now acknowledged that researchers are often both partial insiders and partial outsiders and that this is a result of the interaction between the researcher and the community (and not just the prerogative of the researcher to decide); it is at the same time about power and representation (Clifford & Marcus, 1986).

Notwithstanding these developments, this insider/outsider query in the study of religion (or related fields such as spirituality) is a stubborn one (Jensen, 2011). The debate is about how to manoeuvre studying a religious or spiritual community if the researcher is not from within and what the challenges might be if the researcher is from within (Arweck, 2002; Chryssides & Gregg, 2019). Whereas some argue that the distinction is problematic and might obscure more than it reveals (Jensen, 2011), others argue that these terms can best be perceived as a "series of relationships" that can move from distant to close opening up possibilities while also causing confusion; perceiving them as such might bring us "close to the messy reality of fieldwork" (Bowie, 2019, p. 125). It is important to keep in mind that trying to pin down the researcher in either one of these positions only creates a dichotomy that "essentializes" both the researcher and the research community (Collins, 2002, p. 91). More importantly, it glosses over the possibility that the researcher is neither a "believer" nor a "sceptic" (Bowie, 2019, p. 111).

The Ethnographic Family: Organizational Ethnography and Autoethnography

Ethnography is part of what I prefer to call a larger family of ethnographic approaches. These include, organizational or workplace ethnography, autoethnography and organizational autoethnography. Each of these could be relevant for the study of workplace spiritualty. Table 19.1 below addresses what makes each of these approaches unique in their own way and what each implies for the main aim of the research, the roles of the researcher and researched, and what the intended outcome might be. The table also provides examples of potential research topics in the field of workplace spiritualty and MSR, and some core resources.

The overview in Table 19.1 below indicates that while there is a common interest among these ethnographic approaches, namely understanding culture, moving from ethnography to autoethnography shifts the focus towards a more intense examination of the self. This researcher-as-subject in autoethnography and organizational or

Table 19.1: Ethnographic approaches.

	Ethnography	Organizational ethnography	Autoethnography	Organizational autoethnography
Aim	Understanding cultural understandings held by others	Understanding organizational / workplace life (or organizations and organizing)	Exploring personal experiences to illustrate facets of cultural experience	Probe personal experiences of, with and within organizations or workplaces
Research participants	Interactive engagement dialogical; main source of knowledge creation	Interactive, dialogical: how organization members go about their daily working lives and how they make sense of their workplaces	Are part of the social and cultural context through which (or within which) the researcher examines him or herself	Are part of the organizational context through which (or within which) the researcher examines him or herself
Researcher	Is participant observer in situ (fieldwork, long period of time; living with and living like); conscious of own impact but generally more of an outsider	Is participant observer in situ (fieldwork, less long); conscious of own impact but generally more of an outsider	Is subject of research, examines him or herself (use of memory); explore social processes from an insider perspective; can be combined with stories of others; researcher is an embodied participant	Is subject of research, examines him or herself (use of memory); understanding organizational processes from a persona and insider perspective
Outcome	Thick description of a culture (written representation of a culture)	Showcase the complexities of the everyday in organizational life	Make characteristics of a culture familiar for insiders and outsiders	Insightful and emotionally-rich readings of organizational life
Potential research topics	The meaning of worship; Religious youth clubs; Understanding the Paranormal	Managing a mega church; Marketing of spiritual goods in a Monastery; Spiritual values in the workplace	What does it mean to be spiritual (identity related questions);	What does it mean to be a spiritual leader in an organization; Religious identity work in a family firm

Table 19.1 (continued)

	Ethnography	Organizational ethnography	Autoethnography	Organizational autoethnography
Examples	Bendixsen (2013); Bowie (2016)	Todd (2012); Marie-Catherine Paquier (2019); Azouz et al. (2021)	Zempi (2017)	Cullen (2011)
General references	Van Maanen (1988); Zilber & Zanoni (2020)	Ybema et al. (2009); Ciuk et al. (2018)	Ellis et al. (2011); Winkler (2018)	Sambrook & Herrmann (2018)

Source: Adapted from Koning and Moore (2020, p. 98).

workplace autoethnography creates some unique challenges due to exposing often highly personal experiences and revealing inner musings about the (one's own) cultural setting, which can be a place of work or spiritual/religious community. In the following sections I will address the features of these 'other' ethnographies and support these with examples from workplace spirituality and/or MSR to highlight how it has been picked up by some (indeed only a few) and what it has to offer to the wider field.

Organizational Ethnography

Organizational (or workplace) ethnography is a research approach that explores organizational life from within the organization. It is attuned to understanding how organization members go about making sense of their daily organizational lives and its activities and practices. In this process attention often goes to unpacking hidden dimensions such as emotions, power and politics (Ybema et al., 2009) but it can also study humour to understand organizational identity creation (Huber & Brown, 2017), the implementation of a spiritual leadership program (Cullen, 2011) or the role of religiosity in a family firm and its impact on non-family members (Azouz et al., 2021). Different from the image of the anthropologist traveling to far away and unknown places, the organizational ethnographer might stay closer to home "finding themselves stuck with the familiar and the mundane" but it is this ordinary workplace "that the ethnographer needs to approach with curiosity, respect and inquisitiveness" (Ciuk et al., 2018, p. 272).

As argued by Burton et al. (2018, p. 4), organizational ethnography is well-suited to study the management and organizational practices of religious organizations because these are "explored in the context of the specific traditions of belief and practice within which they are embedded". The unique features of workplace spirituality and/or religiously inspired organizations is the relationship between faith, beliefs, organization, and activities (Hinings & Raynard, 2014). An ethnographic approach, focused as it is on experience, detail, context/culture and complexity, is quite appropriate for straddling attention to both the spiritual/religious and the organizational elements. Deconstructing boundaries (sacred/secular or insider/outsider) is part and parcel of the approach. I will use Todd's (2012) study on how and why religious networking organizations work for social justice in their local community to offer insights into such an organizational ethnography.

Todd (2012, p. 229) discusses the result of "over a year and a half of ethnographic participation in two separate religious networking organizations focused on community betterment and social justice" and has special interest in exploring the role of "religious settings in promoting social justice". Todd (2012, p. 233) has a separate section labelled 'researcher' in which he addresses such issues as his own religiosity, his assumptions towards the two religious network organizations he had selected (a Christian and an Interfaith network) and his interest in liberation theology. He is careful in explaining that these personal revelations are not meant to "be bracketed off" but are a way to acknowledge how these are part of his lens and how he "continually attended to how his social location influenced his interpretation of the data" (ibid.). As addressed above, reflexivity is an important feature in ethnographic research. Todd's paper is a good example of how this can be acknowledged.

A particular useful section in the paper is where Todd (2012) explains the role of field-notes in his ethnographic research as a way to guide the observations, particularly the inclusion of sensory information and physical features deserve attention. This being an organizational ethnography, the overview shows what features of the organization and its members were captured.

> The notes focused on the guiding research questions of how the networking organizations understood and worked for social justice. Thus, the observations and field notes focused on (a) the topics of discussion, (b) significant processes that occurred in the setting like how decisions were made, (c) how organizational members interacted, (d) key events or incidents, (e) variations or exceptions to an emerging pattern, (f) how people attached meaning to their own actions and experiences, (g) sensory information such as sights or sounds, (h) the physical organization of the room, (i) language use, (j) anecdotes and quotes, (k) personal reactions, and (l) any other observations that appeared relevant (Todd, 2012, p. 234).

Of relevance is the addition Todd adds to this section, explaining that these field-notes were accompanied by personal reflections on what he observed.

The result section, offers the rich description that an ethnographic research would be expect to convey, offering the reader an immediate insight into the organization and its members such as:

> Moreover, at network meetings individuals would introduce themselves with their name and congregational affiliation. Meetings began with a devotion that always included reading from religious scripture and meetings ended with verbal group prayer, both of which often focused

> on community betterment and justice. Personally, members described being active in their congregations and seeking to live according to their religious faith (Todd, 2012, p. 239).

Reflecting back, Todd (2012, p. 242) highlights that one of the qualities of his ethnographic approach is to be found in "the in-depth participation that allowed for the qualitative observation of process across time". This *longue durée* is not often heralded as an important feature of organizational ethnography but worthwhile to highlight here in particular as in most cases the ethnographer wants to gain an understanding of a culture or a cultural phenomenon which are never easy to notice or uncover such as the alignment of religion and social justice in an organization's mission, or the development of a spiritual leadership program – on which more in the next section.

Autoethnography and Organizational Autoethnography

Autoethnography sits at the intersection of autobiography (self) and ethnography (culture); it uses personal experience ("auto") to describe and interpret ("graphy") cultural texts, experiences, beliefs, and practices ("ethno") (Adams et al., 2011, pp. 1–2). It often focuses on particular turning point moments in life and how these impacted the life course (Winkler, 2018). However, this is always focused on understanding a particular social-cultural context or setting (for instance an organization, congregation, community) through personal experience and immersion (Kempster & Stewart, 2010; Haynes, 2011). It can shed light on, for instance, the experience of an academic career change from within, where the autoethnographer (via thick description in autoethnographic vignettes) shares with the reader "some of the pleasure and pain associated" with such a change within academia (the cultural setting) (Humphreys, 2005, p. 842).

In the field of workplace spirituality, autoethnography is seldom used. However, there is one study that I will address in detail here as it is a great example of the richness of this research approach and how it can offer novel insights into workplace spirituality. It concerns the research by John Cullen of a Spiritual Management Development (SMD) initiative in a large Irish services organization in an attempt to enhance the personal effectiveness of its managers. Cullen (2011) explains that his research had the aim to understand the organization and organizational culture, and the program and its participants. In his 2011 paper he addresses the ins and outs of using autoethnography (referred to in his paper as auto/ethnography). Since the paper offers a wealth of insights and reflections on using autoethnography in workplace spirituality research, I want to address a few of these here.

Cullen (2011, p. 145) explains why he decided not to study the SDM with a more general ethnographic lens:

> Applying an ethnographic generic template to the research would risk doing violence to how I reported these experiences, and instead I chose to "craft" a piece of research that was more suited to developing a vivid picture of the phenomenon under study. In trying to represent the phenomenon, I had to represent it on its own terms and not slavishly follow evaluative templates inherited from other ethnographic genres.

Based on this consideration, he decided that his own experiences of the organization and the program would be important and so he opted for what he refer to as auto/ethnography:

> I used the term auto/ethnography to refer to the fact that my account of a workplace spiritualization initiative is based on an ethnographic account of the initiative, and my own autoethnographic account" and "to understand how the SMD program might affect the self-hood of participants, I needed to understand how it would impact on my own (Cullen, 2011, pp. 147–148).

He also reveals that experiencing it as co-participant, he was able to reveal and understand why the program ran into problems,

> The process of auto/ethnography, when applied to workplace spiritualization programs such as SMD, gets researchers closer to the experiences of managers undergoing such initiatives and opens up greater opportunities for data collection which may not necessarily become available using more traditional approaches. My experience with DSB's program created a deeper understanding of why participants struggled with implementing its teachings in their own working lives (Cullen, 2011, p. 160).

And finally, he explains what he sees as a core benefit of his chosen approach,

> The key benefit of utilizing auto/ethnography is that it is respectful, in practical terms, of the participants and interviewees. Auto/ethnography can assist in the removal of barriers which so often present when researchers enter an organizational site to undertake cultural research Cullen, 2011, p. 161).

Cullen (2011, p. 158) concludes by stating that autoethnography is about weaving together personal narratives of experience with existing theory of the cultural phenomenon under study and that the aim is to produce "rigorous and convincing accounts of areas of experience which are otherwise "hard to reach", or cannot be vividly articulated via a detached authorial voice". It is such 'hard to reach' experiential dimensions that offer workplace spirituality research a way forward; a way beyond attempts to measure outcomes (on performance for instance) and to offer as Cullen does in his study, a richer and more complex picture of the meaning of workplace spirituality.

In conclusion: Workplace Spirituality and the Ethnographic Gaze

In conclusion, this chapter hopes to inspire the use of ethnographic approaches in the study of workplace spirituality or religious beliefs in the workplace. It has outlined the various ethnographic genres to choose from and the features they share and the features that makes each also unique. What they have in common is to be able offer an 'inside' view layered with experiential richness that provides the reader with an understanding of what spirituality or religion in the workplace might mean for both the organization and the members. This level of richness and complexity can be said to be currently lacking from the field in its drive to 'become' scientific and measure effectiveness of spiritual values, leadership or programs on organizational outcomes. Clearly there is now also a growing discussion on whether these matters are measurable at all. Where the broader business and management field has opened up to embrace ethnographic approaches, it is time that workplace spirituality does the same. It is still hard to find good ethnographic research in this field and it would be a great step forward if this is what the next decade of workplace spirituality research starts to develop. With its interests in spiritual/religious/faith 'experiences' what better way to study workplace spirituality than through an 'experiential' lens? It requires braveness and reflexivity on the part of the researcher but as others have shown, ethnographic studies enrich the field and our understanding.

References

Adams, T. E., Ellis, C., & Bochner, A. P. (2011). Autoethnography: An overview. *Historical Social Research*, *12*(1), 273–290.

Arweck, E. (2002). *Theorizing Faith: The Insider, Outsider Problem in the Study of Ritual*. Univ. PressThe University of Birmingham Press.

Azouz, A., Antheaume, N., & Charles-Pauvers, B. (2021). An ethnography of fairness perceptions among non-family employees: Does religion matter? *Journal of Family Business Strategy*. https://doi.org/10.1016/j.jfbs.2020.100375

Bate, S. P. (1997). Whatever happened to organizational anthropology? A review of the field of organizational ethnography and anthropological studies. *Human Relations*, *50*(9), 1147–1175. https://doi.org/10.1177/001872679705000905

Bendixsen, S. (2013). *The Religious Identity of Young Muslim Women in Berlin: An Ethnographic Study*. Brill.

Benefiel, M. (2003a). Irreconcilable foes? The discourse of spirituality and the discourse of organizational science. *Organization*, *10*(2), 383–391.

Benefiel, M. (2003b). Mapping the terrain of spirituality in organizations research. *Journal of Organizational Change Management*, *16*(4), 367–377. https://doi.org/10.1108/09534810310484136

Benefiel, M. (2005). The second half of the journey: Spiritual leadership for organizational transformation. *The Leadership Quarterly*, *16*(5), 723–747. https://doi.org/10.1016/j.leaqua.2005.07.005
Bowie, F. (2016). How to study religious experience: Historical and methodological reflections on the study of the paranormal. In B. Schmidt (Ed.), *The Study of Religious Experience* (pp. 13–32). Equinox.
Bowie, F. (2019). Negotiating blurred boundaries: Ethnographic and methodological considerations. In G. D. Chryssides & S. E. Gregg (Eds.), *The Insider/Outsider Debate: New Perspectives in the Study of Religion* (pp. 110–129). Equinox.
Burton, N., Koning, J., & Muers, R. (2018). Organizational ethnography and religious organizations: The case of Quaker decision-making. *Journal of Management, Spirituality & Religion*, *15*(4), 349–367. https://doi.org/10.1080/14766086.2018.1496469
Burton, O., Miller, D., Tackney, C. T., Ewest, T., & Issa, T. (2017). Guest editorial. *Management Research Review*, *40*(8), 822–823.
Chryssides, G. D., & Gregg, S. E. (2019). *The Insider/Outsider Debate: New Perspectives in the Study of Religion*. Equinox Publishing Limited.
Ciuk, S., Koning, J., & Kostera, M. (2018). Organizational ethnographies. In *The Sage Handbook of Qualitative Business and Management Research Methods* (pp. 270–285). SAGE Publications.
Clifford, J., & Marcus, G. E. (1986). *Writing Culture: The Poetics and Politics of Ethnography*. University of California Press.
Collins, P. J. (2002). Connecting anthropology and Quakerism: Transcending the insider/outsider dichotomy. In E. Arweck & M. Stringer (Eds.), *Theorizing Faith: The Insider/Outsider Problem in the Study of Ritual* (pp. 77–95). University of Birmingham Press.
Cullen, J. G. (2011). Researching workplace spiritualization through auto/ethnography. *Journal of Management, Spirituality & Religion*, *8*(2), 143–164. https://doi.org/10.1080/14766086.2011.581813
Cunliffe, A. L. (2003). Reflexive inquiry in organizational research: Questions and possibilities. *Human Relations*, *56*(8), 983–1003. https://doi.org/10.1177/00187267030568004
Cunliffe, A. L. (2010). Retelling tales of the field: In search of organizational ethnography 20 Years On. *Organizational Research Methods*, *13*(2), 224–239. https://doi.org/10.1177/1094428109340041
Davies, J. (2010). Introduction: Emotions in the field. In J. Davies & D. Spencer (Eds.), *Emotions in the Field: The Psychology and Anthropology of Fieldwork Experience* (pp. 1–31). Stanford University Press.
Ellis, C., Adams, E., & Bochner, A. P. (2011). Autoethnography: An overview. *Historical Social Research*, *36*(4), 273–90.
Fotaki, M., Altman, Y., & Koning, J. (2020). Spirituality, symbolism and storytelling in twentyfirst-century organizations: Understanding and addressing the crisis of imagination. *Organization Studies*, *41*(1), 7–30. https://doi.org/10.1177/0170840619875782
Hall, A. M. (2013). *Ethnography in congregations*. Adult Education Research Conference. http://newprairiepress.org/aerc/2013/papers/21
Haynes, K. (2011). Tensions in (re)presenting the self in reflexive autoethnographical research. *Qualitative Research in Organizations and Management: An International Journal*, *6*(2), 134–149. https://doi.org/10.1108/17465641111159125
Hinings, C. R., & Raynard, M. (2014). Organizational form, structure, and religious organizations. In P. Tracey, N. Phillips, & M. Lounsbury (Eds.), *Research in the Sociology of Organizations* (Vol. 41, pp. 159–186). Emerald Group Publishing Limited. https://doi.org/10.1108/S0733-558X20140000041013
Huber, G., & Brown, A. D. (2017). Identity work, humour and disciplinary power. *Organization Studies*, *38*(8), 1107–1126. https://doi.org/10.1177/0170840616677632

Humphreys, M. (2005). Getting personal: Reflexivity and autoethnographic vignettes. *Qualitative Inquiry*, *11*(6), 840–860. https://doi.org/10.1177/1077800404269425

Jensen, J. S. (2011). Revisiting the insider-outsider debate: Dismantling a pseudo-problem in the study of religion. *Method & Theory in the Study of Religion*, *23*(1), 29–47. https://doi.org/10.1163/157006811X549689

Kempster, S., & Stewart, J. (2010). Becoming a leader: A co-produced autoethnographic exploration of situated learning of leadership practice. *Management Learning*, *41*(2), 205–219. https://doi.org/10.1177/1350507609355496

Koning, J., & Moore, L. (2020). Autoethnography. In P. Jackson & E. Cox (Eds.), *Doing Coaching Research* (pp. 91–111). Sage.

Koning, J., & Ooi, C. (2013). Awkward encounters and ethnography. *Qualitative Research in Organizations and Management: An International Journal*, *8*(1), 16–32. https://doi.org/10.1108/17465641311327496

Koning, J., & Waistell, J. (2012). Identity talk of aspirational ethical leaders. *Journal of Business Ethics*, *107*(1), 65–77. https://doi.org/10.1007/s10551-012-1297-3

Lin, J., Oxford, R. L., & Culham, T. E. (2016). Introduction: The urgent need to develop a spiritual research paradigm. In J. Lin, R. L. Oxford, & T. E. Culham (Eds.), *Toward a Spiritual Research Paradigm: Exploring New Ways of Knowing, Researching and Being* (pp. ix–xix). IAP.

Lips-Wiersma, M. (2003). Making conscious choices in doing research on workplace spirituality: Utilizing the "holistic development model" to articulate values, assumptions and dogmas of the knower. *Journal of Organizational Change Management*, *16*(4), 406–425. https://doi.org/10.1108/09534810310484163

Lund Dean, K., & Fornaciari, C. J. (2007). Empirical research in management, spirituality & religion during Its founding years. *Journal of Management, Spirituality & Religion*, *4*(1), 3–34. https://doi.org/10.1080/14766080709518644

Lund Dean, K., Fornaciari, C. J., & McGee, J. J. (2003). Research in spirituality, religion, and work: Walking the line between relevance and legitimacy. *Journal of Organizational Change Management*, *16*(4), 378–395. https://doi.org/10.1108/09534810310484145

Miller, D. W., & Ewest, T. (2013). The present state of workplace spirituality: A literature review considering context, theory, and measurement/assessment. *Journal of Religious & Theological Information*, *12*(1–2), 29–54. https://doi.org/10.1080/10477845.2013.800776

Neal, J. (2018). Overview of workplace spirituality research. In S. Dhiman, G. Roberts, & J. Crossman (Eds.), *The Palgrave Handbook of Workplace Spirituality and Fulfillment. 1st ed. Switzerland Cham: Palgrave Macmillan* (pp. 3–57). Palgrave Macmillan. https://doi.org/10.1007/978-3-319-61929-3_45-1

Paquier, M.-C. (2019). The monastic product's biography, a sacralization wave. *Journal of Management, Spirituality & Religion*, *16*(1), 76–108. https://doi.org/10.1080/14766086.2018.1445549

Sambrook, S., & Herrmann, A. F. (2018). Organisational autoethnography: Possibilities, politics and pitfalls. *Journal of Organizational Ethnography*, *7*(3), 222–234. https://doi.org/10.1108/JOE-10-2018-075

Tackney, C. T., Chappell, S., Harris, D., Pavlovich, K., Egel, E., Major, R., Finney, M., & Stoner, J. (2017). Management, spirituality, and religion (MSR) ways and means: A paper to encourage quality research. *Journal of Management, Spirituality & Religion*, *14*(3), 245–254. https://doi.org/10.1080/14766086.2017.1316764

Todd, N. R. (2012). Religious networking organizations and social justice: An ethnographic case study. *American Journal of Community Psychology*, *50*(1–2), 229–245. https://doi.org/10.1007/s10464-012-9493-y

van Maanen, J. (1988). *Tales of the Field: On Writing Ethnography*. University of Chicago Press.

van Maanen, J. (2001). Afterword: Natives 'R'us: Some notes on the ethnography of organizations. In D. Gellner & E. Hirsch (Eds.), *Inside Organizations: Anthopologists at Work* (pp. 233–261). Routledge.

van Maanen, J. (2010). A song form my supper: More tales of the field. *Organizational Research Methods*, *13*(2), 240–255. https://doi.org/10.1177/1094428109343968

Winkler, I. (2018). Doing autoethnography: Facing challenges, taking choices, accepting responsibilities. *Qualitative Inquiry*, *24*(4), 236–247. https://doi.org/10.1177/1077800417728956

Ybema, S., Yanow, D., Wels, H., & Kamsteeg, F. H. (2009). *Organizational Ethnography: Studying the Complexity of Everyday Life*. Sage.

Zempi, I. (2017). Researching victimisation using auto-ethnography: Wearing the Muslim veil in public. *Methodological Innovations*, *10*(1). https://doi.org/10.1177/2059799117720617

Zilber, T. B., & Zanoni, P. (2020). Templates of ethnographic writing in organization studies: Beyond the hegemony of the detective story. *Organizational Research Methods*. https://doi.org/10.1177/1094428120944468

Cécile Rozuel

20 Psychodynamics and the Field of Management, Spirituality and Religion: Deciphering the Unconscious, Mapping the Soul

Situating Psychodynamic Theories

The notion of psychodynamics originates with early studies on personality, emotions and cognition. Although the term is most notably associated with Sigmund Freud's psychoanalytical studies as well as the theories of Carl Gustav Jung (Analytical Psychology), Alfred Adler (Individual Psychology) and several of Freud's followers including Melanie Klein and Donald Winnicott (Object Relations approach), its premises lie in the explorations of early psychologists in the late nineteenth and early twentieth century. The work of French psychologist Pierre Janet (1859–1947) notably helped frame the idea of subconscious (or preconscious) and unconscious dynamics influencing personality and behaviour.

Core to this idea is the postulate that the mind is best understood as a complex field of psychic energy (referred to as 'the libido'), whose intensity and quality determines how we process and express the experiences we live. In other words, the mind (or the psyche) is ruled by complex dynamics, many of which occur outside of our conscious awareness, and whose manifestations are very real, be they through the display of emotions, of psychological or somatic disorders, or of patterns of behaviours and personality traits in response to social stimuli.

Of particular interest to psychodynamic psychotherapists are the experiences of conflicts and tensions emerging from this rich, partly unconscious and autonomous inner life of the person. When these conflicts and tensions manifest, they are assumed to be significant and meaningful in the context of the person's unique life, and they are dealt with in a variety of ways ranging from defence mechanisms (from a Freudian lens) to symbolic enactments (from a Jungian lens). The ability to consciously shed light onto the unconscious etiology of our inner turmoil is the main focus of psychodynamic approaches to therapy and to human development. Indeed, by understanding what occurs within ourselves, we start to grasp and address what occurs outside of ourselves, because much of our inner world is arguably projected onto and mirrored through our social world.

https://doi.org/10.1515/9783110711349-020

Psychodynamics and MSR: Conceptualizing the Self, the Soul and Patterns of Behaviour in Organizations

The more notable engagements between the respective fields of psychodynamics and of Management, Spirituality and Religion (MSR) have been around the conceptualization of the (psychological) self in relation to the (spiritual) soul, and the critical analysis of what this means and implies for the study of management and organizations (e.g. Powley & Cameron, 2006; Roberts, 2007). Doing so has enabled scholars to consider in greater details the normality of emotions and the significance of pathological, unhealthy or harmful behaviours within an organization. It has also paved the way for further ethical reflections on the self-other relationship, touching on notions of meaningfulness and transcendence in a more psychologically-informed manner.

Each psychodynamic tradition comes with its own conceptualization of the self which can help refine, enrich or contrast the views of the self from spiritual traditions, or which can question the outline of the self offered by social science traditions, including management and organizational studies. How we define the self informs how we frame organizational agents, how we interpret the social world, how we make sense of human experiences. It helps us determine whether these experiences are in essence psycho-emotional, socio-political or spiritual, or all at once.

Looking at the past ten years of MSR contributions, we can distinguish three main perspectives that claim a clear anchoring in psychodynamics, namely a Freudian approach, a Jungian approach and, to a lesser extent, a Lacanian approach. Each offers a different perspective on the psyche and on spirituality, outlined below.

Freudian Psychodynamics and MSR

The Freudian psyche is characterized by an inherent tension between the pleasure principle (rooted in the unconscious, conceptualized as the 'id', leading to fantasies and phantasms) and the reality principle which the conscious ego learns to recognize in order to mediate passions and instincts. The superego emerges through an identification with the lost love-object (the initial parental figure) and leads to the emergence of conscience as a now-internalized moral agency. Our conscious life, then, sees our ego constantly working towards mediating the demands of the id with the censoring power of the superego, all the while negotiating its understanding of 'reality' in order to guide and assess behaviour.

When it comes to spirituality, Freud was famously reluctant for most of his life to grant much value to religious and spiritual endeavours, referring to it as a "crutch" from which some people find comfort out of the chaos and uncertainty of life, but conceding little evolutionary need for a transcendent experience as such (Walborn, 2014). Although Freud softened his view on the purpose of religion in his final years, his approach to psychodynamics somehow limits the scope of connections with the MSR field. This means that scholars who position themselves within a Freudian view have had to reach beyond the strict structure of a preconscious mind to find ways to explore more collective, humanistic phenomena. This has essentially taken the form of storytelling as a method for studying organizational life.

The most significant contributions in the framing of a dialogue between Freudian psychodynamics and MSR have been made by Gabriel and colleagues. Grounded in an attention to the stories and various narratives that populate work organizations, these writings focus on exposing deep emotions at play (e.g. Fineman & Gabriel, 1996; Gabriel, 1995, 1997, 1999, 2000, 2004). The study of *what* emotions are experienced, *why* they might be experienced *then* and *there*, *how* they are expressed and *how* they are received, make up a great deal of this scholarship. Over the past decade, we can list the study of disappointment (Clancy et al., 2012) and anger (Lindebaum & Gabriel, 2016), anxieties around consumption choices (Nixon & Gabriel, 2016), disgust and 'miasma' (Gabriel, 2012), blame and the need for compassion (Gabriel, 2015), or the fragmentation of our self-identity in the context of unemployment (Gabriel et al., 2013).

These contributions have helped bring nuances to our understanding of organizational life, reinforcing the need to adopt a more historical and holistic view of the self beyond its identity or its role as an organizational agent. The importance of understanding a self in context, of defining a self through its own history and its own stories (be they fantasies or realities), and of recognizing the significance and the normality of seemingly disruptive emotions within a so-called rational organizational system, are major inputs that echo the efforts of MSR scholars to rehabilitate a non-dual, non-simplistic view of human nature. They converge towards an understanding of organizations as complex, at times paradoxical, living systems in which live fragile, yet adaptive and resilient, human beings.

The constant interaction between individuals and systems, shaping one another in constructive or compensatorily destructive ways, therefore becomes a critical dimension of management thinking: in other words, to manage effectively and responsibly, it is essential to account for the various conscious emotional patterns at play, the unconscious (compensatory) motives and needs unveiled, and the capacity of the organization to respond to these conscious and unconscious dynamics. Furthermore, these interactions, even those seemingly disruptive to the smooth running of the organization, are conceived as meaningful, in so far as they reflect people's unconscious desires and aspirations for a collective ideal. Management is no longer seen as a science but rather as a delicate craft of deciphering, validating, and even co-constructing meaning and identities.

From this follows a timid interest in rituals and symbolic enactments, both deeply spiritual practices, as integral to organizational life and as necessary for the psycho-emotional well-being of organizational members. This does not quite echo Freud's own view of psychodynamics, because Freud himself did not show much interest in the ongoing need for rituals if one is sufficiently well-adjusted. This stands in contrast with Jung's own view on rituals as symbolic liminal spaces for growth.

Jungian Psychodynamics and MSR

The Jungian psyche positions the ego as the centre of consciousness whose function is primarily to filter through (or discriminate) the numerous information emerging from the unconscious. The unconscious is partly personal and time-bound (akin to Freud's preconscious state) and, more importantly, partly collective and timeless. This collective unconscious serves as the repository for the entire human experience, recording and carrying forward the instinctive knowledge and intuitive understanding of our ancestors from an archaic time to our present day. For Jung, the collective unconscious, populated by archetypes, shapes a great deal of our lives, including but not limited to, our emotions and our symbolic enactments. Emotions here can be conceived of as cues about our conscious ego's varied attempts to make sense of, compensate for, or relate to the unconscious contents (or archetypal patterns) that present themselves continuously.

The collective unconscious is, in fact, the source of all that we experience consciously, and the reason behind our specific way of making sense of these experiences. Adopting a teleological view, Jung argued that the main drive behind human existence is the ego's conscious reconnection with the archetypal Self, the ultimate symbol of wholeness. From this standpoint, the ego initially emerges out of the collective unconscious (like an original matrix) and develops a growing ability to differentiate from its collective origins, until it realizes the need to return to its collective roots, but this time maintaining a conscious appreciation of that process. This dynamic, to which Jung refers as 'individuation', is not only psychological but also deeply spiritual in so far as it posits the need to transcend the apparent 'consciousness-unconsciousness' duality while recognizing that this tension itself is creative, generative, fruitful, and necessary. This is because without consciousness emerging out of the initial unconscious matrix, there would be no human experiences as such, and therefore no possibility to know what we know. In the collective unconscious, through the experience of the archetypal Self, we can catch a glimpse of the Soul of the World (the *Anima Mundi*), of 'God' in the sense of something transcendent, of whatever unknown potential lies beyond our consciousness.

The Jungian psyche is therefore the most open framework for psychodynamic explorations in the MSR field because it is inherently spiritual as well as psychological. Jung had strong concerns regarding the dogmatic excesses of religion (Jung, 1957/1970), but he recognized that human beings are driven by holistic, spiritual and meaningful needs which pervade a great deal of our interactions and behaviours. Despite this natural fit, works grounded in a Jungian perspective and exploring MSR issues are relatively few. Amongst those, some studies are systematically anchored in a Jungian psychodynamic framework, while others simply borrow some Jungian concepts to enrich their analysis of other organizational literature, but do not embrace the inherently spiritual worldview that a Jungian framework provides. Only those studies that adopt a comprehensive Jungian approach have been reviewed in this section.

Jungian psychodynamics applied to management and organizational studies can be traced back to the 1980s, with notable papers from Denhardt (1981), Mitroff (1983), followed in the 1990s by Bowles (1989, 1990, 1991, 1993a, 1993b, 1997), Jacobson (1993), and Aurelio (1995). These initial contributions each examined, in their own way, the inner dynamics of business organizations and the business world as whole, hinting at the risks of a disconnected, one-sided, soulless business paradigm for the well-being of individuals and groups. By and large, these scholars outlined primarily the significance of myths and the power of archetypes in the design of organizations and the practice of management, and only secondarily did they examine the manifestations of such dynamics amongst organizational members.

They were followed by a few significant articulations of Jungian psychodynamics to organizational life, with Hart and Brady's publication (2005) a notable attempt at including spirituality at the forefront of their analysis. The works of Moxnes (1999, 2013; Moxnes & Moxnes, 2016) also showcase how Jungian psychodynamics applies to management and leadership studies, although he is much shyer at addressing the spiritual implications of the archetypal dynamics under scrutiny.

In the past decade, a range of contributions have continued to build upon the notion of archetypes to explore the impact of unconscious collective patterns upon the conscious lives of organizations and organizational members (e.g. Kostera, 2012). Aspects of personality types (Lemmergaard & Howard, 2013), the concept of individuation and development (Brown et al., 2013; Ladkin et al., 2018), the significance of the shadow – our so-called dark side – (Chappell et al., 2019; Ketola, 2012), the persona – our social mask – (Rozuel, 2010), and the archetypal dynamic of the feminine/anima and masculine/animus qualities (e.g. Jironet, 2011, 2019; Rozuel, 2020) have been other modes of engagement with Jungian ideas. In the works cited above, the unconscious is indeed defined as symbolically rich, but the idea that 'Self equates Soul' is rarely acknowledged in clear terms.

Rozuel (2014a, 2019; Rozuel & Kakabadse, 2010) is the main author who has explicitly confronted MSR issues from a Jungian psychodynamic perspective. Following Jung in adopting the language of alchemy to decipher the psyche, Rozuel (2014a) notably articulates the nature of wounded soul of organizations and examines the roots and consequences of such a state, before calling for the re-awakening of the *Anima Mundi* through individual and collective soul-work. The lens of alchemy is further applied to organizational tensions (Rozuel, 2019), this time positioning organizational members as alchemical vessels, and arguing for the re-sacralization of work and the re-enchantment of our worldviews.

On a more interpersonal and intrapersonal level, the Jungian psychodynamics scholarship also contributes to redefining the ethical debate by addressing the ambiguity of unexamined moral aspirations (Kociatkiewicz & Kostera, 2012; Rozuel, 2011a, 2011b, 2013a, 2016a) and by positioning the imagination as a source of moral insights grounded in the 'Self as Soul' (Rozuel, 2012, 2014b, 2016b)). The source of ethics or of individual moral reflection is no longer restricted to cognitive processes but is presented as a multi-layered psycho-socio-spiritual experience (Rozuel, 2013b, 2016a). The responsibilities of individuals and organizations are more clearly and more honestly articulated, avoiding the recurring trap of blaming the 'bad apples' or the 'bad barrels' alone for wrongdoings, or of sounding too naïve in prescribing moral rules that ignore psychological complexity and ambiguity.

The possibilities of dialogue with religious or spiritual traditions on MSR matters become evident, especially when engaging the imagination to confront and contrast the stories and narratives that infuse both organizational cultures and religious practices. More precisely, this scholarship supports critical reflections on the fact that deep social transformation must be approached creatively from *both* an individual standpoint (i.e. each person has a responsibility for change) *and* a collective standpoint (i.e. unconscious patterns influence what each person believes is possible or not). Jungian psychodynamics therefore enable the MSR field to grow out of studies focused on individual experiences of spirituality and religion, as well as out of studies aiming to ground economic principles into spiritual and ethical tenets. It holds that one informs the other, necessarily, and one helps meaningfully transform the other, eventually.

Furthermore, emotions and tensions in organizational life are understood as not only normal but as manifestations of transformative possibilities. These possibilities are approached imaginatively, creatively and inclusively: if Freudian psychodynamics outline a pathway to decipher the unconscious, then Jungian psychodynamics extend this pathway by providing not only a map of possible meanings, but also a toolbox of symbols with which we can creatively go and explore the soul.

Lacanian Psychoanalysis and MSR

Another distinct scholarship, derived from the Freudian psychoanalytical tradition, has engaged to some extent with issues pertaining to the MSR field. Building upon the works of Lacan, whose own interpretation of classical psychoanalysis led him to develop an approach emphasizing language and semi-conscious constructions of the self, this scholarship has gained popularity in the field of critical management studies (e.g. Arnaud, 2012; Arnaud & Vidaillet, 2018). Driver (2005, 2007) has been the main contributor to the conversation between Lacanian psychoanalysis and the MSR field, exploring the ambiguities and contradictions behind organizational spirituality discourses.

The Lacanian psyche is not so much focused on deep dynamics, but rather on the scope and scale of social interactions (be they constructive, repressive, idealized or fantasized) involved in the experience of the self. The self is viewed as being constructed through language and evolving as an imaginary unity that may appear authentic but ends up constraining the full expression of a more fragmented, yet more authentic, ego. The purpose of the ego is, in a Lacanian view, to come to terms with the fact that the image of a unified, stable and all-powerful self is an illusion, and that true subjectivity and creativity is found through the acceptance of an inherently fragmented human nature. This, in turn, paves the way for the emergence of various alternative discourses about the self.

Lacanian psychoanalysis has especially appealed to critical management or organizational scholars because of its central focus on the power play, bridging the socio-political angle with a psychoanalytical angle (e.g. Contu et al., 2010). Indeed, it denounces dominant discourses as potentially oppressive, misappropriated, exploitative or alienating. The authentic spiritual expression of the ego, rather, comes out of that ego stating its struggles with being authentic and with experiencing its spirituality (e.g. Driver, 2010, 2013–2015).

It is worth noting that while the Lacanian perspective does provide a framework for examining social structures around the ego-self, it does not offer a detailed mapping of the inner dynamics of the psyche nor does it leave a space for articulating what a transcendent soul would be like – in fact, those very terms would likely be criticized as alienating and empty. In this regard, the contributions of this scholarship to the MSR field have largely targeted the 'dark side of spirituality' or the deconstruction of a problematic discourse or of an ambiguous identity-making process through the use of short narratives or illustrative vignettes (e.g. Driver, 2009, 2017, 2019; Hudson, 2014).

Many Crossovers, Few Encounters: The Missed Conversations Between Psychodynamics and MSR

In reflecting upon the past and the way forward, it becomes clear that there have been many missed conversations between psychodynamic traditions and the MSR field. More precisely, while only three distinct approaches have engaged with MSR topics as outlined above, a great many more have crossed over to management and/or organizational studies for decades. Yet, none of these crossovers have recognized, let alone explored, the spiritual dimension of human needs and human experience in their study of what lies 'below the surface'.

Many more Freudian psychoanalytical approaches to management and leadership than the works cited earlier (e.g. Brunning, 2014; Fotaki et al., 2012; Gabriel & Carr, 2002; Stein, 2011, 2013, 2015, 2016) have shed light upon the darker side of organizational life, be it the experience of trauma, of scapegoating or of narcissistic inflation. They have demonstrated the need to move beyond the binary view of 'good behaviour' versus 'bad behaviour' in organizations, advocating a more nuanced perspective that recognizes behaviours as shaped through compensatory manifestations of deeper unconscious patterns and that points to the possibility of the constructive development of individuals and organizations *if* these patterns are indeed recognized as such. Yet, the eventual *spiritual* drive for such understanding and development is not discussed, and the analysis remains strictly psychoanalytical. In a somewhat similar vein, Kets de Vries's writings on leadership (e.g. Kets de Vries, 2011, 2014, 2019) examine the inner workings of organizational members, some of which deeply unconscious and anchored in compensatory power struggles, but they hardly mention the symbolic or spiritual dimension of leadership – with one notable exception where Kets de Vries (2016) positions leadership coaching as a practice of 'self-retrieval' as akin to the respective shamanic practice and Jungian process of 'soul-retrieval'.

Numerous studies also build upon the Kleinian perspective of Object Relations psychodynamics, sometimes mixed with a classical psychoanalytical grounding (e.g. Petriglieri & Stein, 2012; Stein, 2019) and spearheaded by the Tavistock Institute in London, England. Yet, they too give little room for explicit considerations of spiritual values or worldviews in their analysis of human relations at work. By and large, these studies focus on framing in a 'psychosocial manner' the emotional and affective experiences of organizational members as mirroring the early relationships with the objects of identification (e.g. Fotaki, 2010; Fotaki & Hyde, 2015; Kenny & Fotaki, 2014; see Fotaki et al., 2020 for a rare explicit reference to spirituality).

A further development from this standpoint is the growth of literature on systems psychodynamics (e.g. Gould et al., 2006) which focus on examining the organization as a dynamic psycho-social system whose complexity can be critically grasped through the lens of psychoanalysis. The influence of both Klein's work on early childhood attachment patterns, and Bion's work on groups as well as, to a lesser extent, that of positive psychology, is noticeable in the studies anchored in systems psychodynamics, though once again little is said on the spiritual or religious dimension of the human experiences under scrutiny.

Equally rare are scholarly works which have embraced an Adlerian approach to study management and organizational life, irrelevant of any mention of spirituality (see Ambrus, 2013; Nelson, 1999). This is somewhat surprising given how much the Adlerian self is construed as socially oriented, motivated to act by the various expressions of an inferiority complex, and striving for conscious self-expansion through the realization a chosen goal.

Conclusion and Future Directions

Psychodynamics and MSR remains a niche research area with demonstrated potential for future growth. Psychodynamic approaches ground MSR conversations through their ability to articulate models of the self, of identity, of ego-consciousness, and of unconscious experiences. They help normalize emotions in organizations. They help dig up tensions and make sense of individual and collective behaviours in context. They critically assess the value of spirituality at work. They provide a framework for imagining and constructing inclusive organizations and workspaces which hold us accountable to our ethical values. They bridge inner human experience with transcendent experience.

In this purview, more can be done to position management and leadership practices as legitimately intuitive, emotionally reflexive and contextual, and not merely rational or instrumental. Indeed, if interpersonal relationships are best described as conscious and unconscious energy flows, then there is little relevance for 'one-size-fits-all' models of organizational interventions, management training or leadership development. Instead, more attention is called towards understanding the rich emotional cues on display, the hidden needs behind the words, the symbolic meaning of images and stories that pertain to individuals and to groups. This work necessitates a greater acceptance of intuition and feeling as sources of insights and knowledge on par with 'factual' perceptions and rational analysis. Without it, the surprise element so constitutive of the human experience and of human creativity is lost (Gabriel, 2013).

Another area of desirable collaboration targets the need to re-sacralize and re-enchant the world with greater consciousness. Business organizations are typically viewed as the poster child for postmodern disenchantment, yet work is so intrinsically spiritual that we can question how much of that argument is founded (Rozuel, 2019). Psychodynamics have proven useful in the crafting of deeply meaningful rituals, symbols and words that guide and heal people and communities. MSR studies can certainly work more closely with suitable psychodynamic approaches to explore how spirit or soul can be reinfused in organizations without this process being naïve, forceful, nor scornful (Rozuel, 2020).

Reflections on work and organizations as sacred spaces lead us further into the moral territory. As we have noted, considering the psychodynamics of the self is inseparable from discussing how these impact others – other selves or other institutions (Rozuel, 2016a). As MSR scholarship attempts to develop more encompassing ways for people to uphold the virtues and values they endorse, psychodynamics can shed light on why moral ambiguity remains, and on what responsibility actually means for individuals and collectives. Building from there, I envision further connections with the workplace well-being agenda and with research on embodiment or psychosomatic experiences at work.

It is however important to underline that not all psychodynamic approaches lend themselves to a fruitful conversation with MSR. More than ever, as we grow our field with the necessary rigour and integrity it deserves, our diligence in ensuring an ontological and epistemological compatibility between the frameworks we use – especially when we mix spiritual worldviews with psychological frameworks – is critical. This rigour will further inform the methodologies we use, and the opportunity to ground systematic research in arts-based, creative and participative studies. I argue that the nature of psychodynamics, especially the Jungian perspective, fits Braud's description of "an appropriate tool for exploring topics in more intuitive, holistic, and nonverbal ways" (Braud, 2009, p. 72). The psyche is, just like the soul, a wondrous field of unconscious unknowns and not-yet-knowns, and we can only do it justice if we learn its unique language.

References

Ambrus, Z. (2013). Public administration in the perspective of Alfred Adler's individual psychology. A discussion. *Acta Universitatis Sapientiae. Social Analysis*, *3*(2), 215–232.

Arnaud, G. (2012). The contribution of psychoanalysis to organization studies and management: An overview. *Organization Studies*, *33*(9), 1121–1135. https://doi.org/10.1177/0170840612448153

Arnaud, G., & Vidaillet, B. (2018). Clinical and critical: The Lacanian contribution to management and organization studies. *Organization*, *25*(1), 69–97. https://doi.org/10.1177/1350508417720021

Aurelio, J. M. (1995). Using jungian archetypes to explore deeper levels of organizational culture: Facing your organization's psyche. *Journal of Management Inquiry*, *4*(4), 347–368. https://doi.org/10.1177/105649269500400407

Bowles, M. L. (1989). Myth, meaning and work organization. *Organization Studies*, *10*(3), 405–421. https://doi.org/10.1177/017084068901000306

Bowles, M. L. (1990). Recognizing deep structures in organizations. *Organization Studies*, *11*(3), 395–412. https://doi.org/10.1177/017084069001100304

Bowles, M. L. (1991). The organization shadow. *Organization Studies*, *12*(3), 387–404. https://doi.org/10.1177/017084069101200303

Bowles, M. L. (1993a). The gods and goddesses: Personifying social life in the age of organization. *Organization Studies, 14*(3), 395–418. https://doi.org/10.1177/017084069301400304
Bowles, M. L. (1993b). Logos and eros: The vital syzygy for understanding human relations and organizational action. *Human Relations, 46*(11), 1271–1290. https://doi.org/10.1177/001872679304601101
Bowles, M. L. (1997). The myth of management: Direction an dfailure in contemporary organizations. *Human Relations, 50*(7), 779–803. https://doi.org/10.1023/A: 1016912507723
Braud, W. (2009). Dragons, spheres, and flashlights: Appropriate research approaches for studying workplace spirituality. *Journal of Management, Spirituality & Religion, 6*(1), 59–75. https://doi.org/10.1080/14766080802648557
Brown, M. L., McDonald, S., & Smith, F. (2013). Jungian archetypes and dreams of social enterprise. *Journal of Organizational Change Management, 26*(4), 670–688. https://doi.org/10.1108/JOCM-Sep-2012-0146
Brunning, H. (2014). *Psychoanalytic Essays on Power and Vulnerability*. Routledge.
Chappell, S., Cooper, E., & Trippe, G. (2019). Shadow work for leadership development. *Journal of Management Development, 38*(5), 326–335. https://doi.org/10.1108/JMD-08-2018-0216
Clancy, A., Vince, R., & Gabriel, Y. (2012). That unwanted feeling: A psychodynamic study of disappointment in organizations: that unwanted feeling. *British Journal of Management, 23*(4), 518–531. https://doi.org/10.1111/j.1467-8551.2011.00780.x
Contu, A., Driver, M., & Jones, C. (2010). Editorial: Jacques Lacan with organization studies. *Organization, 17*(3), 307–315. https://doi.org/10.1177/1350508410364095
Denhardt, R. (1981). *Is the Shadow of Organization*. University Press of Kansas.
Driver, M. (2005). From empty speech to full speech? Reconceptualizing spirituality in organizations based on a psychoanalytically-grounded understanding of the self. *Human Relations, 58*(9), 1091–1110. https://doi.org/10.1177/0018726705059038
Driver, M. (2007). A "spiritual turn" in organizational studies: Meaning making or meaningless? *Journal of Management, Spirituality & Religion, 4*(1), 56–86. https://doi.org/10.1080/14766080709518646
Driver, M. (2009). Struggling with lack: A lacanian perspective on organizational identity. *Organization Studies, 30*(1), 55–72. https://doi.org/10.1177/0170840608100516
Driver, M. (2010). Learning as lack: Individual learning in organizations as an empowering encounter with failed imaginary constructions of the self. *Management Learning, 41*(5), 561–574. https://doi.org/10.1177/1350507610374427
Driver, M. (2013). The lack of power or the power of lack in leadership as a discursively constructed identity. *Organization Studies, 34*(3), 407–422. https://doi.org/10.1177/0170840612463003
Driver, M. (2014). The stressed subject: Lack, empowerment and liberation. *Organization, 21*(1), 90–105. https://doi.org/10.1177/1350508412464897
Driver, M. (2015). How trust functions in the context of identity work. *Human Relations, 68*(6), 899–923. https://doi.org/10.1177/0018726714548080
Driver, M. (2017). Never social and entrepreneurial enough? Exploring the identity work of social entrepreneurs from a psychoanalytic perspective. *Organization, 24*(6), 715–736. https://doi.org/10.1177/1350508416665474
Driver, M. (2019). Who will I be when I retire? Introducing a Lacanian typology at the intersection of present identity work and future narratives of the retired self. *Human Relations, 72*(2), 322–343. https://doi.org/10.1177/0018726718761553
Fineman, S., & Gabriel, Y. (1996). *Experiencing Organizations*. Sage.
Fotaki, M. (2010). Why do public policies fail so often? Exploring health policy-making as an imaginary and symbolic construction. *Organization, 17*(6), 703–720. https://doi.org/10.1177/1350508410366321

Fotaki, M., Altman, Y., & Koning, J. (2020). Spirituality, symbolism and storytelling in twentyfirst-century organizations: Understanding and addressing the crisis of imagination. *Organization Studies*, *41*(1), 7–30. https://doi.org/10.1177/0170840619875782

Fotaki, M., & Hyde, P. (2015). Organizational blind spots: Splitting, blame and idealization in the National Health Service. *Human Relations*, *68*(3), 441–462. https://doi.org/10.1177/0018726714530012

Fotaki, M., Long, S., & Schwartz, H. S. (2012). What can psychoanalysis offer organization studies today? Taking stock of current developments and thinking about future directions. *Organization Studies*, *33*(9), 1105–1120. https://doi.org/10.1177/0170840612448152

Gabriel, Y. (1995). The unmanaged organization: Stories, fantasies and subjectivity. *Organization Studies*, *16*(3), 477–501. https://doi.org/10.1177/017084069501600305

Gabriel, Y. (1997). Meeting God: When organizational members come face to face with the supreme leader. *Human Relations*, *50*(4), 315–342. https://doi.org/10.1023/A: 1016938410023

Gabriel, Y. (1999). *Organizations in Depth*. SAGE Publications.

Gabriel, Y. (2000). *Storytelling in Organizations: Facts, Fictions, and Fantasies: Facts, Fictions, and Fantasies*. Oxford Univeristy Press.

Gabriel, Y. (2004). *Myths, Stories, and Organizations: Premodern Narratives For Our Times*. Oxford University Press.

Gabriel, Y. (2012). Organizations in a state of darkness: Towards a theory of organizational miasma. *Organization Studies*, *33*(9), 1137–1152. https://doi.org/10.1177/0170840612448154

Gabriel, Y. (2013). Surprises: Not just the spice of life but the source of knowledge. *M@ N@ Gement*, *16*(5), 719–731.

Gabriel, Y. (2015). Beyond compassion: Replacing a blame culture with proper emotional support and management comment on "why and how is compassion necessary to provide good quality healthcare?" *International Journal of Health Policy and Management*, *4*(9), 617–619. https://doi.org/10.15171/ijhpm.2015.111

Gabriel, Y., & Carr, A. (2002). Organizations, management and psychoanalysis: An overview. *Journal of Managerial Psychology*, *17*(5), 348–365. https://doi.org/10.1108/02683940210432600

Gabriel, Y., Gray, D. E., & Goregaokar, H. (2013). Job loss and its aftermath among managers and professionals: Wounded, fragmented and flexible. *Work, Employment and Society*, *27*(1), 56–72. https://doi.org/10.1177/0950017012460326

Gould, L. J., Stapley, L. F., & Goregaokar, H. (2006). *The Systems Psychodynamics of Organizations: Integrating the Group Relations Approach, Psychoanalytic, and Open Systems Perspectives*. Routledge.

Hart, D. W., & Brady, F. N. (2005). Spirituality and archetype in organizational life. *Business Ethics Quarterly*, *15*(3), 409–428.

Hudson, R. (2014). The question of theoretical foundations for the spirituality at work movement. *Journal of Management, Spirituality & Religion*, *11*(1), 27–44. https://doi.org/10.1080/14766086.2013.801031

Jacobson, K. H. (1993). Organization and the Mother archetype: A Jungian analysis of adult development and self-identity within the organization. *Administration and Society*, *25*(1), 60–84. https://doi.org/10.1177/009539979302500104

Jironet, K. (2011). *Female Leadership: Management, Jungian Psychology, Spirituality and the Global Journey Through Purgatory*. Routledge.

Jironet, K. (2019). *Feminine Leadership: Personal Development Beyond Polarities* (2nd ed.). Routledge.

Jung, C. G. (1957). The undiscovered self. In C. G. Jung (Ed.), *Civilization in Transition* (2nd ed., Vol. 10). Princeton University Press.

Kenny, K., & Fotaki, M. (2014). *The Psychosocial and Organization Studies: Affect at Work*. Palgrave Macmillan. https://books.google.at/books?id=zQ5HBQAAQBAJ
Ketola, T. (2012). Losing your self: Managerial persona and shadow pressures killing responsible leadership. *Journal of Management Development*, *31*(5), 470–487. https://doi.org/10.1108/02621711211226051
Kets de Vries, M. F. R. (2011). *Reflections on Groups and Organizations*. John Whiley & Sons.
Kets de Vries, M. F. R. (2014). *Mindful Leadership Coaching: Journeys Into the Interior*. Palgrave Macmillan.
Kets de Vries, M. F. R. (2016). The shaman, the therapist, and the coach. *Organisational and Social Dynamics*, *16*(1), 1–18.
Kets de Vries, M. F. R. (2019). *Down the Rabbit Hole of Leadership: Leadership Pathology in Everyday Life*. Palgrave Macmillan.
Kociatkiewicz, J., & Kostera, M. (2012). The good manager: An archetypical quest for morally sustainable leadership. *Organization Studies*, *33*(7), 861–878. https://doi.org/10.1177/0170840612445124
Kostera, M. (2012). *Organizations and Archetypes*. Edward Elgar Publishing.
Ladkin, D., Spiller, C., & Craze, G. (2018). The journey of individuation: A jungian alternative to the theory and practice of leading authentically. *Leadership*, *14*(4), 415–434. https://doi.org/10.1177/1742715016681942
Lemmergaard, J., & Howard, C. (2013). Do it my way: A study on type, leadership and emotions. In J. Lemmergaard & S. Muhr, *Critical Perspectives on Leadership* (pp. 59–85). Edward Elgar Publishing. https://doi.org/10.4337/9780857931139.00011
Lindebaum, D., & Gabriel, Y. (2016). Anger and organization studies: From social disorder to moral order. *Organization Studies*, *37*(7), 903–918. https://doi.org/10.1177/0170840616640848
Mitroff, I. I. (1983). Archetypal social systems analysis: On the deeper structure of human systems. *Academy of Management Review*, *8*(3), 387–397. https://doi.org/10.5465/amr.1983.4284373
Moxnes, P. (1999). Deep roles: Twelve primordial roles of mind and organization. *Human Relations*, *52*(11), 1427–1444. https://doi.org/10.1177/001872679905201104
Moxnes, P. (2013). The Hero's dream and other primordial patterns of imagery: Archetypal influences on organisational fantasies and ideations. *Journal of Organizational Change Management*, *26*(4), 638–653. https://doi.org/10.1108/JOCM-02-2013-0023
Moxnes, P., & Moxnes, A. (2016). Are we sucked into fairy tale roles? Role archetypes in imagination and organization. *Organization Studies*, *37*(10), 1519–1539. https://doi.org/10.1177/0170840616634135
Nelson, M. D. (1999). Applying individual psychology to the study of organizational dynamics. *Individual Psychology*, *55*(2), 200–208.
Nixon, E., & Gabriel, Y. (2016). 'So much choice and no choice at all': A socio-psychoanalytic interpretation of consumerism as a source of pollution. *Marketing Theory*, *16*(1), 39–56. https://doi.org/10.1177/1470593115593624
Petriglieri, G., & Stein, M. (2012). The unwanted self: Projective identification in leaders' identity work. *Organization Studies*, *33*(9), 1217–1235. https://doi.org/10.1177/0170840612448158
Powley, E. H., & Cameron, K. S. (2006). Organizational healing: Lived virtuousness amidst organizational crisis. *Journal of Management, Spirituality & Religion*, *3*(1–2), 13–33.
Roberts, C. (2007). Executives' fractured spirit and dissociation at work. *Journal of Management, Spirituality & Religion*, *4*(2), 160–186. https://doi.org/10.1080/14766080709518656
Rozuel, C. (2010). Moral tension in the psyche: A Jungian interpretation of managers' moral experiences. *EJBO Electronic Journal of Business Ethics and Organization Studies*, *15*(1), 36.

Rozuel, C. (2012). Moral imagination and active imagination: Searching in the depths of the psyche. *Journal of Management Development*, *31*(5), 488–501. https://doi.org/10.1108/02621711211226060
Rozuel, C. (2019). Unearthing gold from the mud: Alchemy and organizational tensions. *Journal of Management, Spirituality & Religion*, *16*(2), 178–198. https://doi.org/10.1080/14766086.2018.1524785
Rozuel, C. (2020). Rushing fools and wise women: Tales for organisations aiming to improve lives. In M. Schwartz & H. Harris (Eds.), *Research in Ethical Issues in Organizations* (pp. 101–122). Emerald Publishing Limited. https://doi.org/10.1108/S1529-209620200000023006
Rozuel, C. (2014a). Calling to the Anima Mundi: On restoring soul within organizations. *Journal of Management, Spirituality & Religion*, *11*(2), 123–142. https://doi.org/10.1080/14766086.2013.801320
Rozuel, C. (2016b). Challenging the 'million zeros': The importance of imagination for business ethics education. *Journal of Business Ethics*, *138*(1), 39–51. https://doi.org/10.1007/s10551-015-2639-8
Rozuel, C. (2013a). Daimon and psyche: Ethical reflections on a numinous marriage. *International Journal of Jungian Studies*, *5*(3), 211–225. https://doi.org/10.1080/19409052.2013.795182
Rozuel, C. (2013b). Exemplarity as commitment to the self: Insights from spiritual healers. *Research in Ethical Issues in Organizations*, *10*, 117–151. https://doi.org/10.1108/S1529-2096(2013)0000010010
Rozuel, C. (2016a). Jung's insights on ethics in business and work organisations: Examining the 'moral nature of present-day man.' *International Journal of Jungian Studies*, *8*(3), 141–158. https://doi.org/10.1080/19409052.2016.1200110
Rozuel, C. (2014b). Otherness in self and organisations: Kafka's "the metamorphosis" to stir moral reflection. In M. Schwartz & H. Harris (Eds.), *Research in Ethical Issues in Organizations* (Vol. 11, pp. 25–50). Emerald Group Publishing Limited. https://doi.org/10.1108/S1529-209620140000011002
Rozuel, C. (2011a). The moral threat of compartmentalization: Self, roles and responsibility. *Journal of Business Ethics*, *102*(4), 685–697. https://doi.org/10.1007/s10551-011-0839-4
Rozuel, C. (2011b). Transcending business ethics: Insights from Jung and Maslow. *EJBO Electronic Journal of Business Ethics and Organization Studies*, *16*(1), 41–47.
Rozuel, C., & Kakabadse, N. (2010). Ethics, spirituality and self: Managerial perspective and leadership implications. *Business Ethics: A European Review*, *19*(4), 423–436. https://doi.org/10.1111/j.1467-8608.2010.01603.x
Stein, M. (2011). A culture of mania: A psychoanalytic view of the incubation of the 2008 credit crisis. *Organization*, *18*(2), 173–186. https://doi.org/10.1177/1350508410390071
Stein, M. (2013). When does narcissistic leadership become problematic? Dick Fuld at Lehman Brothers. *Journal of Management Inquiry*, *22*(3), 282–293. https://doi.org/10.1177/1056492613478664
Stein, M. (2015). Double trouble: Sibling rivalry and twin organizations in the 2008 credit crisis: Double trouble. *British Journal of Management*, *26*(2), 182–196. https://doi.org/10.1111/1467-8551.12072
Stein, M. (2016). 'Fantasy of fusion' as a response to trauma: European leaders and the origins of the eurozone crisis. *Organization Studies*, *37*(7), 919–937. https://doi.org/10.1177/0170840615622070
Stein, M. (2019). The lost good self: Why the whistleblower is hated and stigmatized. *Organization Studies*, 017084061988056. https://doi.org/10.1177/0170840619880565
Walborn, F. (2014). *Religion in Personality Theory*. Academic Press.

List of Figures

https://doi.org/10.1515/9783110711349-021

List of Tables

https://doi.org/10.1515/9783110711349-022

About the Authors

Dorothea Alewell is a full professor of human resource management at the University of Hamburg, Germany. After an education in business administration, she specialized in human resources. Some of the topics she worked on during past years are the socio-economic analysis of labor law, internal labour markets, firm's investment in training and personnel development, gender stereotypes and firm's decisions on personnel services. Currently, she is head of the cooperative and interdisciplinary research network on good labour standards at Hamburg, and one of her more important research topics is spirituality at work.

Yochanan Altman is the Founding Editor of the *Journal of Management, Spirituality & Religion* (https://www.ingentaconnect.com/content/jmsr/rmsr20), Editor of the same named book series (https://www.degruyter.com/serial/MSR-B/html) and Founder and Chair of the International Association of Management, Spirituality and Religion (www.IAMSR.org) He has made significant contributions to the establishment and development of this scholarly domain. A globetrotter by nature and intent he held core faculty positions in three countries and visiting appointments in more than a dozen geographies throughout his career. Presently Yochanan Altman is extending his academic work during retirement as Visiting Professor with WU Vienna, Austria and an Honorary Research Fellow at the University of Haifa, Israel. His current focus, in addition to supporting work in Management, Spirituality & Religion, is to develop scholarship on Antisemitism at the workplace.

Puneet K. Bindlish Assistant Professor, Hindu Spirituality at the Faculty of Religion and Theology, Vrije Universiteit Amsterdam, The Netherlands. Earlier he taught at the Department of Humanistic Studies, Indian Institute of Technology (BHU) Varanasi, India. He brings a blend of academic, consulting and entrepreneurial experience across healthcare, telecom, technology, banking & insurance, education, sports, public sectors. His fields of interest are: Spirituality, Leadership, organisational behavior, entrepreneurship and integrative intelligence.

David M. Boje is what Foucault calls a 'specific intellectual', an international scholar confronting and deconstructing the 'regimes of truth' with his own storytelling paradigm. David has contributed 27 books and over 150 journal articles to studying one problem for 45 years: He introduced the now widely used concept of antenarrative, a prospective sensemaking (foresight) and intuitive world (the beyond of spirit) in the field of storytelling systems research. David and his wife Grace Ann Rosile built more work/research around indigenous storytelling and ethics, and that lead to current work on ensemble leadership, and ensemble storytelling. His most recent books are: *True Storytelling* with Jens Larsen and Lena Bruun, and *Doing Conversational Storytelling Interviewing for Your Dissertation* with Grace Ann Rosile. He retired in 2018 from New Mexico State University, earning Regents Professor, and Distinguished Scholar Professorship, and is currently Professor Emeritus. He immediately became professor at Aalborg University, Denmark. He teaches qualitative storytelling science methods at Cabrini University in Philadelphia (with Grace Ann).

Jim Cater is a Professor of Management and the Director of the Center for Family and Small Enterprises in the Soules College of Business at The University of Texas at Tyler. He is a Fellow of the Family Firm Institute. Jim managed his family's retail furniture business in south Florida before returning to school for his doctoral studies in Management at Louisiana State University. Jim has published articles in the *Family Business Review, Business Horizons, Journal of Business Ethics, Management Decision, Journal of Family Business Strategy, Journal of Family Business Management*, and other journals.

https://doi.org/10.1515/9783110711349-023

Léo-Paul Dana is Professor at Dalhousie University. He is also member of the Entrepreneurship and Innovation Chair, which is part of LabEx Entreprendre at the Université de Montpellier.A graduate of McGill University and HEC-Montreal, he has served as Marie Curie Fellow at Princeton University and Visiting Professor at INSEAD.He has published extensively in a variety of journals including *Entrepreneurship: Theory & Practice, International Business Review, International Small Business Journal, Journal of Business Research, Journal of Small Business Management, Journal of World Business, Small Business Economics,* and *Technological Forecasting & Social Change.*

Guiseppe Delmestri (Dr.rer.pol. Universität Mannheim) is Full Professor and Chair of the Institute of Change Management & Management Development in the Management oDepartment of WU Vienna University of Economics and Business. He previously held positions in Milan, Bergamo and Linz. He cofounded Organizational Scientists for Future (#OS4Future) and is member of Scientists4Future. He studies change in and around organizations and markets with special attention on evaluation (status, stigma, reputation) and on the role of social and climate movements such as Extinction Rebellion, veganism and animal rights. He published in journals such as *Administrative Science Quarterly, Organization Studies, Journal of International Business Studies, Journal of Management Studies, Human Relations, Higher Education, British Journal of Management, International Journal of Human Resource Management*, and *Journal of Arts & Cultural Management*.

Roger Gill is Visiting Professor of Leadership Studies at Durham University Business School, Durham University, UK, and an independent scholar. He previously served as Professor of Business Administration (Organizational Behaviour & Human Resources Management) and Director of Executive Development Programmes and subsequently as Visiting Professor of Leadership Studies at the University of Strathclyde Business School in the UK, Director of the joint Strathclyde/ Leadership Trust MBA in Leadership Studies programme, at the State University of New York at Binghamton, USA, and as Director of the Research Centre for Leadership Studies at the Leadership Trust in the UK. Roger has also worked as a human resources manager in the UK and as a management consultant in the UK, USA, Russia, Middle East and Far East, including 10 years based in Singapore. Roger is a UK Chartered Psychologist and a graduate of the universities of Oxford, Liverpool and Bradford.

Marie Holm is an Associate Professor of INSEEC School of Business and Economics in the Department of Management and Human Resources. She completed a Doctoral degree in Management Science from Sorbonne Université and a PhD from ESCP Europe under the direction of Dr. Isaac Getz, followed by a Post-Doctorate at Grenoble École de Management. She explores themes of workplace spirituality, especially new age religions, within sociology and anthropology. Of particular interest to her are alternate states of mind cultivated through contemplative practices, and how these relate to wider society and contributing to the greater good. Her research appears in peer-reviewed academic journals including *Organization*, and the *Journal of Environmental Planning and Management*, and she serves as a reviewer for *Organization*, *M@n@gement*, the *Journal of Management, Spirituality and Religion*, and others. On the spiritual side, Dr. Holm is a certified Holistic Healer, Medium and Minister of the Norwegian Spiritualist Foundation.

Jeffery Houghton is Professor of Management at West Virginia University. His research interests include leadership, self-leadership, and shared leadership. He holds a Ph.D. in organizational behavior, human resource management and labor relations from Virginia Polytechnic Institute and State University. He has published more than 70 journal articles, books, and book chapters, and his work has been cited more than 5800 times in academic journals.

Juliette Koning is Professor of Business in Society at the School of Business and Economics, Maastricht University, the Netherlands. She has a background in social anthropology (PhD, University of Amsterdam, the Netherlands) from which she investigates the role and meaning of religion, ethnicity, kinship, identity, ethics, relationality, gender, and generations for organizational leadership, business conduct, small business development and entrepreneurship. Recent research focuses on the privatization and organization of security. She has published in such journals as *Organization Studies; Journal of Business Ethics; Entrepreneurship, Theory & Practice; Management Learning; Entrepreneurship & Regional Development; Journal of Management, Spirituality & Religion*. Her latest edited volume is *New Religiosities, Modern Capitalism and Moral Complexities in Southeast Asia* (Palgrave, with Gweneal Njoto-Feillard). Juliette is also Associate Editor of *Human Relations*.

Payal Kumar is Dean of Research and Management Studies, Indian School of Hospitality, India. She is an award-winning academician and prolific writer who has published several papers and 12 books so far. She is also the series editor of the Palgrave Studies in Leadership and Followership, a 5-volume series with volume editors spanning USA, Austria, Australia and India. As a thought leader she is frequently invited to write for media publications such as the *Hindu and the Economic Times*. Payal is the advisory member of several international, peer reviewed journals and is Senior Reviewer, *Journal of Organizational Behavior*, Wiley. Another feather in her cap is that she is the inaugural recipient of the Andre Delbecq and Lee Robbins MSR (Academy of Management) Scholarship. In an earlier avatar she was Vice President Editorial and Production at SAGE Publications India Pvt Ltd.

Wolfgang Mayrhofer is Full Professor and heads the Interdisciplinary Institute of Management and Organisational Behaviour, WU Vienna, Austria. He previously had full-time positions at the University of Paderborn, Germany, and at Dresden University of Technology, Germany. He conducts research in comparative international human resource management and work careers, and systems theory and management and has received national and international awards for outstanding research and service to the academic community. He authored, co-authored and co-edited 32 books and more than 150 book chapters and 90 peer reviewed articles. Wolfgang Mayrhofer is a member of editorial or advisory boards of several international journals and research centres. His assignments at all levels of teaching and his role as visiting scholar have led him to many universities around the globe. He regularly consults to both private and public sector organisations and conducts trainings in HRM, leadership, teams, and self-development, partially by outdoor training/sailing (www.championSHIPs.at).

Guillermo Merelo has a strong background in public policy, and has worked as a senior officer, columnist, lecturer and academic researcher in Latin America, Europe and New Zealand. His research revolves around migrants' integration and inclusion. He is also a People and Culture specialist with more than twenty years of experience organisational development and change. Brought up in a family of strong women and being a member of the LGBTQ+ community, he is convinced that diverse workplaces have the potential to unleash individual and organisational growth and make our world a better place. He is currently Head of Research and Innovation at Diversity Works New Zealand.

Sharda Nandram is Full Professor Hindu Spirituality and Society at the Vrije Universiteit Amsterdam and an Associate Professor at the Nyenrode Business University in the field of Business and Spirituality. She has earned two Bachelors and two Masters at the University of Amsterdam: one in Psychology and the other in Economics. She has graduated from her

PhD in Social Sciences at the Vrije University in Amsterdam. She is an adjunct professor at Banasthali University in Jaipur, India. Her fields of interest are: Hinduism and Spirituality, Business and Spirituality, Entrepreneurial behavior, organisational innovation and integrative intelligence.

Judi Neal received her Ph.D. in organizational behavior from Yale University and served as an internal consultant to Honeywell for eight years. Judi then taught management at the University of New Haven. Her research focused on business leaders who have a strong commitment to their spirituality (www.edgewalkers.org), and she began studying how they bridged the spiritual world and the material world of business. Judi was founding director the Center for Spirit at Work, a nonprofit organization, and later became the founding director of the Tyson Center for Faith and Spirituality in the Workplace at the University of Arkansas. She the President of Edgewalkers International, a coaching and consulting firm. Judi has published nine books on workplace spirituality and transformation. She is a co-founder of the Management, Spirituality and Religion (MSR) interest group at the Academy of Management and co-founder of IAMSR. She serves on the boards of MSR, IAMSR, AITIA, and the Conscious Leadership Guild.

Christopher Neck is currently an Associate Professor of Management at Arizona State University, where he held the title "University Master Teacher". From 1994 to 2009, he was part of the Pamplin College of Business faculty at Virginia Tech. He received his Ph.D. in Management from Arizona State University and his M.B.A. from Louisiana State University. Dr. Neck's research specialties include employee/executive fitness, self-leadership, leadership, group decision-making processes, and self-managing teams. He has over 100 publications in the form of books, chapters, and articles in various journals.

Richard Oxarart is a Ph.D. candidate at West Virginia University. He graduated with his undergraduate in psychology and management from Illinois State University, where he also received his MBA. His research focuses on organizational behavior theories and how these can be used to improve HR and work life. Furthermore, he is involved in cross-level projects that examine OB concepts and how these can affect macro-organizational outcomes.

Kathryn Pavlovich is a professor of strategic management at the University of Waikato Management School, Hamilton, New Zealand. Her teaching and research focus on systems change – through relational forms of organising, and the development of purposeful leaders and enterprises, with spirituality and sustainability at the core of human flourishing. She has published in leading journals such as the *Journal of Business Venturing, Journal of Business Ethics, Long Range Planning, International Small Business Journal* and *Tourism Management.* Kathryn is a past Chair for the Management, Spirituality and Religion interest group of the Academy of Management; editor-in-chief of the *Journal of Management, Spirituality and Religion*, associate editor for the *Journal of Management Education* and on the editorial board of *Journal of Business Ethics* and the *Academy of Management Learning and Education.*

Edwina Pio is a recipient of a Royal Society medal, Fulbright alumna, Edwina Pio is New Zealand's first Professor of Diversity, and University Director of Diversity at the Auckland University of Technology. Her research encompasses the intersections of work, ethnicity, Indigenous studies, religion and pedagogy. A thought leader, recipient of a Duke of Edinburgh Fellowship, trustee of the national Religious Diversity Centre, Chair of the Academic Advisory Board of Te Kupenga the Catholic Theological Colleges of New Zealand, widely travelled and published, she is known for her praxis in action and rationally compassionate work on diversity and inclusion in a pluri-ethnic, pluri-religious, volatile world. Many aspects of Edwina's life-worlds have been structured by the complexity of being a scholar of colour and a passionately engaged multi-faith ethnic minority migrant woman educator.

James Campbell Quick is a Distinguished University Professor and Professor Emeritus, the University of Texas at Arlington and former Professor, AMBS, The University of Manchester, England. He is co-author of *Ending Sexual Violence in College* (Johns Hopkins University Press, 2021). Jim is a Fellow of the American Psychological Association and former Chair, APA Publications and Communications Board. He graduated from Colgate University with Honors, was a George Cobb Fellow and later recognized with The Maroon Citation. Colonel Quick retired after 27 years of active service, his highest decorations are the Legion of Merit and the Meritorious Service Medal, and served 3 years on the DOD Defense Health Board. Jim and his wife, the former Sheri Grimes Schember, are members of the Presidents' Club, Colgate University, the Ashbel Smith Circle and Chancellor's Council, The University of Texas System, the Carlisle Society, UT Arlington; and Paul Harris Fellows, The Rotary Foundation.

Veland Ramadani is Professor of Entrepreneurship and Family Business at Faculty of Business and Economics, ***South East European University, North*** Macedonia. His research interests include entrepreneurship, small business management and family businesses. He authored or co-authored around 140 research articles, 11 textbooks and 20 edited books. He has published in *Journal of Business Research, International Entrepreneurship and Management Journal, International Journal of Entrepreneurial Behavior & Research, Technological Forecasting and Social Change, Management Decision* among others. Dr. Ramadani is co-Editor-in-Chief of *Journal of Enterprising Communities* (JEC). He has received the Award for Excellence 2016 – Outstanding Paper by Emerald Group Publishing. In addition, Dr. Ramadani was invited as a keynote speaker in several international conferences. He also is a member of Supervisory Board of Development Bank of North Macedonia.

Cécile Rozuel is an Assistant Professor at Saint Paul University, Ottawa ON, Canada. Her research is grounded in Jungian psychology. Through that lens, she explores the conscious and unconscious dynamics shaping human behaviour and examines the ethical nature of the psyche in both its individual and collective dimension. In her published works, she has written about the psyche in relation to business ethics, self and moral agency, spirituality, alchemy, imagination and storytelling. She is currently an Associate Editor for the *Journal of Management, Spirituality and Religion*, as well as the co-founder of the Research Group on Imagination, Storytelling and Spaces (https://imaginestories.space).

Doris Schneeberger is a University Assistant at the Institute for Change Management and Management Development at the Vienna University of Economics and Business. She obtained a PhD degree (Philosophy) as well as two Master's degrees (Philosophy, English and American Studies) at the University of Salzburg. She wrote her philosophical doctoral dissertation on possible future universal declarations of nonhuman animal rights. In her current research, she focuses on the role of nonhuman animals in organizations. She has presented her work at diverse international conferences and has also contributed to public discourse with talks in non-academic settings. She has been a visiting researcher at Georgetown University (Washington D.C.) and Princeton University.

Julia Storberg-Walker is an Associate Professor in the Department of Human and Organizational Learning, Graduate School of Education and Human Development, at the George Washington University. After serving in various leadership capacities at Deloitte & Touche and Deloitte Consulting (1985-1999), she shifted to the non-profit sector and received her PhD in Work, Community, and Family Education from the University of Minnesota in 2004. She has been recognized for her critically-informed teaching, research, and activism/service as the recipient of multiple awards including the *R. Wayne Pace Book of the Year Award* by the Academy of Human Resource Development (2019), and the *Outstanding Research Award* from the International Leadership Association (2015). She was inducted into the *Academy of Outstanding Faculty Engaged in Extension* by North Carolina State University. She is a former Vice President and Board member of the Academy of Human Resource Development, former Editor-in-Chief of *Human Resource Development Review,* and currently serves on the Executive Committee of the Management, Spirituality and Religion Interest Group of the Academy of Management.

Kasturirangan Sudarshan is a dual-qualified lawyer and a chartered accountant based out of Chennai, India. He also has a Masters in International Tax Law from the Vienna University of Economics and Business as a Foundation of International Taxation Scholar. He is currently pursuing his doctoral studies with the BML Munjal University, India focusing on International Space Law and Space Taxation. On the professional front, he has advised matters on international economic laws and sports law. He is also a guest faculty on tax and investment laws at various universities and professional institutions across India and Europe. With hybrid exposure to academics and practice, he undertakes legal policy advice through his think tank – Global Tax Laboratory, where he undertakes policy advice and research for developing countries, business associations and government bodies. He has international and domestic publications to his credit.

Nurit Zaidman is an Associate Professor of Management at Ben-Gurion University of the Negev. She serves as the Chair of GGFB Faculty Teaching Committee and as the Head of Strategy and International Management Program at the Department of Business Administration. She has initiated and teaches the doctorate seminars in the Faculty. She is an Associate Editor of the *Journal of Management, Spirituality and Religion*; and Member of European Academy of Management (EURAM) Scientific Council.

Laszlo Zsolnai is professor and director of the Business Ethics Center at Corvinus University of Budapest, Hungary, and associate member of Las Casas Institute for Social Justice, Blackfriars Hall, University of Oxford, UK. He is also president of the European SPES Institute in Leuven, Belgium. He has been a guest professor/visiting scholar at University of Cambridge, University of Oxford, University of California at Berkeley, Georgetown University, University of Richmond, Concordia University Montreal, University of St. Gallen, Bocconi University Milan, and the Netherlands Institute for Advanced Study. Laszlo Zsolnai's books include *Ethics, Meaning and Market Society*, *Caring Management in the New Economy*, *The Routledge International Handbook of Spirituality in Society and the Professions*, and *Responsible Research for Better Business*.

Index

https://doi.org/10.1515/9783110711349-024

1 2nd of 530 religious studies journals and in Q1 in HR & OB journals (*Scopus*, 2021) 2nd out of 317 religion journals (*Clarivate*, Journal Citation Indicator, 2021).

https://doi.org/10.1515/9783110711349-025